LABOR'S NEW VOICE:
UNIONS AND THE MASS MEDIA

COMMUNICATION AND INFORMATION SCIENCE

A series of monographs, treatises, and texts
Edited by
MELVIN J. VOIGT
University of California, San Diego

Recent Titles:

Alan Baughcum and Gerald Faulhaber • Telecommunications Access and Public Policy
Herbert Dordick, Helen Bradley, & Burt Nanus • The Emerging Network Marketplace
Sara Douglas • Labor's New Voice: Unions and the Mass Media
William Dutton & Kenneth Kraemer • Modeling as Negotiating
Fred Fejes • Imperialism, Media, and the Good Neighbor
Glen Fisher • American Communication in a Global Society
Howard Frederick • Cuban-American Radio Wars
Edmund Glenn • Man and Mankind: Conflict and Communication Between Cultures
Gerald Goldhaber, Harry Dennis III, Gary Richetto, & Osmo Wiio • Information Strategies
Bradley Greenberg, Michael Burgoon, Judee Burgoon, & Felipe Korzenny • Mexican Americans and
    the Mass Media
W. J. Howell, Jr. • World Broadcasting in the Age of the Satellite
Heather Hudson • When Telephones Reach the Village
Robert Landau, James Bair, & Jean Siegman • Emerging Office Systems
James Larson • Television's Window on the World
John Lawrence • The Electronic Scholar
Kenneth Mackenzie • Organizational Design
Armand Mattelart and Hector Schmucler • Communication and Information Technologies
Robert Meadow • Politics as Communication
Vincent Mosco • Policy Research in Telecommunications: Proceedings from the Eleventh Annual
    Telecommunications Policy Research Conference
Vincent Mosco • Pushbutton Fantasies
Kaarle Nordenstreng • The Mass Media Declaration of UNESCO
Kaarle Nordenstreng & Herbert Schiller • National Sovereignty and International Communication
Everett Rogers & Francis Balle • The Media Revolution in America and in Western Europe
Dan Schiller • Telematics and Government
Herbert Schiller • Information and the Crisis Economy
Herbert Schiller • Who Knows: Information in the Age of the Fortune 500
Jorge Schnitman • Film Industries in Latin America
Jennifer Daryl Slack • Communication Technologies and Society
Keith Stamm • Newspaper Use and Community Ties
Robert Taylor • Value-Added Processes in Information Systems
Sari Thomas • Studies in Mass Media and Technology, Volumes 1-3
Barry Truax • Acoustic Communication
Georgette Wang and Wimal Dissanayake • Continuity and Change in Communication Systems
Frank Webster & Kevin Robins • Information Technology: A Luddite Analysis

In Preparation:

Susanna Barber • News Cameras in the Courtrooms
Lee Becker, Jeffrey Fruit, & Susan Caudill • The Training and Hiring of Journalists
Thomas Lindlof • Natural Audiences
David Paletz • Political Communication Research
Jennifer Daryl Slack & Fred Fejes • The Ideology of the Information Age
Lea Stewart & Stella Ting-Toomey • Communication, Gender, and Sex Roles in Diverse Interaction
    Contexts
Tran Van Dinh • Communication and Diplomacy in a Changing World
Tran Van Dinh • Independence, Liberation, Revolution

LABOR'S
NEW VOICE:

UNIONS
AND THE
MASS MEDIA

Sara U. Douglas
University of Illinois at Urbana-Champaign

ABLEX PUBLISHING CORPORATION
NORWOOD, New Jersey 07648

Printed in the United States of America

Library of Congress Cataloging-in-Publication Data
Douglas, Sara U.
  Labor's new voice.
  (Communication and information science)
  Bibliography: p.
  Includes index.
  1. Trade-unions and mass media—United States—
History. 2. Amalgamated Clothing and Textile Workers
Union—Case studies. 3. J. P. Stevens & Co.—Case
studies. I. Title. II. Series.
HD6490.P82U54 1986   659.2′933188′0973   86-3373
ISBN 0-89391-352-9

Ablex Publishing Corporation
355 Chestnut Street
Norwood, New Jersey 07648

Contents

LIST OF TABLES

LIST OF FIGURES

CHAPTER I

Introduction

The earliest labor union newspaper in the United States of which any copies are preserved today is the *Mechanics' Free Press,* first published in 1828. The very early history of the labor press includes newspapers published by unions and newspapers published by labor parties that comprised the political arm of the American labor movement. Between 1828 and 1834, 61 labor parties were founded in the United States and 68 labor newspapers, many of them dailies, were established.[1] All were created and developed in response to the paucity of reliable information addressed to the particular needs and interests of working people. Like the parties with which most of these journals were associated, their content varied from radically militant to relatively docile. Most slipped into and out of existence depending on the degree of governmental and employer repression of labor, the level of general activity of the labor movement, and the availability of finances. Between 1863 and 1873, for example, 120 daily, weekly, and monthly journals appeared, "attesting to the urgency of a new national drive toward organization."[2]

Socialist publications formed another part of the labor press history in the nineteenth century. Some of these, such as *The Workmen's Advocate* and *Der Sozialist,* official papers of the Socialist Labor Party, tended to emphasize political activity; others like the *Volkszeitung* stressed union activity. Differences between the labor press and the socialist press widened with the formation of the American Federation of Labor in 1886. The AFL's primary organizer and long-time president Samuel Gompers was not unfriendly to socialism, and the early AFL has been described as being more *non*socialist than antisocialist.[3] There were, however, groups within the AFL (largely from Germany and Eastern Europe) who were socialists. These groups formed foreign language federations and published a number of their own newspapers and newsletters.

The use of the press by labor in the nineteenth century was followed in the present century by continued use of communications media in a variety of ways. The following examples, derived mainly from convention reports and proceedings, illustrate this variety and provide evidence that organized labor historically has made more extensive use of the media than generally has been recognized.

1

- In 1926 the Chicago Federation of Labor established an AM radio station, WCFL. The station was owned and operated by the Chicago Federation of Labor until 1979 when it was sold to Mutual Radio of Chicago, Inc.
- In the early 1930s, the International Ladies' Garment Workers' Union began producing radio programs that were distributed to stations that broadcasted in areas where there was large ILGWU membership.
- Early in the 1950s, the International Mine, Mill and Smelter Workers financially supported the filming of *Salt of the Earth,* directed by Hollywood's Herbert Biberman. The film, about a union strike, won acclaim abroad but was blacklisted in the United States.
- During the 1950s, the United Automobile Workers produced and distributed programs to a number of midwest radio stations in addition to owning and operating two FM stations.
- In the late 1950s, Senate investigations by the McClellan committee engendered publicity that was almost entirely unfavorable to unions and their leaders. The AFL-CIO reacted to this unfavorable attention by instituting a $1.2 million public relations program.
- In the spring of 1981, the American Federation of State, County and Municipal Employees initiated a series of television advertisements that vehemently criticized President Ronald Reagan's budget and tax-slashing program. This series was part of a $1 million media campaign by AFSCME directed at major cities throughout the country and also includes radio and newspaper advertising.
- The United Automobile Workers applied to the Federal Communications Commission for permission to establish low-power television stations in 1981, the year the new broadcast service was established.
- Since October, 1982, the AFL-CIO's Labor Institute of Public Affairs has been actively producing video materials for distribution to union members and the general public via broadcast television, cable, cassettes, and satellites.

The interaction of organized labor and the mass media historically has been uneven, and, from labor's point of view, peripheral to the major concerns and activities of unions. Yet labor has ventured numerous attempts to utilize the media. The explicit purposes of its efforts have varied, but the common theme that unites all of them is the desire of organized labor to communicate effectively with its own members and with the general public in ways that enhance labor's visibility, credibility, and legitimacy.

Few avenues have been overlooked in labor's attempts to inform and persuade its audiences. Newspaper, radio, and television utilization is regarded as essential by many labor leaders today. And although a few unions have used various new communications technologies almost as soon as they became available, many labor officials remain disappointed in the quality and results of labor's communications programs. Some believe the opportunities to use the business-owned media in ways that serve labor's interests are few; some say that labor has been hampered by inadequate financial resources; others criticize labor itself saying that, as an institution, labor has far too long overlooked the importance of communications and now is too uneasy with the technology to use the media effectively. Such discontent provided the major impetus for the creation of the Labor Institute of Public Affairs in 1982. Currently a number of labor leaders are focusing attention on the labor-media relationship in more systematic ways than ever before.

This book examines and appraises the relationship between organized labor and the mass media in the United States. In so doing it provides some basis for better understanding the extent to which not-for-profit associations of all types in American society are affected by their relationships with mass media. More specifically, the historically uneven interaction between organized labor and the media is approached from four perspectives. First, there is an attempt to understand the broad context or total environment in which labor operates in terms of its public relations. Analysis of the labor-media relationship is combined with an exploration of relevant history, legal and regulatory factors, economic constraints, organized labor's internal structure, and labor's short- and long-term goals.

Second, in order to examine the relationship between labor and media in a specific situation, the context is narrowed to an in-depth case study of the Amalgamated Clothing and Textile Workers Union's (ACTWU) campaign against the J. P. Stevens Corporation. Labor leaders feel that often the union-media relationship is at its worst during periods of union-management bargaining, times when a good relationship is most needed. During these times, media alliances can be especially critical to labor's objectives. Consideration of the case allows analysis of the ways in which the important participants in this situation—the Amalgamated Clothing and Textile Workers Union, J. P. Stevens, the media, and third parties—interacted.

Third, the case study is analyzed in terms of a framework that allows conceptualization of the relationship between labor and media in a labor-management conflict situation. This conceptualization facilitates the formulation of generalizations about the labor-media relationship during such times that might prove practically useful to labor and heuristically useful to future researchers.

Finally, certain aspects of the structure of the media systems in the United States in terms of their accessibility and responsiveness to organized labor are considered. The findings, even in tentative formulation, have important implications for future labor-media relationships.

Little academic literature is addressed to the relationship between organized labor and the communications media, although there are some notable exceptions. One of these is an article written by Gerald Pomper that appears in 1959–60 in the *Public Opinion Quarterly*.[4] Pomper provides a summary of labor's public relations activities and evaluates these activities. He suggests that because of the ownership structure of the media, it may be necessary for labor to have partial ownership in order to gain better recognition and acceptance by the general public.

The work of the Glasgow University Media Group is another exception, and though their research deals with the labor-media situation in Great Britain, a number of parallels can be drawn between the relationship that exists there and the relationship that exists in the United States. This group's extensive study of the historical and social factors that shape the manner in which television news is presented in Great Britain emphasizes coverage of the country's industrial and economic news. Their research has resulted in the publication of three books on the subject.[5] The first of these includes a chapter that deals specifically with unions and the media, in which the authors assess the manner in which union structure and development affects the union-medium relationship. In this context, they look at differences in approach between white-collar unions and blue-collar unions. The authors use a series of case studies to investigate the relationship and demonstrate how the media manipulate news and display considerable bias in many industrial-economic news stories. Their work is discussed further in Chapter VIII.

Members of the Glasgow University Media Group also made contributions to a book edited by Peter Beharrell and Greg Philo.[6] This collection of essays emphasizes mass media ownership and control in Great Britain. All essays support the thesis that union public relations activities tend "to be rendered meaningless by isolation within a framework of reporting that is fundamentally hostile to the aims which trade unions represent in industrial society."[7] The editors stress the importance of monitoring the media on a full-time basis and lay out proposals for establishing a permanent monitoring/research unit financed and organized by labor.

A number of articles dealing with labor's media relationships have been published in the labor press. The purpose of these articles is largely to provide information about communications technology and public policy to union members and ideas about ways unions can make the best use of media.[8] Recently, labor in the United States has been engaging in some of the monitoring activities mentioned in the Beharrell and Philo book. The best example of this is the International Association of Machinists' research done on television's treatment of labor.[9] This study is discussed in greater detail in Chapter III.

CONSTRAINTS ON LABOR'S UTILIZATION OF THE MEDIA

Labor leaders' earliest attitude toward the media might best be described as aloof. To the extent that they wanted to use media, they preferred that the media outlets be labor-owned and operated. The general press was viewed with distrust by labor leaders, and they saw no reason to have anything to do with the medium. They did perceive a need to communicate internally and to this end established the labor press early in the history of the labor movement in this country. Today most of the international and national unions publish either a newspaper or magazine, and many have more than one regular publication.

Labor's initial reaction to radio technology was the same. Union officials recognized the usefulness of owning their own stations, and some even had hopes of someday establishing a labor radio network. Because this plan did not materialize, but even more importantly because labor leaders began to see a need to communicate with the general public, their next approach was a rather complete about-face. From their aloof position, they moved to a civic/patriotic participation in promoting labor's image to the general public. Their energies were directed toward obtaining media attention that portrayed organized labor as an integral part of American society—a democratic institution working with other organizations to help achieve economic vitality and growth.

Much of this attitude persists in labor circles. More recently, however, it seems to be losing ground to another attitude—that of advocacy. That is, labor is using the media to defend specific political, economic, and social positions that generally enjoy minimal popularity because they deviate, however slightly, from the conventional.

Labor's aloof, participatory, and advocacy attitudes toward the media and the media relationships generated by them have been shaped by labor's evolving goals and objectives. These goals, not always formulated explicitly, developed in response to the environment in which the labor movement finds itself and are constrained by a number of factors. The related events and situations that give significance and meaning to union policies and activities include discrete historical incidents, economic and political trends inside and outside of labor, and legal and regulatory issues.

In order to enhance understanding of these contextual factors, Chapter II presents an historical survey of relationships between the AFL-CIO and the media, and Chapter III describes the public relations activities of four unions that have been active in this area: the International Ladies' Garment Workers' Union (ILGWU), the United Automobile Workers (UAW), the International Association of Machinists (IAM), and the American Federation of State, County and Municipal Workers (AFSCME). Data for this historical survey primarily come from union documents, convention reports and proceedings, the labor press, memos, letters, and pamphlets. These materials are supplemented by personal interviews with present and former AFL-CIO staff members, international union staff members, and individuals from public relations firms and other organizations that contribute in various ways to labor's communications efforts.

Another area that is examined as part of the environment that affects labor's media relationships is relevant internal issues in the labor unions themselves. For example, do internal conflicts or occasional lack of congruency between union leaders' interests and the preferences of rank and file members have implications for public relations? And to what extent do public relations campaigns stimulate greater cooperation—or competition—among labor unions? A variety of internal issues that affect unions' use of the media are explored. The discussion is based mainly on data generated by questionnaires sent to public relations directors of a quota sample of AFL-CIO-affiliated international unions. The objective of the questionnaire was to learn more about the public relations of AFL-CIO affiliates of various sizes and to pinpoint some of the costs and benefits, strategic considerations, and other problems perceived by labor leaders. This information provides further insight into unions' public relations goals in general; more specifically, it helps establish, at least roughly, the extent to which ACTWU, the subject of the case study, is similar to other labor organizations in its public relations approach. In providing information and opinions concerning media use by their own unions, the respondents raised certain other questions that are discussed in relationship to the entire study.

Legal and regulatory issues have long affected the context in which labor operates in its media relationships. Labor often is frustrated in its attempts to gain media access for its viewpoints on important issues and to present these viewpoints fully and fairly in the nation's press, on radio, television, cable, and other new forms of the electronic media. The difficulties labor and certain other groups and institutions have had in achieving these goals have caused the question of media access to be of increasing concern to a number of individuals and groups. Unions have been involved in some of the court cases in which the conflict between two fundamental First Amendment rights, freedom of the press and freedom of speech, have been the central focus; frequently the court cases appear to have been resolved by judicial ad hoc balancing. Consequently, a number of commentators have urged that major changes in relevant public policies be made.[10] In order to develop an understanding of the legal and regulatory issues, numerous court cases, Congressional hearings, federal agency rules, reports and symposia, and labor policy resolutions and reports were analyzed.

Advertising provides obvious, overt indications of the directions that an institution desires to take in its public relations. It is therefore emphasized to some extent in examining the labor-media environment in the various ways described above. Labor has advertised through the media on numerous occasions. During the last 40 years, unions have made some use of newspaper, radio, and television advertising in their attempts to inform and/or persuade the public at large, labor in general, or narrower segments of the labor population.

The dominant themes of civic participation and advocacy come through especially clearly in the advertising that unions have done and are doing. All of these advertisements can be categorized with little difficulty as being either image advertising or advocacy advertising—in accordance with generally accepted usage. Union image advertising is advertising done with the objective of making the public more aware of the union and/or creating a more favorable image of the union in public opinion. When unions attach primary importance to civic participation, their advertising is usually image advertising. The advertisement is designed and copy is worded with the objective of "selling" the institution, in much the same way that products and services are "sold" through advertising. Controversial issues are not addressed except perhaps inadvertently and incidentally. While it may be argued that all advertising is essentially image advertising, certainly not all of it is explicit image advertising that seeks only to "sell" the institution.

Union advocacy advertising refers to that advertising intended to promote and engender support for a union's social or economic point of view, to counter an opposing point of view, or to endorse alternatives or action regarding a controversial issue. Probably no term for advertising of this type is devoid of definitional problems. *Advocacy advertising* is used here because it seems to have no potentially misleading connotations (as "propaganda" does, for example) and because it seems to be more accurate than the term *controversy advertising* (which is often confused with public service advertising).[11]

The terms image advertising and advocacy advertising are also functional in that they indicate the sponsor's purposes. Examples of each type have been provided recently by (among others) the two major textile and apparel workers' unions, the ILGWU and ACTWU. These two international unions have been among the leaders in organized labor's efforts to utilize mass media. The ILGWU's "Look for the Union Label" television advertising campaign is an example of an image advertisement. Emphasis is on promotion of the union, and the high quality and value of American-made apparel. The advertising that ACTWU did during its J. P. Stevens campaign clearly took a different focus in its "Boycott J. P. Stevens Products" theme. The advertisements promoted public support for the union against a major United States corporation and urged the public to show support by boycotting the corporation's products. These were classic advocacy advertisements.

In general, advertising is still a relatively uncommon labor union practice. In ordinary usage, the term advertising is understood in a fairly restricted sense: it is a public communication paid for by business and utilized as a tool to promote products and services and thus, ultimately, to generate profit. The usage is understandable because by far the greatest amount of advertising has precisely these characteristics. Advertising oriented toward objectives other than immediate corporate profit is becoming more common, however. It has been estimated that approximately 10 percent of total advertising expenditures are made by nonprofit organizations.[12] A wide variety of individuals and organizations are included in this category. Local, state, and federal government agencies, for example, spend impressive sums on advertising. Organizations that receive both government and private funding, such as universities, hospitals, and museums, increasingly have been using advertising as part of their effort to market their services. Philanthropic organizations, as well as groups advocating various social causes, are spending larger amounts of their budgets to transmit messages through mass media advertising. And candidates for political offices are spending millions in national elections on advertising.

Union advertising, such as that done by the ILGWU, ACTWU, and others reveals a paradox that parallels the ambiguous political status of American organized labor. Labor leaders need to show their members that they are vigorous, aggressive leaders, and usually this means advocating change in the political and economic status quo. On the other hand, participation in image advertising and public relations campaigns in general betrays an interest in creating an impression of moderation and responsibility, the apparent aim being to integrate unions more fully into American life. Can these two goals be accomplished simultaneously? If so, how? The emergent relationship between unions and advertising has some interesting and perhaps far-reaching implications for the role of labor in American society.

THE CASE STUDY: ACTWU AND J. P. STEVENS

The survey of the general relationship between labor and the media as described above is supplemented by a more intensive case study of the Amalgamated Clothing and Textile Workers Union campaign against J. P. Stevens, the nation's second largest textile manufacturer. In this campaign, ACTWU demonstrated new levels of innovativeness and sophistication in its media utilization. The case will undoubtedly become a classic example of a union going beyond established and conventional union techniques (such as collective bargaining) in its relations with other social, political, and corporate groups. The campaign not only touches on most of the issues examined in the entire research project, but also raises questions about future directions.

The case is a recent one, though its beginnings go back to the early 1970s when the Textile Workers Union of America initiated a concentrated organizing effort in J. P. Stevens plants. These efforts were greatly strengthened in June, 1976, when ACTWU was formed by a merger of the Textile Workers with the Amalgamated Clothing Workers of America. ACTWU leaders, in order to show that they intended to pursue the newly stated union goals actively, immediately announced a massive product boycott against J. P. Stevens, a company that then employed 45,800 workers, none of whom was a union member.

As so often happens, the conflict broadened to include other institutions and it aroused the opinion of publics both hostile and friendly to the union. The difficulties of such a situation are familiar to labor because they are typical of any strike situation. Less familiar, however, and of particular interest to this study, is the advocacy campaign planned and maintained by ACTWU throughout. The union's leadership perceived themselves as too disadvantaged to expect ordinary bargaining to be productive. In a developing situation that had many of the characteristics of the "protest" situation described below, they turned increasingly to media-related strategies.

The ACTWU-J. P. Stevens campaign is relatively familiar to many people, both because of its duration and the media attention it received. It was a dramatic episode in the evolving strategies of both labor and management in their quest for advantage—or, in some cases, survival—within a pluralistic society that encourages the exploitation of technological resources for particularistic purposes. In spite of this, there has been no systematic academic analysis of the campaign, and no examination of the roles the media played in effecting the outcome of how the media came to play such roles. This book illuminates these issues and the possible long-term consequences of ACTWU's efforts.

THE ANALYTICAL FRAMEWORK

Trade unionism in the United States is approaching its two hundredth anniversary, yet it still faces uncertainty about its role in this capitalist democracy. Like socialism, it fits uneasily, if at all, into the dominant American ideology that in spite of an abundance of lip service to equality gives highest priority to *individual* achievement, initiative, and freedom.[13] Achievement especially contradicts equality in the economic sphere; the resolution of this conflict in American ideology has favored achievement over equality, interpreting the latter in terms of equality of opportunity only. Alan Wolfe takes the argument a step further, contending that democracy is no longer defined by equality and Rousseauian standards of individual participation of each citizen in political decision making, but rather by the existence of formal institutions and characteristics such as elections, a constitution, and agreed-upon rules of political discourse.[14] In its efforts to counteract the popular distrust that has emerged because of repression from government agencies at all levels and possibly for a variety of other reasons,[15] labor in the United States has gradually become less militant, especially since the 1940s.[16] Negotiations and collective activity are undertaken by labor in order to obtain a larger share of the corporate income; however, such actions are conducted "responsibly," within the system, in seeming recognition that private investment provides jobs and economic growth. In the words of one social scientist: "The unions are caught in the contradiction of having to make demands against the very industry whose good fortunes they depend upon."[17] As long as the overall system incorporates a capitalist bias, this contradiction applies to all workers except those who favor a genuine revolution.

When viewed in the context of their role in the total American culture, unions are relatively powerless because they often do not possess sufficient resources with which to bargain with management. Traditionally, they have had only their own labor power, and when that can be replaced little is left. Such a degree of powerlessness, according to political scientist Michael Lipsky, encourages protest as political activity. In his book *Protest in City Politics*,[18] Lipsky explores the politics of protest through a study of the rent strike movement that occurred in New York City between 1963 and 1965. The important theme connecting the present study and Lipsky's research is the need for relatively powerless groups or institutions that are engaged in protest activity to activate third parties to enter into the conflict in ways that will aid the protestors. Lipsky's powerless group comprised New Yorkers involved in rent strikes; the powerless group in this study is ACTWU. In both settings the relative powerlessness of these groups impelled them to seek to broaden their support through effective media utilization.

In Lipsky's model of the dynamics of protest politics (Figure 1), media are the key to mobilization of support from reference publics. When the ACTWU-Stevens conflict is conceptualized in terms of the model, ACTWU becomes "protest leader" and J. P. Stevens is the "protest target." (Figure 2 shows ACTWU-J. P. Stevens labels on Lipsky's model.) Before and during its campaign against Stevens, ACTWU wanted to enter into a bargaining situation with J. P. Stevens, but the union was relatively powerless in that it had nothing that Stevens wanted and thus could not bring about the bargaining situation. A strike was not feasible because workers felt they could and would simply be replaced. As an alternative, ACTWU found it necessary to create political resources by activating other groups to enter the situation. "Protest constituents," a third element of the model, can be activated relatively quickly because they share certain values with the protest leader. These were, in the case of ACTWU, civil rights groups, women's groups, student groups, and so on. But even with the support of these groups, the union was unlikely to possess enough power to gain the desired rewards from the protest target.

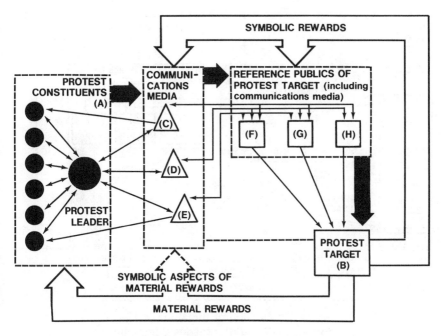

A Model of Influence Through Protest

FIGURE 1.   A Model of Influence Through Protest. Source: Michael Lipsky, *Protest in City Politics: Rent Strikes, Housing and the Poor* (Chicago: Rand McNally and Company, 1970), p. 5.

ACTWU therefore had to induce "reference publics" of the protest target to place some pressure on that target. The reference publics represented groups and institutions that shared few or no goal orientations with ACTWU, but did share goal orientations with J. P. Stevens. The reference publics were not susceptible to direct influence from the protest leader, but they might be sensitive to allies of the protest leader and to media coverage of the issue. Examples of reference publics in the ACTWU case were retailers who carried J. P. Stevens products and financial institutions with whom J. P. Stevens had business relationships.

In Lipsky's model, information concerning the protest leaders' goals has to be taken to the reference publics through the mass media. In explaining this, Lipsky says:

> To the extent that successful protest activity depends upon appealing to, and/ or threatening, other groups in the community, the communications media set the limits of protest action. If protest tactics are not considered significant by the media, or if newspapers and television reporters or editors decide to overlook protest tactics, protest organizations will not succeed. Like the tree falling unheard in the forest, there is no protest unless protest is perceived and projected.[19]

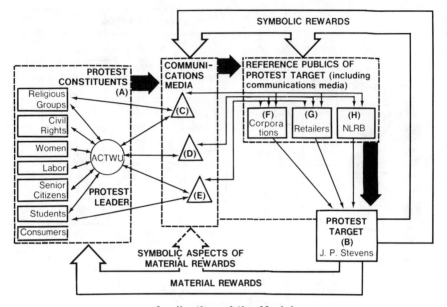

**Application of the Model
to the ACTWU/J. P. Stevens Campaign**

FIGURE 2.   Application of the Model to the ACTWU/J. P. Stevens Campaign

What complicates this need for protest noises to be projected, of course, is the necessity for them to be projected in the right way. The right way, from the protestors' point of view, is in a manner that stimulates protest constituents and reference publics to act in ways that will help the protestors.

Lipsky's model asserts that protest activity is usually undertaken in order to obtain certain tangible rewards. In the ACTWU situation, the desired tangible reward was a meaningful contract with J. P. Stevens. The granting of the material rewards by the protest target may be shared with the communications media ("symbolic aspects of material rewards") and communicated by them to the public. In the J. P. Stevens case, this aspect of the model did play an important role. At Stevens' request, the contract included clauses requiring that the communications media be informed of actions taken and that anti-J. P. Stevens activity had reached a conclusion.

Lipsky's model also allows for dispensation of symbolic rewards by the protest target. The importance of symbolic rewards was first elucidated by Murray Edelman, who observed that symbolic rewards may reassure publics regardless of the absence of material dispensations.[20] That is, appearances of attention to a problem on the part of the protest target may substitute for or supplement action that provides the tangible rewards desired by protest leaders. Press releases and annual reports are mentioned by

Edelman as among the most obvious kinds of symbolic dispensations. This is an important part of the framework because, to the extent that the protest target can provide acceptable symbolic assurances to other actors in the situation, action aimed at gaining tangible rewards can be delayed or diverted. And, as the model suggests, media are likely to be directly involved in the transmission of symbolic rewards.

Lipsky's model contributes a good deal to the ordering and interpretation of the data collected in the present study. And when the data and the model do not coincide perfectly, the reason for the incongruity tends to emerge with exceptional descriptive and theoretical clarity. For example, the relationship between the protest leader, its constituents, and the reference publics in this case was significantly constrained by secondary boycott laws and restraint of trade laws. ACTWU could not enlist the aid of the reference publics directly—not only because of widely divergent goal orientations, as Lipsky's framework suggests, but also because such action could have been illegal. This fact obviously adds to the importance of the roles of the protest constituents and the mass media in the model. This and other divergencies between data that emerged in the ACTWU case study and the Lipsky model led to a revised version of that model (Chapter VIII) and an analysis of the relationships suggested by the revisions.

MEDIA STRUCTURE

The mass media today are big businesses that, in the minds of some, increasingly are controlled by a few groups of corporate executives. The interests of media owners and managers are often opposed to those of organized labor, both economically and politically. Interestingly, the same dominant ideology mentioned above and so revered by these owners and managers prescribes that media ownership and control should not affect media access or the kinds of messages that are communicated; but as so often happens when dominant ideology conflicts with powerful interests, the ideology does not describe reality.

Lipsky's framework does not portray the media as having autonomy apart from the actors in the protest situation. This is misleading as Lipsky himself seems to recognize. He mentions, for example, the "maintenance and enhancement needs" of newspapers that explain their organizational behavior and direct them toward certain projects, and the "role requirements of reporters, editors, and others who determine newspaper policy."[21] He elaborates little, however, and does not justify the fact that his model neglects the potential effects of such crucial factors.

In exploring this and related matters, this book seeks to provide a measure of practical value through explanation of the environment in which labor operates and through the more detailed analysis of a specific labor-media situation. It is also intended to provide some refinement of concepts so that the relationship between labor and the media can be better understood in general, as well as in terms of labor's short- and long-term objectives.

The approach in Chapters II and III is primarily historical. Chapter II focuses on the AFL-CIO and its media usage. Past usage is examined and recent developments and proposed directions are included. Chapter III is similar, but it concentrates on four international unions that are currently active in public relations: the United Automobile Workers, the International Association of Machinists, the International Ladies' Garment Workers' Union, and the American Federation of State, County and Municipal Employees. Some of these unions have a long history of activity; some have become active only very recently. Both of these chapters assume a relatively broad focus and provide details for contrast and comparison with information provided in later chapters.

Chapter IV examines factors internal to labor that affect the labor-media relationship. Much of the information in this chapter was provided by a mail questionnaire sent to public relations directors in various international unions. A more legalistic and documentary methodology is used in Chapter V in order to determine the ways in which legal and regulatory constraints, in conjunction with structural factors, affect media access.

Chapter VI considers three cases in which labor organizations effectively utilized the media prior to the ACTWU-J. P. Stevens campaign. These three are the grape strike in the late 1960s that was undertaken by two groups of farm workers who later joined to form the United Farm Workers of America, the boycott of Farah products initiated by the Amalgamated Clothing Workers of America in 1972, and a labor coalition campaign against proposed right-to-work legislation in Missouri in 1978. Together these three cases provided a foundation upon which ACTWU was able to build its Stevens campaign.

Chapter VII presents the in-depth case study of ACTWU's campaign against J. P. Stevens and the union's media relationship during this time. This period of very directed and intense activity is different from the typical experience of internationals having ongoing or occasional public relations programs designed to achieve other objectives. But difficult and even critical situations can be anticipated in many sectors of organized labor, and the lessons of the J. P. Stevens case surely will be relevant and instructive.

Finally, Chapter VIII evaluates and proposes improvements in the analytical framework applied mainly in the case study. What can be learned through the case study and the application of the framework is outlined and placed in the context of current directions organized labor appears to be taking in its public relations programs.

NOTES

[1] Sidney Lens, *Radicalism in America* (New York: Thomas Y. Crowell Company, 1960), p. 74.

[2] Herbert Harris, *American Labor* (New Haven: Yale University Press, 1938), p. 63.

[3] Lens, *Radicalism in America*. See pp. 179–87.

[4] Gerald Pomper, "The Public Relations of Organized Labor," *Public Opinion Quarterly* 23 (Winter, 1959–60), pp. 483–94.

[5] Glasgow University Media Group, *Bad News,* vols. 1, 2: *More Bad News* (London: Routledge and Kegan Paul, 1976, 1980); and *Really Bad News* (London: Writers and Readers, 1982).

[6] Peter Beharrell and Greg Philo, eds., *Trade Unions and the Media* (London: The Macmillan Press Ltd., 1977).

[7] Ibid., p. 136.

[8] See, for example, "Tuning Out the Public Voice in Radio and TV," *Solidarity,* June 18, 1979, pp. 16–17; and Dave Elsila, "TV: Can We Change the Channels of Communication?," *Solidarity,* June, 1981, pp. 12–14.

[9] International Association of Machinists and Aerospace Workers, *IAM Television Entertainment Report, Part II: Conclusions and National Summary of Occupational Frequency in Network Primetime Entertainment for February, 1980,* June 12, 1980. Also International Association of Machinists and Aerospace Workers, *Network News and Documentary Report: A Member Survey and Analysis,* July 30, 1980.

[10] For example, FCC chairman Mark Fowler has proposed that the trusteeship model that currently guides government regulation of broadcasting be replaced with a marketplace approach. Under Fowler's tenure, the FCC has steadily moved toward decreased regulation and numerous broadcast and cable deregulation bills have come before Congress. See "Quotations from the Chairman," *Broadcasting* (July 12, 1982), p. 30; and "Fowler on the Flip Side," *Broadcasting* (May 7, 1984), pp. 41–42. Others favor changes in directions that would come primarily through law and the nation's courts. See Jerome A. Barron, *Public Rights and the Private Press* (Toronto: Butterworths, 1981); Don R. LeDuc, "Deregulation and the Dream of Diversity," *Journal of Communication* (Autumn, 1982), pp. 164–78; Henry Geller, "FCC Media Ownership Rules: The Case for Regulation," *Journal of Communication* (Autumn, 1982), pp. 148–56; National Association for Better Broadcasting, *Broadcasting Law and the Consumer,* series of ten papers (June, 1979–March, 1982).

[11] The definitions selected for union image advertising and union advocacy advertising are based primarily on the thorough discussion of terminology and definitional problems presented in International Advertising Association, *Controversy Advertising: How Advertisers Present Points of View in Public Affairs* (New York: Hastings House, 1977). Also helpful was S. Prakash Sethi, *Advocacy Advertising and Large Corporations* (Lexington, Massachusetts: Lexington Books, D. C. Heath and Company, 1977).

[12] Philip Kotler, *Marketing for Nonprofit Organizations* (Englewood Cliffs, New Jersey: Prentice-Hall, Inc., 1975), p. 202. See also M. Mushkat, Jr., "Implementing Public Plans: The Case for Social Marketing," *Long Range Planning* (August, 1980), pp. 24–29.

[13] For a complete discussion of these two basic American values (equality and achievement) and the conflict between them, see Seymour Martin Lipset, *The First New Nation: The United States in Historical and Comparative Perspective* (Garden City, New York: Doubleday and Co., Inc., 1967), especially chapter 5.

[14] Alan Wolfe, *The Limits of Legitimacy: Political Contradictions of Contemporary Capitalism* (New York: The Free Press, 1977).

[15] There are a number of interesting interpretations of why American labor has largely

rejected "radical unionism and class consciousness" and moved in the direction of what has been called "business unionism" and "job consciousness." One of these is Daniel R. Fusfeld, *The Rise and Repression of Radical Labor USA—1877–1918* (Chicago: Charles H. Kerr Publishing Company, 1980). See especially pp. 3–5. A review of related literature is provided in Fusfeld's "Notes on Resources," pp. 41–46. Also see Robert Justin Goldstein, *Political Repression in Modern America: 1870 to the Present* (Cambridge/New York: Schenkman Publishing Co., Inc., Two Continents Publishing Group Ltd., 1978).

[16] The militancy of the U.S. labor movement has also received scholars' attention. Goldstein, *Political Repression,* states that "American labor is generally regarded historically as among the least ideologically militant labor movements in the industrialized world," (p. 4) and quotes Richard Hofstader and Michael Wallace, eds. *American Violence: A Documentary History* (New York: Vintage, 1971), p. 19 more at length on the topic: "The rate of industrial violence in America is striking in light of the fact that no major American labor organization has ever advocated violence as a policy, that extremely militant class conflict philosophies have not prevailed here, and that the percentage of the American labor force organized in unions has always been (and is now) lower than in most advanced industrial countries. With a minimum of ideologically motivated class conflict, the United States has somehow had a maximum of industrial violence."

[17] Michael Parenti, *Power and the Powerless* (New York: St. Martin's Press, 1978), p. 153.

[18] Michael Lipsky, *Protest in City Politics: Rent Strikes, Housing and the Power of the Poor* (Chicago: Rand McNally and Company, 1970).

[19] Ibid., p. 169.

[20] Murray Edelman, *The Symbolic Uses of Politics* (Urbana: University of Illinois Press, 1964).

[21] Lipsky, *Protest in City Politics,* p. 170.

CHAPTER II

Historical Foundations: AFL-CIO Public Relations

INTRODUCTION

Organized labor is aware of the need for attaining and maintaining good public relations. The enemies of labor have sought to isolate our free democratic trade unions from the rest of the community, in order better to attack our objectives and our activities. These hostile forces have sought to cloak and minimize the constructive achievements of our labor movement in the hope that the public will develop an erroneous and hostile concept of the functions, purposes, and accomplishments of trade unions.[1]

This statement from the *Proceedings* of the AFL-CIO Constitutional Convention in 1955 confirms that union leaders have, for a relatively long period of time, been aware of the existence of negative public opinion and have felt a need to try to correct the situation. Even prior to 1955, the year of the merger of the American Federation of Labor and the Congress of Industrial Organizations, both organizations had public relations departments. Although in many cases their public relations efforts have been upgraded since the merger, many national and international unions have public relations departments that date back to the 1940s and some have departments that predate this.

Why is it then that the general public seems so little aware of the efforts made by these departments? Answers may be many and diverse, but some of the explanation surely must be derived from the context in which labor unions developed as institutions in the United States. This chapter reviews the history of the relationship between the AFL-CIO and the mass media.

American institutions are evaluated largely in terms of their perceived relationship to democracy and a capitalist economy. To those who view industrial growth as a sign of a thriving, healthy economy, and who have a strong belief in the free market, the protection of the rights of private property, and the traditional concept of individualism, the labor unions, with their persistent emphasis on the right to organize and to bargain collectively, must appear generally threatening if not subversive.

Moreover, until the 1930s and 1940s, labor leaders did not seem particularly concerned about attempting to change such perceptions. As one long-time labor expert says:

> There was a time in the labor movement's comparatively recent past when labor leaders did not care very much what the "capitalist" press thought about them or their unions. In fact, union people felt that favorable mention in the general press was somehow a reflection on their militancy and dedication to the cause of working people. This was an attitude not limited to the socialists and the radicals, but reflected the sentiment of union leadership generally. Their world was the labor movement and what counted was their standing in their own world. This was a reaction to the uneasiness and insecurity that most union leadership felt in their relationship to the community at large—even the most secure union leaders.[2]

Formation of a labor press early in the history of union development was wholly consistent with such sentiments. The primary purpose of labor publications was to provide labor leaders with outlets for their opinions and to reach the union rank and file. Such early labor newspapers, often in the form of newsletters, largely ignored the relationship between labor and the rest of society—rarely were two sides of any issue printed. In fact, perusal of early labor newspapers provides few examples of evidence that there were any opposing views within the union itself. Meanwhile, the general circulation daily newspapers were viewed by labor leaders as either biased or largely inaccessible or both, and for many years this perceived bias or inaccessibility was simply tolerated.

There were, of course, exceptions to the internal focus of most of organized labor. One of these is particularly notable and worthy of individual attention because of its apparent effect on the subsequent focus of union public relations programs. This exception was the establishment in 1926 of a radio station by the Chicago Federation of Labor. The experiences that the Chicago Federation of Labor underwent serve as a good introduction to this chapter because they illustrate the dynamic nature of the labor-media relationship that typifies the historical record.

The possibility of the acquisition of radio stations by organized labor had been suggested in 1925 by the AFL Executive Council. Although interest was shown by some unions, the initiative taken by the Chicago Federation of Labor actually resulted in the creation of WCFL, the voice of labor in Chicago. The station was owned and operated by a corporation composed of and controlled by labor representatives. For the most part, the station was run in much the same way as other radio stations in terms of programming and advertising. The primary difference lay in what was seen as its most significant purpose, which was to "insure the full observance of labor's ideals, principles, and policies . . . and carry labor's constructive, beneficial and humanitarian voice to all parts of our land and into every home."[3] Establishing the station, however, proved to be no easy task.

In the late 1920s licenses to operate radio stations were granted by the Secretary of Commerce, and wave length was regulated only by voluntary agreements between stations. This situation was due to a legal tangle followed by court decisions and Congressional inaction. Courts disagreed on the responsibilities and duties of the Department of Commerce in regard to station licensing. The Attorney General, asked by the Department of Commerce to define the situation, held that the Department did not have the power either to enforce or deny wave length usage or to fix the power of individual stations. Until Congress acted, an applicant for a license selected a wave length and it was expected that voluntary agreements between stations would settle wave length interference problems. As the situation developed, however, stations began to have proprietary interests in their respective wave lengths and threatened legal action against any station using a wave length that interfered with them.[4]

In 1927 there were approximately 732 broadcasting stations operating on 90 channels; interference was a common occurrence. The airwaves were in a chaotic state when the CFL became involved. Both the AFL Executive Council and the CFL found themselves quickly and inevitably embroiled in the situation.

By 1928, although Congress had created the Federal Radio Commission and given this agency responsibility for wave length assignment, the struggle for desirable wave lengths continued. Labor leaders found themselves at a disadvantage. They had only the one station owned by labor and operated in labor's interests and that station was assigned by the Federal Radio Commission a wave length that permitted operation neither after 8:00 p.m. nor with power in excess of 1000 watts ("thus treating the station as though it were purely local in interest and usefulness . . .").[5]

In the years between 1928 and 1939, while labor wrestled with this situation, there is strong evidence in the AFL *Convention Proceedings* that the leadership wanted to use the airwaves to transmit "labor's message" not only to labor but also to the general public. This is an important change in direction, though it is one that occurred gradually. *Convention Proceedings* in 1928, 1929, and 1931 reveal increasing concern.

Radio broadcasting presents new potentialities for publicity, so great as to challenge the imagination. It is a medium through which all sorts of propaganda may be carried directly into the privacy of the very homes of the people in a great number of ways. . . . There is grave danger that this great field of publicity may be placed under the control of a few corporations which will then be able to dictate what may or may not be broadcast and thus materially affect public opinion to suit the pleasure of such corporations. Steps must be taken to make certain that this great avenue of publicity will not be closed to organized labor . . . [1928].

Just as the Labor Movement must have the recognized right to own, publish and control its papers and magazines, limited in circulation only by the financial means of the trade unions and the willingness of the people to subscribe and read, so it must obtain and hold the right to own, operate and control its own broadcasting facilities, limited only by its financial and managerial ability to maintain the necessary stations and the willingness of the listeners to "tune in". . . . The AF of L endorses the efforts of Broadcasting Station WCFL to secure the unlimited use of a radio frequency, with adequate power and time of operation, in order that it may serve the Labor Movement and the general public by the promulgation of the principles and policies and ideas of Organized Labor . . . [1929].

The AF of L hereby petitions the Congress of the United States to appoint a joint committee of Senators and Representatives to investigate the Federal Radio Commission's allocation of channels, wave lengths, and radio facilities, and to inquire into the administration and interpretation of the radio laws of the United States by the Federal Radio Commission and recommend to the Congress of the United States appropriate legislation whereby Organized Labor will receive its proper share of radio channels, wave lengths, and facilities equal to that of any other firm, company, corporation or organization [1931].[6]

The 1931 petition was followed in 1934 by a directive requesting the Executive Council to petition the Federal Communications Commission, asking that agency to allocate 50 percent of radio station licenses to not-for-profit organizations.

Station WCFL was successful in obtaining more power and more on-air time from the Federal Communications Commission, which replaced the Federal Radio Commission in 1934, but concern still existed about the future of labor radio.

Available information is conclusive that the ownership and control of radio broadcasting is rapidly passing into the hands of the daily newspaper publishers. . . . Newspaper publishing and radio broadcasting are rapidly passing under a more centralized control. While the Constitution guarantees a free press it is observed only in maintaining freedom of expression for those who own and operate newspapers and those whose utterances the publishers desire to admit to their columns. Radio and newspapers and all sorts of public information should be freed from monopolistic control and operation.[7]

This involvement and concern about the media and changing media technology by the CFL and the AFL Executive Council alerted other labor leaders to the possibility that their internal focus was inadequate. The institution of organized labor did not and could not exist in a vacuum. It was closely related to other social, political, and economic institutions in an active way. During the 1920s, labor leaders had paid little attention to statistics on newspaper ownership in this country. Labor did, after all, own its own presses and publish its own newspapers. But the growing monopolization of media by private interests gradually became a serious concern of the labor movement. Part of this concern undoubtedly stemmed from awareness of the encounter of the Chicago Federation of Labor with the Federal Radio Commission and later with the Federal Communications Commission. This episode made it clear that corporations not only owned many of the general circulation newspapers, but were, in addition, quickly acquiring a number of radio stations. Moreover, because the majority of labor newspapers were read only by labor union members, labor was communicating primarily with itself while corporations were communicating not only with themselves, but with the general public. Unless labor leaders wanted private interests to speak for the labor movement, access to and/or ownership of the general circulation dailies, in addition to radio stations, seemed necessary.

1900–1940

Between about 1900 and the beginning of the Depression in the 1930s, organized labor endeavored to achieve two essential objectives: (1) the legal right to form unions and to bargain collectively through them, and (2) the right to use the economic weapons of strikes, pickets, boycotts, and other concerted activities. Although labor was allowed to organize before 1930, the Sherman Act was used as a basis for many injunctions against union practices alleged to be in restraint of trade. For about 50 years after the passage of the Sherman Act in 1890, the Supreme Court affirmed its applicability to unions. Perhaps of even greater importance, especially with regard to organizing, were the numerous nonlegal restraints, such as coercion and intimidation, with which unions were confronted.

> Prior to 1930, the degree of union success could be characterized as a century-long winning of reluctant tolerance for unions as institutions, but as institutions whose existence was not actively encouraged and whose activities were subjected to varying but substantial degrees of restraint.[8]

In the 1930s, however, public policy toward labor underwent a change. Both the Norris-LaGuardia Act (1932) and the National Labor Relations (or Wagner) Act (1935) were essentially pro-union and met the union demands for the right to organize and the right to use economic methods. The pro-union climate during this period occurred almost in spite of the unions themselves, who were making few, if any, efforts in the direction of stating their case to the general public. Persuading the public was not important given the magnitude of the economic depression through which the country was going. What union leaders did was to seize the opportunity provided by the Depression and by the Roosevelt administration and to press for political solutions to their problems.

The Norris-LaGuardia Act greatly limited the scope of federal injunctions in labor disputes. Yellow dog contracts (agreements between employers and employees in which workers promised not to join or assist unions, or participate in group action against their employers) were declared illegal. The National Labor Relations Act was intended to correct an inequality of bargaining power between employees and employers. It gave workers the right to join labor unions of their choice and to bargain collectively through them. Unfair labor practices were specified, and the National Labor Relations Board was established. This act was then followed in 1938 by the Fair Labor Standards Act that involved the government in fixing standards such as wages, hours, and child labor conditions.

This legislation and the climate that promoted its passage did a great deal to make unions "acceptable." Statistics show that union membership in 1935 was just under 4,000,000. By 1947, the year in which the Taft-Hartley Bill was passed, union membership had grown to over 14,000,000.[9] This growth was accompanied by a rapid spread of collective bargaining.

All of these developments helped in large measure to relieve the uneasiness and insecurity felt by labor leaders and encouraged their change to a more external focus. They came through the 1930s with a better understanding of their relationship to other institutions; and with this understanding came greater confidence in their ability to be accepted in terms of the values of society. And what may initially have been a desire to be "accepted" because of the importance of public policy and the value of political strategic maneuvering became more than that. As Jack Barbash says, unions wanted to be "well-liked,"[10] and they wanted to translate that popularity into positive social support.

THE 1940s

In 1942 a proposal was put forth in the American Federation of Labor to establish a public relations department

> to widen all avenues of contact between the organized labor movement and the general public; to interpret the true economic and social aims of the millions of organized workers to the American people, and to present to our fellow countrymen in every walk of life an undistorted picture of trade unionism as a constructive force in the national life and the national economy.[11]

The proposal seems to have been in response to several anti-union propaganda drives that were activated in the early 1940s in response to departures by independent unions from the no-strike policy that had been adopted by affiliated unions. Such drives urged repeal of labor legislation. The proposed public relations department would have restructured the AFL's Publicity and Information Service in order to provide more adequate financing and to broaden contact between labor and the general public. It was not until 1947, however, that the idea of an organized, financed public relations program really seemed to gain broad support, and even thereafter the program developed slowly.

During the war years, a number of corporations used advertising to inform the public about their activities related to the war effort. The AFL employed similar advertising strategies, although Executive Council reports indicate they did so only in self-defense, in response to the aforementioned anti-union propaganda drives.

> Shortly after the war began a huge and sinister propaganda campaign was initiated to deprive Labor of its democratic rights and freedom and to deprive American workers of the great social gains which were won by years of untiring effort on the part of the trade union movement. This propaganda found full expression in the anti-Labor press. The most vicious example of newspapers actually fomenting war against Labor took place in Oklahoma and neighboring states, where the most nefarious methods were used to put pressure on members of Congress to repeal social labor legislation.
>
> This situation became so critical that the American Federation of Labor was compelled in self-defense to take out full page advertisements in a selected number of newspapers, including some of those which were most hostile to the cause of Labor. The purpose of these advertisements was to bring home the fact to the readers of those newspapers that those responsible for the anti-Labor campaign were "Sixth Columnists" who were not inspired by patriotic motives but trying to hurt the Administration as much as Labor. The advertisements cited Labor's magnificent war record and presented an incontrovertible array of facts in defense of the 40-hour week, overtime standards and the voluntary no-strike policy of Labor.
>
> The American Federation of Labor was forced to go to the expense of buying this space in the newspapers because, as the advertisements themselves stated, a great majority of the newspapers in this country do not and will not print the truth about Labor.[12]

Interestingly, this may have been the AFL's first venture into advertising. It appears to have been done on a relatively small scale when compared to advertising that was done in 1947 when Congress was considering passage of the Taft-Hartley Bill.

In addition to these ads, both the AFL and the CIO took advantage of radio time made available to them without charge, as a public service, by the National Broadcasting Company. The two labor organizations broadcast a series on alternate weeks—"Labor for Victory"—which presented programs intended to inform the public of labor's contributions to the war effort.

At the war's end, several new programs were produced and broadcast during time made available by the networks as a public service. The AFL judged these new programs to be immensely popular among both Federation members and the general public, based on "a large volume of favorable mail and independent checks taken by networks."[13] One of these programs, "America United," achieved higher listener ratings than were given to any other noncommercial program on the air; NBC subsequently increased its time allotment from 15 to 30 minutes.

A small amount of radio advertising was undertaken by international unions at this time as well. The United Steelworkers of America, for example, used paid network radio time to state their case for a wage increase in 1946. This was followed by other, coordinated advertisements in large metropolitan newspapers. Like their counterparts in business, however, union advertisers were frustrated by the difficulty of evaluating such efforts realistically. Illustrative of this sentiment is the remark attributed to nineteenth century merchant John Wanamaker: "I know half the money I spend on advertising is wasted, but I can never find out which half."[14] A public conviction that what an ad says is true is influenced by many factors. For ads that advocate action of some type, inferences regarding the ad's effectiveness can be based on some action taken—for example, buying a product, voting for a candidate. Ads that simply state a case, however, are even more difficult to evaluate.

The gains made in public opinion toward organized labor through the radio series were set back during the wave of industry-wide and multifirm strikes that occurred across the country from 1945 to 1947. This situation caused labor leaders to take note of the fact that when the public is inconvenienced and provoked by strikes, it is likely to forget rapidly other things that labor has accomplished. Shortly before the 1945–47 strikes, a labor commentator remarked:

> It is unfortunate that labor's primary economic weapon against employers should carry with it such inconvenience and sometimes real hardship to the public. The general tendency of the public is to blame labor whenever a strike occurs, though the underlying cause may be the unduly low standards of the employer and an unwillingness to raise them unless compelled to do so by strike action.[15]

Ongoing public relations programs differ from the kind of public relations needed in a strike situation for several reasons. One is simply because the issues are different. Another is due to the fact that strikes involve others, and therefore labor's opponents become more vocal and visible during strikes. In AFL-CIO Executive Council Reports to the conventions in 1944 and 1946, reference is made to the attacks that were made through the public media by labor's opposition, especially the National Association of Manufacturers. A 1946 resolution declares that "the forces of extreme wealth, spearheaded by the National Association of Manufacturers, have by their vicious and virulent campaign of vilification against organized labor created a monstrous libel on our traditionally democratic labor unions."[16] Such publicity resulted in several other resolutions that called for the creation of an AFL public relations department.

By 1947 an enlarged publicity campaign was underway in the AFL as a direct result of the strikes, the negative publicity that resulted from them, and congressional consideration of the Taft-Hartley Bill. The Executive Council reported to the convention

> on the special advertising and radio campaign which was resorted to in order to combat anti-labor propaganda being leveled by the press and radio during the period when the Taft-Hartley Bill was being considered by Congress. It was pointed out that this was the first time in the history of the Federation when the organization "was compelled to buy space in newspapers and time on the air, day after day and week after week, to express its views in a way that would command public attention."[17]

Earlier advertising efforts, such as those undertaken during the war years, were not mentioned. This 1947 campaign appears to have been more sustained and was, of course, more expensive. Approximately $1 million was collected by a voluntary assessment of members and used for extensive radio and newspaper advertising.

The Taft-Hartley Bill was passed in 1947 in spite of labor's strong opposition and efforts against it. The passage of this bill, also known as the Labor Management Relations Act, marked the end of the twelve-year period characterized by relatively favorable government policy toward labor. During the latter part of this period, labor's increasing power began to generate a good deal of public apprehension. The strikes that followed the war came during a time of high consumer demand; to many people they provided ample evidence of labor's ability to incapacitate the nation. The National Labor Relations Act and other prolabor legislation of the 1930s was seen as having tipped the balance of power onto the side of labor rather than having achieved its intended effect of equalizing the bargaining power between labor and management.

Congress responded to this concern by passing the Taft-Hartley Act, an act intended once again to "adjust the imbalance." The Taft-Hartley Act allowed greater legal and governmental intervention in labor actions and, in addition, defined a variety of "unfair labor practices" by unions against employers and workers. Although its passage was an extremely discouraging event for the labor movement, the changes it engendered did not mean a return to the even more restrictive policies of the pre-1930s. Moreover, in the aftermath of the bill's passage, most AFL leaders insisted that resources expended for publicity had not been wasted. The Executive Council report states: "The fact that the Taft-Hartley Bill was eventually enacted over President Truman's veto does not detract from the effectiveness of the educational campaign against it which was carried on by the American Federation of Labor."[18] No basis for this statement is provided in the report; it could well have been made simply as an attempt to justify earlier policies. It is also used to argue for the need to establish and maintain a permanent public relations program. The Council report indicates that such a program was especially necessary in order to offset future antilabor propaganda. Leaders expected one source of this to be, once again, the National Association of Manufacturers which had allocated $2,000,000 for a public relations program for 1948.[19]

Not all of labor's public relations efforts in the second half of the 1940s were directed specifically to the strike and legislative situations. Community project work that had engendered good radio and newspaper publicity was regarded as helpful even though the strikes had caused some setbacks. Labor believed that public relations programs should be continued, systematized, and strengthened. After 1945–47, unionists felt the need for programs that would give them legitimacy and a good reputation in other "solid" American institutions—schools, churches, communities, and social agencies. Carefully planned, long-range efforts were viewed by a number of labor leaders as being innovative and worthwhile.

In 1948 the AFL entered into an agreement with a public relations firm, Owen and Chappell, Inc. of New York, to provide an "extended and comprehensive public relations and education program. This public relations plan calls for a constructive program of ever-increasing publicity work in radio, motion picture, magazine, and newspaper fields."[20] This action was taken, according to the Executive Council, because of the numerous resolutions calling for such a program that had been adopted by central labor bodies, locals, and other affiliated units. There appears to have been a good deal of internal agreement on the need for such action.

During the same period the Political Action Committee of the CIO undertook the task of educating members of locals on "how-to-use-radio." They asserted that, since the airwaves belonged to everyone, they should be used and used well by labor. Pamphlets were published containing information on the rights of nonprofit organizations with regard to radio time, including both free time (how to get and use free time) and purchased time that could be used to present topics of specific union interest. If denied time, union leaders were advised to protest vigorously to the station and to the FCC and to inform CIO-PAC.

During the 1940s, the structure of radio ownership underwent some interesting changes associated with the increased usage of the FM band. Among labor unions, only the Chicago Federation of Labor had obtained an AM broadcasting license. Interest in the potential of FM, however, led to renewed interest in radio on the part of labor. Frequency modulation, or FM, is a wide-band system that offers a number of advantages over the AM, or amplitude modulation, system. Of primary importance to many applicants was the fact that the new system was able to offer more channels than AM and thus seemed to offer them a "second chance" to get into radio. Additional attractions were the relatively static-free quality of FM, little interference from other transmitters, and inexpensive equipment requirements.

One major barrier that dramatically delayed the rapid spread of FM radio was the fact that FM equipment—both transmitting and receiving—was not the same as AM equipment. In the 1930s large corporations such as RCA, General Electric, and Westinghouse were deeply and profitably involved in AM technology and were beginning to become involved in television; the prospects of complications caused by FM were not welcomed. These large AM radio corporations sought to delay the spread of FM while they explored means of retaining industry dominance, and the ensuing battle raged for years. In 1933 Edwin H. Armstrong was issued four patents covering the FM system; during the next 35 years, 20 FM patent infringement suits against Armstrong had to be settled in court. Between 1933 and 1968, the year when Motorola settled the final case by paying the last of some ten million dollars to Armstrong's widow, a continuous battle was being waged for the survival of FM.

The struggle took place in U.S. courts, where the issue was FM patents, and it took place in governmental hearings in both the Federal Communications Commission and in Congress. Few FM receivers were produced before the outbreak of World War II and few FM licenses had been approved by the FCC. Further progress came to a virtual halt during the war years when it was even difficult for licensed FM stations to go on the air due to the scarcity of needed electronic parts.

In 1945, partially on the excuse that any necessary changes in FM had to be undertaken immediately, before many FM stations had received licenses, the FCC made several judgments that significantly affected the development of FM radio. The most critical of these was the decision to shift the spectrum assignment of FM radio to a higher band. The reason given, in spite of controversial and inconclusive technical evidence, was that the higher band would provide less skywave interference.[21] The FCC made the ruling in June, 1945, anticipating the number of license applications that the war's end would bring. The spectrum reallocation made all existing FM receivers and transmitters obsolete. This fact, plus a faster public acceptance of the rival medium television, impeded the growth of FM radio further.

In the summer of 1946, fully 13 years after the FM system had been patented, there were only 55 FM stations on the air[22] and the anticipated deluge of license applications lay on FCC desks. FCC licensing-granting policy for FM stations had never been precisely formulated nor freed from bureaucratic entanglements. The agency has been criticized not only for its inefficient (and unexplained) methods of processing the applications, but also for granting the majority of licenses to owners of AM stations and newspapers. In its 1947 annual report, the FCC stated: "As of March 1, 1947, three-fourths of all FM applications were from standard broadcast interests, and one-third were from newspapers, 23 percent of which were in the standard broadcast field. These groups are in a position to support the new industry until it reaches profitabïlity."[23] Concern over the monopolistic tendencies in FM broadcasting came from small business concerns, labor unions, and community groups. Organized labor had developed an active interest in FM during the early 1940s. While many unions still found costs out of reach, a number of unions and groups of unions did apply for licenses or bought stock in cooperative stations with backers friendly to labor.

> Labor's serious entry into the FM field was marked by applications filed with the FCC by the United Automobile Workers, the Amalgamated Clothing Workers, the International Ladies' Garment Workers Union, the National Maritime Union and the Chicago Federation of Labor (AFL). In New York City a substantial number of CIO unions, the IWO and other progressive groups, formed the Peoples Radio Foundation, Inc. for the purpose of establishing an FM metropolitan station. There were also rumors that the United Steel Workers of America-CIO, and other big unions were studying FM with an eye to filing applications. Progressive groups were organizing other cities to establish projects similar to the Peoples Radio Foundation in New York.[24]

In spite of the fact that, according to the 1947 FCC statistics given above, only about 15 percent of FM licenses were held by persons with neither AM nor newspaper interests, a news magazine estimated in 1949 that about 75 stations were either owned and operated by unions or were run by people friendly to labor.[25] This is a surprisingly large estimate; no source was cited, and both FCC and industry records (e.g., *Broadcasting Yearbook*) at that time lacked the information needed to be precise about such a figure. The magazine's estimate appears especially questionable because of the difficulty of defining "people friendly to labor." However, even if the figure was totally accurate, stations friendly to labor would have represented only 10 percent of the total of 737 FM stations on the air in 1949.[26]

The fact that it takes money to run a broadcasting station was just as true of FM stations as AM stations. By 1949 a number of stations were finding they simply could not continue to incur large financial losses and many stations that had made it onto the air were going off. Necessary support from advertisers simply was not there. In 1949, however, the labor stations received an unexpected windfall when Kaiser-Frazer (an automobile producer) signed a contract with a network of six union FM stations for a commercial program.[27] For many labor leaders and especially for those who had invested a great deal of time and effort in the development of labor communications via radio, this contract represented the beginning of what they hoped would develop into a network of union-controlled stations.

EARLY 1950s—PREMERGER

The AFL Executive Council reports in the early 1950s continually praised the participation of members in community projects as a means of developing good community relations. Members' activities included the development and support of public schools, playgrounds, and recreational facilities, slum clearance and housing, welfare and health projects, care for children and the aged, improvements in registration and voting procedures, and work in community planning of economic development and growth. These efforts were not centralized, however, through the AFL. The programs were centered in communities and were usually planned and funded by locals and central labor bodies.

While these activities resulted in good press relations and some publicity, and while most large daily newspapers had at least one reporter who was assigned to cover labor news, the distance that labor leaders perceived between themselves and the press was little diminished. Local media people were not difficult to talk with when the topic involved some "safe" subject such as labor's support of playground improvement; negotiations and other labor-management-related problems presented an entirely different situation, however. In spite of increased community involvement, the problems thus remained essentially unchanged from the late 1940s. Gordon Cole, editor of the newspaper put out by the International Association of Machinists, explained the feelings of a number of union members who were closely involved:

> I believe it is fair to assume that the newspapers are almost never going to applaud unions in their bargaining efforts with management. . . . As long as newspapers are supported by the advertising of business corporations, the newspapers are always going to favor the employer in any showdown. Furthermore, the management of almost every newspaper is in almost constant negotiations with one or another of the Printing Trades Unions or the Newspaper Guild, representing the newspaper's employees. No newspaper that I know of takes a position editorially that would raise the cost of its own operation. That's one reason why newspapers rarely favor higher wages.
>
> This is the basic fact of life in the operation of any union public relations department. An impartial statement of union demands may be published in a newspaper. But when negotiations approach a climax, the newspaper will almost always be found on the side of the employer. If the union wants to argue its case before the public at that point, it should buy advertising space or radio time in which to tell its own story.[28]

Cole, however, advocated community involvement and other service activities outside the union. He felt it was necessary to try to get good public relations *between* negotiations and he discussed the importance of continued emphasis on all other union activities. Regarding more extensive use of advertising (in times when negotiations were not being conducted), he said, "If we had unlimited funds, we could advertise, but we can never expect to compete with management in this field. This means we must aim our story at the news and feature columns and the special events broadcasts."[29]

Before they merged in 1955, both the AFL and the CIO did have some notable, broad-based projects underway, although their efforts to reach the nonunion public were almost entirely restricted to radio. Both labor organizations had started to sponsor evening radio news broadcasts. The goal of the AFL program, which was first undertaken as early as 1949, was "to establish a standard of full and accurate coverage of the news, fair presentation of the news and intelligent interpretation of the news from the liberal point of view."[30] The program, with Frank Edwards as commentator, was on the Mutual Network five nights a week and was regarded as the "main channel of communications between the AF of L and its members and the public generally."[31] Edwards was heard on 176 stations, including the six FM stations and one AM station then owned by labor unions. According to a 1950 Executive Council report, the program cost $350,000 and reached seven million listeners weekly in 44 states.[32] Although Edwards was fired four years later for incompetent reporting, a new series was initiated soon after, this time with Edward P. Morgan on the ABC network.

The CIO ventured into the sponsorship of a nightly news program in 1953 under a contract with ABC. This program had a purpose similar to that of the AFL's and featured John W. Vandercook as commentator. In 1953, Vandercook was heard on about 150 stations nationwide. The CIO *Proceedings* mention the intention of the organization's leaders to place the program in areas where CIO membership was strongest; it is unknown whether the reason for this was to reach CIO members or to bolster CIO local relationships with the general public in those areas; perhaps both reasons applied.

Commercial time on these programs was used by the labor organizations to give various messages to the listening audience. Gerald Pomper, who examined the public relations of labor unions in the late 1950s, categorized four types of commercials used on the news programs: community services, legislative issues, organization, and special.[33] Pomper's research showed that most commercials aired on the Morgan news program fell into his "organization" category; these concerned union organization matters, right-to-work laws, wage/inflation relationships, praise of union activities, and general explanations of the nature of the labor movement.

The commercials in all these categories appear to have been oriented largely toward public service, and the relationship between the main subject of the commercial and organized labor was touched on only briefly, if at all. For example, some commercials were devoted to the promotion of the activities of other nonprofit organizations, such as the Boy Scouts. The "special" category referred to by Pomper was used for charity drives, elections, and other topics associated with particular and passing circumstances. Even the commercials prepared during campaigns were often public service messages (for example, "remember to register to vote") rather than appeals for the support of a particular candidate. This was true also of the commercials on the Vandercook program. The AFL utilized its own public relations department for the preparation of its commercials; Henry J. Kaufman and Associates, an advertising agency, prepared the CIO "announcements."

LATE 1950s—POSTMERGER

After the merger in 1955, the AFL-CIO sponsored two radio news programs for several years. Commentators continued to be Edward P. Morgan and John W. Vandercook. Both programs were highly praised; in 1957 Morgan won a Peabody award for outstanding reporting and interpretation of the news. The AFL-CIO *Proceedings* also noted: "The citation, for the first time, went out of its way to commend the sponsor and the public-spirited 'commercials.' "[34] On several later occasions the Federation also received recognition for "complete non-interference" with the contents of the news program. The Vandercook program was terminated in 1961 because of the commentator's illness; the Morgan program continued until June of 1967 when Morgan decided to join the educational television network. Because of Morgan's departure, the AFL-CIO Executive Council decided to suspend—at least temporarily—the Federation's activities in commercial broadcasting.

The labor organization also heeded the advice it gave its affiliates and utilized free time that was made available by the radio networks in order to meet FCC requirements for the provision of public service time. The program "As We See It" was considered the most valuable by labor leaders and was the longest lasting. This regular interview series, airing news and views of labor on ABC, was begun in 1950 and continued, with some format changes, for 17 years. Other free time radio shows being broadcast in the late 1940s and early 1950s were "America United" (a 30-minute roundtable discussion program on NBC), "Viewpoint, U.S.A." (which replaced "America United" on NBC in 1952, but was shortened to 15 minutes), "Special Report from Washington" (an interview program produced by the AFL's Labor's League for Political Education), and "Cross-Section—

U.S.A." (a CBS program on which national problems were discussed). Except for the "As We See It" program, these shows all had lost ground by 1953. They had been cut in time, station coverage, or frequency of presentation by the major networks. No reason for these changes is cited in public relations department reports.

The Federation used free radio time again to address public disquiet that arose, first from the merger itself, and second from the McClellan investigations of 1957. One program, broadcast for 26 weeks on a non-network basis, was "Labor Reports to the People." A second program, aired for 13 weeks, was entitled "Labor Answers Your Questions."

Labor regained more regular use of free time in the 1960s when "Labor News Conference" and "Washington Reports to the People" were initiated. The first of these, sponsored by the Mutual Broadcasting System, was continued until 1982. Since the topics of these programs sometimes did catch the attention of those who wrote for general circulation newspapers, the programs had the potential of gaining additional media coverage. They were terminated, however, because surveys taken at regional labor conferences showed that only a few union members had ever heard of the program. A limited number of small city radio stations were carrying the program and most of these carried it when the listening audience was small.[35] As a partial replacement for the radio program, the Federation in 1982 initiated a telephone news service. This system, called the AFL-CIO Audio Service, responds automatically to telephone callers and provides up-to-date statements of labor positions on a variety of issues, and in technical quality good enough to be recorded for use on the air. This system, although relatively new, apparently is well-used both by labor leaders and media personnel.

Television also has been used by labor for many years. The CIO first made direct use of television in 1952 when members of the organization produced 13 quarter-hour films entitled "Issues of the Day." Time for this series was purchased by various unions, groups of unions, or state and/or city CIO councils. The CIO *Proceedings* (1952) relates worries about high costs, both in terms of time and production:

> Television has demonstrated itself to be, perhaps, the most effective medium of communication now available. On the other hand, the problem of cost of production and of time is extremely grave and not always easily borne within the budget of unions or Councils. It is clear, however, that the CIO and its affiliated unions cannot afford not to make use of television in the future. Unless some other method of financing such programs is developed, there is grave danger that the wealthy conservative and big business propaganda agencies will use this medium to present, uncontested, their reactionary viewpoints.[36]

At the time, CIO leaders apparently felt that it was not feasible to ask for free television time because there were only a limited number of stations in operation and intense competition existed for airtime.[37] They recommended, however, that CIO unions give thought to requesting free television time when the FCC had granted licenses for more television stations.

In 1953 the AFL produced 14 "experimental" programs that were shown weekly between March and June over ABC television stations. Entitled "Both Sides," the program dealt with public issues in a debate format. Although judged by labor leaders to be highly popular, the program was not continued after the initial "test" period. No explanation for discontinuation was provided in union records. In 1953 the Executive Council recommended that the convention delegates give authorization to AFL officers to sponsor another series because of the favorable response to the first series and because the television medium was reaching a large public audience.[38] Evidently, however, the recommendation was never acted upon.

In addition to its broadcasting activities, the AFL-CIO has continued to be extensively involved in publishing efforts. The AFL and the CIO both published newspapers before the merger; after the merger the papers were combined into the weekly *AFL-CIO News*. This paper, now in its thirtieth year, is sent to subscribers, most of whom are labor union members. Subscriber lists also include schools, libraries, and other organizations or individuals interested in labor. The AFL-CIO also provided weekly news service to the labor press, and published an official monthly magazine, the *American Federationist*. In addition, numerous pamphlets and leaflets were printed and distributed by the Federation. All these diverse publications were directed primarily to union members. The news service and other publications are activities that extend to the present time; in 1982 the *Federationist* was converted into a weekly magazine supplement to the *AFL-CIO News*. The *Federationist* name has been retained, as have the analytical, in-depth articles.

Additional public relations work was done by AFL-CIO departments other than the Public Relations and Publicity Departments. The Departments of Organization, Education, and Research engaged in some public relations directly associated with their purposes. Some of the AFL-CIO trade and industrial departments have also been active in public relations; these departments, subordinate to the Federation, are made up of appropriate affiliated national and international unions, and manage and finance themselves. Examples include the Industrial Union Department and the Union Label and Service Trades Department. Both are experienced in specific types of public relations and publicity. The Union Label and Service Trades Department organized national activities designed to develop and increase the demand for union products and services from the general public. The Union-Industries Shows, which display the products and skills of American labor, have been presented annually in cities across the country by this department and undoubtedly have done a great deal to present favorably the aims and purposes of the labor movement to the public. In a similar vein, the department also organized Union Label Week, an annual event that was created for the purpose of increasing public familiarity with and demand for goods marked by union labels and for services identified by shop cards and service buttons. Emphasis in these efforts was on presenting the importance of labor's contribution to and position in the country's economic life, on high quality, and the values that come from buying U.S.-made products. In addition, they sometimes resulted in some favorable attention by the mass media that was considered an important complement to the efforts of the public relations department. More recently, the Union Label and Service Trades Department has supported the efforts of a coalition of industry associations and international unions who embarked in July, 1983, on a Buy American campaign.

LATE 1950s—THE MCCLELLAN INVESTIGATIONS

The 1957 to 1959 period was especially critical for organized labor's public relations programs because of the McClellan investigations and hearings and the passage, in 1959, of the Landrum-Griffin Act (or the Labor-Management Reporting and Disclosure Act).

The Select Committee on Improper Activities in the Labor or Management Field was named in January, 1957, and was almost immediately generally referred to as the McClellan Committee, after its chairperson, Senator John L. McClellan. During 1957, 1958, and 1959, this committee was in session for 270 days of hearing, heard 1,526 witnesses, and produced 46,150 pages of testimony.[39] The purpose of the committee was to investigate improper activities in the labor-management field in order to determine what legislation was needed in the area of labor-management relations.

Although the committee interviewed a number of businesspeople as well as unionists, and discovered that over 50 companies, some of them well-known, had engaged in unethical, even illegal, behavior in dealings with unions, it was the revelations of corrupt union internal affairs that generated most public attention. Hearing proceedings were relayed to the public by means of detailed press coverage and by televised coverage of some of the hearings. There can be little doubt that the hearings and the ensuing publicity caused organized labor to be faced with serious public relations problems and to examine more closely their relationship with media.

An investigator who researched the case of the Bakery and Confectionary

Workers International Union (one of the unions expelled during the period by the AFL-CIO) concluded:

> [A] Senate investigating committee with no formal punitive powers may, in some instances, and under certain conditions effect punishment through its ability to arouse public concern. There appear to be three conditions which enabled the McClellan Committee to influence 'public opinion' in 1957: (1) there was a shock situation, i.e., the revelations were (or were made to appear) sensational, contrary to expectations; (2) the substance of the investigation— union corruption—was of pertinence to a large segment of the public; and (3) the press was willing, perhaps even eager, to carry sensationalistic headlines.[40]

According to 1957 Gallup Poll results, the hearings apparently did have a significant effect on what that organization calls the public approval of labor unions.

> In February, 1957, just prior to the beginning of the McClellan Committee hearings, pro-union sentiment had reached an all-time high, when 76 percent of the general public said they approved of labor unions.
> The public's acceptance of labor unions—after six months of hearings— took a dramatic drop of 12 percentage points to 64 percent approval in September of that year.[41]

Labor's response to the investigations came with little delay. From the outset of the hearings, AFL-CIO President George Meany had expressed labor's desire to aid the investigations in every possible way. In an effort to show strong union sentiment against corruption, the AFL-CIO Executive Committee established an Ethical Practices Committee in 1957. This committee drafted a code of ethical practices for the organization that every union and union officer was asked to accept and abide by. Those unions that did not correct abuses and eliminate corrupt influences would be expelled. In the months that followed the declaration of this plan, a Federation committee conducted its own hearings into the ethical practices of its members. As a result, eight unions were charged with corrupt practices; five of these took reform measures, three were expelled (the Bakery and Confectionery Workers International Union, the Teamsters, and the Laundry Workers). These expulsions were widely endorsed in the mass media, as were the suspensions of individuals. After the Executive Council suspended Dave Beck (the controversial head of the Teamsters Union), Secretary of Labor James P. Mitchell was quoted as saying the action would "help labor to regain public confidence" that had been lost in the course of the hearings.[42]

But such actions were not universally popular. "The AFL-CIO has no police powers. It can dissociate itself from unions that do not meet decent standards. But it cannot make them meet such standards."[43] Indeed, the Teamsters survived expulsion with little difficulty and remained a powerful union (although this cannot be said about the Bakery Workers and the Laundry Workers, both of which were hurt by the action). Excepting only the Bar in the State of Tennessee, the AFL-CIO was the only group investigated by the committee that took steps to maintain standards; this is in spite of the fact that at least 15 attorneys and 50 companies and corporations had been shown to be involved in improper activities.[44]

During the November, 1957 convention, an alarm was sounded in a resolution submitted by the Committee on Resolutions about the McClellan Committee hearings.

> We view with concern the practice which the Committee has indulged in of trying individuals in the press and by television; we deplore the practice of repeating questions for publicity purposes to which it is known that no answer will be made; we do not condone the issuance of announcements to the press, in advance of hearings, of the conclusions to be drawn from testimony not yet heard; we do not approve the publication of evidence obtained in violation of Federal law.[45]

Concern was also expressed about the direct role of the mass media. One labor press editorial stated that the general press was tucking stories of management corruption away on inside pages and concentrating its headlines and front pages on the "handful" of officials who had misused union funds.[46]

Of all the strategies undertaken by the AFL-CIO to meet the challenges presented by the McClellan investigations, however, one in particular is of great interest and relevance. In October, 1957, the AFL-CIO Executive Council approved a quite impressive increase in its public relations budget. The money was intended for the "execution of a new, broad and comprehensive public relations program, designed to bring the facts and the truth about the AFL-CIO aims, aspirations and accomplishments to the general public."[47] Between July 1, 1956 and June 30, 1957, the AFL-CIO spent $753,023 on its total public relations program (this figure excludes publication costs, most of which went to publish the *AFL-CIO News* and the *Federationist,* and expenditures on public relations of such other departments as Organization, Education, and Research). About 86 percent of the total was spent on radio programs. The budget was increased in the following year (July 1, 1958 to June 30, 1959) to $1,187,410, an increase of about 58 percent. This amount represented approximately one-third of the total amount budgeted for programatic departmental expenses (this excludes administrative departments; it includes departments for organization, public relations, publications, research, education, social insurance, legislation, legal, and international affairs) and about 13 percent of the total AFL-CIO budget.

Between October of 1957 and the following April, an AFL-CIO committee tried to decide how to allocate the public relations budget. As a *Wall Street Journal* headline announced, "AFL Goes Madison Avenue, Mulls How to Spend $1.2 Million to Sell Unionism." And one Federation official is quoted as complaining, " 'It's not like selling soap. You can't just sing a jingle that says "Love that AFL-CIO." ' "[48]

For the first time, the AFL-CIO was coming to grips with the complexities of image advertising. The union committee discussed appropriate media, sponsorship of programs, and public perceptions of valuable services that labor might provide. Their purpose was to make unionism more palatable to the public. The final decisions of this group are revealed in the budget figures of the next convention; the 1957–58 budget contains several notable differences when compared with the previous year. Two new categories appeared in the 1957–58 budget year: a Speakers Bureau and films. The Speakers Bureau was established in February, 1958, as part of a program (the rest was a direct mail campaign) to reach "opinion makers." Union officials contacted and spoke on topics about organized labor before nonunion groups, mainly colleges and universities.

The most remarkable budgetary change, however, was not in the new opinion maker categories, but in the area entitled "television programs." In the 1955–56 year, this category accounted for about $9,600; the following year, virtually no money was spent for television ($32). In 1957–58, however, the figure soared to $252,182. The major venture for which this money was expended was a series of 15-minute films entitled "Americans at Work" and intended for weekly use on television. Each film was built around a single trade or industry and presented

> in dramatic simplicity the skill, talent, training and toil that union members bring to the job and to portray the importance of the worker.
>
> These films, offered to television stations for presentation on public service time, are now being shown on more than 100 stations. The viewing time, if purchased, would have cost well over $700,000.[49]

Later convention reports indicate that the public relations committee evaluated this endeavor as being highly successful. This judgment appears to be based upon the large number of television stations that continued to use these public service spots and upon the length of time they were used. A total of 104 films were produced between 1958 and 1960. They were shown on television until 1967, when the AFL-CIO decided to withdraw them because they were outdated. At that time, however, more than 100 stations were still using them. An additional factor that was used in evaluating the films was the fact that the United States Information Service used them abroad.

At the same time, the budget for radio actually declined (though at $489,751, it was still substantially above television). Sponsorship was continued for the Morgan and Vandercook news programs (the latter program was reduced to five minutes); "Washington Reports to the People" and "As We See It" were produced for broadcast on radio's public service time.

The apparent success of these efforts was not consistent with the passage of the Landrum-Griffin Act in 1959. This act provided comprehensive federal regulation of many internal union affairs (for example, union elections and use of union funds). Convention *Proceedings* (1959) reflect the frustration organized labor felt regarding this bill. Several labor-related bills had been introduced in the 86th Congress, each primarily as a result of the McClellan hearings. The AFL-CIO supported Representative John F. Shelley's bill because it provided antiracketeering measures without the antilabor provisions of the Landrum-Griffin bill.

> Throughout this period, direct and indirect lobbying rose to an intensity not equalled within the memory of most members of Congress. Simultaneously, a propaganda campaign more extensive and more vicious than any in the last decade, aimed at legitimate union operations, was launched by America's anti-labor bloc.
>
> This campaign was carried on not only by the traditionally anti-labor newspapers, which used their news and editorial columns to spread the lies of labor's opponents, but by radio and television as well. The concept of public service time, for the frank and full discussion of all sides of a controversial issue, was subverted. Radio and TV broadcasters misused a powerful weapon placed in their trust—the public air waves—to aid the National Association of Manufacturers, the Chamber of Commerce and the American Retail Federation—in their attack on organized labor.[50]

THE 1960s AND 1970s

Such antimedia sentiment continued to be strong in the 1960s, as reflected by a variety of statements contained in the Federation's conventions.

> Big business, in alliance with right-wing politicians and frequently supported by an anti-labor press, has redoubled its efforts to shackle the trade union movement.[51]
>
> Anti-union forces strategically located in mass communications media have helped create an atmosphere generally unfavorable to successful organizing. . . .[52]
>
> The public media of communication, including press, radio, and television are now almost completely controlled by people who oppose the philosophy and the basic objectives of the labor movement. . . .[53]

[L]avishly-financed reactionaries and extremists dominate the "opinion" phase of broadcasting, especially on radio. Although the FCC has promulgated a "fairness doctrine," supposedly insuring equal treatment of all issues and the right of any person or organization to rebut an attack, the doctrine is ignored by the hate-mongers and never adequately enforced by the FCC.[54]

Such statements preceded resolutions whose purposes ranged from the implementation of an invigorated and expanded public relations program to the need for the FCC to show more responsibility to its public interest obligations, especially as related to the fairness doctrine.

Budget allocations, however, did not reflect the continuation of an "invigorated and expanded" public relations program in the 1960s and 1970s. The budget reached a high of $1,407,420 in the fiscal year ending in June, 1960; at this time it was 14 percent of total AFL-CIO expenses. (See Figure 3.) After June, 1964, the percentage steadily decreased and dropped sharply in 1968 to two percent. Between 1968 and 1980, public relations expenditures remained at one to two percent of total expenses. A jump to about six percent in 1980 and 1981 was due more to internal reorganization than to an actual monetary increase. This figure fell to five percent in 1982, and then rose to seven and a half percent in 1983, when the Labor Institute of Public Affairs became part of the Department of Information.

It is interesting to compare the AFL-CIO expenditures to the *Gallup Report* that shows trends in public support of labor unions. (See Figure 3.) These polls show that the high point of public approval (76 percent) occurred in 1957, just before the start of the McClellan hearings. By June, 1979, approval had dropped to 55 percent, the lowest point in 43 years. Results of the latest poll, taken in August, 1981, show approval at the same 55 percent level. A similar poll was conducted in October, 1983. Rather than asking about approval of labor unions, this opinion index measured confidence in a variety of institutions, one of which was labor unions. The percentage of those persons who responded that they had either a great deal of confidence in labor unions or quite a lot of confidence was 26 percent, down two percentage points from 1981.[55]

The 13 percent and 14 percent budget allocations made in the years 1958 and 1960 may have helped win some public support, but in May of 1961 there was a drop in approval to 63 percent. In 1963–64 the Federation increased its allocation some, and there was, just after this, some increase in popular support. Between 1965 and 1980, as Figure 3 shows, popular support and budgetary allocations to public relations diminished more or less concurrently.

Although the relationship indicated by these data is suggestive, it is far from conclusive. The Gallup survey provides only one measure of attitudes toward unions; one would like to see responses to alternatively worded and more specific questions. Moreover, however accurate the polls' assessment

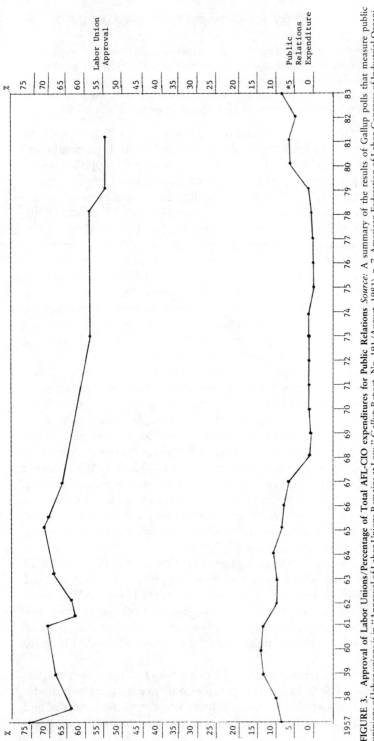

FIGURE 3. Approval of Labor Unions/Percentage of Total AFL-CIO expenditures for Public Relations *Source:* A summary of the results of Gallup polls that measure public opinions of labor unions is in "Approval of Labor Unions Remains at Low," *Gallup Report*, No. 191 (August, 1981), p. 7. American Federation of Labor-Congress of Industrial Organizations Expenditures are taken from the AFL-CIO, *Executive Council Reports of the AFL-CIO, 1957–1983*. Figures were calculated by dividing the total public relations budgets given for the July to June fiscal years (see Financial Reports, Statements No. 2; 1983, Schedule No. 3) by the total expenses for the fiscal year (see Financial Reports, Statements No. 2; 1983, Statement No. 3).

*The reason for the increase in expenditures in the 1980 and 1981 fiscal years is due largely to the fact that the AFL-CIO Public Relations and Publications Departments were combined to form the AFL-CIO Department of Information. Earlier calculations were based only on public relations expenditures and so did not include costs for the newspaper, magazine, and so on. In 1983, the larger budget includes the Labor Institute of Public Affairs.

40

of public opinion may be, the levels and trends reported obviously are influenced by an array of variables of which labor's utilization of the media is only one. The virtual impossibility of demonstrating the effect of labor's advertising efforts means that decisions about the extent and nature of such efforts must be based on something other than reliable, "hard" evidence. The most determinative factors, including a substantial dose of intuition, are explored in the discussion of labor's media-related decisional processes in Chapter IV.

Few new projects were initiated in the AFL-CIO public relations program during the 1960s and 1970s. Sponsorship of radio programs declined rapidly; as mentioned above, the Vandercook program was canceled in 1961 due to illness of the commentator and the Morgan program was discontinued in 1967 when that commentator decided to join the educational television network. In spite of Morgan's status as a highly regarded and frequently-honored reporter and the AFL-CIO's recognition for sponsorship characterized by "noninterference," Morgan's resignation brought an end to the Federation's activities in commercial broadcasting.

"As We See It" continued to be produced as a public service radio program until it went off the air in 1967 (after more than 17 years). A new program called "Labor News Conference" was begun in 1960 and continued until 1982. Each show provided an interview of an AFL-CIO leader by two journalists; the show was carried by the Mutual Broadcasting System and aired nationally. Annual Labor Day messages to the public by AFL-CIO officers are also usually broadcast by the radio networks.[56]

THE 1980s

Until 1983, the AFL-CIO did not attempt to replace its successful "Americans at Work" films, which were made for television and shown until they were withdrawn in 1967. Between 1967 and 1983, the organization continued to produce films, however, and while some gained television time, common practice was simply to circulate them to union locals which rented them to show at union meetings. Network television also aired occasional interviews of labor leaders and often carried the AFL-CIO president's Labor Day speech or Labor Day interviews of union officers.

The Report of the Department of Public Relations that was presented to the 1979 Convention is relatively brief, routine, and notable only in that it lacks creativity and vigor. The report claimed, in fact, that the department's most important tool was the telephone; this instrument was used informatively, to contact major national newspapers, wire services, and networks, and defensively, to counter unfair attacks on labor.

The need for an energy-boosting injection of some type into the AFL-CIO's public relations efforts must have been apparent to a number of labor leaders. In 1980, AFL-CIO President Lane Kirkland announced the establishment of a new Department of Information combining what had been the Departments of Public Relations and Publications. This new department was given responsibility for all contacts with the mass media, the briefing of AFL-CIO officials, the AFL-CIO News Service, and all AFL-CIO publications.

This reorganization was followed by further changes. In 1982 a new director, journalist Murray Seeger, was hired, AFL-CIO publications were restructured, and the telephone news service was begun. Then, following a proposal by a reestablished Committee on Public Relations in the summer of 1981, the Executive Council approved the establishment of the Labor Institute of Public affairs (LIPA). The institute became a reality in 1982 as a nonprofit organization under the Department of Information and governed by the AFL-CIO Executive Council. Its purpose is to develop long-term communications strategy for labor. Part of the initial funding of LIPA was provided by increased per capita dues from AFL-CIO members as approved by delegates at the convention in November, 1981. The AFL-CIO's initial budget allocation for LIPA was $3 million; in fall, 1983, the Federation approved a $6 million budget for LIPA for 1984 and 1985. This figure indicates the AFL-CIO's support of the new organization. Staff members point out, however, that it is small in comparison to the $20 million budget used for rival BizNet, the highly successful satellite-delivered closed circuit information service operated by the U.S. Chamber of Commerce.

LIPA director Larry Kirkman and his small staff, all experts in electronic media and new communications technology, have been given the responsibilities of (1) providing the labor movement with a permanent, consistent, visible, and effective voice in the electronic media, and (2) improving the ability of the AFL-CIO and its affiliates to take full advantage of electronic communications. Those responsibilities have involved program production, distribution, the preparation of advisory materials, the devising of ways to improve internal communications, and issue, audience, and market research. Major projects that have been undertaken at LIPA are (1) production of a 12-part television series entitled "America Works"; (2) production of spot advertising for use on television; (3) the Labor Video Bulletin, a video-cassette service that regularly provides news, information, background stories, and special reports at no charge to every AFL-CIO affiliate, state federation, and regional office; (4) the Labor Communications Resource Service, a regularly-updated looseleaf notebook that contains information on different aspects of electronic media; (5) a newsletter, *Relay;* and (5) Cableline, labor's $1 million venture into cable television.

Eight of the "America Works" series came out in July, 1983; the last four programs of the first series were shown starting in January, 1984. Some negotiating had to be done to put together labor's television network and this task fell to two New York-based syndication firms, Fox-Lorber Associates and All American Television. About 80 percent of the stations that agreed to carry "America Works" were independent stations; managers of several network owned-and-operated stations explained that their stations carried only network-produced public affairs programs. In addition to being paid for running the series, each of the 36 stations that carried the programs was allowed to keep revenues generated from three minutes of local advertising time. In order to enhance sales to local unions, LIPA made three "generic" commercials. One of these received some attention because it featured John Riggins, who, after being named most valuable player in the 1983 Super Bowl, had turned down various offers to advertise commercial products. As an active union member in the National Football League Players Association, Riggins agreed to appear for the AFL-CIO.

LIPA itself sold the three remaining minutes of commercial time to national advertisers to help offset production and distribution costs. Early hopes of sales to a number of commercial establishments did not work out; Pan American Airlines was the only commercial sponsor. Other sales were made to affiliated international unions. In spite of all its problems, however, LIPA's network finally provided outlets in 19 of the 20 largest television markets and potential reach to about 60 percent of people in the United States.

The purpose of each segment of the "America Works" series was to explain and gain support for labor's position on a variety of current issues. Topics addressed included toxics in the workplace, job retraining, pay equity for women, health care for senior citizens, and voter registration. Each program adopted a similar format: a documentary segment in which the key issue was explained by workers, followed by a discussion and debate among national experts. Moderator was Marie Torre, a producer and reporter at WCBS in New York. In order to comply with the fairness doctrine which requires equal time for opposing views, panelists holding opposing views always were included. In addition, Henry Geller, former counsel of the Federal Communications Commission, was retained as a consultant on fair and balanced coverage. Six new programs in this series premiered in September, 1984, on over half of all public television stations in the country.

Cableline was introduced in Atlanta, Pittsburgh, and Seattle from October to December, 1983. This experimental series ran seven days a week, mostly in prime time, and featured labor-oriented films, specials, documentaries, entertainment, news, and public affairs programs. It included an original hour-long labor news magazine—"Laborvision"—and programs from the "America Works" series. The cities used for testing the series were chosen because each has a well-established cable system and a high number of union households that subscribe. Based on market and audience research conducted while Cableline was running, LIPA staff decided to continue this endeavor in fall, 1984. Work on program development began in the spring when former Disney Channel publicity director Harvey Kahn was recruited. While LIPA intends to maintain a good deal of program variety, there is a new focus on entertainment, an unusual move for a "special interest" group and one undoubtedly intended to counter that label to some extent. Included among Kahn's tasks will be the production (in California) of a 90-minute monthly variety show with talent supplied by show business personalities who are also union members. Eventually it is hoped that LIPA will serve as an independent producer and packager for worker-oriented news, public affairs, drama, and entertainment programs.

In addition to its new "fall programming," the AFL-CIO launched a $1 million advertising campaign in September, 1984. The advocacy ads, labeled as a "Campaign for America's Future" focused on advocacy of issues, union members, and union organizations and leadership. The three major networks judged the campaign controversial and, fearing that opponents might demand equal time, refused to sell prime time to the Federation. LIPA put together its own "network," as it had with the "America Works" series by buying time from local network affiliates in 24 U.S. cities.

All of this flurry of activity in the AFL-CIO Department of Information—and especially the establishment of LIPA—obviously signals the beginning of a new era in the history of organized labor's public relations. It is also a sign of renewed commitment by the AFL-CIO to utilize new communications technology to achieve its organizational goals.

SUMMARY AND CONCLUSIONS

During the past 25 years, AFL-CIO officials have learned a great deal about public relations and about labor's relationship with the media. Labor unions are relatively visible in the United States today and most people appear to have a ready response when asked for their opinions on labor unions. But organized labor's capability to influence that response remains problematic. When Federation officials needed to intensify education and public relations efforts in the late 1950s, they looked for "themes," for the types of messages that would seem to broaden labor's base of support in this country. What the public relations committee came up with was a plan to associate the labor movement, in the public mind, with concepts that were strongly American in connotation. Illustrative of this approach, as mentioned by Pomper, is the way Edward Morgan opened his radio newscast regularly: "Thirteen-and-a-half million Americans bring you Edward P. Morgan and the news. This program is sponsored by the thirteen-and-a-half million men and women who make up the AFL-CIO—your friends and fellow citizens who are working to keep America strong and free."[57]

This emphasis on participation was neither original nor new. It was an extension of the kinds of ideas that labor had promoted ever since the days when they first decided they needed to communicate with the general public. This theme lay behind early community projects, later more systematic community efforts, and the commercials used on the sponsored radio news programs. As early as 1945, one labor leader explained his idea of a good public relations program as one that would get "across to the people the fundamental truth that trade unionism is an integral part of the American way of life, that the achievements of labor are a major contribution to democracy, and that the aims and aspirations of the labor movement have their rightful place in the future of America."[58]

The well-used theme has serious inherent problems, however, and Gerald Pomper identified them in 1960 when the intensified program was well under way.

> When they perform their tasks properly, unions by their very nature are disturbers of the status quo. . . . The process of collective bargaining is normally initiated by demands on the part of unions; improvements in contracts must first be sought by unions before they are granted by managements. Those outside the situation, the public, are more concerned that there be some settlement to a disturbing situation than they are with the merits of the particular settlements proposed. The union, which in the dutiful exercise of its responsibilities has most commonly caused the instability, therefore must bear a heavier burden of explanation than management, which is usually satisfied with the status quo. In politics as well, unions generally support new legislation to change current economic and political relationships. Such reformist activity may tend to bring into question the identity of unions and "Americanism."
>
> Ideally, unions would like to carry on past activities, including disturbance of the political and economic status quo, while gaining public agreement that such activity is the truly American way.[59]

The contradiction between union action and union communications efforts was apparent. The Federation had launched itself into a public relations campaign that was, in essence, designed to better acquaint the public with certain positive characteristics of unions. More controversial issues were not addressed. The portion of the public relations budget that was spent for advertising was spent for *image* advertising. And leaders eventually found that, indeed, unions could not be promoted in the same way soap was promoted. Perhaps even more frustrating, after their sizeable financial outlays, was the fact that they were unable to assess the results of their efforts. There was no sure way to tell if any changes in public opinion were due to their campaigns or to other, quite separate, factors or to some combination of the two.

Perhaps these were the reasons that in the 1960s and 1970s the Federation backed away from the public again. Perhaps union leaders realized that emphasis on an all-American image might signal or at least encourage a retreat from the economic tools that they had developed over the years—the rights to organize and bargain collectively, and to strike, picket, and boycott. And such a turn would have been taken just after the passage of the Landrum-Griffin Act, an act that already required the restriction of certain picketing and boycott tactics. Instead of pursuing a public relations program that would have reinforced a trend toward moderation and even passivity, labor leaders shifted their attention to internal communications. This is not to say that the shift resulted from a unanimous and deliberate recognition of the problem in these terms, however.

Projects undertaken by the public relations department increasingly focused on union members—on the internationals, on the locals and central bodies, on the labor press. Union leaders certainly did not revert to a posture of total disregard for what appeared in the mass media. As the report from the 1979 convention indicates, the media continuously were monitored and the public relations department responded when they thought inaccurate stories were published or broadcast. But the department was far more passive than it had been in the late 1950s and early 1960s, and budget allocations for public relations decreased regularly.

One man, Albert J. Zack, directed the AFL-CIO public relations program through this entire period, from 1958 until 1980. He was the person who, in 1957, was responsible for the $100,000-a-month budget, who had looked over the proposals submitted by 50 to 60 advertising agencies in early 1958,[60] and who administered a program that was later largely abandoned. When Zack retired, he articulated the reasons for the directions his department had taken over the years in its public relations with media.

> [P]ublic relations professionals are addicted to panaceas—a massive public relations campaign, utilizing television, radio, billboards, print advertising, songs, blimps, movies and what-have-you. Well, that just won't work. The first time a union is forced to strike and the public is inconvenienced, all that contrived good will vanishes. Public relations people have confided to me that, if the labor movement renounced the strike, its "image problem" would disappear. Of course, so would the labor movement.[61]

Zack had come to the conclusion that while there was a definite need to improve public understanding of the role labor played in society, it should begin in the schools and with its own members. ("[w]hen the men and women who carry a union card speak up, it's more effective than any gimmick Madison Avenue can dream up.") He stressed the importance of the labor press, how he had seen it improve, and how it was essential that it continue to improve.

In view of this internal analysis, it is not surprising that defensive-style strategies began to characterize labor's contacts with the mass media. On the other hand, there remained considerable sentiment for a more positive attack on the "ignorance" of media personnel, an additional problem cited by Zack in his retirement speech. Emphasis on this aspect of labor's public relations difficulties is apparent in a resolution passed by the California Federation of Labor and referred at the 1979 AFL–CIO Convention to the Executive Council:

> Whereas, Public perceptions of the American labor movement are predominantly determined by coverage in the mass media, and
>
> Whereas, Television, radio and the printed medium are owned by private corporations which shape and dominate the coverage of news events and the discussion of vital public issues, and
>
> Whereas, The concerns of organized labor include not only the immediate bread and butter issues of full employment, wages, hours, and working conditions, but extend to broad public policy positions on such issues as progressive taxation, comprehensive health care, environmental and economic balance, quality education, investment in mass transportation and development of all possible energy sources, and
>
> Whereas, These positions and policies of the American labor movement are consistently ignored by the mass media, and
>
> Whereas, The cost of radio and television time or advertising space in printed publications are astronomically high and beyond the financial capacity of local unions and central bodies for any substantial coverage; therefore, be it
>
> Resolved: That the AFL-CIO establish a special media education fund to be financed by national and international unions for presentation to the nation of labor's positions and policies on the central collective bargaining, economic, social and political questions of the day.[62]

While this resolution, introduced by John F. Henning, convention delegate from California, was not adopted in 1979, it provides an example of what was becoming an increasingly popular item of discussion at all levels of the labor movement. It was this growing concern that led to the conception, planning, and eventual funding of the Labor Institute of Public Affairs.

The issue that separates the apparent positions of Albert Zack and John F. Henning is whether reporter ignorance (Zack's view) or media ownership (Henning's view) is the crux of the problem that exists between organized labor and the mass media. If one adopts Henning's thesis, education of reporters will achieve little because the private corporations that own the media "shape and dominate" news and public issue coverage. The education fund, according to this perspective, would be better used to buy space and time, to gain access to the media, in order to educate not the reporters but the public.

The actions of the new AFL-CIO Department of Information would seem to indicate that someone there listened to *both* Zack and Henning. And, under the direction of Murray Seeger, the Federation is moving systematically to combat what, in Seeger's view, are the two problems the AFL-CIO has with the media: bias and ignorance.

AFL-CIO investment in LIPA has been used primarily for production and for media access. Labor is confronting media bias by itself going to members and the public. The messages that are being disseminated are designed to combat ignorance—not by building an image of labor, but by addressing issues and informing on labor's positions and actions regarding those issues.

NOTES

[1] American Federation of Labor—Congress of Industrial Organizations (AFL-CIO), *Report of the First Constitutional Convention Proceedings* (Washington, D.C.: AFL-CIO, 1955), p. 37.

[2] Jack Barbash, *The Practice of Unionism* (New York: Harper and Brothers, 1956), pp. 287–88.

[3] American Federation of Labor (AFL), *American Federation of Labor History, Encyclopedia and Reference Book*, 3 vols. (Washington, D.C.: AF of L and CIO, 1919–60), 3 (1960):1994.

[4] See Murray Edelman, *The Licensing of Radio Services in the United States, 1927–1947: A Study in Administrative Formulation of Policy* (Urbana: University of Illinois Press, 1950).

[5] AFL, *History, Encyclopedia and Reference Book*, 3:1994.

[6] Ibid., pp. 1994–96.

[7] Ibid.

[8] E. Wight Bakke, Clark Kerr, and Charles W. Anrod, "Industrial Relations and the Wider Community," in *Unions, Management and the Public*, 3rd ed., eds. E. Wight Bakke, Clark Kerr, and Charles W. Anrod (New York: Harcourt, Brace and World, Inc., 1967), p. 649.

[9] U.S. Department of Labor, Bureau of Labor Statistics, *Directory of National Unions and Employee Associations, 1979*, Bulletin 2079 (Washington, D.C.: U.S. Government Printing Office, 1980), p. 58.

[10] Barbash, *The Practice of Unionism*, p. 288.

[11] AFL, *History, Encyclopedia and Reference Book*, 3:1935.

[12] AFL, *Report of the Executive Council of the American Federation of Labor to the Sixty-second Annual Convention* (Washington, D.C.: AFL, 1942), p. 112.

[13] AFL, *Report of the Executive Council of the American Federation of Labor to the Sixty-fifth Annual Convention* (1946), p. 68.

[14] S. Watson Dunn and Arnold M. Barban, *Advertising: Its Role in Modern Marketing*, 4th ed. (Hinsdale, Illinois: The Dryden Press, 1978), p. 287.

[15] Joel Seidman, "Responsibilities of Unions to the Public," in *Unions, Management and the Public*, 1st ed., eds. Bakke, Kerr, and Anrod (1948), p. 903.

[16] AFL, *History, Encyclopedia and Reference Book*, 3:1937.

[17] Ibid., p. 1939.

[18] AFL, *Report of the Executive Council of the American Federation of Labor to the Sixty-sixth Annual Convention* (1947), p. 71.

[19] Ibid.

[20] AFL, *Report of the Executive Council of the American Federation of Labor to the Sixty-seventh Annual Convention* (1948), p. 169.

[21] Erwin G. Krasnow, Lawrence D. Longley, and Herbert A. Terry, *The Politics of Broadcast Regulation*, 3rd ed. (New York: St. Martin's Press, 1982).

22 U.S. Federal Communications Commission (FCC), *Thirteenth Annual Report* (Washington, D.C.: Government Printing Office, 1947), p. 20.

23 Ibid.

24 Eugene Konecky, *Monopoly Steals FM from the People* (New York: Provisional Committee for Democracy in Radio, 1946), pp. 8–9.

25 "Union Network," *Business Week*, December 17, 1949, pp. 92–93.

26 FCC, *Fifteenth Annual Report* (1950), p. 39.

27 "Union Network," p. 92.

28 Gordon Cole, "The Union's Public Relations," in *The House of Labor: Internal Operations of American Unions*, eds. J. B. S. Hardman and Maurice F. Neufeld (New York: Prentice-Hall, Inc., 1951), p. 207.

29 Ibid., p. 206.

30 AFL, *Report of the Executive Council of the American Federation of Labor to the Seventy-third Annual Convention* (1954), p. 63.

31 AFL, *Report of the Executive Council of the American Federation of Labor to the Seventy-first Annual Convention* (1952), p. 158.

32 AFL, *Report of the Executive Council of the American Federation of Labor to the Sixty-ninth Annual Convention* (1950), pp. 181–82.

33 Gerald Pomper, "The Public Relations of Organized Labor," *Public Opinion Quarterly* 23 (Winter, 1959–60), pp. 483–94.

34 AFL-CIO, *Proceedings of the AFL-CIO Third Constitutional Convention*, 2 vols. (Washington, D.C.: AFL-CIO, 1959), 2:314.

35 Murray Seeger, Director, AFL-CIO Department of Information, "Report to the Public Relations Committee," press release, May 27, 1982.

36 Congress of Industrial Organizations (CIO), *Proceedings, Fourteenth Constitutional Convention* (Washington, D.C.: CIO, 1952), p. 183.

37 The FCC had issued a "freeze order" in 1948 that halted processing of applications for new television stations until new rules could be adopted based on engineering reports on coverage and interference. This "freeze" lasted until July 1, 1952. (FCC, *Eighteenth Annual Report*, 1953, p. 110.)

38 AFL, *Report of the Executive Council of the American Federation of Labor to the Seventy-second Annual Convention* (1953), p. 88.

39 U.S. Congress, Senate, *Final Report of the Select Committee on Improper Activities in the Labor or Management Field*, pts. 1–4, S. Rept. 1139, 86th Cong., 2d sess., 1960, 4:868.

40 Gregory Allen Barnes, "The Impact of the McClellan Investigations on the Bakery and Confectionery Workers International Union of America," (M.S. thesis, University of Illinois, 1959), p. 95.

41 *Champaign-Urbana Courier*, February 7, 1959, p. 10 as quoted in Barnes, "McClellan Investigations," p. 80.

42 *AFL-CIO News*, April 6, 1957, p. 16.

43 "Labor Violence and Corruption," *Business Week*, August 31, 1957, p. 90.

44 Robert Kennedy, *The Enemy Within* (New York: Harper and Brothers, 1960), p. 318.

45 AFL-CIO, *Proceedings of the Second AFL-CIO Constitutional Convention*, 2 vols. (1957), 1:479.

46 "News Is What You Make It," editorial, *AFL-CIO News*, November 2, 1957, p. 4.

47 AFL-CIO, *Proceedings* (1959), 2:282.

48 "Madison Avenue Techniques Considered by AFL-CIO," *Wall Street Journal*, February 6, 1958, p. 5.

49 AFL-CIO, *Proceedings* (1959), 2:283.

50 Ibid., 2:371–72.

51 AFL-CIO, *Proceedings of the AFL-CIO Fourth Constitutional Convention*, 2 vols. (1961), 1:225.

[52] Ibid., 1:180.

[53] Ibid., 1:521. (This is also repeated in the *Proceedings*, 1965.)

[54] AFL-CIO, *Proceedings of the AFL-CIO Seventh Constitutional Convention*, 2 vols. (1967), 1:366.

[55] "Confidence in Organized Labor," *Gallup Report*, No. 217, October, 1983, p. 13.

[56] On Labor Day, 1981, however, CBS radio broke a 35-year tradition and refused to broadcast Lane Kirkland's annual message. The network claimed that the text, which had been taped earlier, dealt with "controversial issues of a political nature." This action by the network drew a charge of censorship from Kirkland. Susan Dunlop, "Kirkland Hits CBS Refusal to Air Labor Day Broadcast," *AFL-CIO News*, September 12, 1981, pp. 1 and 3.

[57] Pomper, "Public Relations," pp. 488–89.

[58] "Public Attitudes Toward Labor Unions," *Labor and Nation*, October, 1945, as quoted in Barbash, *The Practice of Unionism*, p. 289.

[59] Pomper, "Public Relations," p. 491.

[60] See "AFL-CIO Plans $1,200,000 Promotional Drive," *Advertising Age*, April 14, 1958, p. 1.

[61] "Labor Press Has Critical Task of Keeping Labor Members Informed," *AFL-CIO News*, January 26, 1980, p. 5.

[62] AFL-CIO, Proposed Policy Resolution, *Proceedings* (1979), 1:153–54.

CHAPTER III

Historical Foundations: Public Relations of Selected International Labor Unions

INTRODUCTION

There are, in the United States, three distinct levels of union government (Figure 4). At the top is the federation, the AFL-CIO. Federation policies are determined at biennial conventions; between conventions the governing body is the Executive Council, composed of the president, the vice-presidents, and the secretary-treasurer. The national AFL-CIO headquarters, located in Washington, D.C., is comprised of a variety of departments, one of which is the Department of Information. As the historical survey in Chapter II suggests, this department is continuously challenged in its task of casting a gloss of cohesiveness onto a truly diverse movement.

Media relations at the federation level, however, constitute only a fraction of labor's public information efforts. The second and third layers of union governance, the nationals/internationals and the locals, operate separate and generally autonomous programs. The affiliated nationals or internationals form the foundation of the federation. While the federation has no substantive structure without these affiliates, a number of national and international units can and do exist with no federation affiliation.[1] The AFL-CIO international affiliates are relatively independent units rather than being subordinate to the federation.

The four international unions that are the subject of this chapter are the International Ladies' Garment Workers' Union (ILGWU), the United Automobile, Aerospace and Agricultural Implement Workers of America (UAW), the International Association of Machinists and Aerospace Workers (IAM), and the American Federation of State, County and Municipal Employees (AFSCME). The objective of this chapter is to provide an appreciation for the different directions and variety of approaches that have been used by international unions to gain favorable recognition and attention from the general public and other target groups. Through a survey of these four unions it also will be shown that some duplication of efforts results from the structure of the labor movement, and this problem is compounded when one adds the public relations activities of local labor units and other intermediate labor bodies. While some of this duplication may provide reinforcement to efforts

51

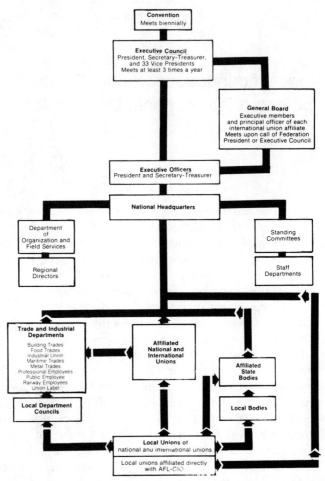

FIGURE 4.   Structure of the AFL-CIO. Source: *Directory of U.S. Labor Organizations: 1982–83 Edition,* ed. Courtney D. Gifford (Washington, D.C.: The Bureau of National Affairs, Inc., 1982), p. 7.

by other bodies, it is not necessarily the most efficient means of communicating to all or part of the public.

The local union ordinarily does function in subordination to its international union. Locals are important primarily because they provide accessibility and immediate contact for every individual member. The societal role of these local labor units has evolved, partly in response to changes in business organization. When local businesses dominated the economy, local labor federations were well situated to accomplish labor's objectives. As corporations became national, however, so did union organization. Larger bodies thus became operative centers for labor. The present relationship between local units and the international units is dependent on a number of factors and varies from union to union. Intermediate levels of governance between the locals and internationals are common, and typically include district or regional units, often called joint boards, and state organizations.

Development of media relations probably has been quite varied, and portrayal of any given model as representative in terms of timing and stages would be misleading. Moreover, such an approach, in providing an overview of what is typical, would afford less insight into the more active and successful media relations programs. There are, at least by reputation, a handful of internationals that lead the others, qualitatively and quantitatively, in their attempts to utilize the media. The four whose historical progress in this area is sketched in this chapter are not necessarily at the very top of any particular scale of media relations; but they are four that, in rather different ways, have directed considerable resources toward communicating with various audiences through the mass media. Their innovations and relative success in this area provide a basis for further analysis and comparisons in subsequent chapters.

INTERNATIONAL LADIES' GARMENT WORKERS' UNION
(ILGWU)

The International Ladies' Garment Workers' Union was formed and chartered by the American Federation of Labor in 1900. Its history includes an impressive list of accomplishments in areas where no other union had attempted to penetrate, or had attempted but failed. David Dubinsky, who was president of the union from 1932 until 1966, believed that the purpose of the union went far beyond negotiations over wages and hours; it extended to improving the standard of living and quality of life of its members in numerous ways. Further, he believed that the worker "is part of the larger community, and so the union must be part of that larger community, making its own contribution to the welfare of the community and also broadening opportunities for effective participation and enjoyment of its members."[2]

The ILGWU has a reputation for being more than a trade union. "It is also a welfare agency, an educational institution, a philanthropic society, and a kind of experimental station for the amicable adjustment of industrial disputes."[3] It comes as no surprise that this union has led the way in the establishment of pension and welfare funds, union health centers, adult education programs, the organizing of management engineering and research departments, and generous monetary contributions to philanthropic and labor causes. Most recently, the ILGWU opened a day care center in New York's Chinatown for children of members; it is the first center that combines public and private funding, and the first to serve children of workers in a single industry.

The union has also made some unique contributions in the public relations area. The ILGWU became involved in labor press activities early in its history. A newspaper called the *Ladies Garment Worker* was started in 1914. This publication was the predecessor of *Justice,* the name given to the paper in 1918 and under which it continues to be published monthly. Because of the exceptionally large numbers of immigrants who were employed in this union, the newspaper was published not only in English, but also in Italian, Spanish, French, and Yiddish; the Italian and Spanish editions of *Justice* still are being published. Convention reports note that the publication has, at various times, received recognition both from the International Labor Press Association and from the general press through reprints of features and editorials from its pages. In 1974 an editorial from Justice was reprinted on the OpEd page of the *New York Times,* giving it the distinction of being the first trade union publication editorial to be chosen.[4]

While proud of such recognition, the union has perhaps been even prouder of its ability to "win widespread public notice . . . by its deeds and achievements."[5] By deeds and achievements, members are referring not only to contract renewals, but also to community endeavors and political action. Evidence of such public notice is provided in several convention reports by means of lists of articles, special features, and editorials about the ILGWU that have appeared in various publications.

The garment industry in the United States has always been concentrated in New York City. It is, in fact, the largest single industry in that city. Because the economy of New York City is so heavily dependent on garment production, its political importance can hardly be overstated. Union activities have traditionally received a large amount of space in the New York City press, but relations between the ILGWU and the New York press generally are uneven. Union convention reports, however, rarely mention instances when labor officials have been displeased with press coverage; they frequently note their "good copy" and instances of press editorials and tributes to the union and union leaders that were made on special occasions such as anniversaries and conventions. One of these occasions was the union's thirtieth convention, in 1959. To mark this event, the ILGWU staff prepared a 20-page advertising supplement, devoted to their union and in honor of convention delegates, for inclusion in the *New York Times* as a special supplement. The supplement contained a history of the ILGWU, a number of pictures, and a variety of articles by labor leaders. Union reports claimed that "This marks the first use by a union of such a medium to convey to the public an accurate picture of what a union is and what it stands for."[6]

Another activity for which the ILGWU has received attention from the mass media is the staging of plays, an accomplishment that represents another "first" for this union's record. Most notable among these is the production of *Pins and Needles*. The impetus for this unusual accomplishment came from David Dubinsky, who states that the idea stemmed from his attendance of an international Socialist Congress in Vienna in 1931. At this meeting thousands of trade unionists participated in a pageant that was performed in a huge stadium before a large audience. As Dubinsky says: "The whole thing was most impressive. I could not get it out of my mind— the mood it created of unity and hope, the friendship it built."[7]

With the aid of New Yorkers who had theater experience, Dubinsky established a department of recreational activities in the union; this department provided lessons in dancing, acting, and painting to union members. The enthusiasm with which union members responded to the establishment of this department led to the purchase, by the union, of a small theater in the center of the garment district in New York City. A group of men and women shopworkers devoted weekends to performances of the group's first major production, a serious drama about a steel strike, written by playwright John Wexley. The play continued for six months and enjoyed only mediocre success, but enough to encourage a second undertaking.

This time the play was *Pins and Needles,* a story with a different and demonstrably effective approach. First performed in November, 1937, the play was "a zany commentary on the politics of world, nation, city and labor movements and on depression life in general, all as seen through the rollicking imagination of Harold Rome. Every member of the cast was recruited from behind a sewing machine, a shipping cart, or a cutting table."[8] Critics' reviews and a schedule change from weekend-only performances to nightly performances were responsible for a gradual shift in audience composition, which originally had consisted primarily of union members.

> And now the general public began to flock to the revue. The critics raved. Big manufacturers would call in their shop chairmen and force on them hundreds of dollars for tickets: the buyers, it seems, insisted on being taken to *Pins and Needles*. The cast trooped down to Washington for a command performance at the White House. A gala performance was given in Hollywood. Two companies went on the road for four years. New editions of the revue were presented in New York in the course of a phenomenal run of almost 1200 performances. The total box office receipts were nearly $1,500,000.[9]

Pins and Needles continued to be performed until May, 1941. A more basic restructuring of the script was necessitated by the outbreak of World War II, after which the play was entitled *New Pins and Needles.*

> *Pins and Needles* had a profound effect on the educational policy of the International. The experience confirmed Dubinsky's feeling that the educa-

tional work of a labor union should emphasize the cultivation of sound public relations. *Pins and Needles* created an enormous reservoir of good will for the ILGWU. And this lesson was not forgotten after *Pins and Needles* closed its doors.[10]

A similar noteworthy project was the ILGWU production of the film *With These Hands,* prepared for the union's Golden Jubilee in 1950. This was not the union's first attempt at film production, but it was a larger, Hollywood-type undertaking. *With These Hands,* once again written by Harold Rome and starring Arlene Francis and Sam Levene, portrayed the drama of the establishment of the ILGWU by immigrants and the struggles of the workers to achieve dignity and respect. It was first shown to convention delegates, and later leased to a theater on Broadway. After this it was shown by ILGWU local units across the country and distributed to universities, high schools, and community groups. Television time was acquired for its showing in some communities. The film, ultimately translated into 12 languages, was used abroad by the United States Information Service, and was evaluated by the ILGWU Executive Board as having marked a high point in union cultural and educational activity, just as *Pins and Needles* had earlier. This evaluation was based on critical acclaim received in newspapers, numbers of requests for the film, the number of language translations, and the general attention it received in the three years after its production. The ILGWU Promotion Department did the publicity work for the film, including advertising done in advance of television showings.

Specific artistic endeavors and their promotion thus represented one means by which the ILGWU utilized mass media. There were other, more structural approaches. As mentioned in Chapter II, the ILGWU was one of the few unions that applied during the 1940s for FM broadcasting station licenses. However, the attempt to operate three FM stations proved financially debilitating to the union. The reasons, as viewed by the General Executive Board, were presented to the convention in 1953.

> We are out of the radio field. Our venture into radio broadcasting, to be specific, into FM (Frequency Modulation) radio, proved a failure. In assessing this failure, we could point with reasonable accuracy to more than one cause. Unquestionably, we got and accepted faulty direction and advice on installation costs, maintenance budgets and expansion policy from sources which, while competent on the programmatic side of broadcasting, did not prove to have similar competence in the business, operational and fiscal policies which are fundamental to the success of radio broadcasting.
>
> We entered radio at a time when many broadcasters and institutions were in a race to obtain FM licenses. We thought we were lucky when we succeeded in getting six licenses for six stations in cities we considered good strategic spots from a union viewpoint. Fortunately, we launched our radio projects in three instead of six places. [The three ILGWU FM stations were located in Los

Angeles, Chattanooga, and New York.] As it happened, however, the arrival of FM practically coincided with the phenomenal boom and the wide public acceptance of television, amounting to a virtual revolution on the airwaves. Television pulled the rug out not only from under FM but has cut deeply into old established AM stations.

Still another factor militating against FM entered into the picture. It was hoped at the time FM had made its bid for a substantial share of the radio audience toward the end of the war, that the big manufacturers of radio receivers would turn toward exploiting the new FM medium in a big way. Instead, the makers of radio sets, as soon as the war was over, swamped the market with regular AM receivers, practically ignoring FM, even though the latter medium offered superior reception in most population centers the country over.

It is in place to state here, as we reported to the 1950 Convention, that we had no illusions concerning the money-making potential of our stations; that, in fact, we anticipated losses during the trial years of their operation. Still, while our attitude in this respect was based on the fundamental objective of our radio enterprise, namely to promote educational, cultural and community service programs and to utilize the airwaves for the welfare of our union and its membership, we, nevertheless, sought to secure, on a carefully selected basis, commercial programs to help out in the maintenance budgets of our stations. The failure of the radio industry to promote FM, however, made the obtaining of paid-for programs increasingly difficult.[11]

This account clearly shows the frustrations felt by the union leaders in regard to this unsuccessful endeavor. There might have been some consolation in the fact that they were not alone. By mid-1950, the number of FM stations on the air was 691, a decrease from the previous year's total by 46 stations.[12] And the decline continued; by mid-1954 there were only 569 commercial FM stations on the air.[13] Certainly the early 1950s was a bleak period for FM radio and a time of rapid expansion for television. Reasons given by the Federal Communications Commission for the downward FM spiral were that many FM licensees were experiencing receiver supply problems and/or financial losses.[14] The major reason underlying these difficulties, not mentioned by the FCC, goes back to that agency's 1945 decision to shift the FM spectrum. That decision, while based on technical grounds, was resulting in the long-term economic situation that had been forecast by its critics. It was enhancing the position of established interests such as RCA, whose hopes for rapid development of television were being fulfilled, and was impairing the positions of groups such as the ILGWU, relative newcomers to radio ownership that lacked the ability to have much influence on FCC policy. At any rate, the ILGWU failure reveals why the hoped for "labor network" never materialized.

The FM disappointment notwithstanding, ILGWU personnel were experienced in radio programming and their competence in that area had been demonstrated by earlier successful endeavors. The union had produced radio programs, primarily for the purpose of political education, in the early 1930s, long before they applied for their FM licenses. Funds for this purpose came from voluntary contributions by union members. In addition, several locals produced and/or sponsored radio programs. An example of one that was especially successful was a weekly one-hour program produced by Local 89, the Italian Dressmakers' Union. The program, "Voice of 89," was initiated in 1934, primarily to serve members of the "largest single organization of people of Italian origin in the country, . . ."[15] The program, in the Italian language, was broadcast over an eastern network of five stations. Programs were educational and artistic, and included talks by union leaders, politicians, and special broadcasts from Italy. According to a union report, the program was "recognized as the most influential Italian-language radio program in the country. It reaches not only the members of Local 89, but their families and most Italian-American communities in the East as well."[16]

Today the ILGWU is fairly widely recognized for advertising that promotes name-recognition of the union and its label. These advertising efforts go back to 1959 when a resolution requested the convention and the General Executive Board to approve a large-scale advertising and promotion campaign to publicize the union label as a symbol of industrial democracy.

> In recent years, one of the most dramatic changes has been the growth in power and impact of the advertising and public relations industry. That industry will now be working for us. Its tools and techniques will enable us to bring the message of the label to every corner of the country.[17]

The request for such a venture came only after some initial testing of the water. Resolutions introduced at the 1956 convention had strongly recommended widespread use of the union label. The ILGWU label campaign subsequently grew rapidly. In May, 1958, the General Executive Board appropriated a $2 million budget to promote the label for an initial two-year period. The 1959 convention voted to assess each ILGWU member 25 cents per month to finance label promotion. On March 4, 1959, Doyle Dane Bernbach, Inc. was selected as the advertising agency to handle the label promotion drive. The union hoped for a long-range program that would involve members and the consuming public. The first ad appeared May 10, 1959, just prior to the opening of the ILGWU convention.

Fifteen different advertisements for the union label appeared in 154 newspapers a total of 833 times between 1959 and 1961. The ads were targeted both for the trade (insertions in *Women's Wear Daily*) and for ultimate consumers (insertions in *McCall's, Good Housekeeping, Women's Day,* and *Ebony*). Advertisements were also placed in foreign language newspapers and in the trade union press.[18]

Concern among top union leaders regarding the effectiveness of the campaign prompted a change in agency in 1961 from Doyle Dane Bernbach to the Wexler Agency and a request to Louis Harris and Associates that the campaign be evaluated. In 1962 the union was presented a report based on interviews with 1,506 women in ten cities. In general, the survey results were encouraging: "As a symbol of decency to labor, the union label is powerful, believable, and can be made to work. As a symbol of good working conditions, the label can receive unchallenged, but deeply emotional support."[19] The report made a number of helpful suggestions based on its findings and ILGWU continued its advertising efforts. In 1963 eight advertisements appeared in a combined total of 777 newspapers and in 1964, six ads appeared in 331 newspapers. The print advertising campaign was used in conjunction with radio and television campaigns. The ILGWU produced fashion films that were provided to television stations for showings on a public service basis in the early 1960s. The union's newspaper *Justice* reported that the first five of these films were telecast 783 times to a combined audience of 22,000,000.[20] In addition, the films were shown in motion picture theaters and schools, and to a variety of organizations. By 1965 union members were paying three dollars per year to promote the label; between 1962 and 1965, the label fund had an income of $3,544,220. Of this $1,286,653 was spent for advertising in newspapers and magazines.[21]

In the early 1970s the Union Label Department put out a series of advertisements aimed more specifically at the problem of imports. These ads appeared first in the labor press, and later were circulated as subway posters and leaflets. Spot announcements on CBS radio during peak annual shopping seasons were considered highly successful based on response to ILGWU's offer for free booklets. Additional advertisements were placed in *Women's Wear Daily* and other trade publications aimed at retailers and manufacturers, and some direct mail was sent to retailers.

The campaign that most often is given credit for pioneering the way for organized labor's television advertising is ILGWU's familiar "Look for the Union Label."

> At its October 1975 meeting, the GEB authorized a proposal to begin a series of unprecedented TV and radio commercials that would put the ILGWU's look-for-the-union label message squarely before the American public.
>
> A program had been drawn up that would use real ILGWU members in a brief TV-radio "spot" urging people to buy women's and children's clothing made in America by union members. On November 11, 1975 millions of Americans saw and heard the union's first televised commercial message. It did not take very long for the catchy "Look for the Union Label" song to take hold.[22]

As developed for the ILGWU by Green Dolmatch Inc. (now Paula Green Advertising), the campaign included tie-in radio and newspaper spots (Figures 5 and 6) and cost the union over one million dollars its first year. That year, 1975–1976, 12 commercials were included on 10 network programs. Program selections were based on perceived wide public appeal. For example, the first program, in November, 1975, was a Flip Wilson variety spe-

Sunday, February 17, on "60 Minutes," a woman is going to stand before a national TV audience and say: "I'm from Kilgore, Texas and I belong to the International Ladies' Garment Workers' Union."

Think of it. Kilgore, Texas.

How many people do you think know the ILG makes clothes in Kilgore, Texas? Most of them think we're in just a few big cities.

For five years now, we've been talking to them on TV and radio. Millions of Americans who never thought about who made their clothes are singing "Look for the Union Label."

They know who we are now, and what we do, and why we want them to look for the union label. They know it means our jobs.

But how many of them know the jobs we're talking about are right in their backyards?

We're not just talking about a union. We're talking about their neighbors. We're talking about people just like them who work for a living, support families, and pay taxes in towns and cities up and down and across the country.

Anything that affects our jobs is going to have an effect on the places we live and the people around us.

So when Georgia Lohr stands up and says she's from Kilgore, Texas and she belongs to the ILGWU, when she tells them we also make clothes in 37 states all over the country, she's telling them something about us that a lot of them didn't know.

We told them once before, on the

Perry Como Christmas Show. Now we're telling them on one of the most important programs on TV. "60 Minutes" is the only public affairs broadcast ever to rank consistently among the nation's top 10 TV network programs. It attracts an audience of 19,380,000 families every Sunday. Even better, it's an audience of the most aware and concerned viewers in the country.

So tune in to "60 Minutes" Sunday, February 17, at 7 PM/EST on the CBS-TV network.

Sing along with the ILG as we bring our message home to all the places we call home.

FIGURE 5.   Advertisement in *Justice*, January 1980, p. 14; ad sponsored by ILGWU.

FIGURE 6. Advertisement in *Justice*, September 1980, p. 5; ad sponsored by ILGWU.

cial; the second, in December, 1975, was a telecast of the drama "The Homecoming."

At the 1980 ILGWU convention, the campaign was summarized as increasingly effective and very successful, not only for the ILGWU but for the entire union movement.

> One of the highlights of the presentation in the convention's third day was the showing of two films which illustrated the impressive impact of the union label campaign. One of the films traced the history over the last three years and showed our inclusion in such "blockbuster" shows as the Lucille Ball, Perry Como and Ann-Margret specials. The other film traced the enormous amount of free publicity the union has received from spoofs of its ads by such comedy professionals as Carol Burnett and the Crew of "Saturday Night Live."
>
> The executive vice president [Wilbur Daniels, who directs television activities] cited a survey taken in 1978, three years after the start of the campaign, which showed "awareness of the union label was still going up." Also up were the number of Americans who said they were more inclined to buy domestic apparel and those who rated our union as "one of the best."
>
> The executive vice president also brought delegates up to date on the campaign of the last three years. "Since the last convention, our TV messages have aired 31 times on 21 programs," he said. Although this exposure is "a drop in the bucket" compared with the efforts of large corporations, "they would all like recognition like ours," Daniels asserted.
>
> The message has reached over 71 million families, 91 per cent of all American families. We have had our commercials on the two highest rated programs of all time, Daniels indicated, "Roots," and just recently, "Shogun."[23]

In 1983, the ILGWU spent only one-tenth as much on the union label media campaign as in 1975; television spots were shortened and moved to less-popular shows. The familiar look-for-the-union label line was continued, and a new line, "Think of it as a little American flag in your clothes," was added (Figure 7). Network television rejected the inclusion of this line initially on the basis that it was too controversial, but later reversed this decision. In spite of the budget cutbacks, the ongoing success of the label campaign was recognized in a 1984 article in *TV Guide* where look-for-the-union-label was credited with being the best known labor advertisement in television history.[24]

A more generic form of advertising was implemented in December, 1983, when the ILGWU launched its Christmas appeal over the radio in 16 cities and on leaflets distributed at retail stores: "Make it an American Christmas . . . and maybe next year we'll all have something to celebrate." This attempt to encourage consumers to make all their purchases American-made products seems to be a logical extension of, first, the union-made label campaign, and then the buy American-made clothing campaign.

While best known for union label advertising, the union has sponsored

FIGURE 7.   Advertisement in *Illinois State AFL-CIO Newsletter,* May 12, 1984, p. 2; ad sponsored by ILGWU.

other kinds of messages as well. Advocacy advertising was used in 1958 when a large group of ILGWU affiliates, the Dressmakers Joint Council, was striking against anti-union jobbers. During this strike, the union placed ads in the *New York Times,* the *Herald Tribune,* and *Women's Wear Daily,* appealing to retailers to take sides with union manufacturers against the "anti-social, privilege-seeking few."[25] Union reports indicate that this ad was refused by the *Daily Mirror, Daily News, Journal-American, World Telegram and Sun,* and the *Post.* These newspapers said the content of the ad was too controversial and they would only print it if the copy was revised.[26]

Another example of the variety of types of advertisements placed by the ILGWU is an award-winning ad that appeared in October, 1962. This full-page ad appeared in 79 newspapers having a total circulation of almost 14 million.[27] Beginning with the words "All babies are beautiful," its purpose was to express the union's "belief in and support for the ideals of true democracy and brotherhood."[28] In the spring of the following year, this advertisement won the "mass media brotherhood" award presented by the National Conference of Christians and Jews and the Advertising Writers Association of New York. The award was presented jointly to the Wexton Agency and the ILGWU.

A discussion of the mass media relationships of a large apparel union would be incomplete without some mention of commercial films. Undoubtedly the best known of these, *Norma Rae,* concerns the Amalgamated Clothing and Textile Workers Union and is discussed in Chapter VII. *Norma Rae* is the successor to two other widely distributed films that dealt with the life of garment workers and their unions. These were Warner Bros.' *Pajama Game* (1956), a musical comedy, and Columbia's *The Garment Jungle* (1957), a drama.

Both the film and the Broadway musical *Pajama Game* were based on a book by Richard Bissell, entitled 7½¢. The story concerns the efforts of workers in a garment factory to obtain a 7½¢ per hour salary increase. The ILGWU newspaper *Justice* summed up *Pajama Game* as a story in which "[l]ife, love and labor in a garment factory are depicted in snappy tunes and hilarious hi-jinks."[29]

The Garment Jungle, based on a *Readers' Digest* article, deals with an ILGWU organizer's efforts to unionize a company that has hired gangsters to keep the union out. The ILGWU provided a good deal of technical assistance for this film, much of which was shot on location in New York and in the ILGWU offices. It was given high praise in May, 1957 by Paul Patrick, who wrote a regular column on films for the *AFL-CIO News.*

> This is an earthy, realistic drama reminiscent of some of the great black-and-white movies of years ago and also of the more recent "On The Waterfront."
>
> It is almost documentary in its approach, with the exception of a melodramatic ending. . . .
>
> This is a movie that all unions and union members should attempt to sell by word-of-mouth advertising to their friends and neighbors. Let's make sure it does well at the box office. Be sure to go see "The Garment Jungle."[30]

In 1981 another author, a union organizer, looked back at a number of U.S. films that involved labor unions and was far more critical of most of these than earlier reviewers had been. He found that most of the films reviewed presented a negative image of unions to the public. Concerning *Pajama Game,* this author comments on the ineffectuality of the union:

> The unions are so incredibly reasonable and docile it appears Hollywood was presenting a model for real unions to follow. . . . While the film presents a

union that is likable enough, it is not the kind of organization a worker could trust to get much done. Once again someone in management brings home the bacon for the workers.[31]

The Garment Jungle is seen as a somewhat better representation of the union, perhaps reflecting the technical assistance given by the ILGWU.

> [A] union organizer is finally portrayed as respectable, reasonable, dedicated, intelligent, firm and concerned with the wishes of the workers.
>
> The union too is shown as honest and human. There are union dance classes, a union housing project, and . . . a mass union funeral. Unfortunately the film has a weak ending, both dramatically and from a pro-union viewpoint. Returning to the long movie tradition, the *Garment Jungle* has the owner's son, moved by [the union organizer's] dedication and sacrifice, intervene on behalf of the workers. Even in films that endorse unions, the boss is only a problem for the workers temporarily, if at all.[32]

While the public relations story of the ILGWU has been deemed a successful one by many commentators, it has not been without its critics. Some of these believe that the union has achieved minor successes while ignoring other union issues that are far more important. An author writing in 1976 commented on ILGWU problems and referred to a 1962 article in which the ILGWU was accused of having two "faces."

> One was the public relations image that the ILGWU had carefully nurtured, of a "socially-conscious," "progressive" organization bringing order to its industry, the New York City-based ladies' garment industry, and recreational services to its members. The "other face" of the ILGWU was "of a trade union controlled by a rigid bureaucracy that long ago lost contact with its rank and file members; a bureaucracy that has more in common ethically and socially with the employers than with the workers it is supposed to represent."[33]

The extent to which the ILGWU leadership—or that of any other union—is representative of and responsive to the membership is indeed a problem. And the way in which media utilization expresses and influences such internal dynamics will be considered, however tentatively, in Chapter IV. Whatever the political alignments and motives within the union and its policy-making leadership, the ILGWU clearly has established an exceptionally vigorous and visible public relations program.

UNITED AUTOMOBILE, AEROSPACE AND AGRICULTURAL IMPLEMENT WORKERS OF AMERICA (UAW)

In many respects the United Automobile, Aircraft and Agricultural Implement Workers of America is an unusual union. Built from the bottom up, it has continued to maintain considerable vigor, missionary zeal, and pioneering qualities, despite the elimination of the turbulence and factionalism that characterized the first dozen years of UAW's existence (1935–1947). The dynamic quality of this union stems partly from its early struggles and partly from the idealism and progressive character of its leadership.[34]

The relatively late organizational date for the UAW was caused by the problems that grew out of the differences between industrial unions and craft unions. The AFL was made up of craft unions; for the auto industry, however, division on the basis of crafts would have necessitated the existence of a number of different unions within the industry, a situation that would make effective bargaining difficult. Early association with the AFL disillusioned workers; in 1937, with other industries that perceived the need for a different form of organization, the UAW split from the American Federation of Labor and the Congress of Industrial Organizations was formed.

The person whose name is most closely associated with the UAW, Walter Reuther, became president in 1946. After that year, opposition within the fraction-ridden union gradually diminished. In fact, in a discussion of democracy within the UAW, one commentator notes that there was no organized opposition to Reuther's policies that was of any consequence.[35] Reuther has been called a number of things—among them controversial, effective, influential, and an exceptional leader. One long-time observer of the labor scene inserted the following paragraph in a chapter whose subject was influential AFL-CIO leaders:

> The other great personal figure in the AFL-CIO is Walter P. Reuther, president of the UAW, the Industrial Union Department of the federation, and, before the merger, of the CIO. He is the established leader of what is still the most dynamic national union in the American labor movement and the leader of the old CIO forces. Reuther is a product of industrial unionism, functioning in one of the strategic sectors of the economy. The high priority given to political action and public policy and to the formulation of rational bargaining programs in Reuther's scheme of unionism is directly traceable to his automobile industrial-union, mass-production environment. Reuther also has a flair for dramatizing and galvanizing action in behalf of original and wide-ranging programs. The intensity and comprehensiveness of the federation's interest in public policy owes much to Reuther's influence.[36]

Reuther remained unchallenged in his position as president of the UAW until his death in 1970. During that time he achieved some notable successes in collective bargaining battles, especially in the areas of wages and fringe benefits. Reuther's "original and wide-ranging programs" included several emphasizing social needs—health care, urban renewal, vocational retraining, civil rights, and problems of immigrant workers, for example. In his philosophy that the union should devote itself to high and idealistic goals, Reuther was similar to David Dubinsky.

In 1968, dissatisfied with George Meany's dominance in the labor federation and what Reuther felt was exceptionally slow progress in the area of social needs, the UAW disaffiliated from the AFL-CIO. It remained separate until July 1, 1981. Reuther was succeeded by Leonard Woodcock and, after Woodcock's retirement in 1977, Douglas A. Fraser was elected president. Fraser proved to be a popular leader who, before retiring in 1983, won the respect and acclaim of both labor and business leaders. Owen Bieber succeeded Fraser as UAW leader. The UAW, with over one million members, remains one of the largest unions in the United States, although membership has been falling. It is governed by a biennial convention and, in the interim, by the International Executive Board (IEB).

Of the parallels that might be drawn between the ILGWU and the UAW, only two relate especially directly to union public relations. Just as the ILGWU is deeply rooted in New York City, so is the UAW centered in Detroit. Because of the size of these industries in these cities, the economies of New York City and Detroit rest heavily upon developments in the two industries. The two unions get a sizeable amount of local media attention in these cities. Second, the UAW, like the ILGWU, has long emphasized the importance of working *with* communities, and has seen the importance of convincing the public that union goals are closely—and compatibly—associated with community goals.

Even before the merger of the AFL and the CIO the UAW-CIO had three departments whose responsibilities were to interpret union actions and policies to the community. These were the departments of community relations, publications and public relations, and radio-television. At the present time, the radio-television department is part of the public relations department, whose tasks are to produce official union publications and to assume responsibility for news activities, including contacts with communications media.

The UAW magazine and official publication is *Solidarity,* until 1957 entitled *United Automobile Worker.* In 1962, during Reuther's presidency, *Solidarity* was described as follows:

> The UAW newspaper, which varies from eight to twelve pages in size, gives heavy emphasis to legislative, political and international news. There are also occasional lengthy feature articles on such subjects as the Jane Addams Centennial, gerrymandering of congressional districts, and Tom Mboya, Kenya labor leader and statesman. The bulk of *Solidarity* is generally devoted to collective bargaining news, accounts of UAW conferences, National Labor Relations Board rulings, arbitration decisions, local educational and recreational activities, and other stories with direct appeal to UAW members. In contrast to the factional period and the early years of the Reuther presidency, when the UAW newspaper was an important administrative propaganda weapon, *Solidarity* now carries little news of a strictly partisan internal politi-

cal nature. Photographs and articles about activities of Reuther, Mazey, Woodcock and other executive board members appear frequently. But this is more a reflection of "men who make UAW news" than a calculated effort to "build up" the officers. On the other hand, *Solidarity* makes no attempts to present any union views other than those of the administration. It is frankly an administrative organ engaged in promoting the interests of the UAW as seen through the eyes of the leadership.

Reuther takes considerable interest in the UAW newspaper. One week before publication, he and Public Relations Director Frank Winn see a brief outline of the items to be included in each issue of *Solidarity* and the amount of space to be devoted to them. Reuther frequently has suggestions on "how to play" a certain subject and additional items to be included. He rarely orders anything eliminated, although this may be necessary if his suggestions regarding additions are to be followed.[37]

A look at recent issues of *Solidarity* reveals that many of the characteristics of the paper in 1962 remain essentially unchanged today. The newspaper has grown in length and is now usually 24 pages long. There is still a heavy emphasis on legislative, political, and international news, a variety of feature articles, and a great deal of union news. This union news, however, includes a fairly small amount of information on internal UAW affairs, other than that which deals directly with organizing and bargaining. There is little to be found, for example, on what the Education Department is doing or who directs and staffs it.

A clue to the union's opinion of the relationship between advertisers and the press may be gleaned from the fact that the UAW usually does not accept paid advertising in its newsletters and newspapers, a policy that appears to be typical of the labor press in general. What ads are seen are those for UAW books or dress patterns. Advocacy ads also have been present in the form of labor product boycott promotions, political ads (pro-labor law reform, pro-ERA, and pro-health care reform, for example), and economic ads (Figures 8 and 9).

Ads promoting an economic point of view have been sponsored by a coalition called Americans for a Working Economy, composed of several international unions, including the UAW, and various other organizations such as the Consumer Federation of America, Friends of the Earth, the Scientists' Institute for Public Information, and the U.S. Conference of Mayors. The group was formed in 1977 primarily in order to counter a media campaign by the Advertising Council that was based on an Ad Council Booklet, "The American Economic System . . . and your part in it," that had been judged as "biased" and "misleading" by a number of economists.[38] Advertising for Americans for a Working Economy was prepared by The Public Media Center and was placed in newspapers and on radio and television, as well as in the labor press.

FIGURE 8.   Advertisement in *Solidarity,* October 16–31, 1976, p. 24; ad sponsored by Americans for a Working Economy

The Radio-TV Department was the department whose responsibilities included the direction of the two FM stations that the UAW built and operated. These were established in 1949 and located in Detroit and Cleveland. The history of the UAW's involvement with FM is almost identical to that of the ILGWU, though the stated reason for giving up the stations was not mainly financial. In 1952 WDET-FM in Detroit was given to Wayne State University; the station in Cleveland was abandoned. Reuther's

FIGURE 9.   Advertisement in *Solidarity*, March 1981, p. 24; ad sponsored by UAW.

official report to the convention in 1953 included the following statement regarding reasons for giving up WDET-FM:

> The decision to offer the complete facilities of WDET to Wayne State University had been made only after careful review of the Union FM operation by the International Union Executive Board. WDET had under Union auspices established a distinguished record of public service broadcasting. Its fine music, discussion of public issues, and presentations of programs of a cultural and spiritual character had won the respect of thousands of listeners in Southeastern Michigan. Its contribution to community service and to community

understanding had been attested to by hundreds of letters from individuals and organizations of widely varying interests.

However, the International Union Executive Board felt that since "the UAW-CIO established WDET not as a commercial venture but to make a contribution to the advancement of the cultural and educational activity of our community, it is our sincere belief that these purposes can be more effectively carried out by an institution of higher education."

"We offer the facilities of WDET to Wayne, because we are confident that the use of these facilities by the University will advance the principles and philosophy of the UAW-CIO which are founded on the belief that no group within a community can make progress except as the community moves ahead together. WDET, as an instrument of Wayne University, can contribute to the creation of a spirit of mutual understanding and responsibility toward the common problems of our community and of the world."[39]

These reasons seem ideologically sound, but not totally adequate. With its great desire to reach the public and to portray a favorable image, it seems unlikely that the UAW would have given up the station if it had been as popular as the report indicates. Another commentator laid the blame on the fact that the station was not reaching union members.

Although less than 25 per cent of all UAW members owned FM sets, the leadership considered this a good investment because it expected FM to replace AM in time. By 1952 it was apparent that the leadership had been mistaken. FM programs which featured classical music, discussions of public issues, and cultural and spiritual subjects were enthusiastically received by professionals, intellectuals, and middle-class people but reached very few automobile workers.[40]

It is not difficult to believe that the station was not reaching many auto workers. Still, by reaching other segments of the population, the UAW had a channel through which it could make an important contribution to the community as well as present its point of view to people it did not reach in other ways. Doubtless, no one factor provided the reason for giving up the station. If one is to be selected, however, it seems plausible that the union was simply discouraged with the entire FM situation. Financially they may have been somewhat hurt, but the UAW has long been a wealthy union and early in 1953, leaders took tentative steps in the direction of another communications medium. This time the license application was for a television channel, but nothing came of these early plans; the UAW has never operated a regular television station.

At the time of the AFL-CIO merger in 1955, the UAW was sponsoring a number of radio programs. The nightly news commentary by Guy Nunn, director of the Radio-TV Department, was in its sixth year. It was broadcast on three stations—CKLW in Windsor, WILS in Lansing, and WAKR in Ohio (where it was sponsored by the United Rubber Workers—CIO)—and surveys had shown that there were close to half a million listeners to CKLW alone. "Eye-Opener," an early morning news program, had been initiated in 1954; its target audience was UAW members on their way to work the day shift. A similar audience was targeted for the "Shift-Break" program, begun in 1954 in Flint, Michigan. "This program is an innovation in union broadcasting, since it is on the air for a total period of 90 minutes, reaches a potential of more than 95 per cent of all auto workers driving to—or leaving—work, and features news, local union announcements, music and sports."[41] Time was also reserved on these news programs for local unions in the area of the broadcast to insert announcements and items of local interest.

A Sunday afternoon television program, "Meet the UAW-CIO," had been broadcast since 1951. These regular efforts were supplemented by the production of a number of special programs and production assistance for other programs broadcast in Michigan.

These radio-television endeavors by the UAW, which were expanded after the AFL-CIO merger, were cut back during the union austerity program instituted in 1958 (the union wanted to build up a strike fund in preparation for negotiations on several major automobile contracts that were due to expire in mid-year). "Shift-Break" continued with high listener ratings; "Telescope," a daily television program, replaced "Meet the UAW-CIO," and "Eye-Opener" continued, but was heard in only 17 cities rather than 40 as in 1957.[42] All of these were intended to inform, educate, and entertain primarily union members, secondarily the general public. The programs covered a wide range of ideas and ideals not limited to specific union causes.

Because of the austerity program, the UAW could not respond to negative publicity engendered by the McClellan hearings with any special public relations program of its own. Even after that period, however, when the series of hearings that had begun in August, 1959 caused a good deal of negative publicity specifically about the UAW, their programming remained essentially unchanged, anchored by the regulars, "Eye-Opener," "Shift-Break," and "Telescope." These were deemed successful, however, and certainly represented more than most international unions were doing.

> The membership can be proud that its union is the only one in this country which maintains a radio and television operation of this size and scope.
>
> As an international organization arrayed against powerful, anti-union forces commanding great resources and the bulk of the nation's communication facilities, the UAW has obvious need of this close, daily contact within its ranks.[43]

In 1981 the UAW applied to the FCC for several licenses to operate low-power television (LPTV) stations in high-membership areas. It was the first union to take this step, and may be the only one. Well over 12,000 applications have been received by the FCC. Many of these have not yet been processed; FCC personnel hoped to have completed the major portion of this task by the end of 1984. When LPTV was conceived, its advocates thought that, because of its relatively low equipment costs, LPTV would be an ideal medium for many groups who had experienced difficulties gaining media access. Unfortunately, the FCC received far more applications than expected, had too few available outlets, and few guidelines for deciding how to allocate the licenses. The system decided upon was a lottery, a decision that made neither established broadcast interests nor the smaller groups—minorities, women, community organizations, labor unions—happy. UAW leaders plan to take no action on any one of their applications until they know whether all other applications have been granted or denied.

The Public Relations and Publications Department of the UAW has a staff of approximately ten full-time people. In comparison with a number of other international unions, especially those that are smaller and less wealthy, this is a large department. It is also quite experienced. The departmental budget is used for a variety of activities—*Solidarity* and other informational pamphlets and newsletters to members, a news service for its locals, and press conferences. Radio and television media are still utilized, especially via public service time when it can be obtained, and occasional purchases of time in order to present union views on public affairs issues. Because this union has frequently utilized the fairness doctrine as a means for obtaining broadcasting time, and because it also has occasionally been denied access to the media, the public relations staff has kept itself well-informed on communications legislation and media technology.

Radio and television stories appearing in *Solidarity* provide examples of the staff's interests in these areas and their desire to inform and gain the support of UAW members. For example, a piece entitled "Tuning Out the Public Voice in Radio and TV" (1979) discussed the threat from proposed deregulation of the broadcast industry as seen by union leaders.

> With the tacit support of the White House, some politicians in Congress are moving to hand the airwaves over lock, stock, and barrel to the giant communications companies that already control most radio and TV programming in the U.S. Many of these corporations are part of still-larger financial giants who see in "deregulation" a chance to strengthen their control over news and public-affairs broadcasting that sometimes threaten to expose corporate politics.
>
> The UAW, other unions, and a large body of public organizations are strongly opposing this giveaway.
>
> "For more than 40 years," says UAW President Douglas A. Fraser, "our country has regarded the airwaves as a scarce public resource. We have required that those who make private profit from that resource at least serve the

public interest in certain ways as well. We need to reform our communications laws in America, but the goal should be greater responsiveness to the public, not less."[44]

The article goes on to explain station licensing requirements ("[s]tations today must show that they have aired a minimum amount of news and public-affairs programs"), the fairness doctrine ("requires radio and TV stations to air both sides of a controversial issue"), the equal-time rule ("stations that run political ads favoring a candidate or ballot issue must grant equal air time to opponents of that candidate or ballot issue"[45]), the public-interest standard, and equal employment guarantees, and proposes changes for each. In order to support the argument against deregulation, the article quotes UAW legislative director Howard Paster who had recently testified before the House Communications Subcommittee.

> We flatly reject elimination or dilution of the fairness doctrine or equal-time rule. Rather, they should be beefed up and made to work much more quickly and effectively.
>   The chief argument of deregulators like Van Deerlin is that "marketplace forces" (i.e., public demand) will ensure broadcasting that meets the public interest. This argument is rooted in a fiction—namely, that there is a competitive market in radio and TV ownership and programming.[46]

Another article in *Solidarity* (1981) explained new media technologies— cable, low-power stations, direct-to-home broadcast satellites, closer spacing of stations on TV and radio bands—that "could make it possible for thousands of new stations to fill the airwaves and wires, with a proliferation of new voices, contrasting ideas, and a variety of formats. But like most new technologies, the most serious question remains unresolved: who will control it?"[47]

Such articles as these two are relatively unusual in union newspapers. Other union papers may have short news stories or editorials, especially concerning proposed legislation. The UAW stories, however, differ. Because of the format of *Solidarity,* more a magazine than a newspaper, longer feature stories are common. The articles are also written on a personal level—bringing in related quotes and experiences of UAW members, and explaining how individual UAW members can respond to the situation in an advocate's role if they so desire. In its 1983 excellence in journalism contest, the International Labor Communications Association awarded *Solidarity* first place for general excellence for the second consecutive year.

While at the forefront in such journalistic efforts to inform members, the UAW entered the advertising arena more slowly. The union did very little mass media advertising before 1980. In 1978, it did contribute financially to the call for help from organized labor in Missouri when a coalition there began to utilize innovative communications to help defeat the "right-to-

work" proposal (discussed in Chapter VI). At the UAW's twenty-sixth convention in 1980, delegates voted in favor of a constitutional amendment
that permitted setting aside up to half the interest and dividends earned by
the union's strike insurance fund for a new organization, education, and
communications fund.[48]

Results of this action were immediately visible. In November, 1980, the
UAW began an extensive newspaper and radio advertising campaign. Three
full-page ads were placed in daily papers in Michigan, Indiana, New York,
California, Washington, D.C. and elsewhere; their focus was trade reform
(Figure 10).

> [Consumers] are being urged to give North American-built cars a fair
> chance before buying a new auto and they're being warned that the country's
> "free trade" policy is not fair to millions of working families in auto and
> supplier industries across the nation.
>
> The ads are part of a major new campaign to communicate the views of
> UAW members to their neighbors and fellow citizens on economic and social
> issues. The first series was developed to help point out the crisis faced by
> domestic industry due to the flood of low-wage imported cars from Japan and
> elsewhere which are taking a growing share of the market.[49]

As with some of the ILGWU advertising, the purpose of this campaign was
to call attention to unemployment and the short-term relief that could come
through import restrictions and the long-term benefits that could be gained
through strengthening the industrial base of the economy.

The UAW moved its advertising campaign to television in December,
1981, and January, 1982. Emphasis in these 30- and 60-second spots, aired
on both local and network stations, was again the commitment to quality,
the need for job security, and the need for a change in the direction of the
nation's economy.

Solidarity describes one of these ads, which was produced by the Public
Relations and Publications Departments after research that involved interviews of local leaders and rank and file members to determine what issues
should be brought to the attention of a nationwide audience:

> The camera focuses on a man walking through a farm field. An array of
> shiny new tractors, built by UAW members, comes into view.
>
> The camera comes closer. Standing next to one of the new models, the man
> turns to face the TV audience and you hear the following message in one of the
> first three 30-second UAW TV ads:
>
> *"United Auto Workers built this machine. It's not as flashy as a new sports
> car. But this happens to be one of the best tractors made in the world today.*
>
> *"The point is . . . If United Auto Workers can build fine farm equipment
> like this . . . if we can build the space shuttle, we can also build the finest cars.*
>
> *"Sure, there've been problems. But now there's a new commitment by the*

FIGURE 10.   Examples of full-page ads sponsored by UAW and placed in metropolitan daily newspapers; *Solidarity*, November 1980, p. 3.

companies to design cars right and engineer 'em right. And we're committed to building 'em right.

"A secure job is an important part of this. It strengthens our commitment to quality.

"The UAW wants to help make America work again."[50]

All three advertising campaigns (newspaper, radio, and television) were intended to educate and to inform. Union leaders also believed the ads would make people more aware of the UAW and helped create a more favorable union image. The television campaign focused on geographic areas containing large numbers of UAW members and potential UAW members, an indication that it was also intended to be of some help in organizing efforts. But, perhaps most importantly, the message was intended to communicate to the general public the economic importance of buying American products. The UAW has continued to advertise. In 1983, ads supporting the Domestic Auto Content Bill were released. Just before contract negotiations in 1984, the UAW introduced a series of television commercials intended to inform the public about the need to keep auto industry jobs in this country and the efforts of the union to do so. The first spot was aired on NBC's "Today" show in late August.

INTERNATIONAL ASSOCIATION OF MACHINISTS
AND AEROSPACE WORKERS (IAM)

A third international union occupying a leadership role in the area of mass media communications is the International Association of Machinists and Aerospace Workers.

The history of the IAM goes back to 1888 when the name of the organization was the United Machinists and Mechanical Engineers of America. As early as 1890 the first Canadian lodge was admitted and the name was changed to International Association of Machinists. The union is now not only one of the oldest unions in the United States, but one of the largest in the United States and Canada. Originally a group of railroad machinists, IAM members now include aerospace workers, automechanics, airline employees, technicians, and tool and die makers, as well as machinists. The union prides itself on its democratic form of government. Control by the members stems from a constitution written by members, an executive council nominated and elected by members, free and open conventions (usually held every four years) with delegates chosen in local lodge elections, and an open system of reporting that emphasizes keeping members informed about activities and finances.

It was in order to facilitate the latter that the first IAM publication, a magazine called the *Machinists' Monthly Journal,* was initiated. The first issue of the *Journal* came out in 1889 and the publication was continued without interruption until 1956. It provided current information and education and historical material to members; issues were also mailed to libraries, schools, heads of various federal and state agencies, and labor and public leaders abroad.

In 1945 the decision was made to publish, in addition to the *Journal,* a weekly newspaper for members. This paper, like the *Journal,* enjoyed a substantial circulation among a variety of people and a reputation as a leading labor newspaper. In 1956 delegates at the regular IAM convention decided to discontinue publication of the *Journal,* primarily because of costs. There was also a certain amount of duplication in the two publications and a number of members desired, if funds were available, to improve the new *Machinist* newspaper and to utilize radio and television more frequently to communicate with the general public.

Leaders of IAM saw the years 1956–1960 as being very difficult for labor. The president's opening address at the 1960 convention dealt with the subject of the extreme antilabor climate caused by the McClellan hearings, the Landrum-Griffin Act, and the current recession, high unemployment, and inflation.

> Unfortunately—with a few honorable exceptions—the nation's press, including most of the major magazines, radio and television outlets, has wittingly or unwittingly cooperated in the campaign to reduce the economic and political effectiveness of every union in our countries [the United States and Canada]. . . . The efforts of our labor papers and magazines and other media of public contact have actually been puny compared to the efforts of the vast array of daily newspapers, magazines, radio, television and other means of communications used to convey the propaganda and half-truths against us.[51]

The IAM was proud of the fact that it was the only union to publish a weekly paper. By 1964 it was spending more than $1,000,000 per year on the award-winning *Machinist*. In the 1970s, however, high costs forced the union to cut the *Machinist* back to fewer pages, and in 1976, though the publication was doubled in size, it was cut from 48 to 12 issues per year. The move was necessitated primarily by printing costs and the rapidly increasing postal rates for not-for-profit organizations.

Like UAW's *Solidarity*, no paid advertising was (or is) accepted in the *Machinist*. Free space was provided for members to buy, sell, and trade. And, especially recently, the *Machinist* has published image advertisements prepared by the IAM Communications Department and disseminated to the union's district and local units for placement in local daily newspapers (Figure 11).

In 1980 the *Machinist* underwent some format and style changes in order to provide more space for

> in-depth analysis of key social and political issues facing IAM members in today's society. Some of the issues examined in recent editions have included the increasing power of corporate America, the growing imbalance of income and wealth in the USA, the inequities of so-called free trade, new trends and methods in union-busting, Social Security, women in the work force, and the continuing battle for safer and more healthful work places.
>
> While feature articles have been given more scope and depth, sweeping changes have been made in graphics and design. These changes, in content and packaging, have won for *The Machinist* staff the approval of their peers in the labor press. We have been awarded top honors by the International Labor Press Association for graphics and front page design as well as top honors for editorial excellence in both of the last two years.[52]

THE BEST OF HOLIDAYS

from the union that brings you the best all year round

The holiday season is here.

It's a great time of year, one that traditionally generates happiness and goodwill. People become more people-oriented than at any other time of year.

And, as always, we're hard at work to help make this holiday season enjoyable for you.

We're the nearly one million members of the International Association of Machinists and Aerospace Workers, a trade union. Like other unions, it's an organization run by people for people—nearly a million of them.

We come in all sizes, shapes and colors.

We have a wide range of jobs in virtually every industry in our society.

We have different lifestyles; and, especially during the holiday season, we enjoy a variety of customs and traditions.

But nearly everything we do, regardless of how different those things may be, touches the lives and lifestyles of all Americans.

For example, we build and service the commercial airplanes that bring families closer together for these important holidays. If you're traveling by rail, or by bus, or even in your own family car, chances are good that an IAM mechanic contributed his or her skills to make your holiday safer and more pleasant.

Our members manufacture many of the modern appliances, tools, toys, recreation equipment and thousands of other items that will be given as gifts from people to be enjoyed the year round and for years to come.

As you can see, the nearly one million members of the Machinists Union do a lot to make your holiday season happy, comfortable and secure.

But we'd like to make a person-to-person appeal for you to do us— and yourself—a favor. When you're making your holiday plans this year, please use and buy products and services of American workers.

You'll be getting the best there is. And, just as important, you'll have the satisfaction of knowing that you've done something for another person—an American worker—a friend, a neighbor, possibly even a relative whose job directly or indirectly touches you this holiday season.

On behalf of the officers and the nearly one million members of the IAM, we extend our best for a happy, healthy and safe holiday season to all.

William W. Winpisinger, INTERNATIONAL PRESIDENT

International Association of Machinists and Aerospace Workers, AFL-CIO

FIGURE 11. Advertisement in *Machinist*, December 1982, p. 16; ad sponsored by IAM.

Budget cuts necessitated reducing the paper from a 16-page format to a 12-page format in 1983. Content also has changed, with a good portion of the newspaper now used for regular news of the major industrial branches of the union. Industry newsletters, which formerly filled this function, have been discontinued.

The IAM traditionally has published a wide variety of pamphlets, leaflets, and other types of materials primarily intended to keep members informed and also to help local units in efforts to publish materials. Convention reports continually mention the importance of telling the union story to the public at every level. Every lodge (local and district unit) is urged to have a public relations chairperson, to get news to the local media, and to print a regular newsletter. For a number of years the IAM has helped in this effort by preparing a monthly packet of news features and pamphlets that are sent to local units. At the 1980 convention, the Communications Department reported that this monthly news press service, called *Keeping in Touch*, had

> been tripled in size with the addition of news and art service from Press Associates, Inc. (PAI). This is a Washington-based service that functions for labor publications as Associated Press does for daily commercial newspapers. Its features and news reports emphasize the labor movement and the world of work. Every local or district that furnishes Grand Lodge with copies of its publication regularly receives *Keeping in Touch* along with the PAI packet.[53]

Another regular publication is *Report from Headquarters*, a biweekly newsletter targeted toward local and district union leaders, which contains a summary of important union news and legislative developments. To supplement these, the IAM distributes monthly videotaped messages and occasional special videotapes on particular topics—all for use at local and district meetings.

The Machinists have also produced a number of public relations films since 1952. These have included *My Dad J. R.*, a film shown in commercial theaters; *POSSE,* a story of a *Journal* editor, shown at lodge meetings; *Anatomy of a Lie,* a documentary that countered an anti-union film whose subject was a particular strike; and *Union Headquarters*, a cinematic tour of the Machinists' Building in Washington.

By 1964 the IAM was producing a five-minute radio news program twice a week entitled *The World of Labor.* At that time a few districts and locals sponsored the show in several cities across the United States. By 1968 the program was broadcast regularly in 72 cities and the Communications Department was pleased with the increased amount of air time the union was receiving. At the same time, departmental concern was expressed about

> the withdrawal of the AFL-CIO from virtually all radio broadcasting activities and by its failure to develop any method which would enable the labor movement to use the medium of television.

We urge our district and local lodges through their representatives in the city central bodies and state federations to introduce resolutions urging the AFL-CIO to step up its communications and public relations activities and especially to develop some kind of television programming that could be sponsored locally by Central Labor Bodies. We urge the AFL-CIO to resume radio broadcasting.[54]

As recently as the end of 1981, many public relations directors for international labor organizations still felt that the AFL-CIO did not utilize the media satisfactorily, and that it should do more on behalf of organized labor as a whole.[55] Such sentiments, however, were rarely expressed during the 1960s, and it was even more unusual to find a publications committee urging union members to take specific action in order to change the situation. These opinions emphasize the importance of the need for the various structural levels of organized labor to put forth a concerted effort in their public relations programs.

The importance that the IAM places on public relations can be inferred from the amount of money allocated to public relations endeavors. In 1972 the Communications Department report stated: "No union spends more effort or money to keep its members informed."[56] At the time the union was spending about 1 percent of its general revenue on public relations and another 5–6 percent on its newspaper, then still a weekly.[57] The change to a monthly newspaper in 1976 did lower that percentage to approximately 3 percent, but this decrease has been made up for by constant increases in the public relations budget (approximately 2½ percent of general revenue in 1979),[58] showing that the IAM accomplished what it wanted to do when it was forced to cut the annual number of newspapers—that is, to utilize the money in other public relations efforts. By 1981, the total percentage of general revenue allocated to the Communications Department was up to approximately 7½ percent. However, that same year IAM membership began a precipitous decline and the union had to cut its budget in a number of areas, not the least of which was communications.

The IAM radio program was discontinued in 1969 because many districts and locals that had been purchasing air time were unable to continue their financial support. The international's efforts to broadcast the program nationally had been unsuccessful.

During the five years that *The World of Labor* was on the air, we tried repeatedly to purchase network air time to air it nationally. Although professionally acceptable, the program was rejected by each network in turn on the grounds that only the owners have the right to decide what will be broadcast as news over their networks. The so-called fairness doctrine of the Federal Communications Commission does not require any broadcaster to sell time to permit a trade union to speak for itself on controversial matters.[59]

It was because of this setback that the IAM moved toward "advertising"; that is, they produced some commercials, but did not have to pay for air time:

> In place of the twice-weekly news program, we have developed four sets of 60-second commercials. They were produced for the IAM by John Henry Faulk and Cactus Pryor of Austin, Texas. Using humor, Faulk and Pryor wrote and voiced spot announcements supporting trade union campaigns. The subjects were: occupational health and safety, the fight against pollution, registering to vote and the importance of voting. Each series consisting of five announcements was aired as a public service on more than 800 radio stations. The only cost to the IAM was for talent and reproducing the tapes. They were mailed in most states with the cooperation of the IAM State Councils.[60]

When William Winspisinger became IAM president in 1977, he announced that one of his major goals was the overall improvement in image of workers and unions. This statement marked the beginning of several significant changes for the union, the most important of which was the redirection of the expanded Communications Department's time and effort to electronic media. Throughout the 1970s, IAM officials had noted the importance of television and obviously had felt some frustration over inability to gain much access even for commercials because of the costs.

> [Television] requires more funds than we ever expect to have available under normal circumstances. The present cost of a 60-second commercial message on a major network—NBC, CBS or ABC—is $100,000 a minute. Filming the message is an additional cost.
> However, this year's Labor Coalition Clearing House, formed to encourage the election of union delegates to the recent national political conventions, proved something that could be useful in union communications. It proved that a number of unions can organize a successful program to raise funds for necessary trade union purposes. We feel that a labor coalition for TV is both practical and possible in the near future. We intend to try for it.[61]

It might be that the IAM couldn't drum up support among other unions for this idea, or that they were diverted by their new president and some ideas they liked better. Perhaps they simply put the idea on a back burner. It appeared to have potential to unify union communication strategy and also make it more feasible for smaller, less wealthy unions to become actively involved. Perhaps this coalition idea was a precursor of the Labor Institute for Public Affairs. At any rate, by the end of the 1970s, the efforts of IAM leaders who were trying to seek out more opportunities to get on the air were rewarded; the union at that time managed to obtain more publicity than it had ever had in the past—on local news and feature programs as well as on such nationally broadcast programs as "Meet the Press" and "Sixty Minutes."

While the cost of any kind of sustained sponsorship or programming on the commercial networks is prohibitive, we have used cable TV enough to recognize its promise as a means of communicating with our members and the public. In April, 1979, the IAM hosted a special 90-minute show on foreign trade [Figure 12]. The highlight of the program was the airing of the IAM-produced film, "We Didn't Want It To Happen This Way," a true life portrayal of what actually happens to people when a plant closes and moves American jobs overseas. The film, which took the top award for documentaries at the 1979 New York Film Festival, sparked a lively discussion among panelists, which included President Winspisinger. The panelists were joined in their discussion—for the first time in television history—by phone calls from viewers around the nation. The two-way live communications was made possible with the help of a satellite orbiting 24,000 miles above earth.

A second IAM cable TV 90-minute special on the energy crises [sic] was aired in December, 1979. These three hours of television time cost about the same as one sixty-second spot advertisement during prime time on any of the major networks.[62]

Name recognition continues to be important to the IAM, primarily because it helps with organizing campaigns, but leaders also want the general public to remember the union. In order to increase public recognition of its name, the IAM has, for a number of years, distributed a variety of items such as matchbooks, pens and pencils, key chains, posters, buttons, and stickers, all imprinted with the union name and emblem. In November of 1981, the union staged what is probably the ultimate in union billboard advertising. For an entire month, including the time that the AFL-CIO convened in New York City, the IAM rented the huge electronic sign on Times Square to publicize its name. This sign, made up of computer-synchronized lights which produce moving pictures, was programed to give the IAM's full name and logo and read, "The Machinists' Union, The Big Apple of Trade Unions—Proud of Our Past; Excited About Our Future."

Perhaps the best known of all the activities of the IAM staff and its communications department is the IAM Media Project, an unusual program launched in 1979. In August of that year the IAM decided to monitor the news and entertainment on the three major television networks in order to answer the general question, "What is television doing for workers in America?" Or, as the *IAM Television Report* stated, what is television doing *to* workers in America? In the next few years, the project produced results that received wide media attention and caught the interest of a number of other unions.[63]

Probably one reason for the success of the venture is the careful planning that went into it initially. Such an undertaking would have been out of the question for the majority of U.S. unions because of the expense involved, estimated to be about $100,000. At the outset even some IAM members must have questioned the value of spending so much for such a project,

THE RUNAWAYS:

Since 1969, over one million factory workers have lost their jobs as U.S. factories closed down and moved to foreign countries. These runaway shops, seeking the advantages of cheap labor and low overhead, are selling off our technology and creating unemployment for workers here at home.

A live public affairs broadcast will be aired on cable TV channels throughout the country via satellite on Sunday, April 29, 1979 from 12:00 to 1:30 P.M.

During this important broadcast, you will have the opportunity to:

WATCH . . . . . the film, "We Didn't Want It to Happen This Way," a 30-minute documentary which looks at the impact on seven American workers and their families when a runaway shop takes away their jobs.

HEAR . . . . . a distinguished panel discuss the business and the economic and social issues raised by runaways. Panelists will include:

> **William Winpisinger**, President of the International Association of Machinists and Aerospace Workers;
>
> **Robert T. Hall**, U.S. Assistant Secretary of Commerce for Economic Development;
>
> **Robert Lekachman**, Professor of Economics, Lehman College, New York City;
>
> and others.

SPEAK OUT . . . . . to the panelists through a toll-free phone number, available across the country during this important cable-TV broadcast.

IS AMERICAN LABOR BECOMING OBSOLETE?

REMEMBER! April 29, 1979 is an important date for you and your family. On Cable TV channels Sunday April 29, 12-1:30 P.M.

The International Association for Machinists and Aerospace Workers, in cooperation with the Center for Non-Broadcast Television, is the first American union to bring important issues before the American public through a network of cable TV systems and the RCA Satcom I satellite (1) (1) (1)

FIGURE 12. Advertisement in *Machinist*, March 1979, p. 16; ad sponsored by IAM.

innovative but perhaps of questionable value. According to the assistant director of the IAM Communications Department, the project developed after an unsuccessful attempt to sell the networks on the idea of a series of IAM-sponsored documentaries depicting the lives of trade unionists. The union then decided "to try to get a handle on the identity problem."[64]

The IAM utilized the professional assistance of William Young and Associates of Chicago, a media consulting firm. This firm developed a monitoring form and a training program to be used by IAM local lodge monitors around the country. The training manual was designed to give IAM members and their family members who had volunteered to help with the program basic information not only about the project and the methods that were to be employed, but also about the television industry, communications regulations, citizen recourse to improper broadcasting procedures, and effective action that can be taken by the public.

The monitoring forms utilized by the IAM were designed to accomplish the following:

1. [aid monitors] to critically view the content of the particular program
2. sensitize the viewer to stereotyped images of union leaders, members and the blue collar workers
3. sensitize the viewer to unfair or inaccurate reporting, editorializing of news and documentaries
4. provide solid facts for inclusion in letters to local stations, networks, advertisers, and the FCC
5. provide solid facts to IAM to illustrate objections or praise for future media actions, such as petitions to deny.[65]

Separate monitoring forms were developed for entertainment programming and for news programming. The former poses the following general questions:

What is the image of American workers on television programs? Television is a powerful public persuader. Is it convincing the public that workers are valuable, concerned people? Or foolish and clumsy? Or victims and criminals? Are they of central importance to American life, or very minor?[66]

The actual monitoring was done during the entire month of February, 1980, by 1,500 volunteers in 43 states.

The survey of entertainment programs, which included 53 series, 24 films, and 24 specials, found that only 14 percent of major characters in series had unionized occupations and that the majority of labor roles were nameless background characters. The following are summary statements of the conclusions of the *IAM Television Entertainment Report:*

1. Unions are almost invisible on television. Despite unionized occupations as the basis for plots and characters, the role unions continuously play in

improving the quality of life and working conditions for those workers is never illustrated.

2. Television depicts unions as violent, degrading and obstructive. . . .
3. Occupational prevalence on television is grossly disproportionate to reality. . . .
4. Television's denial of the importance of production and trades which produce goods is hazardous to the nation's economy. . . . As the public, and especially young people who are selecting an occupation, view television, they see the importance and value of services and the devaluation of goods production. . . .
5. Television continues to portray workers in unionized occupations as clumsy, uneducated fools who drink, smoke and have no leadership ability. . . .
6. The majority of workers in unionized occupations on television may as well be robots. They are nameless, personalityless cab drivers and waitresses who take orders, do their job and disappear. . . .[67]

A separate report on network news programming was released by the IAM in August, 1980. It included an issue analysis, news profiles of each network and its editorial policy, documentary analysis, and news magazine analysis. On IAM-selected priority issues (which included inflation, energy, foreign trade, health care, and tax reform), the IAM found that corporate America's views prevailed through selection of interviewees, visuals used, or reporter comments on almost every issue. "It is this distortion which consistently erodes labor's confidence in the media," states the report.[68] The following specific conclusions come from this report:

1. Machinists' issues are not receiving coverage in the network news.
2. Union issues which receive most attention are strikes.
3. Reasons for strikes and backgrounds are not given in strike stories.
4. Labor positions are not sought out for expression on national issues.
5. Network news provides more visual entertainment than information and awareness of national and international concerns.
6. Political campaign coverage fails to provide helpful voter information for candidate comparisons on labor and other issues.
7. When networks take time to do in-depth reports, they are appreciated by viewers.
8. There is great need to expand national and international news; it is impossible to give adequate attention in 24 minutes.
9. There are too many commercial interruptions.
10. Viewers know nothing about international situations in which there is not a violent, hostile action. More international information is needed in an unbiased way before a crisis. International reports showed too few opinions. If Americans are media-fed only one point of view, it is very little different from the controlled media in some other nations.

11. Media should help viewers improve their lives—offering information
and solutions to problems in the lives of American workers. Health and
safety information were the most frequently listed types of direct and
immediate benefit.[69]

After results of the project were in, President Winspisinger personally
visited each of the network presidents. He familiarized these people with the
data, discussed the scope and intensity of the problem as the union saw it,
and asked that changes be instituted in broadcasting policy at every level.
Winspisinger also encouraged local IAM members to follow up the project
by visiting local television station managers in order to present them with
the data and request more diligent efforts to promote change.

A *Machinist* report indicates that a limited number of positive developments have occurred at local levels as a result of the project. For example,
union representatives have been included on local station advisory boards in
some cities (viz., Hartford, Connecticut; Oklahoma City; Wichita, Kansas;
and Portland, Oregon). As board members, these people are asked to review
editorial content and contribute to programming decisions. Station KNXT-
TV, a CBS-owned and operated station in Los Angeles, announced it would
sponsor a seminar for union representatives; the seminar was intended to
acquaint unionists with ways to obtain better responses from television
news departments and thus get union viewpoints onto the air more frequently.[70]

While such changes were welcomed by the IAM, results of a second
monitoring project, undertaken in April and May of 1981, were more discouraging. For the second project the IAM received volunteer support from
two other major unions, the International Union of Operating Engineers
and the Bakery, Confectionary and Tobacco Workers; 2,000 volunteers
worked in 36 states and watched both entertainment programs and local
and network news programs.

The summaries of entertainment programming showed that union people
were even less visible in the second monitoring period than in the first.
Other conclusions reached in 1980 remained essentially unchanged after the
1981 survey:

Television continues to depict unions as violent, degrading and obstructive. . . .

Occupational prevalence on television is grossly and dangerously disproportionate to reality. . . .

Today, as the nation is faced with a critical need for increased goods
production, television continues to emphasize service occupations to a degree
that is hazardous to the nation's economy. . . .

Television's answer to nation problems is less goods production and more jokes. . . .

Television continues to draw more negative portrayals of unionized occupations. . . .

The majority of workers in unionized occupations on television may as well be robots. They are nameless, personalityless people who take orders, do their jobs and disappear. . . .[71]

The report is somewhat more encouraging for network news coverage. While all three major networks still expressed corporate views most of the time, the frequency of coverage of labor priority issues (these were the same as previously noted with one exception—plant closings and job losses replaced foreign trade) rose by at least 25 percent for all three networks when compared with the 1980 results. Network bias toward what the IAM called "Corporate America" was found to have increased on ABC and CBS since the Reagan administration began, but to have decreased on NBC; CBS expressed corporate views six times as often as union views, ABC five to one, and NBC three to one.

Of course it is important to note that this monitoring project was being done by a group that could be described as "non-objective"—monitors were all prolabor and were instructed to look for examples of antilabor reports. As William Winspisinger's letter to trainers that appears in the training manual states: "Television, as a powerful persuader and educator, is too often guilty of presenting Organized Labor in an unfavorable light. These negative messages are conveyed to the American public, miseducating them and creating unfavorable public reaction."[72]

At the AFL-CIO convention in 1981, delegates expressed support for IAM's work and it was reported that more international unions indicated a desire to participate. However, since that time no further systematic monitoring of television entertainment or news has been conducted. This can be explained both by IAM's dwindling financial resources and the creation and subsequent activities of LIPA (Labor Institute of Public Affairs). LIPA has conducted no media monitoring, but, rather, seems to be taking for granted the bias that IAM's project reported and is trying to move forward from there by producing programs itself. These efforts will not change existing media bias—at least not directly. And labor may want to engage in further monitoring in the future; for the present, however, IAM can be given credit for being the moving force behind a media study that had great interest to labor, and LIPA can be credited with assuaging some of the frustrations the study engendered.

Of course, the IAM and labor are not the only groups to accuse the media of bias. "Corporate America" has done the same thing. In direct opposition to IAM, however, business claims the media bias exists against its views rather than in favor of them. Kaiser Aluminum and Chemical Corporation, for example, became upset over the implication on ABC-TV's "20/20" program that it intentionally marketed unsafe house wiring. In protest, corporation leaders not only developed full-page newspaper ads to present their side and to call attention to what they called "trial by television," but they also hosted, in April, 1980, a meeting to discuss with 20 other companies ways greater television access could be gained. Out of this meeting came a 24-page booklet, *At Issue: Access to Television Denied,* that states Kaiser's point of view on the issues.

The Kaiser affair was followed by a study done by The Media Institute in California. This group is composed of 300 individual and corporate members, including Mobil Oil, Westinghouse, General Electric, and Twentieth Century Fox. Its primary function is to monitor television news coverage of business and economics. A spokesperson for the Institute states that its research has found little antibusiness bias in network news broadcasts. When this group extended its monitoring activities to prime time entertainment programs, however, it found that business executives were often portrayed as villains (e.g., J. R. Ewing of "Dallas") and that only 3 percent of business executives on television were portrayed as engaged in socially or economically productive behavior.[73]

A slightly different type of survey was conducted by Richard Manville for Brouillard Communications, a division of the advertising agency J. Walter Thompson. This research utilized a mail questionnaire sent to advertising and public relations directors of the top 1,000 industrial corporations and the top 50 nonindustrial corporations in the categories of insurance, banking, diversified financial, transportation, utilities, and retail. Although the response rate was a low 30 percent, results showed senior executives in these companies participated frequently in news interviews with the participation percentage increasing as the annual company sales increased. This study concluded that alleged hostility between business executives and the electronic news media is greatly exaggerated.[74]

The debate between unions and corporations on these issues doubtless will continue, especially while Congress continues to discuss the need and methods for updated federal communications legislation.

AMERICAN FEDERATION OF STATE, COUNTY AND MUNICIPAL EMPLOYEES (AFSCME)

The American Federation of State, County and Municipal Employees is unique among U.S. labor unions in a number of ways. Its membership is composed of people from a diversity of occupations that ranges from zookeepers, gravediggers, and sanitation workers to librarians, architects, and social workers—all of whom work for the government. Equally troublesome, at least from a labor union point of view, is the fact that it is not unusual for employer authority to reside not in one person, for example, a mayor, county commissioner, or governor, but in a state board or a state legislative committee. And, all too often, the legal employer is not clearly defined.

The National Labor Relations Act excludes government workers on the theory that a government cannot bargain because it cannot share its power. The international union does not control jobs or job security and in only a few states are public employees given the legal right to bargain collectively (though the number of these is growing). Public employees are often denied the right to strike and have no legal protection against unfair labor practices by employers. Because the union does not control jobs, individuals as well as entire locals can move in and out of membership with ease, and most of AFSCME's local and district units are highly autonomous in bargaining efforts.

In spite of all this, during approximately the last 30 years, AFSCME has been the fastest growing union in the AFL-CIO. One reason for the growth spurt is simply that between 1950 and 1980 the numbers of people employed by local, state, and national governments almost tripled. Another reason was that, in the 1950s, government salaries and benefits began to lag, and, pressured by city employees, Philadelphia and New York finally agreed to bargain. In 1961, New York teachers won the right to bargain, and, in 1962, an executive order from President John Kennedy gave Federal civilian employees limited collective bargaining rights. A number of state and local governments followed this example.

A drop in membership was noted at the 1980 AFSCME convention for the first time since 1951. Numbers of government jobs disappeared in 1977 and 1978 because state and local governments, influenced by unhappy citizens, imposed tax cuts or spending limits upon state and local governments; the trend continued in 1981, aggravated by higher expenses due to inflation and revenues that have been hurt by recession. As a result of the ensuing membership decline, AFSCME has initiated major new political and organizational campaigns.

The union was formed in Wisconsin in 1933 when that state's civil service system was threatened. A small group met in Madison to discuss what might be done to help the state's public employees. At the time, while the American Federation of Government Employees existed for employees of the federal government, no group was devoted to the interests of state and local government employees. The group obtained a charter from the AFL and by 1935, 30 similar groups existed in other states. Delegates from these states met and adopted a constitution. The group was a department of the American Federation of Government Employees but this status lasted only a year, after which a separate charter was applied for and obtained from the AFL.

Early growth was slow, primarily due to widespread resistance to the idea of a union existing among this segment of the population and especially for white-collar workers. Change came gradually, but efforts and progress gained momentum after Jerry Wurf was elected president in 1964. A constitutional convention was held in 1965, after which the union experienced its greatest growth period. Wurf, a skilled organizer, quadrupled AFSCME membership before 1980.

The unique aspects of this union, its growth and potential, and Jerry Wurf himself made AFSCME attractive to media in the 1970s. An AFSCME booklet cites a 1972 series on American labor done by the *Washington Post* in which the union is credited with being a "model of vitality and democracy" and one that "works incessantly at communicating with its members and in espousing causes that many other unions shun."[75] (See Figures 13 and 14 for AFSCME's government and structure.) Wurf, president until his sudden death in December, 1981, has been compared to Reuther in terms of his social activism, his reputation as an intellectual, his leadership abilities— and his independence. An oft-quoted excerpt from a *Time* magazine article states: "At meetings of the AFL-CIO executive council, . . . the vote usually ranges from 25–1 to 34–1, depending on how many other union chiefs are present to vote down Jerry Wurf."[76]

In comparison with other international unions examined in this chapter, AFSCME had a slow start in its public relations efforts. It did have an official journal, the *Public Employee,* that was being sent to members, public officials, other labor unions, libraries, journalists, and political leaders before the AFL-CIO merger in 1955. The journal was intended to improve union public relations, both internally and externally. And the international urged its local units to observe an annual Public Servants' Week, started in 1947, and intended as a time when special efforts should be made to publicize the work being done by public employees; suggestions regarding methods that might be utilized to accomplish this were published in the journal.

The need for better and more systematic efforts directed toward union public relations was recognized at the convention in 1954. An argument in support of changes was made by the chairperson of the Committee on Education and Public Relations:

> No organization is as directly affected by public opinion toward organization or more dependent on general acceptance of the idea of trade unionism as part of the life of our over-all community and country. As public employees we need to acquaint the general public and public officials more fully with the benefit and values in public employee organization.[77]

Action on the suggestion came by means of a resolution passed at the same convention requesting the executive board to create an international depart-

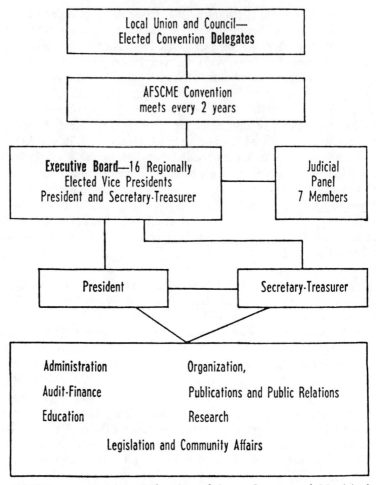

FIGURE 13. American Federation of State, County and Municipal Workers: Government. Source: American Federation of State, County and Municipal Workers, *Officers' Manual,* pamphlet (Washington, D.C.: AFSCME Publications Department, n.d.), p. 46.

ment of public relations and publicity and staff it with one or more qualified and experienced experts.

On April 1, 1956, this new department came into existence. Its inception was accompanied by numerous and creative ideas, but these seemed to be offset by a lack of financial commitment and discouraging reports of waning interest even in Public Servants' Week. By 1958, however, the department finally seemed to be moving in a forward direction with a larger staff, more publications, and more emphasis on Public Servants' Week, renamed

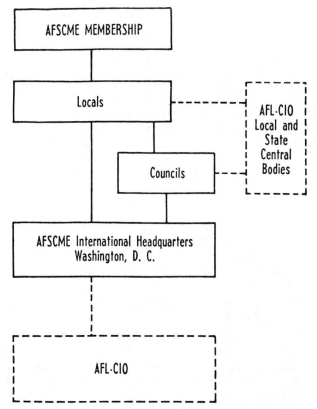

FIGURE 14.   American Federation of State, County and
Municipal Workers: Structure. Source: American Federation of State, County and Municipal Workers, *Officers'
Manual*. pamphlet (Washington, D.C.: AFSCME Publications Department, n.d.), p. 47.

Public Employees' Week. Public relations efforts still had little pattern and
direction at the international level, but the locals were credited with sustain-
ing excellent efforts that had resulted in an increased media visibility for the
union.

In the late 1950s and early 1960s, in spite of the fact that the department
was restricted by lack of money, it provided technical assistance to the AFL-
CIO series, "Americans at Work," succeeded in getting more enthusiastic
participation in Public Employees' Week, and became affiliated with the
Union Label and Service Trades Department. For a period during 1960–61,
publication of the *Public Employee* was curtailed due to lack of funds.
When it returned, it did so as a tabloid newspaper, printed every other
week. In spite of continued financial difficulties, delegates to the 1962 con-

vention demonstrated concern for the lack of an adequate public relations program by passing several resolutions that indicated the desire to expand communications and publicity as soon as financially feasible.

The publications division of the union department faced fewer difficulties in the 1960s than the public relations division. The staff was responsible for the publication of numerous pamphlets targeted toward AFSCME locals and councils, as well as a variety of material for other international departments. In addition, they issued a brochure that related the "AFSCME story," established a system for issuing press releases, and continued to increase participation in Public Employees' Week. Many locals and councils were even able to utilize radio and television.

In spite of all these successful endeavors, the department found it necessary for financial reasons to cut back on the number of annual issues of the *Public Employee,* and the newspaper became a monthly publication. In 1965 the department name was shortened to Department of Publications, and public relations efforts were turned over to the firm of Maurer, Fleisher, Zon and Associates, Inc., specialists in public relations counseling and activities for labor unions and not-for-profit organizations. It was hoped that with the firm's help, the union could improve its ability to communicate with the public and develop closer media contacts. This arrangement was short-lived, however. By 1968, for reasons undisclosed in the department's biennial convention report, its name had reverted to the one used previously—Publications and Public Relations. Maurer, Fleisher, Zon and Associates were retained, but only to help with public relations activities of a "specialized nature."

It was also in 1968 that the publications division underwent a crisis that forced its staff to adopt some new procedures, to learn to operate under pressure, and to gain valuable experience in working with the media. In April of that year Martin Luther King, Jr. was assassinated in Memphis, Tennessee, where he had gone to support striking AFSCME sanitation workers who were seeking higher pay. The situation had received a good deal of publicity even before the assassination and, after that, even those Americans who had only marginal interest in striking workers focused their attention on the situation in Memphis.

The publications staff found that the monthly *Public Employee* was inadequate to keep members apprised of events, and they began producing and distributing a daily newsletter to AFSCME members. The staff also had to accelerate greatly their normal activities with the media.

> The Memphis Strike was a major challenge to the Department. The Department expended every effort to keep the news media of the nation informed of fast-breaking developments, making certain that AFSCME's role in the situation was made clear.
>
> The national—and international—attention that was given the struggle of

the 1,300 striking public works employees in Memphis before and after the tragic assassination of Dr. Martin Luther King, Jr. brought great demands on the department. Inquiries from the press, television and radio were answered on a round-the-clock basis.[78]

Such a crisis situation had to have an effect on a public relations department, and the effect was apparently positive in this case. Staff members proved to themselves that they could operate and operate effectively in such a situation. Throughout the following year AFSCME received good press publicity—in *Life, Time, Newsweek, U.S. News and World Report,* the *Wall Street Journal, Business Week, Fortune,* the *New York Times,* and the *National Observer.* Some publicity was based on AFSCME news releases, and some on interviews with union officers, especially Jerry Wurf. A subject of continuing interest to the press was AFSCME's collective bargaining policies, a subject that AFSCME was also eager to publicize. The union's phenomenal growth also stimulated attention.

Throughout the 1970s the department experienced structural change and reorganization as the union experimented with the most efficient way to deal with what its leaders saw as three major areas: external relations, organization, and publications. Some of the structural difficulties were simply due to the rapid growth of the union, the reverse of the situation being experienced by a large portion of organized labor. The AFSCME publications division was separated from public relations again, but again only briefly. Field offices were established and full-time AFSCME public relations staff members were based in selected states across the nation (e.g., Illinois, California, Ohio, Florida). Responsibilities of the field staff usually included local press relations as well as newspaper, television, and radio advertising during an organizing campaign in a specific area.

In order to aid these efforts, the Department of Public Affairs produced a series of 15 public service broadcast announcements for national distribution in 1972. The intent of these announcements was to stress the character of government employees and to develop "public appreciation and support for public employee causes."[79] The report of the AFSCME Public Affairs Department in 1974 indicates that AFSCME was the first union to produce spots for national distribution. As explained above, however, IAM was doing the same thing in 1971 and 1972. Either the AFSCME report was referring to the fact that IAM's spots were not actually written by staff members or this confusion is another example of lack of communication among labor organizations about their media relations. AFSCME may have had an easier time than IAM in lining up its public service airtime, however, simply because AFSCME was not considered a "traditional" union by many because of the unique aspects of its membership. The degree of public interest in AFSCME was high at this time, and the numerous national magazines and newspapers that were publishing articles about AFSCME were largely sympathetic in that they indicated an increased receptivity to the idea of public employee unionism.

The 1974 report of the Department of Public Affairs illustrates the extent to which AFSCME press had been good. The report states that probably the most controversial AFSCME-related article appeared in the *Washington Post* on October 14, 1973, just prior to the opening of the AFL-CIO convention. The author, interestingly, was President Jerry Wurf. The department report summarizes the article briefly:

> The article started a debate within the labor movement that promises to echo for years to come. It said that labor's influence, while formidable, is slipping; that too many workers do not belong to unions and that too many unions squander their resources in inter-union rivalry rather than seeking to organize the unorganized.[80]

This occurrence is surprising only because inter-union and intra-union difficulties usually do not appear in the labor press, and many labor leaders do not like to see accounts of such problems in general circulation newspapers. On the other hand, the article is not surprising because such outspokenness was typical of Jerry Wurf:

> When Jerry Wurf isn't squabbling with his own members or their employers, the chances are that he is embroiled in some kind of a dispute with his colleagues in organized labor. At AFL-CIO headquarters in Washington, old line union leaders—in particular George Meany—don't seem to know what to make of an international union president whose alliances extend outside the labor federation and whose militance is sometimes turned against it.[81]

Public receptivity to public employee unionism, whether real or imagined in the early 1970s, did not continue for the entire decade. A large segment of the public seemed to be uncomfortable with the idea. In 1937 Franklin Delano Roosevelt, a recognized friend of labor, wrote: "All government employees should realize that the process of collective bargaining, as usually understood, cannot be translated into the public service."[82] And William Buckley, debating Jerry Wurf in 1975, quoted an even stronger statement from Roosevelt:

> A strike of public employees manifests nothing less than an intention on their part to obstruct the operations of government until their demands are satisfied. Such action, looking toward the paralysis of government by those who have sworn to support it, is unthinkable and intolerable.[83]

Because Roosevelt was a strong labor supporter, these phrases were quickly seized upon and widely used by those who opposed collective bargaining for public employees. Roosevelt's actual position on the matter is somewhat unclear, for he has also been credited with encouraging the organization and improvement of working conditions of public employees. At any rate, opposition to the legitimation of such a form of collective bargaining seemed to regain vitality almost 40 years later when, in 1976, a Public Affairs Department report noted an "intense assault by politicians, bankers and the media against public employees' rights, their benefits, and even their jobs."[84]

The department responded by initiating several projects. One of these was the retention of the services of a clipping agency in order to provide the department with an overview of nationwide newspaper articles related to the union and its activities. Such a service would seem to be especially useful to AFSCME because of its diverse membership and decentralized structure. AFSCME staff members responded to clippings that were judged as being unfair to public employees by means of a coordinated campaign in which attacks were answered in letters-to-editors that stated the union's position on the issues in question. Emphasis was placed on providing the press with facts that supported AFSCME's positions.

AFSCME's interest in what was being reported in the media extended beyond articles that directly mentioned AFSCME and included a variety of topics that were of particular interest or relevance to AFSCME members. A good example of this type of media monitoring and the kind of response that could occur took place in November, 1978. Earlier that year California voters passed Proposition 13, or the Jarvis-Gann amendment, a constitutional amendment that reduced property tax bills in the state by 60 percent. Such tax cuts of course translate into layoffs for state workers. Before and after the California vote, Proposition 13 received a great deal of national attention, resulting in similar tax cut proposals being placed on ballots in other states. Many of these, however, were not actually tax cut proposals but were less drastic spending limitation proposals. Both types of proposal would affect public employee jobs, but the latter would not have as serious a potential effect as the former. AFSCME leaders, upset by inaccuracies that appeared in some media that reported voters around the country had voted for tax cuts rather than spending limitations, responded by calling a press conference, at which Wurf discussed the discrepancies. Wurf was also invited to discuss the issue on the "Today" show.

"Media assaults" on the rights of public employees in the last half of the 1970s also encouraged AFSCME to undertake a newspaper and radio advertising campaign in 1977–78. The advertisements were intended to help AFSCME members and other public workers in their various job-related difficulties. Because of the union's diversity, the problems encountered by members are also diverse—probably far more so than with other unions. Therefore, rather than a nationwide campaign, AFSCME started with local ads that spoke to particular issues. For example, in response to a proposition that would have required all city government employees in Dayton, Ohio, to live in the city, the union mounted a "Vote No" ad campaign arguing that it was unfair for city employees to be required to forfeit rights that other American citizens had. The issue was defeated. In Toledo an ad campaign was designed to try to convince city administrators to adopt a more reasonable wage policy. In Pennsylvania a campaign was directed toward obtaining better support for the state highway system and the state employees who maintained it. The ads were advocacy ads, but of course they also increased AFSCME visibility and, as one member said: "The ads show American citizens that we are a thoughtful organization, involved in matters that affect them."[85]

The following year AFSCME, recognizing the "immediacy and impact" of television, allocated $1.4 million[86] for a television advertising campaign. This campaign differed from the radio-newspaper campaigns primarily in that it centered directly on name recognition and featured a spectrum of services performed by AFSCME members in order to emphasize the importance of public service and the AFSCME members who perform them. The spots were aired in 22 cities across the country in the spring and summer of 1979, primarily on news and public affairs programs. Surveys done by AFSCME following this endeavor revealed a 16 percent increase in public recognition of AFSCME's name and an 11 percent favorable rating increase; AFSCME decided that such results were sufficient reason to intensify its efforts and allocated $2.1 million for advertising in 1980.[87]

The purpose of the next television ad, produced by the J. Walter Thompson advertising agency, was to enhance public employee image and to aid in organizing efforts. This ad was more dramatic than the earlier ads had been. The ad opens with a variety of shots of public workers and descriptions of jobs they perform—in a busy day care center, in a school cafeteria, repairing a highway, clearing a littered park, and providing health care to the elderly. Then the announcer states: "Public employees touch our lives every day. Have you ever thought where we'd be *without* public employees? Think about it." Viewers then see a closed day care center, a street in a state of disrepair, an untended elderly patient. The ad was intended to stress the importance to each and every community of public workers and the services provided by them. The ads were concentrated in eastern states—New York, Pennsylvania, Florida, Connecticut, Maryland, and Washington, D.C., but were also used in areas where bargaining or organizing was occurring.

In the spring of 1981 AFSCME broadened its advertising directions and began to focus on national issues. One million dollars were budgeted for a national television, radio, and newspaper ad campaign critical of the Reagan administration's budget and tax cuts. The ad shows a giant cake decorated with the words "Republican Economic Policy" being sliced up in unequal portions with the wealthy getting the larger pieces. President Wurf explained the purpose of the ad:

> "Our ads point out that vital government services like school lunches, Medicaid, mass transit and social security will be cut back sharply if Reagan's plan gets final approval," . . . .

"The ads show how unfair and unequally distributed Reagan's tax cuts would be."[88]

This spot appeared in a number of cities across the country—Washington, New York, Boston, Dayton, Chicago, Seattle, Pittsburgh, St. Louis, Philadelphia, Milwaukee, and Hartford—but was not aired as widely as AFSCME had hoped. Four network-owned stations in New York and Washington and all television stations in Albany and Des Moines refused to air the ad.[89] AFSCME persisted in its efforts, but, according to the director of the Department of Public Affairs, the final tally showed that about 40 percent of television stations, in about 12 major media markets, refused to carry it. The reason given, in most cases, was that the spots were advocacy ads and station policy did not allow ads in this category to be aired.

In spite of such obstacles, AFSCME leaders believe that advertising can accomplish a great deal—not only by creating a more favorable image of AFSCME, but also by presenting the union's side on various issues, and, when warranted, by urging public actions. The union's national advertising campaign continues to be a major emphasis of the Department of Public Affairs.

In addition to its advertising, AFSCME is devoting a good deal of effort to another project—the Labor News Network. This consists of a satellite transmission service beamed to commercial television and cable systems and commercial and public radio stations nationwide. Production takes place in AFSCME's own in-house studio, and the service offers a variety of features. Local stations can, for example, set up interviews with AFSCME officers or get union response to legislative issues at no cost to the station. Public Affairs Department head Phil Sparks commented at the time the network began: "At a time when two-thirds of Americans get their news from TV and radio, it is critical for organized labor to try new approaches."[90] AFSCME has continued to try new approaches. Since its opening, uses for the union's studio have expanded and now include videotape production, teleconferencing, and rental to other organizations, mostly labor, for similar purposes. While very few labor organizations are fortunate enough to have studio space, both the UAW and IAM do have small studios, used primarily to make videocassettes for internal distribution.

CONCLUSIONS

Examination of the histories of the ILGWU, the UAW, the IAM, and AFSCME at the international level shows that these unions have left few promotional tools untouched. All four publish monthly newspapers that are distributed to members, libraries, community groups, and public figures. The newspapers are supplemented by various booklets, pamphlets, newsletters, brochures, and news services for local and district units.

A look at the labor press—even over only the last 25 years—reveals considerable progress. Publications are highly professional and appear well able to provide readers with a sense of both reliability and credibility. In 1980 retiring public relations director Albert Zack gave his perceptions of why the labor press has steadily improved. He mentioned the following: (1) the continuing attacks on trade unionism; (2) the failure of much of the news media adequately to cover labor news, making it necessary for labor to do the job themselves; (3) the dramatic changes in communications technology and methodology that have caused labor editors to reexamine such journalistic fundamentals as graphics, display, content, and language; and (4) the high turnover among union members, which requires labor papers constantly to reach new readers.[91]

The histories of the four unions examined reinforce Zack's conclusions. The labor press has improved and it must continue to do so in order to survive. Financial pressures have caused even these four large unions many difficulties and have necessitated changes in their news publications. In January, 1982, another jolt came when the U.S. Postal Services Board of Governors announced major increases in postal rates for union journals and other nonprofit publications. These increases had been planned, but on a phased-rate schedule over several years; immediate increases were triggered by Congressional cuts in Postal Service appropriations. This has caused changes in a number of union publications in terms of distribution, content, and frequency of publication.

In spite of the fact that labor unions do distribute their publications more widely than to members only, realistic assessments lead to the conclusion that very few among the "general public" read the labor press. The labor press may well be an instrument of information, education, credibility, and reliability, as well as being a countervailing force to the daily news media— but for union members only. Because of this, the labor press does not serve directly to build the union image for nonunion members. Indirectly, however, it does accomplish this objective. And this goes back again to what Zack said:

> [D]irect communications tailored to specific audiences, reaching union members in their homes, is the most important and persuasive communications tool. . . .
>
> We must give our members the information they need, along with the reinforcement necessary to speak up for the labor movement. I've always thought the greatest ad line of my lifetime was the Packard slogan: ask the man who owns one. The best public relations in the world is the spoken word from one individual to another.[92]

In 1981, in addition to presenting journalistic awards for union publications, the International Labor Press Association (in 1983, the name was changed to International Labor Communications Association) gave awards for its first competition in electronic communications. All four unions have been involved in radio broadcasting and film production. The ILCA awards and the number of entries in these categories (106 in 1981 and 110 in 1984) give some indication of the level of labor utilization of media other than print journalism.

The nature of labor union involvement in radio has undergone a good deal of change. From early hopes of owning and operating FM stations and establishing labor radio networks, the internationals moved to union-sponsored programs. Usually the international union produced the broadcasts and distributed them to their own locals that in turn purchased local air time. In at least one case, there was cooperation between internationals— the United Rubber Workers sponsored the UAW nightly news commentary by Guy Nunn in Akron, Ohio.

Free public service time has also been obtained by all four unions when possible. Again, the usual arrangement has been that the international union was responsible for the production of the radio spots (usually informative, educational spots), and their distribution was handled by state and local councils.

More recently, however, these state and local councils have been encountering difficulties both in finding the necessary resources to sponsor a local program and in obtaining public service time. The same is true of television broadcasting, though individual international unions have never been able to obtain much television time, either by sponsoring shows or by providing tapes for use during public service time. It has been helpful to have an "issue" that brings invitations to the international presidents to appear on network talk shows. The IAM, UAW, and AFSCME have all been fortunate or resourceful enough recently to have been associated with issues that the news media have deemed interesting and newsworthy. This has helped the internationals gain network television time.

Recent changes in the deregulation of radio and television by the FCC have led some labor leaders to predict that air time will be even more difficult for unions to obtain in the future. In 1981, the FCC eliminated or revised a number of rules that applied to requirements for licensees of radio stations. In 1984 the agency deregulated television along similar lines. Under the former rules, licensees were required to provide their audiences with specified amounts of news, public affairs, and nonentertainment programming; this regulation has been dropped. Stations are no longer obliged to air public service announcements. Licensees were limited in terms of how many minutes per hour were devoted to commercials; this is no longer true. Licensees no longer must formally ascertain the needs and interest of the communities they serve. Detailed programming logs previously required of stations have been eliminated. Radio and television broadcast licenses have been extended from three to seven years. License renewal forms have been shortened to a postcard-size form for all AM, FM, and television stations, with the exception of a random sample of about 5 percent who are required to submit a longer "audit" form. Finally, the Commission continues to urge Congress to repeal both the fairness doctrine and the equal time requirement.

Advocates of these changes argue that quality programming does not come as a result of artificial, government-imposed restrictions, but, rather, from the operation of the "marketplace." They claim that radio stations, deregulated three years before television, continue to serve their communities. Critics respond that real diversity does not exist because the networks still control about 80 percent of the prime time audience; and that the burden of proof that a station is not serving the community now rests with the public rather than the station, but the public has lost the tools necessary to provide the FCC with such proof. Final decisions on some of these issues will undoubtedly have to be made in the courts where communications regulations have been examined, and often confirmed, for 50 years.

In addition, public broadcasting, intended to be an alternative to the networks, has suffered reduction of its federal funding in recent years and has been searching for ways to make up the differences. In 1983, after experimenting with advertising on some public broadcasting television stations, the commission in charge recommended that the public stations not accept advertising except in the form of increased corporate underwriting. Public broadcasters are, therefore, becoming more dependent on underwriters, who in turn are in a position to exert increasing influence over prime time programming on public television. As this happens, union leaders see their chances of obtaining coverage of issues and viewpoints they consider important further diminished.

All four of the unions reviewed have engaged in advertising. All of the ads done by these unions have been targeted toward their own union members, potential members, and the general public. The four have utilized a variety of media for their advertising campaigns: the labor press, the daily commercial press, trade publications, national magazines, radio, television, subway posters, leaflets, direct mail, and billboards. All have advertised at the local, regional, and national levels, but emphasis among these has differed. The ILGWU, IAM, and AFSCME have emphasized the national level, while the UAW has done more advertising at the local level. The Auto Workers' December, 1981–January, 1982 move to national television represents a change—perhaps encouraged by its cosponsorship (with AFSCME) of some of the anti-social security cuts newspaper ads that were undertaken on a national level.

Some of the advertisements for these unions have been produced by the international union's public relations staff alone. Others have been prepared by well-known general advertising agencies—Doyle Dane Bernbach, J. Walter Thompson, and Paula Greene, for example. Labor news services such as Press Associates, Inc., have been helpful, as have agencies such as Maurer, Fleisher, Zon (now Maurer, Fleisher, Anderson and Conway) who specialize in public relations for labor and not-for-profit institutions. The Public Media Center, an alternative advertising agency centered in San Francisco, did the advertising for the Americans for a Working Economy. Union public relations staffs are becoming more expert at understanding advertising, and are, at the same time, increasingly aware of the pitfalls that may be encountered. An increasing number of public relations directors believe that if unions can afford it, retention of professionals is wise.

Reasons for the advertising done by ILGWU, UAW, IAM, and AFSCME are diverse. The ILGWU has used ads to promote its plays and films, to promote the union label, and to "convey to the public an accurate picture of what a union is and what it stands for."[93] This union as long ago as 1958 also engaged in advocacy advertising that was refused by some newspapers because of its controversial content. ILGWU's recent advertising campaigns have done more than attempt to create a positive image and familiarity with the label. They have directly addressed the problem of apparel imports and the need to buy American products.

The UAW, IAM, and AFSCME entered the world of advertising much later than the ILGWU. Stated purposes for UAW ads have included education, information, increased awareness, image promotion, trade reform promotion, and opposition to Reagan administration social security cuts. The IAM has aimed at name recognition and support of union interests—occupational health and safety, anti-pollution, and so on. It also has advertised in opposition to deregulation of natural gas prices. AFSCME has produced advertisements that stress the character of government employees, help individual local units in job-related difficulties, highlight the importance of public services and those who perform them, and criticize the Reagan administration budget and tax cuts. Both the UAW and AFSCME have recently been refused media access.[94]

It is interesting to compare and contrast, in retrospect, the apparent success of these ads. Labor advertising campaigns have been criticized by people who perceive that they appear only in times of crisis and speak only to the crisis issue. Examples: the AFL-CIO's ad campaign when the Taft-Hartley Bill was being considered by Congress; the ILGWU's advocacy ads during a strike in 1958; the UAW's campaign to increase sales of American cars in 1980. The ILGWU, however, is given credit for "being different" in this respect. In 1959, after realizing little success with its 1958 advocacy campaign, the ILGWU started its label promotion. Since then, its ads have appeared with regularity—in newspapers, trade publications, labor publications, consumer magazines, on leaflets, subway and bus posters, and on radio and television. The purpose was always the same—to promote the union name, its label, its ideals. In 1975, "look-for-the-union-label" was initiated—a new theme, but intended to achieve the same ends. After five years of exposure to this theme, the public knew it, knew the song, recognized the union. The line, the song, the commercial was teased, parodied, and still the union used it, and *TV Guide* reported that four out of five people reacted positively to it.[95]

ILGWU is still sending the message; now, however, it can be shortened and people fill in missing words automatically. The union has used the time/space gained by the omission to fill in some new lines, lines that emphasize the need to buy American. In purpose, ILGWU's ad campaign is very similar to the UAW's. Yet the UAW's campaign is seen by many as a "crisis" campaign and the ILGWU's as not. Because of ILGWU's consistent theme, regular appearances, and because it is known for image ads, the union can shift to "crisis" appeals and leave many people still thinking they are hearing or seeing image ads.

Each of the four internationals has made some effort to evaluate the success of its advertising. The most common method for such evaluation has been ad posttesting by means of surveys. The ILGWU has cited to a survey done by Louis Harris and Associates. The IAM reports using only its own staff to evaluate ads, the UAW reports using only private research groups, while AFSCME reports utilizing both.

"Concealed" as it may be by ILGWU, there does seem to be a general trend among all four unions toward advocacy advertising. As one advertising practitioner observed, everything today is a public issue, and the public for public issues today is just about everybody. Issues, causes, and ideas will be presented to the public and the "competition's going to be as fierce as any in any product category you can think of."[96] And, just as in product advertising, costs will be high. In 1981, the UAW, IAM, and AFSCME were spending between just under 10 percent to slightly over 26 percent of their total public relations budgets on advertising.[97] With production costs rising as quickly as costs for television air time, it is apparent that only wealthy institutions, groups, and individuals will be able to compete for air time. It was not long ago that a majority of unions refused to consider advertising on any level because they felt it was a financial impossibility to keep up with corporations. For many unions this remains the sentiment. In addition, however, competition is not coming only from corporations, but from many other sources who also have ideas they want to express to the public. For example, after AFSCME initiated its anti-Reaganomics commercials in the fall of 1981, the Republican party countered with a television campaign that cost over five times the amount AFSCME had spent. This GOP action, in turn, caused the Democrats to turn to the fairness doctrine and ask the networks (CBS and NBC) to provide (unpaid) time to them so they could respond. Former FCC chairman and attorney for the Democratic National Committee, Charles Ferris, wrote in a letter to the networks:

> The planned expenditures of funds for these [Republican] commercials far exceeds the funds available to any spokesperson for the opposition viewpoint. . . . Such a result creates precisely the sort of monopoly over the marketplace of ideas that the fairness doctrine was designed to prevent.[98]

The surge in advocacy advertising is coming at the very moment that the future of the fairness doctrine is being debated. If the fairness doctrine is repealed, as Ferris points out, less wealthy institutions, groups, and individuals would have no opportunity to voice opposition to advocacy ads over the air by requesting that the stations provide time.

All four internationals examined in this chapter have used up-to-date media technology—cable television, satellite transmissions, videotapes, teleconferencing, plans for low-power television, and so on. They are relatively unusual in that respect, because many international unions have not done so. Communications technology is complex and it becomes even more complex in the context of advocacy advertising and government policy. And it seems apparent that there has been little horizontal communication among internationals to provide encouragement to those unions that have made no moves in this direction. This chapter provides only a few examples of any kind of media cooperation among international unions. These examples were limited to the following: hopes for a labor FM radio network; the United Rubber Workers' sponsorship of a UAW radio show for a period in the 1950s; the organization of labor and consumer groups into the Americans for a Working Economy; discussion among IAM leaders of the need for a labor coalition for television; and the UAW-AFSCME co-sponsorship of a national newspaper advertising campaign. These examples notwithstanding, a number of references in reports from public relations departments indicated a lack of knowledge about what other internationals were doing, what they had done in the past, which methods they judged valuable and which a waste of time and money. International unions need continually better channels of communication with each other and with the AFL-CIO.

The commitment by the AFL-CIO Executive Council to create the Labor Institute of Public Affairs indicated a renewed desire on the part of labor leaders to form a labor coalition for communications. LIPA and the AFL-CIO Department of Information are focusing on mobilizing efforts to accomplish shared public relations goals. Improved AFL-CIO communications with its affiliates already is being realized. Internationals are being instructed in communications technology; more unions may be able to advertise because of LIPA's generic ads. Horizontal communications should be facilitated because of the increased attention being given to this problem;

there should be less unnecessary duplication of efforts. Concerted action through LIPA is providing additional funding, more effective control of funds, and allowing expenditures to be made on public relations endeavors that benefit the entire labor movement.

However, LIPA and the Department of Information are confronted by a political process in which their influence on legislation will be limited at best. Every year, as new rewrites of the Communications Act come before Congress, labor attorneys present labor's position on regulation, deregulation, the fairness doctrine, equal time rule, and so on. LIPA will need to use its communications expertise and research abilities to accumulate data supportive of labor's position on any communication legislation and be sure that such material is in the hands not only of its attorneys, but also of its affiliates.

NOTES

[1] In 1980, the Bureau of Labor Statistics listed an almost equal number of AFL-CIO affiliated and unaffiliated labor organizations: 101 unaffiliated and 102 affiliates. In spite of the fact that the nation's two largest labor unions, the Teamsters and the National Education Association, are independent, only about 30 percent of all organized workers in the United States belong to independent unions. *Directory of U.S. Labor Organizations: 1982–83 Edition*, ed. Courtney D. Gifford (Washington, D.C.: The Bureau of National Affairs, Inc., 1982) pp. 13, 66. As of July, 1984 as a result of mergers, the AFL-CIO had 95 affiliates.

[2] David Dubinsky and A. H. Raskin, *David Dubinsky: A Life with Labor* (New York: Simon and Schuster, 1977), p. 187.

[3] Herbert Harris, *American Labor* (New Haven: Yale University Press, 1938), p. 193.

[4] International Ladies' Garment Workers' Union (ILGWU), *Report and Record, Thirty-fifth Convention* (New York City: ILGWU, 1974), p. 198.

[5] ILGWU, *Report and Record, Twenty-eighth Convention* (1953), p. 247.

[6] ILGWU, *Report and Record, Thirtieth Convention* (1959), p. 206.

[7] Dubinsky and Raskin, *David Dubinsky*, p. 189.

[8] Ibid., p. 190.

[9] Benjamin Stolberg, *Tailor's Progress: The Story of a Famous Union and the Men Who Made It* (Garden City, New York: Doubleday, Doran and Company, Inc., 1944), p. 297.

[10] Ibid., pp. 297–98.

[11] ILGWU, *Report and Record* (1953), pp. 19–20.

[12] U.S. Federal Communications Commission (FCC), *Sixteenth Annual Report* (Washington, D.C.: Government Printing Office, 1950), p. 109.

[13] FCC, *Twentieth Annual Report* (1954), p. 97.

[14] FCC, *Seventeenth Annual Report* (1951), p. 124; and FCC, *Nineteenth Annual Report* (1953), p. 102.

[15] ILGWU, *Report and Record* (1953), p. 100.

[16] Ibid., p. 101.

[17] ILGWU, *Report and Record* (1959), p. 402.

[18] ILGWU, *Report and Record, Thirty-first Convention* (1962), p. 49.

[19] Ibid., p. 52.

[20] "Boosting the Union Label," *Justice*, May 15, 1962, p. 9.

[21] ILGWU, *Report and Record, Thirty-second Convention* (1965), p. 84.

[22] "1970–1980: New Leaders, New Vistas," *Justice,* June, 1980, p. 16.

[23] "Daniels: TV Ads Help ILGWU Cause," *Justice,* November, 1980, p. 5.

[24] Steven Banker, "Look for the Union Label . . . and Much, Much More," *TV Guide,* March 31, 1984, pp. 30–35.

[25] ILGWU, *Report and Record* (1959), p. 124.

[26] Ibid.

[27] ILGWU, *Report and Record* (1965), p. 86.

[28] Ibid.

[29] "'Pajama Game' Tunes, Capers Air Shop Life," *Justice,* February 15, 1956, p. 9.

[30] Paul Patrick, "'Garment Jungle' True Union Story," *AFL-CIO News,* May 11, 1957, p. 8. See also "Garment Jungle Breaking Box Office Records," *Justice,* June 1, 1957, p. 3.

[31] Ken Margolies, "Silver Screen Tarnishes Unions," *Screen Actor,* Summer, 1981, p. 48.

[32] Ibid., p. 49.

[33] Burton Hall, "Gingold's Law; Or Why Does the ILGWU Continue to Decay," *New Politics* XI:3 (Winter, 1976), p. 69. See also William Serrin, "Ailing ILGWU Is Facing More Problems," *New York Times,* November 29, 1981, p. 29.

[34] Richard A. Lester, *As Unions Mature: An Analysis of the Evolution of American Unionism* (Princeton, New Jersey: Princeton University Press, 1958), p. 92.

[35] Jack Stieber, *Governing the UAW* (New York: John Wiley and Sons, Inc., 1967), Chapter 5.

[36] Jack Barbash, *American Unions: Structure, Government, and Politics* (New York: Random House, 1967), pp. 117–18.

[37] Stieber, *Governing the UAW,* pp. 119–20.

[38] "Americans For a Working Economy Publishes Economics Booklet," *Public Employee,* July, 1977, p. 13.

[39] United Automobile, Aircraft and Agricultural Implement Workers of America (UAW), *Report of Walter P. Reuther, President, to the Fourteenth Constitutional Convention* (N.P., 1953), pp. 219–20.

[40] Stieber, *Governing the UAW,* p. 120.

[41] UAW, *Report of Walter P. Reuther, President, to the Fifteenth Constitutional Convention* (1955), p. 117-D.

[42] Stieber, *Governing the UAW,* p. 121.

[43] UAW, *Report of Walter P. Reuther, President, to the Eighteenth Constitutional Convention,* Part III (1962), p. 153.

[44] "Tuning Out the Public Voice in Radio and TV," *Solidarity,* June 18, 1979, p. 16.

[45] Ibid.

[46] Ibid., p. 17.

[47] Dave Elsila, "TV: Can We Change the Channels of Communication?," *Solidarity,* June, 1981, p. 12.

[48] "Organizing: Union Plans a Counter-Offensive," *Solidarity,* July 11, 1980, p. 17.

[49] "UAW Ads Stress Fair Trade, High Car Quality," *Solidarity,* November, 1980, p. 3.

[50] "UAW Messages Go on Nationwide TV," *Solidarity,* December 16–31, 1981, p. 3.

[51] International Association of Machinists (IAM), *Proceedings of the Twenty-fifth Grand Lodge Convention,* (1960), p. 7.

[52] IAM, *Officers' Report to the Thirtieth Grand Lodge Convention* (1980), p. 29.

[53] Ibid., p. 30.

[54] IAM, *Proceedings of the Twenty-seventh Grand Lodge Convention* (1968), p. 125.

[55] Author's questionnaire.

[56] IAM, *Officers' Report to the Twenty-eighth Grand Lodge Convention* (1972), p. 27.

[57] Ibid., p. 77.

[58] IAM, *Officers' Report* (1980), p. 88.

[59] IAM, *Officers' Report* (1972), p. 32.

[60] Ibid.

[61] IAM, *Officers' Report to the Twenty-ninth Grand Lodge Convention* (1976), p. 27.

[62] IAM, *Officers' Report* (1980), p. 31.

[63] Not all the attention has been favorable. For example, the National Association of Broadcasters reportedly took a dim view of the campaign. An NAB spokesperson is quoted as saying: "To imply that broadcast journalists and those responsible for broadcast entertainment programs slant their stories with an anti-union bias, besides being ludicrous, is a veiled attempt to intimidate the media." *U.S. News and World Report*, October 22, 1979, p. 70.

[64] Russell Shorto, "Machinists Tool Up for TV," *Washington Journalism Review*, September, 1980, p. 9.

[65] *IAM Media Project TV Trainers' Manual* (prepared by William Y. Young and Associates, Chicago, n.d.), p. 145.

[66] Ibid., p. 135.

[67] IAM, *IAM Television Entertainment Report, Part II: Conclusions and National Summary of Occupational Frequency in Network Primetime Entertainment for February, 1980*, June 12, 1980, pp. 11–12.

[68] IAM, *Network News and Documentary Report: A Member Survey and Analysis*, July 30, 1980, p. 2.

[69] IAM, "Network News Fails Union Viewers," *Labor News*, press release, August 30, 1980, p. 2.

[70] "Moving in for a Closer Look at our TV Image," *Machinist*, January, 1981, p. 3.

[71] "Television News Biased!" *Machinist*, December, 1981, p. 8.

[72] *IAM TV Trainers' Manual*, n.p.

[73] Jay Arnold, "Study: TV Has Bad View of Businessmen," *Champaign-Urbana News-Gazette*, April 24, 1981, p. B-8.

[74] "'Antagonism' Between Business and Broadcast News Is a Myth," *Media Industry Newsletter*, November 18, 1981, p. 5.

[75] American Federation of State, County and Municipal Employees (AFSCME), "A Model of Vitality and Democracy," pamphlet (AFSCME, n.d.), p. 2.

[76] "Public Workers' Powerhouse," *Time*, May 21, 1973, p. 90.

[77] American Federation of State, County, and Municipal Employees (AFSCME), *Proceedings of the Ninth International Convention* (1954), p. 99.

[78] AFSCME, *Proceedings of the Seventeenth International Convention* (1968), p. 436.

[79] AFSCME, *Proceedings of the Twentieth International Convention* (1974), p. 337.

[80] Ibid.

[81] Fred C. Shapiro, "How Jerry Wurf Walks on Water," *New York Times Magazine*, April 11, 1976, p. 84.

[82] President F. D. Roosevelt to Luther C. Stewart, President, National Federation of Federal Employees, August 16, 1937 in Leo Kramer, *Labor's Paradox: The American Federation of State, County, and Municipal Employees, AFL-CIO* (New York: John Wiley and Sons, Inc., 1962), p. 36.

[83] AFSCME, "Who Speaks for Public Employees: Jerry Wurf Debates William Buckley," pamphlet (AFSCME, 1975).

[84] AFSCME, *Proceedings of the Twenty-second International Convention* (1976), p. 325.

[85] "Public Sees Ads, Backs Councils," *Public Employee*, March, 1978, p. 27.

[86] "The Pinch on Public Employees," *Business Week*, June 23, 1980, p. 77.

[87] Ibid.

[88] "State-County Ad Campaign Slices Up Reagan Economics," *AFL-CIO News*, May 16, 1981, p. 3.

[89] Ibid.

[90] "AFSCME Labor News Network Transmits Via Satellite," *Public Employee*, September, 1982, p. 7.

[91] "Labor Press Has Critical Task of Keeping Members Informed," *AFL-CIO News*, January 26, 1980, p. 5.

[92] Ibid.

[93] ILGWU, *Report and Record* (1959), p. 206.

[94] Author's questionnaire.

[95] Banker, "Look for the Union Label," p. 30.

[96] Paula Green, "Huge Growth Expected in Issues-Causes Advertising," *Advertising Age*, November 13, 1980, pp. 66–68.

[97] Author's questionnaire.

[98] "Fairness Struggle Taking Shape," *Broadcasting*, October 26, 1981, p. 42.

CHAPTER IV

Perspectives on Public Relations

Not all international unions have as many members as the UAW, AFSCME, IAM, or even ILGWU (the smallest of the four, with a membership of about 300,000), and there is similarly wide variation among international unions in amount of general revenue and ways it is allocated. In particular, whereas some international unions, like those discussed in the preceding chapters, actively cultivate and utilize the mass media, others are considerably less involved in public relations. In order to explore further the opinions of labor leaders regarding public relations and the mass media, a survey was undertaken in the fall of 1981. The survey was designed to provide information on the structure and function of public relations departments and on policy and opinions of labor leaders concerning the media relationships of their own unions, of labor in general, and of the AFL-CIO.

SURVEY DESCRIPTION

A questionnaire was mailed to public relations directors of a quota sample of 30 national/international unions, all AFL-CIO affiliates, in September, 1981. The *Directory of National Unions and Employee Associations, 1979* provided a list of 102 unions then affiliated with the AFL-CIO. Using this list, two labor specialists and two communications specialists judged each union as being either relatively active or relatively inactive in current public relations activities. Twenty-six unions that were to be included in the survey were selected randomly from the resulting active/inactive lists—11 active unions and 15 inactive unions. In addition, questionnaires were sent to each of the four active unions discussed in the preceding chapter, bringing the total to 30. Union size varied. Nine of the selected unions had memberships of over 500,000 (categorized as large), 12 had between 100,000 and 500,000 (medium), and 9 had under 100,000 (small).

Public relations directors or other officers or staff members having public relations responsibilities were contacted by telephone before the questionnaires were mailed; the purpose was to encourage a good response by briefly explaining the project and responding to questions. In some cases the telephone contact was helpful in correcting and updating names and other information about persons responsible for public relations in unions where no name was listed in the *Directory.*

In early November, follow-up letters were mailed to 11 unions that had not yet responded to the questionnaire. Three of these did reply, bringing the total number of responses to 22, a rate of 73 percent. Responses came disproportionately from the larger and more active internationals. Of those that responded, eight were categorized as large and active, one large and inactive, three medium and active, six medium and inactive, one small and active, and three small and inactive. Of the eight that did not respond, one was categorized as medium and active, two medium and inactive, two small and active, and three small and inactive.

FINDINGS

Public Relations Departments: Structure and Functions

Reports indicated that 14 of the 22 responding unions had one or more staff members whose responsibilities were primarily public relations. Of the eight having no such staff, only one report indicated that the organization had no other established way of dealing with public relations. Reports from the seven remaining unions indicated that public relations functions were carried out by other elected or appointed officers or staff members (who assumed them in addition to their other responsibilities) or by independent consultants. Each of these seven unions was categorized as a relatively inactive union, with the exception of two. Both of these two unions retained independent professional consulting firms on a continuing basis.

A variety of publics are important to international unions—for example, their own members and officers, potential members, members and officers of other labor unions, government officials and legislators, the general public, and the AFL-CIO. The fact that the responsibility to communicate with these publics fits naturally into several of the departments that most international unions have, such as organizing or education, complicates the administrative incorporation of public relations functions into the overall organization. Usually, however, any public relations efforts undertaken in, for example, the organizing department, are a means to an end—that is, they tend to be limited to organizing objectives. Of the unions surveyed that had one or more staff people whose responsibilities were primarily public relations, most had them placed in a department that was titled public relations. Another common alternative is to combine public relations with publicity or publications—the department that puts out the union newspaper and various educational pamphlets and booklets intended primarily for members. When the departments are titled public relations or publicity, the responsibilities tended to be broader with public relations an end in itself.

In most of these unions, the public relations department was not new, but has existed between 20 and 50 years. One union was in the process of reorganizing these functions. This international was making some dramatic internal changes, with the objective of professionalizing and placing more emphasis on its mass media activities than had previously been the case.

Public relations staff size ranged from one to as many as 30; however, two-thirds of the unions with public relations departments had between two and four full-time employees.

Information about budgets for public relations is less revealing than might be expected because budgeting procedures and categories vary so much. The public relations budget may, for example, be channeled through other departments. Or public relations allocations may be made as needed from the general fund. Further, as one labor official said, often there is a great deal of budget adjusting and readjusting during the year depending on departmental needs. Notwithstanding these limitations of the survey data, Table 1 suggests that increases in public relations spending were far more common than decreases between 1977 and 1981; and Table 2 gives an idea of the range of activities on which those funds are spent in various unions. (Only the replies of the 14 unions who have internal public relations staffs are reported in these two tables.) Table 3 reports the range of answers—perhaps best summarized as cautious but not pessimistic—to a question about likely future trends in public relations expenditures.

All of the responding unions were spending more on newspaper publication and distribution than on other public relations functions. Because mail costs keep increasing, many expected major increases in expenditures in this area. And it is worth noting that no respondent at that time indicated expectations that this was an area whose budget would probably be cut in the near future.

AFL-CIO Public Relations

One question was included that sought opinions on AFL-CIO utilization of the mass media. Most respondents were not satisfied with what the Federa-

Table 1   Change in Fund
Allocation for Public Relations in
the Last Five Years

	(N = 14)
Increased significantly	36%
Increased slightly	14
No change	29
Decreased slightly	0
Decreased significantly	7
No answer	14

Table 2   Functions Currently Covered by
Public Relations Budget

	(N = 14)
Newspaper to members	100%
Newsletter to members	79
News service for districts and locals	50
Publication of books, pamphlets	86
News releases	100
Press conferences	79
Television time	50
Radio time	50
Film production	50
Advertising	71
Receptions and parties	43
Research expenses	29
Consultants' fees	50
Other	29

tion was doing as of September, 1981 (Table 4), and most were unaware of the proposals for change that were to be presented to the AFL-CIO convention the following month. Some respondents, however, suggested changes along the lines that were to be adopted shortly thereafter. One respondent, for example, expressed the need for the AFL-CIO to allocate more money, obtained through a per capita dues increase, for public relations. Such a recommendation was approved by the 1981 convention. Respondents also indicated that they would like to see the Federation do more in the way of public relations for organized labor as a whole. The Labor Institute of Public Affairs, also authorized by the 1981 convention, was intended to

> enable the AFL-CIO and its affiliates to coordinate their communications programs and to speak with a more consistent voice to a mass audience through the most effective means of all modern media. By pooling their resources, the AFL-CIO and its affiliates can reduce the communications gap which too often complicates and hinders their efforts to reach their members and the general public.[1]

Table 3   Predictions of Future
Expenditures by Union for
Public Relations

	(N = 22)
Considerably more	9%
More	41
About the same	50
Less	0
Considerably less	0

Table 4   Opinions of AFL-CIO Media Utilization

Statement	Agree	(N = 22) Disagree	No answer
AFL-CIO utilization of mass media is usually satifactory	23%	73%	4%
A larger share of public relations should be carried out by the AFL-CIO on behalf of . . .			
. . . organized labor as a whole	86	14	0
. . . individual affiliates in general	55	36	9
. . . individual affiliates with particular public relations requirements	68	23	9

Union officials also expressed interest in increased activity for affiliates with particular requirements and for affiliates in general. Affiliates have been seeing more activity since 1981. AFL-CIO Department of Information staff members have stepped up efforts to help locals and state federations with press relations in several ways. One staff member, for example, spends most of his time helping state federations with press relations during their conventions—calling newspapers and radio and television stations ahead of time to build up the event, attending the conventions and acting as the media contact person, and so on. The state federations benefit from his experience during an important time, and learn enough in the process to do better subsequently on their own. In addition, LIPA (Labor Institute of Public Affairs) is currently providing affiliates with materials to help them better understand the technical and legal aspects of electronic communications, and, on request, provides other information it has that might solve particular problems of individual affiliates. Original plans for LIPA also recognized the need for a central storehouse of information, especially information concerning labor's publics. The plan provides for a staff member who will be qualified to supervise the measurement of public opinion inside and outside of labor's constituency. The institute could then establish an ongoing databank, based on regularly recorded surveyed opinions on labor-related issues for the benefit of the labor movement, and make this information available to affiliates on a cost basis for their own purposes. LIPA has, thus far, not gone far in this particular direction.

Opinions and Use of the Mass Media
It is not surprising to find that union officials' opinions regarding the coverage labor receives in the nation's mass media varies greatly, as does their use of it. As indicated in Table 5, 41 percent of those responding indicated they felt that mass media news treatment of labor and labor-related activities was rarely fair and unbiased. All of these internationals were medium-sized,

Table 5   Opinions of Mass Media News
Treatment of Labor and Labor-Related Activities
and Interests

	(N = 22)
Fair and unbiased the majority of the time	9%
Fair and unbiased about half of the time	50
Rarely fair and unbiased	41

with the exception of one large union. Two-thirds of this group had been categorized as relatively inactive in public relations activities. Fifty-five percent of this group (i.e., those who felt media news was rarely fair and unbiased) had never utilized free public service time on either radio or television, and 44 percent had never purchased time in order to present their own point of view. Some of the problems sensed by these individuals thus may have been associated with lack of initiative or perseverance in these matters. Some, in fact, blamed themselves—especially for not taking advantage of free time. Others blamed the media; one union representative who had not ever purchased time or space said attempts had been made, but the union had been denied access.

Fully half of the respondents said they believed news coverage of union activities was fair and unbiased about half the time. Of this group, 54 percent were large unions with active public relations programs.

Opinions regarding the manner in which print media had treated the respondent's own international union were about even (Table 6). However, the high frequency of no judgment responses is somewhat surprising. Perhaps the neutral alternative was selected because little had been broadcast about those particular unions, though that in itself could reflect broadcasters' bias and thus serve as a basis for judgment.

In principle, organized labor is able to communicate its viewpoints by radio or television at little or no cost; this is usually easier to do when these viewpoints concern issues that are considered in the public interest or public issue categories. However, 50 percent of all the internationals questioned

Table 6   Characterization of Media Treatment of the Union of
Which Respondent is a Member

	(N = 22)		
	Usually good	Usually poor	No basis for judgment
Newspapers and magazines	50%	45%	5%
Radio	23	45	32
Television	23	45	32

had never (at least to the knowledge of the respondent) utilized public service time on radio (Table 7). Even more had not utilized public service time on television. On the other hand, two-thirds of the respondents indicated their internationals had used paid time or space (68 percent) (Table 8). The small inactive unions tended to use neither, though one had used both. The large unions tended to use both, and advertising was used more frequently than free time; only one large international had never advertised. Of all the unions who advertised, 50 percent said they did so only infrequently, 36 percent said they advertised frequently, and 20 percent did not respond to the question. Only one of these frequent advertisers was a medium-sized union; all the others were large. All had been categorized as having active public relations programs.

Respondents who indicated that their internationals did some advertising were asked to describe the point of view expressed in the most recent ads. From their comments, most of the ads (61 percent) appear to have been image ads rather than advocacy ads. The following remarks are examples of the comments received.

"Explanation of position."
"Support for causes of importance to workers."
"Union ready to change with times."
"Organizing campaigns and nice institutional ads."
"Collective bargaining by unions is good."
"One million dollar national TV, radio and newspaper ad campaign to fight Reagan budget and tax cuts."
"Themes: 'We're helping to build the 20th Century.' Mostly institutional in nature, with an 800 call-in phone number for organizing."
"Fighting deregulation of natural gas prices."
"We put an ad in the *Washington Post* protesting the creation of a Federal Education Department."
"Opposing Reagan social security cuts."

Almost half of the respondents indicated that their international had never been denied access to the media (Table 9). In some cases, however, this was because no attempt had ever been made by those unions. Seventy

Table 7   Union Usage of
Public Service Broadcast Time

| | (N = 22) | |
	Yes	No
Radio	50%	50%
Television	41	59

Table 8   Unions That Have
Purchased Media Time/Space

		(N = 22)
Yes		68%
Frequently	36%	
Infrequently	50	
No response	14	
No		32

percent of the internationals categorized as inactive responded that they never had been denied access, while only 25 percent of the respondents for active unions said they had never been denied access.

Those that had been denied access were asked to give reasons for denial. These responses were quite varied and provide an indication of the different ways that unions have tried to gain access. They also provide evidence that media relationships are particularly difficult during a strike.

> "When we have tried, i.e., with news releases or gone with produced paid ads, we have been denied access."
> "Not responsive to presenting our side in strike or negotiating instances."
> "The *Washington Post* has refused even to print our 'letter to the editor' in response to biased editorials on mass transit cost."
> "In organizing campaigns and in boycott activity."
> "Occasional problems for field representatives in getting news of meetings published and/or favorable comments during picketing or strike situations."
> "About 40 percent of TV stations refused to run recent TV ads hitting Reagan economic programs in about twelve major media markets."
> "Denied opportunity to respond to unfair and untrue reporting— KDKA-TV, Pittsburgh. Filed complaint with FCC."
> "Refused to run paid organizing ads."
> "Some of our paid spots were refused by a Chicago radio station."

Table 9   Unions That
Have Been Denied Media
Access

	(N = 22)
Frequently	14%
Occasionally	32
Rarely	9
Never	45

"Broadcaster responding to our request for reply time under fairness doctrine, saying issue was not controversial."

"Example: in a strike, turned down by all available media in Indianapolis."

"Many issues of importance to maritime industry and union seamen (of foreign flagships owned by U.S. corporations, and safety matters) are not considered newsworthy."

The Fairness Doctrine

Half of the respondents said their internationals had never used the fairness doctrine as a basis for requesting radio or television time (Table 10). The respondents who reported that they had utilized the fairness doctrine mostly represented large, active labor unions. All of the respondents who reported never having used the fairness doctrine represented medium and small unions; of this group, 64 percent were categorized as inactive, and 36 percent active.

Utilization of this method to gain access to the airwaves places the organization in a confrontational rather than a cooperative relationship with broadcasters. It requires familiarity with the law and with the process to be followed in order to enforce station compliance. Most staff members and officers of international unions, large and small, are familiar with the laws and the processes. The smaller unions, however, have either a small public relations staff or no staff at all. The fact that the process is time-consuming combined with the other costs and risks of confrontation surely helps explain why small unions tend toward nonutilization of the doctrine.

Opinions regarding the fairness doctrine ranged from the comments, "It is worthless," to "It is essential." Generally, however, while respondents recognized weaknesses of the fairness doctrine and strongly favored updated legislation that would provide some kinds of access guarantees, they assessed the doctrine favorably (Table 11). Almost half of those who considered the fairness doctrine as limiting rather than increasing diversity of

Table 10 Use of the Fairness Doctrine as a Reason for Requesting Radio or Television Time

	(N = 22)
Frequently	14%
Occasionally	18
Rarely	14
Never	50
No response	4

Table 11   Opinions of the Fairness Doctrine

	Agree	(N = 22) Disagree	No answer
We see the fairness doctrine as helpful to our union because broadcasters are not free to ignore controversial issues of public importance.	73%	27%	0%
The fairness doctrine is valuable because it can provide us with media access due to the fact that licensees are required to make air time available for alternate points of view.	77	23	0
Though the fairness doctrine is intended to increase the diversity of opinions presented to the public, we have found that it has the opposite effect; broadcasters use it to exclude particular views.	54	32	14
In spite of the fairness doctrine, network executives have what amounts to absolute power of censorship.	54	37	9
Because it has been outdated by new technology, it needs to be replaced by new, stronger legislation that would provide guarantees of some kind of access to us and similar organizations.	82	14	4
The fairness doctrine, even if updated, is unnecessary because competition alone will insure a diversity of programming and a variety of viewpoints.	9	91	0

public opinion still felt that the doctrine is helpful and valuable to their internationals. The feeling of most respondents seemed to be that although something new is needed, they are not willing to give up what they now have unless and until better legislation is enacted.

Advertising

The advertising portion of the questionnaire elicited responses from all the sampled unions that had advertised (68 percent of the total sample), regardless of whether the advertising function was covered by a specific public relations budget. Of the unions that did not advertise and thus did not answer these questions, 57 percent were medium in size, 29 percent large, and 14 percent small; 43 percent were categorized as active. (As explained above, "active" or "inactive" are categories used only to describe public relations programs.) These figures are not unexpected, but it bears mention that not all large unions advertise and not all active unions advertise.

On the other hand, of those that have done advertising, 47 percent were large, active international unions. Twenty percent of the sample represented small inactive organizations, 20 percent medium and inactive, and 13 percent medium and active. Forty percent of these respondents reported there had been virtually no change in the amount of money allocated to advertising in the past five years. One-third, however, reported that allocations had increased significantly. All unions with increasing advertising budgets were active in public relations, and all were large with the exception of one medium-sized union.

A number of respondents were unsure when their unions had first undertaken advertising. Of those who did know, however, one union reportedly advertised in the mass media as early as 1945, and two unions did not try it until 1980.

Eight percent of the internationals that have advertised have utilized general circulation newspapers, and 73 percent have advertised on the radio (Table 12). Most of these unions emphasized national and local rather than regional and state ad campaigns (Table 13). Several audiences were targeted in this advertising (Table 14), but the audience most frequently mentioned was the general public. Potential union members and current union members also ranked high on the list of frequently targeted audiences. The fact that almost half the unions had advertised to their own members, hoping to enhance their image of the union, may be somewhat surprising because internationals have a variety of less costly ways of reaching their own members. Although the purposes of both advocacy advertising (i.e., promoting social, economic, and political viewpoints, etc.) and image-building can be advanced internally via the labor press, it is the opinion of certain union leaders that the rank and file take a good deal of pride in image ads ostensi-

Table 12   Media Utilized by Unions That Advertise

	(N = 15)
Newspapers, trade publications	47%
Newspapers, general circulation	80
Radio	73
Television	27
Magazines	40
Other*	20

*Mentioned in this category were booklets in labor, women's and political areas, yearbooks, and programs.

Table 13   Scope of
Advertising Campaigns

	(N = 15)
National	47%
Regional	20
State	13
Local	53
No response	13

bly intended for the general public. Howard Samuel, president of the Industrial Union Department of the AFL-CIO, is one labor leader who expressed this view:

> I have doubts about the eventual utility of institutional [image] advertising. It is very expensive and it has got to be a saturation type of campaign no matter what media you are using and we can't afford that. So, it may be doomed. But many unions do use it as institution-building. It looks like institutional advertising. It really isn't. It's really institution-building. It's really aimed at their own members and you've got to understand that.[2]

Table 15 lists purposes for which union advertising might be intended. Making the public more aware of the union and creating a more favorable image of the union in public opinion are both forms of image advertising. Each of these has been a goal of past advertising for 60 percent of the unions that advertise. A slightly higher percentage (67 percent), however, reported that some of their past advertising had aimed at promoting and engendering support for a social, economic, or political point of view, a form of advocacy advertising. Most of the respondents stated that their unions never had tried to measure or evaluate the success of the advertising that had been done (Table 16). Of those who had undertaken evaluation, 55 percent said it had been done internally by their own staff, and 45 percent reported that it had been done by a private research group. The methods used most frequently by the unions who evaluated were advertising posttesting methods—surveys, recall or recognition tests, and so on.

Table 14   Intended Audiences of Union
Advertising

	(N = 15)
Own members	47%
Potential members	53
Labor in general	20
Consumers of own union's products	13
General public	73
No response	13

Table 15   Purposes of Past Advertising

	(N = 15)
To promote and engender support for a social, economic, or political point of view	67%
To make the public more aware of union	60
To create a more favorable image of own union in public opinion	60
To recruit new members	53
To counter an opposing point of view	47
To encourage action on the part of readers	33
To endorse alternatives on a topic of concern	20
No response	7

Of all the unions that have advertised in past years, only two reported that there had been internal objection to doing it. One of these two did not explain the reasons for the objections; the other respondent, however, stated that the objections were not serious objections and had come from union leaders who were concerned about the expenses involved.

All respondents replied to questions concerning future advertising that might be undertaken by their own international unions. The greatest number of these (54 percent) indicated that if an advertising campaign were undertaken in the future, they would prefer that ad preparation be the responsibility of either an outside agency completely or a joint effort on the part of their own staffs and an outside agency. There was a slight preference among these for using a public relations firm—which typically has broader responsibilities—rather than an advertising agency. Forty-one percent of the respondents preferred to give ad campaign responsibility to their own staffs (the other 5 percent did not respond to the question). All of the respondents representing small unions indicated that future ads done by their unions would be prepared by their own staffs. On the other hand, over half of the respondents from large unions wanted their ads created by advertising specialists and only one of these indicated preference for his own staff to work with advertising specialists.

These results are consistent with often-expressed labor sentiments about the mass media in general and advertising in particular. That is, that it is

Table 16   Frequency of
Evaluations of Advertising

	(N = 15)
Never	40%
Rarely	27
Occasionally	33
Frequently	0

becoming increasingly difficult for public relations staff members to do a good job because the media are increasingly complex and advertising professionals have the knowledge that is necessary to produce good results. Most feel that media specialists are necessary in order to take full advantage of media opportunities. As one respondent from a large active union noted:

> Labor complains because it does not understand or know how to use the mass media. The fault lies with labor. They should hire professional people and let them do the job and tell the story *and* have a *policy* role. The area is too inbred with people who feed off labor for their monetary existence and deliver inferior products.

Many internationals, however, do not have budgets that are large enough to support such professionals. The following comment came from an outside consultant who represented a medium-sized union that has been relatively inactive in public relations:

> For the small- and medium-sized unions, big national advertising campaigns—and, often, national public relations programs—are too expensive to warrant serious consideration. Ingenuity is required to get media attention on a news or feature basis—and that is not always possible! So it's an uphill struggle.

The information director of a small, relatively inactive union commented on the special problems of advertising:

> Advertising is really beyond the reach of the average union. Properly done, it would need a coalition of unions sponsoring advertising. Some feel that AFL-CIO budgeting emphasis should be changed to allocate far more for such use as this on behalf of the whole labor movement.

Rather predictably, representatives of small unions generally indicated agreement with the statement that advertising is too expensive to enable labor to compete with business, while those from large unions disagreed (Table 17).

Table 17 reports some opinons held by the respondents regarding advertising. This group felt that past advertising usually has achieved its purpose (though, as indicated earlier, this opinion is not based on formal evaluation of advertising), and that advertising is necessitated by the lack of information on news and public affairs programs, but that advertising alone will not solve media problems. The large number of respondents who agreed with the statement "It can be very valuable and can be used to present our side of issues and to urge public action" (91 percent who either strongly agreed or agreed) indicated that few would approve only of image advertising. Advocacy advertising by organized labor found strong support among the respondents.

Table 17   Opinions About Labor Union Advertising

	(N = 22)		
	Agree	Disagree	No answer
Advertising that has been done by my unit has usually achieved its intended purpose.	59%	9%	32%
News and public affairs programs are currently doing a good job of keeping people informed and therefore advertising is not necessary	4	91	4
Advertising does not solve the problem; what is needed are legislative changes that would guarantee some access to the mass media for the public.	64	32	4
Advertising is too expensive; we cannot compete with business.	54	41	4
Advertising can be very valuable, but should only be used to create a favorable image of our union.	45	41	14
Advertising can be very valuable and can be used to present our side of issues and to urge public action.	91	4	4

A final open-ended question asked respondents, "In your opinion, what public relations strategies will best achieve your goals?" Some representative responses to this question are given below.

"Ad hoc rather than ongoing programs." (medium-sized, inactive union)

"Continued, positive news releases of union activity; spot public relations activity during organizing drives." (large, active union)

"Improved internal communications foremost." (large, active union)

"We must try to change the public's perception of the labor movement." (medium, active union)

"Assume there's much more that can be done if it's worked out properly, with professional public relations methods." (small, inactive union)

"Wide communication of union views, reaching as large an audience as possible." (large, active union)

"Combination of advertising, use of free TV and radio and use of full range of traditional advertising tools." (large, active union)

"An AFL-CIO budget earmarked for public relations and raised through per capita tax." (large, active union)

"Anticipating future needs of industry, government and the labor force in changing society." (medium, inactive union)

DISCUSSION

The view elicited by the responses was one of general concern, some agreement about objectives, and very little consensus about how to achieve these objectives. The survey, plus the written and oral comments that it engendered, proved to be a valuable resource not only for the explicit similarities and differences it brought to light, but also in raising some additional questions and issues that labor leaders will find desirable or necessary to address as they proceed with their public relations plans.

The questionnaire indicated that concern about public relations has not always been translated into action. In the last chapter it was noted that four major international unions had obtained free public service time on radio and television as one component of their extensive and diversified utilization of mass media. Yet results of the questionnaire show that a full 50 percent of the surveyed internationals have never used free public service time on either radio or television. This was especially true of smaller unions. Since this cannot be explained on the basis of cost, it is most likely a consequence of staffing limitations characterizing the smaller unions.

The four unions examined in Chapter III made more use of new media technologies than most of the unions surveyed. Only one questionnaire response referred to technology in mass communications. One public relations director (of a medium-sized union) said his union had organized a Public Broadcasting System teleconference that received enthusiastic response and feedback. The telecast originated in Chicago and was linked by satellite to five studios in other locations. Viewers could call and ask questions of persons in any of these locations or in Chicago. The subject of the teleconference was occupational safety and health. Awareness of the possibilities that new technology presents—and perhaps some uneasiness with the technology—might be implied by the desire of the unions to use professionals and for the AFL-CIO to do more for its affiliates.

Over half of the sampled unions have advertised. In fact, advertising has been used more frequently than free time, a finding that may be explained by labor leaders' complaints that public service time typically was the worst listening/viewing time of the week. In addition, sometimes what a union desires to communicate simply may not fall into the public issue/public interest categories—or may not be considered as such by media managers. At any rate, the data support the notion that union advertising appears to be growing in popularity. Advertising offers the advantages of allowing more control over both the content and the setting of the communication. It also gives labor an opportunity to portray itself in a thoughtful, positive manner.

Those who advertise tend to be large unions, but even many of these do not advertise frequently. Cost is a limiting factor for most internationals, but it is becoming increasingly evident that cost is not the only problem.

Public relations efforts and advertising efforts lead to a variety of internal and external policy problems.

Apparently neither the internal organization structures or decision-making processes relating to public relations and to advertising are well-developed. The roles of the public relations department and the public relations director and staff are far from being well-defined in terms of responsibility and direction. To which public is the director trying to communicate? What priorities have been or should be established? Whose views of what the international is and what it does should be expressed? Those of the president? Those of the executive council? Those of rank and file members? Ideally, these would all be the same; realistically they are likely to diverge. These and related questions are associated with internal problems the union must address in order for its public relations program to move forward in clearly defined, well-organized directions.

Between the 1930s and the 1970s, organized labor in the United States changed from being a militant class movement to an institution integrated, however uneasily, into the corporate economy. Labor unions operate within the capitalist system—seeking recognition and a larger portion of the corporate income. In doing so, labor implicitly recognizes the power of employers. David Dubinsky, former president of the ILGWU, once stated, "Trade unionism needs capitalism like a fish needs water."[3]

A corollary to this axiom has been the structuring of organized labor along lines similar to corporate structure. The position of union officers within this structure is complicated by the fact that, more than in the case of business executives, union leaders strive for a system of internal democracy. Nevertheless, union officers have been criticized for being rigidly bureaucratic; gaps have developed between union officers and members, and between union officers and their own staff people. Such gaps—and related disagreements, power struggles, and so on—become all too evident in public relations policy. Public relations directors can try to ignore them in their public communications, gloss over them, bridge the gap internally, or simply admit differences and strive for public understanding.

The policy of the AFL-CIO Department of Information is to try to remain neutral on issues that divide workers. In spite of the expertise and care of the staff, however, even that Department occasionally finds itself in the center of controversy. An example of one of these situations began on Sunday, August 15, 1982, when a full-page advertisement appeared in the "Week in Review" section of the *New York Times*. The ad incorporated a position statement adopted 10 days earlier by the AFL-CIO Executive Council declaring support for Israel's invasion of Lebanon (Figure 15). The headline of the ad stated, "The AFL-CIO Is Not Neutral. We Support Israel." The policy position, as presented in the advertisement, was entirely correct. The AFL-CIO, however, had nothing to do with the advertisement,

Organized Labor Speaks Out on Lebanon

'THE AFL-CIO IS NOT NEUTRAL. WE SUPPORT ISRAEL.'

For seven years, the people of Lebanon have been subjected to a reign of terror at the hands of the PLO and Syria, which together occupied 60 percent of the country. Nearly 100,000 were killed, another quarter of a million wounded, 800,000 Christians and 500,000 Moslems made homeless. The country's political structure and institutions of authority were shattered.

In Lebanon, the world could see what a PLO state would look like, but little attention was paid to this unfolding tragedy. By contrast, when the Israeli forces moved into Lebanon, there was a global outcry against the civilian casualties.

The AFL-CIO deeply regrets the loss of civilian lives in the present conflict. **The PLO's tactic of deliberately locating its forces in residential areas and storing its ammunition in schools, hospitals and other public facilities has compounded the number of civilian casualties.** In effect, it is holding the civilian population of West Beirut hostage.

The AFL-CIO Executive Council considers the Israeli invasion of Lebanon entirely justified on security grounds. The seizure of vast caches of PLO weapons and ammunition in southern Lebanon is proof of a PLO military buildup which posed a direct threat to Israeli security. **To protect its security, Israel was justified not only in altering its stated objective of removing the immediate threat but in attacking its source—the command structure of the PLO itself.**

In the conflict between Israel, on the one hand, and the PLO and Syria, on the other, **the AFL-CIO is not neutral. We support Israel.** The world should demand that the PLO and Syria leave Lebanon now and allow the Lebanese to proceed with the task of reconstruction and the creation of an independent central government. Upon the departure of those forces, the Israeli forces must also withdraw, as they have committed themselves to do. We call upon the United States government to assist the Lebanese in this task in every way possible and to make humanitarian aid available to the Lebanese and the Palestinians.

In destroying the PLO's military infrastructure, **Israel has not only created the possibility of a free Lebanon; it has dealt a blow to international terrorism and set back Soviet influence in the Middle East—and thus advanced the interests of the Western democracies.**

The weakening of the PLO and of Soviet influence may set the stage for fruitful discussion with moderate Arab forces aimed at a solution of the Palestinian problem. The U.S., through diplomatic and other means, should work toward the creation of conditions for a negotiated settlement of this issue. Toward this end, **the AFL-CIO urges the U.S. government to continue withholding recognition from the PLO** and to refrain from any actions which would encourage the PLO to believe that it can snatch a political victory from military defeat.

The PLO should be denied recognition or legitimacy not only because it is dedicated to the destruction of Israel but because it is a terrorist organization. **To reward it with recognition is to encourage terrorism as a political tactic around the world.**

Adopted by the AFL-CIO Executive Council August 5, 1982, New York City
Presented as a public service by the Ad Hoc Committee for Peace in the Middle East
443 Park Avenue South, New York, NY 10016
A.D. [illegible], Coordinator

FIGURE 15. Advertisement in the *New York Times,* August 15, 1982, p. F7; ad sponsored by the Ad Hoc Committee for Peace in the Middle East.

although many readers were probably left with the impression it did. Rather, an ad hoc group, which included some labor officers, had financed and sponsored the ad.

Three weeks later another ad appeared in the "Week in Review" section of the *New York Times*. This ad, not quite as large, publicly stated opposition to the earlier ad (Figure 16): "As trade unionists, we cannot and will not stand for the identification of the trade union movement and workers of this country with Israeli action in Lebanon." The ad was signed by persons from a variety of labor unions; they, too, had formed an ad hoc committee to advertise.

Department of Information director Murray Seeger "heard a lot" about both ads from unhappy union members and from an angry public. Official policy positions taken by union leaders on such non-"bread-and-butter" issues are certain to be opposed by some members. On this occasion the opposition was made abundantly clear by the second advertisement. This example suggests not only differences between leaders and rank and file members, but also between leaders and those responsible for public relations. In this case, the formation of ad hoc committees removes any organizational responsibility, but the public relations results were detrimental to the Department of Information's program and reputation. (At least one published account of the original ad reported that the AFL-CIO paid half a million dollars to publish it.)

To some extent the problem is inherent in "public group speech." A situation may arise at any time that causes media representatives to ask a union officer to express an opinion on behalf of labor or on behalf of his/her union. What this person says is public group speech in the sense that he or she is taking personal responsibility for expressing the opinions of those who are part of an organization. Advocacy advertising is another form of public group speech; this time the responsibility is usually assumed by the public relations staff or by an outside firm. In such situations, a good deal of responsibility must be assumed by the spokesperson. Whose position is to be expressed? Who decides to express it? Who decides that the expression justifies any necessary allocation of resources? What relationship does the expression establish between the communicator and other publics? As a member of an institution, does an individual give up a portion of his or her own freedom of speech?

All this goes somewhat beyond internal organization and decision making to ethics of group speech. Ethical problems may arise in a variety of ways in institutional communications, and obviously the practice of advocacy advertising, as in the above example and in contrast to the situation with traditional product advertising, tends to create such problems. Certain of these, such as protection of First Amendment rights of persons who disagree with positions taken by institutions and use of union dues and per

FIGURE 16.   Advertisement in the *New York Times*, September 5, 1982, p. E5; and sponsored by the Ad Hoc Committee of Trade Unionists to oppose the Israeli Invasion of Lebanon.

capita taxes to back positions not supported by an individual, are discussed in Chapter V.

Respondents to the survey looked favorably on increased advocacy advertising in spite of its hazards to the organization. Of course public relations officers might have a vested interest in increased advertising of all kinds, and this may even affect their ability to recognize internal objections to advertising. Whether they can maintain this favorable outlook if the trend toward advocacy advertising continues remains to be seen.

Internal union organization structures, decision making, ethics, and legalities all may be classified as issues relating to the perception the union communicates to the general public of itself. Most public relations directors will be well-challenged by such issues alone. These issues, however, actually comprise only about half of what are (or should be) the issues facing public relations directors. The other side of the coin lies in the need for public relations people to be able to provide union officers with the public's perception of labor.

Of course, the public does not have a monolithic perception of labor; rather, various publics have a mixture of perceptions of labor. Murray Seeger remarked on this situation in an address given before the Public Relations Society of America in April, 1982:

> On the one hand, we are seen as part of the economic and political establishment—a tradition-bound organization that plays the role expected of it without causing any surprises. Some of our strongest critics claim we have become irrelevant, that our rhetoric is out-of-date and that we are fighting the battles of the 80s in the same way we fought the battles of the 30s, 40s and 50s.
>
> Our enemies say we are simply another lobby—like so many in Washington—that perpetuates itself for selfish purposes without reflecting the true desires of our members. Reporters regularly claim we are diminishing as a force in the economy, that we can't keep up with what is happening in the country.
>
> In analyzing a recent poll about the position of organized labor in the United States, a Washington Post writer drew the conclusion that a political candidate would be better off to have labor endorse his opponent than himself. Just a few weeks ago, the Vice President of the United States repeated the canard that the officers of the AFL-CIO were out of touch with their membership.
>
> The other side of this mixed perception is this: that same Washington Post poll found that a large percentage of Americans think we are too powerful. Other measures of public opinion regularly cite organized labor as one of the most powerful institutions in the country.
>
> We are regularly attacked by well-financed organizations who want to dismantle the legal structure under which unions function. Employers pay

millions of dollars to so-called consultants to fight union organizers attempt-ing to sign up their workers. More millions are paid to union-busters whose function it is to get rid of organizations which legally won the right to repre-sent workers. . . .

So, for an institution that is supposedly on its last legs, we draw a lot of interest and activity by individuals and organizations who see us as dangerous agitators and trouble makers.

In the same fashion, some of the same writers who claim unions have lost their economic power turn around and blame unions for causing inflation, the deficit in the international balance of trade, the high sales of Japanese cars and just about every other economic ill except the Medfly infestation in Cali-fornia.[4]

Part of Seeger's job—and the job of every union's public relations direc-tor—is to be as thoroughly knowledgeable as possible about the mixed perceptions of the organization that are held by various publics. Further-more, all directors need to be constantly attuned to the public because perceptions undergo constant—and often rapid—changes. Only on this basis can a communications program be planned and executed in such a way that its messages are responsive and meaningful to the public. Such a public relations program would not be confined to what the union wants to tell its publics, but it would also respond to what the publics want to know about organized labor and individual unions.

Independent public relations firms that specialize in labor problems may understand the importance of this side of public relations better than most unions. Personnel of these firms make it their responsibility continuously to monitor relevant publics and store a reservoir of information on public perceptions of labor.[5] This enables them to provide potentially effective public relations programs to labor by sharing the information and articulat-ing it with what union staff and officers want to communicate to their publics. A public opinion databank at the AFL-CIO could provide affiliates with such information; effective use of it would then depend on the skill of public relations personnel.

Even with more help and expertise from the AFL-CIO, organized labor may be hard-pressed to maintain congruence between what it is doing and what it is telling the public it is doing. Congruence is important in order to reduce mixed public perceptions about labor and to maintain institutional credibility. Even the best public relations program cannot be effective if it is not backed up by behavior patterns that are consistent. This is not to say that all officers, locals, and rank and file members must always speak with one voice or behave in exactly the same way. Different commitments and priorities exist at different levels within labor. However, public relations directors view the maintenance of general internal agreement and of consistency between the public relations program and the behavior of union officers and members as important to a successful program. These are not always easily achieved.

Internal consistency may be especially difficult to maintain when labor takes an advocate's position and complex issues are tackled publicly—when, for example, a social or economic point of view is being endorsed, or a certain opposing viewpoint is being countered. Complex issues often do not lend themselves to the simplicity and directness that make some public relations campaigns and most advertising effective. The difficulties that may be encountered in trying to be succinct while clearly explaining a position means that such attempts risk being easily misunderstood. Very complex issues may be addressed more successfully in fora such as press conferences or talk shows where media time and/or space are not too severely limited and where there is a better opportunity for questions and discussion.

Consistency in public relations programs is further complicated because internal consistency is only part of the problem. Communications generated through international unions are certainly not the only communications the public will receive about labor and labor-related issues. In fact, in view of labor's limited control over external consistency, public misunderstanding of organized labor is *less* likely to occur when public relations campaigns and advertising address specific issues, even though they may be complex, than when they strive for general good will. Image campaigns and advertising may indeed fulfill an internal "institution-building" function, but such messages will appear to some outside labor as contrived good will that does, as Albert Zack said (Chapter II), vanish the first time a union is forced to strike and the public is inconvenienced.

Labor is usually considered part of a liberal coalition in this country, however tenuous this coalition may be. Directly addressing controversial issues that affect labor makes sense and is an approach widely understood in a pluralistic society. International unions can make a substantive contribution to public information in their campaigns, and, while avoiding defensive, "crisis" campaigns, they can present regularly unions' positions on issues. Such a communications strategy can be understood and will contribute to the maintenance of an overall consistency. And if the more controversial labor issues can be linked to broader issues—humanitarian, environmental, and so on—the greater the total effectiveness of the message should be.

Organized labor exhibits an internal heterogeneity that obviously is most acute at the top, or Federation, level. Because of this, the AFL-CIO will find it more difficult than international unions to initiate public relations campaigns that deal with controversial issues. It would be addressing issues that affect labor as a whole and speaking for labor as a whole. It can be done, but the existence of great internal diversity means that internal contradictions can occur all too easily and too often. Sometimes the contradictions may be public and purposeful, as exemplified in the anti-Israeli ad by union members; at other times activities of one or more affiliates may unexpectedly lead to inconsistency and cause the public to perceive the labor movement with confusion. Advocacy may be somewhat easier for international unions, but it is just as true for the Federation as it is for internationals that little will be accomplished by undertaking simplistic image-building campaigns or engaging only in irregular, "crisis" campaigns. Advocacy makes just as much sense for the AFL-CIO as it does for its affiliates. The AFL-CIO has a great deal of essential information to give the public, including information on issues that affect all working people in the same or similar ways as well as information that affirms the breadth of labor's concerns, responsibilities, "special interests," activities, and objectives.

NOTES

[1] Murray Seeger, "Report to the Executive Council: Institute of Public Affairs," unpublished report received from Murray Seeger, Director, AFL-CIO Department of Information, May 25, 1982, p.1.

[2] Howard Samuel, President, AFL-CIO Industrial Union Department, interview, Washington, D.C., May 24, 1982.

[3] Quoted in Michael Myerson, "ILGWU: Fighting for Lower Wages," *Ramparts,* October, 1969, p. 55.

[4] Murray Seeger, "Address to the Public Relations Society of America," Washington, D.C., April 20, 1982.

[5] Henry C. Fleisher interview, Washington, D.C., May 29, 1982. Also Victor Kamber, The Kamber Group, interview, Washington, D.C., May 25, 1982.

CHAPTER V

Media Access

INTRODUCTION

Advertising budgets and communications strategies may be necessary components of programs of public relations, but, if union leaders intend to reach beyond the membership to other audiences, particularly the general public, there is an equally fundamental requirement: media access. The ability of a union (or anyone else other than media owners—on this point Liebling's famous quote says it all[1]) to place messages in mass media of communication cannot be taken for granted. The issue is all the more important, intuitively and constitutionally, because obstruction of access affects not only the party wishing to transmit some message, but also the public's interest in availability of information. The countervailing interest is media owners' concern for making a profit. This chapter explores the problem of access—its development as a subject in American communications policy and the constraints it places upon organized labor's utilization of the mass media.

An introduction to the way access has been troubling organized labor and to the analysis of this problem in this chapter is afforded by two judicial decisions handed down in 1970. One of these cases, *Chicago Joint Board, Amalgamated Clothing Workers of America, AFL-CIO v. Chicago Tribune Company*,[2] involved a dispute between the Chicago Joint Board and several Chicago newspaper publishers—the Chicago Tribune Company, the Chicago American Publishing Company, and Field Enterprises, Inc. The basis of the dispute lay in the union's objection to the sale of imported apparel by Marshall Field and Company on the grounds that such activity jeopardized jobs of clothing workers in the United States.

As part of a campaign to limit apparel importation, the union had attempted to place advertisements that explained its position in four Chicago newspapers—the *Chicago Tribune, Chicago Today, Chicago Sun-Times,* and *Chicago Daily News*. All four of these newspapers regularly published Field's advertisements and, by inserting ads in these newspapers, the union hoped to convey its position to the same public that was exposed to Field's ads. Each of the four newspapers refused to publish the advertisement. Refusal was based on alleged failure to meet standards prescribed in the newspapers' Advertising Acceptability Guide that provides, among other things, for rejection of an advertisement that "reflects unfavorably on competitive organizations, institutions or merchandise."[3]

The union took the case to court, asking that newspapers be enjoined to publish the ad. Union lawyers also sought a declaration that the defendants

> may not arbitrarily refuse to publish advertisements expressing ideas, opinions or facts on political or social issues and . . . may not refuse to publish such advertisements if they are lawful and the party submitting the advertisement is willing to pay the usual rate and there is no technical or mechanical reason why the advertisement cannot be published . . . [4]

The U.S. Court of Appeals, Seventh Circuit, decided in favor of the newspaper companies; the court's understanding of the concept of freedom of the press recognized in the First Amendment was at variance with the union's concept. According to the court, the press had no obligation to serve as a public forum and the union's right to free speech did not include the right of making use of the Chicago newspapers' printing presses and distribution system without their consent.

> We glean nothing from the constitutional guarantees, or from the decisions expository thereof, which suggest that the advertising pages of a privately published newspaper may so be pressed into service against the publisher's will either in the contest of a labor dispute to which the publisher is not a party or otherwise.[5]

The second case, *Retail Store Employees Union, Local 880, Retail Clerks International Association, AFL-CIO v. Federal Communications Commission*[6] is similar, although this time the issue was over use of the air waves rather than printing presses. As in the *Chicago Joint Board* case, the labor-management dispute did not involve the mass media. The dispute was between the Retail Store Employees' Union and Hill's Ashtabula, in Ashtabula, Ohio, one of a chain of department stores in Ohio and Pennsylvania. After some months of bargaining in 1965, the union voted to go on strike against Hill's. A boycott of the store was organized in Ashtabula and other Ohio communities.

Hill's advertised on station WREO in Ashtabula "extolling the virtues of Hill's stock, bargains, and service, and on that basis urging listeners to patronize the various Hill's outlets."[7] In February, 1966, the union began an advertising campaign to support its boycott; time was purchased from WREO for one-minute spots that announced the strike and asked listeners to respect the picket line.[8] Between February 16 and April 7, station WREO aired 322 of these spot announcements. The union gradually found it more difficult to purchase time, however, and finally, in April, no station in the Ashtabula area would accept the ads. That same month the Retail Employees filed a complaint with the Federal Communications Commission, charging violations of the fairness doctrine. The FCC responded that broadcasters were not common carriers who were required to accept advertising from all who wished to purchase time; further, there was no controversial issue of public importance involved in this dispute. WREO continued to air Hill's advertisements.

In 1967, when WREO was required to renew its broadcasting license, the union petitioned the Federal Communications Commission to deny, alleging that the station had cancelled the union ad campaign because economic pressure had been applied to WREO by Hill's. The union contended that the fairness doctrine was violated when WREO continued to carry Hill's ads that urged people to patronize its stores, while all union ads were refused.

The Federal Communications Commission's investigation of the matter consisted primarily of letters to the station manager. The manager stated that Hill's had applied no economic pressure, but that the union ads had been cancelled because "continuous repetition of these partisan announcements had become an irritant to WREO's listening audience."[9] This answer satisfied the FCC, but the union appealed and the case reached the U.S. Court of Appeals, District of Columbia, where the decision was made to remand it to the FCC for further proceedings consistent with court opinion.

The court opinion, given by Judge David Bazelon, was that the FCC had acted without proper investigation of either the public interest standard or the fairness doctrine, suggesting that sometimes these two concepts could both serve as independent bases for a right to purchase reply time to answer broadcast ads.

The FCC, in the opinion of the court, should have investigated more thoroughly WREO's ambiguous claims regarding listener irritation over the repetitiousness of the ad. The station also should have explained its own response to the alleged complaints. Did management suggest to the union officers that they advertise less frequently or change their ads more often? Was it station policy to cancel any ad that caused listener complaints because of repetitiousness?

Bazelon wrote:

> In the present case, it seems clear to us that the strike and the Union boycott were controversial issues of substantial public importance within Ashtabula, the locality primarily served by WREO. The ultimate issue with regard to the boycott was simple: whether or not the public should patronize Hill's Ashtabula. From April through December, Hill's broadcast over WREO more than a thousand spot announcements and more than a hundred sponsored programs explaining why, in its opinion, the public should patronize its store. During that same period, the Union was denied any opportunity beyond a single roundtable broadcast to explain why, in its opinion, the public should not patronize the store. We need not now decide whether, as the Union would

have us hold, these facts make out a *per se* claim of a violation of the fairness doctrine. We do believe, however, that the question deserves fuller analysis than the Commission has seen fit to give it.[10]

These two cases illustrate some of the conflicting interests involved in the complexities of media access and are useful in raising issues that have obvious importance for labor. In each case a labor union felt the need to impart significant information to the public. In each case the labor union was unable to do so because it was denied use of the media. The unions were willing to pay in order to be heard by the public, although requests that the media grant nondiscriminatory access for legal advertising are but one way by which access might be gained. Many access cases reached the courts during the 1970s, although the problems surfaced before that decade. Affiliates of the ILGWU were denied access to five newspapers with whom they wanted to place advocacy advertisements in 1958. Demands for media access became increasingly visible during the 1960s, a decade during which social unrest served as a catalyst for stimulating the access concept. Moreover, the issue has not tended to become less visible over time; AFSCME was denied access by numerous television stations when officers attempted to purchase time for advocacy advertising in 1981. It also appears unlikely that the issue will go away in the near future, though media technology may change the nature of the problem.

All sides of the issue are grounded in the constitutional guarantees of free speech and free press. Traditional First Amendment interpretation emphasizes freedom of the press to operate without government intervention. Under this interpretation, imposition of obligations upon the press have been viewed as highly questionable legal practices. But the framers of the Constitution could have had little idea of the rapid changes that would take place in the field of communications. Mass media now include a range of complex electronic systems that exist in a marketplace narrowed by concentration of media ownership and an array of technical and financial limitations.

Such limitations have led to the articulation of less traditional interpretations of the First Amendment. Proponents of media access make the following assumptions:

(1) free expression is vital to the democratic process, (2) monopolistic or concentrated control of access to the dominant media represents a threat to the workings of democracy, (3) traditional interpretations of the First Amendment are inadequate to meet the issue of corporate or private censorship and (4) the government must intervene to encourage free expression.[11]

The interests of media access proponents were greatly advanced in 1969 when the Supreme Court decided freedom of expression in broadcasting involved far greater consideration than that of the rights of broadcasters to air whatever they selected and to exclude whomever they desired. Significantly, the Supreme Court was examining a case that involved a radio station rather than a newspaper. The First Amendment had traditionally been regarded as assuming equality of all media and traditionally providing the same protection for all media. However, it took the issues that lay behind the development of radio and television broadcasting to move the courts to recognize the need for a less traditional First Amendment interpretation. And, when faced with having to choose between the interests of media owners and the rights of the public to participate and to receive information, the Court chose the latter.

> Although broadcasting is clearly a medium affected by a First Amendment interest, . . . differences in the characteristics of new media justify differences in the First Amendment standards applied to them.[12]

> It is the right of the viewers and listeners, not the right of the broadcasters, which is paramount. . . . It is the purpose of the First Amendment to preserve an uninhibited marketplace of ideas in which truth will ultimately prevail, rather than to countenance monopolization of that market, whether it be by the Government itself or a private licensee. . . . It is the right of the public to receive suitable access to social, political, esthetic, moral, and other ideas and experiences which is crucial here.[13]

The basis of the media differences lies in the fact that the air waves are a limited resource. There is only a given amount of space available on the electromagnetic spectrum and there is a scarcity of channels because many people wish to use them. Regulatory policy charges owners and operators of broadcast stations with the responsibility of acting as "public trustees" of the air waves in their communities and of operating to serve the "public interest, convenience, and necessity"[14] and to adhere to the stipulations of fairness, which require the provision of "reasonable opportunity for the discussion of conflicting views on issues of public importance."[15]

Two years after the First Amendment/broadcasting decision, in 1971, a plurality of the Supreme Court for the first time alluded to a need for public access not only to broadcasting, but also to the print media. In a case that centered on libel rather than access, Justice Brennan stated: "Constitutional adjudication must take into account the individual's interest in access to the press. . . ."[16]

Primarily because of different regulatory policy, the issues of access to print media and access to the broadcasting media will be discussed separately in this chapter. The analysis will emphasize the extent to which groups, especially labor organizations, have rights to media access in order to insert image and advocacy advertising. Advertising is an access-gaining route that has been utilized with increasing frequency by a variety of individuals, groups, and institutions. Since litigation is a principal approach through which unions and other groups have sought to improve their media access, the analysis which follows is essentially legalistic; that should not obscure the point—also taken up below—that an underlying political-economic bias causes unions to get inadequate media coverage in the first place and thus occasions the need for advertising.

COMMERCIAL SPEECH AND THE FIRST AMENDMENT

The legal connection between media access and First Amendment interpretations is compounded when advertising is added to the relationship. For many years, advertising was regarded as a "different type" of speech—done only by businesspeople in order to sell a product or service. Because it was different, it was not entitled to First Amendment protection. The arguments against the protection of "commercial speech" are usually based upon the rationale that commercial speech is not associated with the interests that the First Amendment seeks to protect—such interests as political freedom, self-government, robust debate, the exchange of ideas, the search for truth, and so on.

Crucial to the legal issue was a definition of the term "commercial speech." If commercial speech was not protected and other types of speech were protected, what exactly were the characteristics of this unprotected category? The term commercial speech is often used interchangeably with the word advertising; however, the term has never been defined conclusively by the courts. Rather, early arguments usually revolved around similarities between "commercial speech" and "First Amendment" speech. They have been based on the theoretical foundations of the First Amendment in order to compare the goals of protection of free speech with the functions of commercial advertising. One commentator, for example, makes the following points about the social value of commercial speech: (1) it may serve a vital role in aiding an individual's attainment of a materially satisfactory life, furthering the government function of promoting the general welfare; and (2) it simplifies the consumer's task of learning what is offered for sale and thus serves a legitimate educational function. The author argues:

> Sharp distinctions in the application of the first amendment between the political and private sectors take on an air of irrationality with the recognition that much political activity is directed to the betterment of the individual's material welfare. . . . It would therefore appear that present distinctions in the application of the first amendment in the political but not private spheres may well be ill-considered.[17]

United States courts finally did extend protected status under the First Amendment to commercial speech in 1976. However, they still have not developed a comprehensive, coherent framework for dealing with the commercial speech category. And now advertising commonly refers to far more than product and service advertising by businesses for commercial purposes. Since the 1976 court decision, adjudicative struggles with the category have persisted.

Litigation, which provides the formal setting for the introduction of economic evidence and argument, is afflicted with procedural difficulties. Examples of these are the collection and presentation of data in accordance with the rules of evidence, the complexities involved with defining issues in legal terms, the necessity of issuing a judgment that addresses the causes of the violation, and the length of time involved. Often judges must try to understand specialized technical concepts. Influential pressures may come from unexpected directions, and outcomes of various remedies usually are uncertain. As one observer states: "Litigation procedures involve many features which interfere with impartial analysis. They depend greatly on the 'gamesmanship' of the counsel for each side. . . . Although they are regulated by the canons of relevance and judicial impartiality, they do not allow for independent inquiry."[18]

None of these problems of the legal system detracts from the value, to the analyst, of examination of a series of opinions. Cases provide a thorough record of controversies surrounding media access and of the logical arguments that they have generated. Those discussed below have direct implications that relate to the types of advertising in which organized labor is engaged.

The seminal case in the First Amendment/commercial speech controversy was *Valentine v. Chrestensen* (1942).[19] It was in this decision that the Court rather summarily separated speech of a commercial nature from other forms of traditionally protected communication, particularly expressions of political connection or religious belief. Even though the case lacks strength because the severance of commercial speech from other protected forms was accomplished with little analysis and no reliance on either the language or the theory of the First Amendment, commercial speech was positioned as an inferior form of speech.

A number of relevant court cases were recorded between 1942 and 1976 when commercial speech was finally given protected status. During this period, the courts displayed a considerable amount of vacillation and reliance upon a variety of rationales.

There are essentially two ways that the absolute-appearing language of the First Amendment can be weakened. One is through the process of defining-out, the other is a balancing method. Defining-out refers to exempting certain categories of speech from First Amendment protection. Obscenity, defamation, and fighting words all have been defined-out categories in the past. Speech, however, does not fit neatly into such discrete categories, and Supreme Court decisions have substantially eroded each of these categories, with the qualified exception of obscenity. When commercial speech was initially added to the defined-out list, courts attempted to define it by relying on a "primary purpose test." That is, if the "primary purpose" of the speech was a business activity engaged in for the purpose of generating profit, it could not be given First Amendment protection. If, on the other hand, the "primary purpose" of the speech was to convey information or opinions, the speech was protected. However, neither category of expression was explicitly defined by the courts nor was any consideration given to the fact that they might converge.

The primary purpose test was essentially rejected in *New York Times v. Sullivan* (1964).[20] The Court recognized at this point that there often is little relationship between the purpose of the speaker and the value of the communication. Sullivan, a police commissioner from Montgomery, Alabama, sought damages from the *Times* for allegedly libelous statements contained in an advertisement that described a civil rights demonstration in Montgomery, Alabama, and solicited donations for civil rights causes. Sullivan's position was that the newspaper had accepted payment from the NAACP and others to print the advertisement and it therefore could not invoke the First Amendment because as commercial speech, the statement lay beyond the scope of First Amendment protection. The Court denied damages. The justices' rationale was based on content. The commercial speech was found to be valuable because it "communicated information, expressed opinion, recited grievances, protested claimed abuses, and sought financial support on behalf of a movement whose existence and objectives are matters of highest public interest and concern."[21]

This case established that the financial motive of the *Times* as a profit-seeking entity was not sufficient to remove First Amendment protection from statements that would have been covered if printed in editorial form rather than as an advertisement (i.e., information, opinion, grievances). The judgment in this case does not hold that commercial speech should be included in First Amendment protection, but rather that First Amendment speech will not lose protection when presented in commercial form.

After the *New York Times* case, advertising content came into contention again both in *Pittsburgh Press Company v. Pittsburgh Commission on Human Relations* (1973)[22] and in *Bigelow v. Virginia* (1975),[23] though with some interesting variations. In *Pittsburgh Press*, the Supreme Court considered the newspaper's separation of "help-wanted" classified advertisements into sex-designated columns when the jobs advertised did not contain occupational qualifications or exceptions. A section of the Human Relations Commission Ordinance prohibited such advertising practice except when deemed necessary by the Commission. The *Press* argued the case on the following points: information exchange is essential and First Amendment protection should extend to all forms of information, including commercial speech; the government should not involve itself in matters of editorial discretion; enforcement of this ordinance would constitute prior restraint of the press. All of these were rejected by the Court. Regulation of the classified ads was permitted on the basis that they were "classic examples of purely commercial speech."[24] In addition, they proposed illegal discrimination in employment. The decision established, therefore, that one characteristic of content sure to remove First Amendment protection from commercial speech is advocacy of anything illegal.

The minority opinions in this case deserve mention as they appear to have had some effect on later cases and do point out some of the inconsistencies that existed in case law up to this point. The dissents were based upon an alleged misdirection in the suit (employers who engaged in discriminatory hiring practices should have been sued rather than the newspaper that printed the classified advertisements); upon the fact that the *Press was* providing job-seekers with valuable information; and upon the *New York Times* decision that found that the advertising placed in a newspaper could be covered by the First Amendment.

The *Bigelow v. Virginia* case dealt with abortion, which, being an especially controversial issue at the time, made it a less than perfect case to address the commercial speech confusion. Bigelow, a newspaper editor, was charged with a misdemeanor for running an advertisement in his Virginia newspaper for a New York state abortion service; this violated Virginia's law against encouraging abortion. The ruling in this case was that the commercial speech in question was protected to a degree; that is, the advertisement in question contained factual information of clear public interest and the fact that it had commercial aspects or reflected the advertiser's commercial interest did not remove all First Amendment guarantees. The value of content was again used as a rationale, this time to support protection.

Balancing, the second method that can be used to dilute the First Amendment and the method that continues to be the most popular, was used in arriving at this decision. First Amendment freedoms were balanced against other societal interests. This method is no more problem-free than the defining-out method. Some persons, feeling strongly that no interests can be more important than those protected in the Constitution, automatically move toward an absolutist position if one side seems clearly protected. The issue becomes less clear when both sides involve constitutionally protected areas—such as speech and religion. Justice Black argued against employing this method in 1960:

> [The "balancing test"] tells us that no right to think, speak or publish exists in the people that cannot be taken away if the Government finds it sufficiently imperative or expedient to do so. Thus the "balancing test" turns our "Gov-

ernment of the people, by the people and for the people" into a government over the people.[25]

Bigelow is also weakened because the reasons for the support of the "public interest" are not stated. It is true that abortion was the topic of a great deal of public interest and controversy, but the content of the ad in *Bigelow* was not a debate or critique of the matter of abortion. The advertisement proposed a purely economic transaction. The difference between *New York Times* and *Bigelow* is that the *Times* ad was more directed toward an exchange of ideas, while the *Bigelow* ad was directed toward an exchange of products and services. The latter was interpreted as being closer to an exchange of ideas because it dealt with abortion rather than with detergents, toothpaste, or any more ordinary product or service. Therefore, it was easier to interpret it as containing factual material of clear public interest and First Amendment protection was awarded.

In spite of the fact that the public interest standard has deep roots in American history and American public policy, it is an elusive concept and one that consistently poses problems in adjudication. In *Pittsburgh Press* the Court concluded that public interest was not involved, though they could have decided that much of the public was surely interested in job discrimination, or in finding jobs, or even in ease of reading classified advertisements. The difficulties posed by the phrase "public value" are almost identical. Every topic and category of speech provides some degree of interest and/or value to some number of people. The Court in *Bigelow* did attempt some clarification by stating that the advertisement ". . . conveyed information of potential interest and value to a diverse audience—not only to readers possibly in need of the services offered, but also to those with a general curiosity about, or general interest in, the subject matter. . . . "[26] This statement also points out the fact that commercial speech *per se* was less the issue than what product or service was being advertised and the importance this information might have for consumers. This shift toward the interests of consumers set the stage for the reasoning in *Virginia State Board of Pharmacy v. Virginia Citizens Consumer Council* (1976),[27] the case in which the commercial speech/First Amendment issue finally was squarely faced.

The case involved a Virginia statute that prohibited a licensed pharmacist from advertising or promoting prescription drug prices. The content at issue was "purely commercial," involving no editorializing, nothing newsworthy. Mundane price advertising, done for the purpose of generating profit was at issue. The Virginia Citizens Consumer Council maintained that the statute prohibiting such advertising violated its members' First Amendment right to know. A District Court opinion declared the statute void; the decision was upheld by the Supreme Court.

Justice Blackmun delivered the opinion of the Court. Again, public interest was relied upon, but a new definition of the meaning of that term was developed. The problem was whether commercial speech, absent a case-by-case examination of value of particular content, could be said to involve an interest worthy of First Amendment protection. The Court approached the issue by first observing that the relationship of commercial speech to the marketplace of products or services does not make it valueless in the marketplace of ideas, and then by emphasizing the importance of economic issues to the public. Blackmun cited the importance of the social benefits that could be gained through the free flow of commercial information. Dissemination of commercial information can lead to rational buying decisions by individuals that would lead to the most efficient and appropriate allocation of resources, thus benefiting everyone in the long run, contributing to the public welfare, and thereby certainly warranting First Amendment protection.

While a new commercial speech doctrine was born with this decision, the Court maintained that commercial speech is not "wholly undifferentiable" from other forms of speech and this fact suggests that a "different degree of protection is necessary to insure that the flow of truthful and legitimate commercial information is unimpaired."[28] In concluding his delivery of the opinion of the Court in *Virginia Pharmacy*, Blackmun gave brief justifications for certain exceptions to the protected status, stating that "The First Amendment, as we construe it today, does not prohibit the State from insuring that the stream of commercial information flows cleanly as well as freely."[29] The protected status exceptions mentioned were (1) time, place, and manner restrictions; (2) proposed illegal transactions; (3) advertising that causes special problems in connection with electronic broadcasting media; and (4) false, deceptive, or misleading commercial speech.

Judging from Court decisions that have been handed down since *Virginia Pharmacy*, it can be concluded that regulations aimed at suppressing truthful commercial speech are usually not upheld, but the Court still distinguishes between commercial and informative communication. In *Bates v. State Bar of Arizona* (1977),[30] for example, the Court struck down a state ban on advertising by lawyers because the information under consideration was truthful, and the regulatory action chosen by the state would have kept the public in ignorance. On the other hand, regulations aimed at restricting the manner in which such speech may be communicated are likely to be upheld; this is especially true if the manner is interpreted as increasing the potential for deception. A case in point is *Ohralik v. Ohio State Bar Association* (1978),[31] which involved in-person solicitation by an attorney. The Court found the manner of speech to be potentially harmful and thus subject to regulation because in-person solicitation might involve undue influence or intimidation.[32]

One other Supreme Court case bears rather directly on labor union interest in commercial speech. This is the 1978 case of *First National Bank of Boston v. Bellotti,*[33] which affirmed the First Amendment freedom of speech rights for corporations. The Court overturned a lower court decision and ruled that a Massachusetts law abridged expression the First Amendment was meant to protect. The law prohibited banks and business corporations from making contributions or expenditures for the purpose of expressing corporate opinion in order to influence a public vote in two cases: (1) if the public issue was unrelated to the corporation's business; or (2) if the issue involved the taxation of individuals. In this case, a referendum was being held in the state of Massachusetts on the enactment of a graduated personal income tax, an issue the bank wished to oppose. Court opinion focused on the nature of the speech rather than the source of the speech by maintaining that free discussion of governmental affairs fell squarely within First Amendment protection and the only argument remaining was that a corporation was the speaker rather than an individual.

Powell, giving the opinion of the Court, stated: "The inherent worth of the speech in terms of its capacity for informing the public does not depend upon the identity of its source, whether corporation, association, union, or individual."[34] Chief Justice Burger concurred, arguing: "In short, the First Amendment does not 'belong' to any definable category of persons or entities: It belongs to all who exercise its freedoms."[35] This decision has a strong bearing upon institutional advocacy advertising.

Minority opinion arguments were based on the motives of the speech as well as the source of the speech. It was contended that the fact that the Massachusetts statute forbade use of corporate funds to publish views on public issues that had *no* material effect on the corporation, as in this case, was of fundamental importance. Also central was the difference between the motives of profit-making corporations as opposed to the motives of individuals or not-for-profit groups. Much of the argument in this latter area was grounded in the assumption that not-for-profit groups were usually formed expressly to advance ideological causes and that the dissemination of ideas and opinions relating to these causes would be viewed as desirable by all individual members. On the other hand, shareholders in corporations formed to produce a profit do not share a common set of political or social views. While it may be arguable that corporations utilize advocacy advertising because their executives believe it is in the corporation's economic interest to do so, it cannot be concluded that these views are expressive of the probably heterogeneous opinions of their shareholders or that corporate funds should be used to disseminate such opinions. Moreover, in this case, both courts agreed that the personal income tax issue had no material effect on the bank's economic interests. This being true, shareholders' opinions would be expectedly even more diverse.

However, the assumption that the same argument does not apply to not-for-profit groups faces logical difficulties. Such groups may be formed in order to gain certain specific objectives, but total agreement on the means of obtaining the objectives would be rare. There undoubtedly are many among the rank and file in organized labor who object to having a portion of their dues used for advocacy advertising. Powell wrote:

> Nor is the fact that § 8 [the disputed Massachusetts statute] is limited to banks and business corporations without relevance. Excluded from its provisions and criminal sanctions are entities or organized groups in which numbers of persons may hold an interest or membership and which often have resources comparable to those of large corporations. Minorities in such groups or entities may have interests with respect to institutional speech quite comparable to those of minority shareholders in a corporation. Thus the exclusion of Massachusetts business trusts, real estate investment trusts, labor unions, and other associations undermines the plausibility of the State's purported concern for persons who happen to be shareholders in the banks and corporations covered by § 8.[36]

Justice White, dissenting in the *Bellotti* case, supported the Massachusetts statute because it prohibited corporate managers from using corporate monies "to promote what does not further corporate affairs but in the last analysis are the purely personal views of the management, individually or as a group."[37] He contrasted the *Bellotti* case with a Michigan labor-management case[38] in which the Supreme Court ruled that a state may not require individuals, as a condition of employment, to contribute to the support of an ideological cause they may oppose.

> At issue were political expenditures made by a public employees' union. Michigan law provided that unions and local government employers might agree to an agency shop arrangement pursuant to which every employee—even those not union members—must pay to the union, as a condition of employment, union dues or a service fee equivalent in amount to union dues. The legislation itself was not coercive; it did not command that local governments employ only those workers who were willing to pay union dues but left it to a bargaining representative democratically elected by a majority of the employees to enter or not enter into such a contractual arrangement through collective bargaining. In addition, of course no one was compelled to work at a job covered by an agency shop arrangement. Nevertheless, the Court ruled that under such circumstances the use of funds contributed by dissenting employees for political purposes impermissibly infringed their First Amendment right to adhere to their own beliefs and to refuse to defer to or support the beliefs of others. . . . It would hardly be plausibly contended that just because Massachusetts' regulation of corporations is less extensive than Michigan's regulation of labor-management relations, Massachusetts may not constitutionally prohibit the very evil which Michigan may not constitutionally permit. Yet this is precisely what the Court today holds.[39]

It could be argued that the Court is not giving corporate shareholders the right to the same First Amendment freedoms that it has given to labor union members. An extension of the labor case would indicate that corporations should give rebates to dissenting shareholders proportionate to their investment in advertising with which they disagree. By purchasing stock in a corporation, or by joining a labor union and paying dues, individuals usually accept the fact that decisions will be made concerning a variety of matters, including advertising, that are integrally related to business or labor objectives. The problem arises when business and labor unions finance issues seen as unrelated to corporate or union business. Perhaps the only realistic way to protect the First Amendment rights of those who disagree with positions taken by institutions is to ban the right of the institution to speak on issues unrelated to its business.

Another point that Powell makes that deserves comment is that other groups "often have resources comparable to those of large corporations." To the extent that this is true, corporate domination of electoral processes and ideological expression is perhaps of little concern. But to what extent is it true? Corporations exist to further certain economic goals and the corporate laws that apply to them were established to facilitate such goals in order to strengthen the country's overall economy. The right to receive information protects the interchange of ideas. Domination of communications in general and of advocacy advertising in particular will not allow such an interchange.

MEDIA OWNERSHIP AND CONTROL

The concern about media access, and increasingly numerous demands to obtain it, is prompted by increasing centralization and concentration of control of mass communication agencies.

The provisions of the Sherman Act, characteristically applied to business enterprises that manufactured tangible goods, were first applied to mass communication businesses in 1917 when the Motion Picture Patents Company was broken up. The earliest such legal move against the press occurred in the early 1940s. At that time the Supreme Court ruled that the Associated Press was violating the Sherman antitrust laws, even though the Press was engaged, not in the manufacture of tangible goods, but in distributing the sensitive commodities of information, opinion, and ideas.

Justice Black responded to the argument that invocation of the Sherman Act against an association of publishers abridged First Amendment guarantees of freedom of the press:

> The First Amendment, far from providing an argument against application of the Sherman Act, here provides powerful reasons to the contrary. That

Amendment rests on the assumption that the widest possible dissemination of information from diverse and antagonistic sources is essential to the welfare of the public, that a free press is a condition of a free society. Surely a command that the government itself shall not impede the free flow of ideas does not afford non-governmental combinations a refuge if they impose restraints upon that constitutionally guaranteed freedom. . . . Freedoom of the press from governmental interference under the First Amendment does not sanction repression of that freedom by private interests.[40]

In 1978, the Federal Trade Commission sponsored a symposium on media concentration. In his introductory statement, FTC chairman Michael Pertschuk said:

We must examine whether the right of free speech can be disassociated from the economic structure of the media which gives access to that speech. Is there substance to the fear that freedom of speech will be impacted by patterns of corporate change? Is there a relationship between changes in corporate structure and the independence and accessibility of the media? The First Amendment protects us from the chilling shadow of government interference with the media. But are there comparable dangers if other powerful economic or political institutions assume control of the media?[41]

The symposium was held in response to concern over what appeared to be increased merger activity in the newspaper and broadcasting industries. Such merger activity was seen as increasing the degree of concentration not only within industry segments (evidenced, for example, by the increasing number of one-newspaper communities) and cross-media ownership where a single firm owns more than one segment of the industry, but also in the tendency for large corporations outside of the media industry to buy into the media industry. Proponents of access are concerned about such questions as: (1) to what extent is such activity actually taking place? (2) what effect does concentration have on the flow of information? (3) would diversely-held ownership increase media accessibility? (4) would more governmental regulation intended to increase free expression through the implementation of access actually be helpful? or (5) is governmental deregulation the answer, federal intervention being unnecessary because diversity can be gained through cable television and satellite transmissions?

The general industrial trend in the United States toward domination by a few industry giants certainly has not bypassed communication enterprises. In the newspaper industry, the number of group owners has increased, as has the number of dailies they control. Large, well-capitalized chains control about three-fourths of all daily newspaper circulation and continue to acquire small- to medium-sized daily papers. Of the 30 dailies that were sold in 1983, 26 were acquired by chains.[42] The largest of these chains, Gannett, represented 7 percent of total circulation at the end of 1982; the 12 largest groups controlled 42 percent of the total. While no single newspaper or chain dominates news dissemination, national/international news comes through only a few news and wire services. The percentage of communities that have competing daily newspapers is down from more than 60 percent in the early 1900s to less than 2 percent, making monopoly an established fact in American daily newspapers.[43] Even in communities that have more than one newspaper, the papers often are not separately owned and published.

Ben Bagdikian has calculated that 68 corporations share at least half of the audience in all major media:

> Twenty corporations control more than half the 61 million daily newspapers sold every day; twenty corporations control more than half the revenues of the country's 11,000 magazines; three corporations control most of the revenues and audience in television; ten corporations in radio, eleven corporations in all kinds of books; and four corporations in motion pictures.[44]

To borrow a line Bagdikian used in a talk several years ago, the 68 executives who control these corporations constitute a private Ministry of Information and Culture in the United States.

In past years, Federal Communications Commission regulations have, to some extent, inhibited growth in radio and television by specifying the maximum number of stations allowable under common ownership. The radio multiple ownership limit has been seven AM and seven FM stations; the television limit has been seven stations, of which not more than five may be VHF. Over half the television stations are owned by groups, however, and if the FCC drastically changes or drops its "rule of sevens" for ownership limits, as proposed, this percentage undoubtedly will increase rapidly. In July, 1984, the FCC adopted an order that would change the rule of sevens to a rule of twelves (a single entity could own 12 AM stations, 12 FM stations and 12 television stations, with no requirements that any of the television stations be UHFs) and that would eliminate the ownership rules completely by 1990. In response to Congressional criticism, however, the FCC stayed the television portion of its own order until April, 1985 or later. The proposal set off a flurry of activity, however. Some of this was directed at improving the proposal (much opposition comes from the fact that caps are placed on station numbers rather than on allowable percentages of audience reach or market size), and some was directed toward examination of potential antitrust implications. The network groups, ABC, CBS, and NBC, have the largest combined audiences. Combined audience share of the networks is 80 percent and, although it is slowly declining, "the three networks are expected to account for the largest segment of television viewers for the foreseeable future."[45] Among the other major group owners are those involved primarily in communications enterprises such as Metromedia, Scripps-Howard, and Cox Communications, as well as those that are diverse conglomerates, such as General Tire and Rubber Company and Westinghouse.

Radio, which before television arrived on the scene had a distinctly national orientation, now has a more regional/local focus. Overall radio advertising revenues have increased, with local advertising providing the largest chunk—about three-fourths of the total. This local/regional focus and the fact that corporations have been limited legally to owning only seven stations gives an impression of diversity. Nevertheless, according to Bagdikian's measurements of radio audience—which are more difficult to determine than newspaper and television audience—10 corporations dominate the commercial radio audience. Corporations that own all seven of their allowable stations in the largest markets gain large audiences and, again, their audience share will undoubtedly rise if the rule of sevens is abolished.

A significant number of groups have combined media ownership of both newspapers and broadcasting stations. Their holdings often extend to various other communication agencies. Bagdikian narrows his estimated number of 68 corporations that control the media when he discusses combination group ownership:

> [S]ome [corporations] control audiences in more than one medium. In 1980, for example, CBS was among the dominant companies in television, radio, magazines, and books; Capital Cities in newspapers and radio; Hearst, Washington Post, New York Times, and Newhouse in newspapers and magazines; ABC and NBC in television and radio; Cox and Gannett in newspapers and radio; Time, Inc., McGraw-Hill, and Reader's Digest in magazines and books; and Times Mirror in newspapers, books, and magazines. The net result is fifty corporations that share half or more of the audience in the combined major media.[46]

Furthermore, many of these 50 have smaller financial holdings in other media, typically are in partnership with other large industries, and have interlocking directorates with still other huge industries and financial groups.

The effects of the tendency toward concentration and centralization are far more difficult to determine than the trends themselves. Some maintain that economies of scale result from concentration and these will provide better media quality and quantity. They would also argue that the public has access to a large amount of diverse content when overall production of communications industries is considered and therefore the monopoly of communications argument is irrelevant. Others believe that concentration can only result in increased media homogeneity; combined ownership is seen to pose a real threat to objective news reporting and editorial policy because of possible conflicting interests between the responsibilities of journalists to cover newsworthy events and their bosses' economic interests. Moreover, while it is true that the public may subscribe to a variety of papers and magazines, the issue is the extent to which large groups can be reached by diverse ideas and opinions. For those concerned about diversity and access, the ownership statistics continue to engender dismay.

When all analysis and speculation is completed on the effects on media content of media industry competition or the lack of it, two irrefutable facts remain: (1) single newspaper ownership or unaffiliated radio or television station status will ensure *neither* media integrity nor quality; and (2) single newspaper ownership or unaffiliated radio or television station status will not ensure media diversity. This realization has led a number of critics to the conclusion that the entire controversy over increasing media control through ownership concentration ignores the more fundamental question of control by a class of owners. Deconcentration of ownership alone is insufficient; those who favor access require *both* diversification of control *and* the right of access.

ACCESS TO PRINT MEDIA

There is, undeniably, a lack of consistent policy regarding access and First Amendment rights. Adjudicative authorities, perhaps more than other policy makers, operate in the context of historical forces and react relatively slowly to change. Judicial interpretations of First Amendment issues are confusing and offer no clear directions because of the ad hoc, case-by-case decisions that have been handed down.

Because the First Amendment's reference to "freedom of the press" referred to print media when it was written and not to electronic media, the rights of the print media are rather firmly entrenched in American jurisprudence. The rights of these media that have been consistently and often emphatically protected include the right to publish and guarantees of no prior restraints,[47] and the right to exercise editorial discretion about what should be included and what should be excluded from printed pages. The press is doubly protected in the sense that this institution is included in policy written to protect private businesses and also falls under the special constitutional protection provided by the First Amendment.

A range of legal arguments has challenged these institutional guarantees, all attempting to prohibit certain communications because of their substantive content. Justifications given for restraining speech vary widely. They include, for example, attempts to restrain speech against misconduct of public officials,[48] to restrain speech in order to protect jurors from pretrial information that could have an effect on the fair administration of justice,[49] to restrain speech in order to protect privacy,[50] and to protect state secrets.[51]

A legal right of public access to the press has been denied by the courts. Perhaps the most compelling arguments for access have been for the need to balance free press rights with free speech rights. One of the best-known cases in which these rights had to be considered was *Miami Herald Publishing Company v. Tornillo* (1974).[52] It was especially difficult because the type of free speech at issue was clearly "typical First Amendment" speech in that it involved political debate, generally viewed as necessary in order to safeguard the integrity of the electoral process.

The case involved opposition of the *Miami Herald* to the candidacy of Pat Tornillo for the state legislature. Opposition was based on the fact that Tornillo, director of the Classroom Teachers' Association, had led a strike by public school teachers in 1960, a time when such a strike was illegal in Florida. *Miami Herald* editorials referred to Tornillo as a law-breaker and urged readers not to vote for him. In response, Tornillo asked for the right to reply under Florida Election Code; the *Herald* refused and Tornillo filed suit against them. The U.S. Supreme Court overturned the decision of the Florida Supreme Court, which had upheld Tornillo's rights.

The Florida Court based its decision on the public's right to information, especially critical during a political campaign. Disagreement by the Supreme Court was based on the conclusion that the Florida statutes violated the free press guarantee; a decision for the statute might have a chilling effect on newspaper content in that editors might decide the safe course would be to avoid controversy altogether.

> Even if a newspaper would face no additional costs to comply with a compulsory access law and would not be forced to forego publication of news or opinion by the inclusion of a reply, the Florida statute fails to clear the barriers of the First Amendment because of its intrusion into the function of editors. A newspaper is more than a passive receptacle or conduit for news, comment, and advertising. The choice of material to go into a newspaper, and the decisions made as to limitations on the size and content of the paper, and treatment of public issues and public officials—whether fair or unfair—constitute the exercise of editorial control and judgment. It has yet to be demonstrated how governmental regulation of this crucial process can be exercised consistent with First Amendment guarantees of a free press as they have evolved to this time.[53]

In action that is consistent with these views, courts have recognized that the public does have a right to receive the information and opinions that advertising contains, but never has a privately-owned periodical been forced to accept an ad.

> This court holds, therefore, that, in this State, the newspaper business is in the nature of a private enterprise and that, in the absence of valid statutory regulation to the contrary, the publishers of a newspaper have the general right either to publish or reject a commercial advertisement tendered to them.

Their reasons for rejecting a proposed advertisement are immaterial, assuming, of course, there are absent factual allegations connecting them with a duly pleaded fraudulent conspiracy or with furthering an unlawful monopoly.[54]

This position maintains the fundamental arguments given in the *Chicago Joint Board* case discussed above. However, one of the basic arguments in the Chicago case involved monopoly. This was not directly addressed in *Tornillo*. Should—can—the ownership situation make any difference in the position taken regarding the sanctity of the domain of private ownership of the press versus access? The *Chicago Joint Board* access proponents tried to argue that monopoly power existed in an area of significant social concern. The fact is that there are fewer newspapers today and these must serve a larger population than formerly; the press thus wields a great deal of power and influence. In the *Chicago Joint Board* case, Judge Castle, writing the opinion of the court, shows a lack of sympathy with the union position on constraints caused by monopoly:

> The circulation figures for each of the four newspapers published by the defendants (each publishes two newspapers) are set forth in the Union's complaint. The figures clearly establish that neither of these defendant publishers approaches a monopoly position. The figures reflect a relatively high degree of competition between the defendants rather than monopoly control by one of them. And there is no allegation, nor is there any indication in the record, that there was any concert of action between these competitors in the refusal of each of them to accept the Union's advertisement for publication. There was no individual "monopoly power," and there was no exercise of monopoly power by means of combination.[55]

Yet the four daily newspapers were operating under two corporate ownerships and this structure was sufficient to keep the union side completely out of the Chicago press. As Jerome Barron argues when discussing this case, it would appear that monopoly power was indeed at work.[56]

While courts have never forced a *privately* owned periodical to accept an advertisement, they have ruled that public high school and college newspapers and state bar associations cannot refuse advertising simply because the newspaper staff finds it objectionable. In *Lee v. Board of Regents* (1971),[57] for example, the court ruled that the university newspaper at Wisconsin State University violated the First Amendment by refusing to publish an advertisement concerning a university employees' union and an advertisement concerning the Vietnam war. The difference between *Lee* and *Chicago Joint Board* is the fact that the university newspaper is not privately owned, but is published with public funds.[58] So while access for advertising might be gained in newspapers that are not privately owned, the drawback of course is audience. The *Chicago Joint Board* wished to reach the same public that Marshall Field and Company was reaching with its corporate ads and this could not be easily accomplished in any state-funded newspaper.

Could this audience be reached by submitting letters to the editor rather than by advertising? Jerome Barron responds to this question by emphasizing the fact that letters frequently are edited and that no attempt is made to publish all letters received or even a representative sample of them. Barron holds the opinion that the letters page in most newspapers is more a feature item than an attempt to provide balanced presentations of controversial community views.

> Any attempt to change this [editing letters] will be met with the argument that journalistic discretion is being impinged upon. Access to the advertising section of the paper, where the content is traditionally supplied by the advertiser, presents much less of a challenge to the journalist's editorial control—especially since the newspaper is being paid for the privilege.[59]

While it makes sense that access could be more easily supplied in a newspaper that is expandable (at least theoretically) than in broadcasting that operates within a limited number of hours per day, and, while suggestions have been made on how newspapers could expand the use of their presses and place the financial and legal burdens involved upon those who wished to use them, present law is clear. There is no right of public access to the press and no move to provide one either by the press itself or by legislative or judicial policy making.

ACCESS TO BROADCAST MEDIA

Some commentators contend that the First Amendment not only assumes equality of all media and traditionally provides the same protection for all media, it also assigns individual and social responsibilities to all media—print *and* broadcast.[60] If true, print media managers definitely can interpret their responsibilities more freely than broadcast media managers, holders of licenses from the government who have promised to operate in the public interest. The courts have sanctioned governmental intrusions into broadcast management that clearly would be illegal if attempted against the press. The best known of these intrusions is the fairness doctrine, the objective of which is to ensure fair treatment to all sides by the licensees.

It was editorial policies of some radio stations that first attracted Federal Communications Commission attention that ultimately led to the fairness doctrine. In the late 1930s and early 1940s, station WAAB in Boston regularly aired editorials expressing the opinions of its management. When WAAB's license renewal was challenged in 1941, the FCC ruled on editorializing by radio stations:

> [W]ith the limitations in frequencies inherent in the nature of radio, the public interest can never be served by a dedication of any broadcast facility to the

support of [the licensee's] own partisan ends. Radio can serve as an instrument of democracy only when devoted to the communication of information and the exchange of ideas freely and objectively presented.[61]

The FCC changed its position eight years later, however, in a report entitled *In the Matter of Editorializing by Broadcast Licensees,* which states, "overt licensee editorialization, within reasonable limits and subject to the general requirements of fairness . . . is not contrary to the public interest,"[62] as long as the licensee provides opportunity for the presentation of other positions on the matter. The intent of the 1959 fairness doctrine is much the same. It imposed a twofold responsibility on broadcasters: first, they are obliged to cover controversial issues of public importance in their communities; and second, they must provide air time for alternate viewpoints on those issues.

The FCC left much of the duty of defining these ambiguous terms up to the individual licensees. As the fairness doctrine has evolved, a number of court cases have delineated its meaning. One of the best known of these is *Red Lion Broadcasting Company, Inc., v. Federal Communications Commission* (1969).[63] A comparison of this case and *Tornillo* demonstrates the basic differences between print and broadcast media and their public responsibilities.

The *Red Lion* case involves that portion of the fairness doctrine relating to personal verbal attacks in the context of controversial public issues and to political editorializing. The personal attack rule requires that a station must provide an opportunity to reply to a person who has been verbally attacked on the air. Fred Cook, author of *Goldwater—Extremist on the Right,* was discussed and criticized by Reverend Billy James Hargis on a fifteen-minute program aired by a Pennsylvania station in 1964. When Cook heard of the broadcast, he concluded that he had been personally attacked and asked the station to provide free reply time; the station refused. After investigation, the FCC agreed that Cook had been attacked and that the Red Lion Broadcasting Company had not met its obligations under the fairness doctrine. The FCC concluded that public interest required that the public be allowed to hear both sides of an issue, even if the time for reply had to be paid for by the station. The Court of Appeals, District of Columbia Circuit, concurred in the FCC opinion, and ruled that both the fairness doctrine and the personal attack rules were constitutional. The decision was affirmed by the Supreme Court.

It is therefore constitutional for the FCC to require broadcasters to supply free reply time to victims of personal attacks on their programming, but it is an unconstitutional intrusion into editorial discretion to require newspapers to give space to persons attacked in their pages (*Tornillo*).

Red Lion is important to the issue of access because, although the Court relied mainly on the "limited spectrum" approach in order to justify its decision, it also mentioned the right of the public to access and the importance of rules without which broadcasters would have "unfettered power to make time available only to the highest bidders, to communicate only their own views on public issues, people, and candidates, and to permit on the air only those with whom they agreed."[64] In spite of these positive outcomes of *Red Lion*, however, the decision did nothing to strengthen individual rights to access with the exception of individual replies to personal attacks. The FCC saw the *Red Lion* decision as logical and one that should provide broadcasters with no logistical problems because, if they were actually meeting their fairness doctrine obligations, there would be no need to provide access, either free or paid for, to all who requested it.

The FCC reiterated this position in 1970, when two groups, the Business Executives Move for Vietnam Peace (BEM) and the Democratic National Committee, on separate occasions, complained that they had been refused air time requested for editorial advertisements. The FCC ruled that broadcasters who were meeting their responsibilities and providing full and fair coverage on public issues did not need to accept such advertising. The Court of Appeals, using reasoning based on *Red Lion*, reversed the FCC, concluding that a broadcaster should not have a fixed policy of refusing all editorial advertisements, and remanded the case to the FCC.[65] In *CBS, Inc. v. Democratic National Committee* (1973),[66] the issue reached the Supreme Court. It was the decision of the Court that the Court of Appeals had erred in judgment:

> More profoundly, it would be anomolous for us to hold, in the name of promoting the constitutional guarantees of free expression, that the day-to-day editorial decisions of broadcast licensees are subject to the kind of restraints urged by respondents. To do so in the name of the First Amendment would be a contradiction. Journalistic discretion would in many ways be lost to the rigid limitations that the First Amendment imposes on Government. Application of such standards to broadcast licensees would be antithetical to the very ideal of vigorous, challenging debate on issues of public interest. Every licensee is already held accountable for the totality of its performance of public interest obligations.[67]

The Court held that the requirement of access rights for editorial advertising time by means of either the public interest standard or the First Amendment would mean an end to the editorial function in broadcast journalism and, perhaps more importantly, an end to licensee accountability. With this decision and its emphasis on the rights of broadcasters, the momentum gained in *Red Lion* for access rights slowed.

At about the same time, another aspect of the fairness doctrine was arousing controversy; this aspect was the use of the policy in relation to commercial advertising. In 1966 lawyer John Banzhaf urged the FCC to allow free counteradvertising to oppose cigarette advertising. Safety and health issues definitely complicate what otherwise might appear as clear-cut legal decisions.[68] Banzhaf questioned the balance that was occurring between commercials that linked cigarettes to health, vigor, and romance and programming that dealt with the adverse health effects of smoking. To the surprise of many, the FCC held that the licensees' fairness obligations extended to controversial issues "in whatever context they may arise."[69] The FCC emphasized the fact that cigarette commercials presented a "unique situation," however.

When cigarette advertising was banned entirely in 1970, that specific problem vanished, but the FCC discovered that the counteradvertising situation was, after all, not so unique. The applicability of the Banzhaf ruling was tested again in 1970 in the Retail Store Employees Union, discussed above, and in 1971, when the issue was commercials for large displacement automobile engines and lead additive gasolines that polluted the air.[70] The FCC stuck by its decision that cigarettes were "unique" and refused to extend Banzhaf. On both of these occasions, however, the Court of Appeals reversed FCC decisions on the basis that no principled differences were seen to exist between them and Banzhaf. Then, inconsistently,[71] the Court of Appeals ruled that military recruitment ads did not make a controversial statement about the draft and therefore did not require countercommercials[72] and, on a later occasion, ruled that countercommercials need not be used in response to Chevron gasoline additive commercials because the ads did not directly deal with an issue of public importance.[73]

The confusing signals from the circuit court and an increasing number of complaints based on Banzhaf encouraged the FCC, in its 1974 Fairness Report, to clarify its policy. Here the Banzhaf rule was explicitly reversed:

> We do not believe that the underlying purpose of the fairness doctrine would be well served by permitting the cigarette case to stand as fairness doctrine precedent. In the absence of some meaningful or substantive discussion, such as that found in the "editorial advertisements" referred to above, we do not believe that the usual product commercial can realistically be said to inform the public on any side of a controversial issue of public importance. It would be a great mistake to consider standard advertisements, such as those involved in the Banzhaf and Friends of the Earth, as though they made a meaningful contribution to public debate. . . . Accordingly, in the future, we will apply the fairness doctrine only to those "commercials" which are devoted in any obvious and meaningful way to the discussion of public issues.[74]

The "obvious and meaningful way" phrase is ambiguous and subjective in spite of the fact that the FCC hoped its report would provide an objective test for application of the fairness doctrine. In an attempt to clarify the issue the report states:

> [W]hat we are really concerned with is an obvious participation in public debate and not a subjective judgment as to the advertiser's actual intentions.

Accordingly, we expect our licensees to do nothing more than make a reasonable, common sense judgment as to whether the "advertisement" presents a meaningful statement which obviously addresses, and advocates a point of view on a controversial issue of public importance. . . . If the ad bears only a tenuous relationship to that debate, or one drawn by unnecessary inference, the fairness doctrine would clearly not be applicable.[75]

Whether this statement does, in fact, really clarify the situation or whether it only adds ambiguity remains to be seen. The Commission has had to scrutinize its words in several pertinent cases. The first challenge came from a group in Maine who desired to air, in response to television ads for snowmobiles, its view that snowmobiles were dangerous and environmentally destructive. The FCC decided that the fairness doctrine did not apply and this decision was upheld by the First Circuit Court of Appeals. In *Public Interest Research Group v. Federal Communications Commission* (1975),[76] Judge Levin Campbell ruled that the FCC was not acting arbitrarily or capriciously in its ruling because the snowmobile ads were ordinary product ads that did not address public issues in an obvious and meaningful way. The Commission holds to its judgment that usual product advertisements do not realistically inform the public on any side of a controversial issue of public importance. From this, it would appear that the FCC considers institutional and editorial advertisements more likely to be "obvious and meaningful" than "standard product" commercials. The *test* is for "obvious and meaningful," however, rather than for a specific type of advertisement. Therefore, some product ads may be included in the fairness doctrine.[77]

The 1974 *Report* divides commercials into three categories: commercial product and service, editorial, "countercommercial." Editorial commercials, which are of central concern to this study, are defined as those that "consist of direct and substantial commentary on important public issues."[78] Institutional ads are considered a type of editorial advertising:

Editorial advertisements may be difficult to identify if they are sponsored by groups which are not normally considered to be engaged in debate on controversial issues. This problem is most likely to arise in the context of promotional or institutional advertising; that is, advertising designed to present a favorable public image of a particular corporation or industry rather than to sell a product. Such advertising is, of course, a legitimate commercial practice and ordinarily does not involve debate on public issues. . . . In some cases, however, the advertiser may seek to play an obvious and meaningful role in public debate. In such instances, the fairness doctrine . . . applies.[79]

Institutional advertisements are even more difficult to deal with when they *appear* to discuss public issues, but do not *explicitly* address the controversial matter. The problems involved in the ability of "implicit" institutional ads to be "obvious and meaningful" had been faced by the FCC before the issuance of the 1974 *Report* and the agency relied on a specific case to provide an example of its intended meaning. The case, *Wilderness Society and Friends of the Earth* (1971),[80] developed in response to Esso commercials dealing with Alaskan oil reserves, the U.S. need for energy, and Alaskan ecology. While the advertising copy never explicitly mentioned the oil pipeline construction, complainants argued that the commercials presented a statement that favored construction of the pipeline; they asked for time to reply and to present arguments against the pipeline construction. The FCC agreed with the complainants, stating that "since the company's large investment in drilling for Alaskan oil quite obviously is based upon the assumption that transportation of the oil to other parts of the world will be permitted,"[81] the commercials implied a pro-pipeline position.

As used in this book, advocacy advertising could fall into either the editorial category or the institutional category. What is important is to be able to show that the advertisement meaningfully addresses a controversial issue of public importance. This task would obviously seem to be more easily accomplished explicitly, in a "substantial and obvious"[82] way rather than implicitly. The decision regarding whether or not a "meaning-implicit institutional advertisement" raises an issue of public importance is subjective and difficult; the court, in fact, cautions that the "difference between obvious and unobvious advocacy is not obvious."[83] Since the *Fairness Report* and the judicial interpretations of it laid out in *National Citizens Committee for Broadcasting v. FCC* (1977), meaning-implicit institutional advertisements come close to ruling themselves out of fairness doctrine inclusions by definition alone.[84]

That the courts may be moving in a defining-out direction was demonstrated in a relatively recent dispute over United Way spot television advertisements.[85] Complainants charged that the manner in which United Way funds are collected and distributed is controversial, and that its policies do not benefit a number of charitable causes. They contended that United Way spots that ended with the line "Thanks to you it works for all of us . . . The United Way," presented an issue that needed to be balanced. The FCC ruled that the fairness doctrine had not been violated, and, upon appeal, the court agreed.

> In our judgment the ruling by the FCC did not violate its Fairness Doctrine, which applies only when the broadcasted statement amounts to advocacy of a position on one side of an ongoing public debate and obviously and substantially addresses that issue in a meaningful way.[86]

Moreover, the 1974 *Fairness Report* ruled that when there was discussion of one side of an ongoing public debate, opposing views were not required on an individual basis, nor according to a quantitative formula, but only in the course of overall programming over a reasonable period of time. This has led to a ready reply when broadcasters are accused of non-compliance with the doctrine: look at our overall coverage; we *are* being fair. And, if the issue has been mentioned at all, even if briefly, or even if during undesirable time periods, and if this occurred over a "reasonable" period of time, the broadcaster, to the frustration of the complainant, has made his or her case.

The cases cited above are relevant in demonstrating that for unions and for many other institutions, including corporations, who wish to use advocacy advertising, the fairness doctrine is providing a forked path. The cases support the following conclusions: (1) broadcasters have a responsibility to cover controversial issues of public interest; (2) broadcasters have a responsibility to present more than one side of controversial issues of public interest; (3) broadcasters can and should use editorial discretion in deciding what issues to cover, both in their news programs and in the advertising they accept; and (4) if broadcasters accept advertising that expresses in a direct and meaningful way an opinion on a controversial issue, they may be required to provide free time for counterexpression.

Those in favor of access, once very much in favor of the fairness doctrine, are now considering the ways it works against them: (1) broadcasters are not obliged to cover specific controversial issues, but may use their discretion; (2) when a controversial issue is covered, broadcasters decide how, when, and by whom opposing viewpoints shall be presented; (3) broadcasters may decide what advocacy advertising to accept and when to air it. The fairness doctrine is thus responsible for allowing broadcasters to exclude particular persons or views and is responsible for chilling the airing of most advocacy advertising because broadcasters are afraid, if they accept it, they will have to provide free time for replies. The risks and hazards involved for broadcasters have both economic and regulatory implications. The profit maximization goal of licensees makes them reluctant to provide free time, just as it often makes it difficult for them adequately to communicate the views of others on controversial issues. The ambiguity of some FCC policy has resulted in that agency's sometimes ad hoc approach to conflict resolution; this approach in turn has led them to an increased involvement in a range of day-to-day decisions, decisions that the broadcaster would prefer to make alone. However, if broadcasters can avoid the advertising in the first place, and the courts have declared they have that right, the risks and hazards will be eliminated. Therefore some broadcasters, who initially felt threatened by the fairness doctrine intrusion into their freedom, have moved toward favoring it—certainly not over total deregulation, but at least over some alternatives.

Most of the above arguments on the weaknesses of the fairness doctrine were written as long ago as 1973 by Justice Brennan, dissenting in the *CBS* case. He contended that the fairness doctrine *plus* the absolute ban on editorial advertising permitted by that decision would force the public "to rely *exclusively* on the 'journalistic discretion' of broadcasters, who serve in theory as surrogate spokesmen for all sides of all issues."[87] His suggested remedy was a limited scheme of editorial advertising.

At the present time Brennan undoubtedly would find more support for his argument than he did in 1973. Circuit Judge McGowan, in delivering the opinion of the court in *National Citizens Committee for Broadcasting v. FCC* (1977) stated that the FCC decision to limit fairness doctrine applicability imposed upon that agency some responsibility to consider other suggestions that would help ensure sufficient and balanced coverage of important public issues. Two specific proposals were remanded to the FCC for reconsideration. The first of these involved a specific access scheme whereby licensees would devote one hour a week either to the presentation of messages by members of the public or to other public issue programming. Half of this time would be allocated on a first-come, first-served basis; the other half would be apportioned among spokespersons on differing sides of controversial issues. The second proposal would require each licensee to submit annually to the FCC a list of ten controversial issues of public importance it had selected for the most coverage during the preceding year, noting representative programming presented on each issue.

The FCC issued a report in 1979 in which both of these proposals were rejected on the basis that they were not adequate substitutes for the fairness doctrine.[88] In this report, the FCC emphasized that the primary focus of the fairness doctrine is public access to information rather than speakers' access to audiences. It also emphasized the importance of allowing licensees to exercise their journalistic discretion concerning matters of public interest, subject, of course, to usual FCC oversight.

The court thus gives importance to the sufficient and balanced coverage of important public issues, but has left discretion in administration of the fairness doctrine and consideration of change up to the FCC. And, rather than movement toward a system of limited editorial advertising or other specific access schemes, there has been a rather forceful trend away from *any* type of governmental intrusion. Monroe E. Price, speaking at the 1978 FTC Symposium on Media Concentration said:

> What is happening, in terms of First Amendment vibrations, is quite important. Coming almost to the edge of the content regulatory cliff in *Red Lion*, there has been a general retreat. Concerns about concentration, about diversity, about access remain intense, perhaps justifiably so, but something deep inside was suggesting that the progress of the law was moving headlong in an erroneous direction. There is more of a search for alternative approaches.

Structure has been identified as a prime candidate for reform, replacing content regulation as a method for achieving First Amendment goals.[89]

Price goes on to give three reasons for the shift toward structural reform: (1) it is not evident that the fairness doctrine is accomplishing its intended goal of enhancing the discussion of controversial issues; (2) legal decisions appear to be evolving in the direction of a concept of editorial autonomy that is inconsistent with some regulatory forms; and (3) new technology provides hope for increased diversity and access.

The 1980s have witnessed steady growth of support for structural change and various proposals from the FCC and members of Congress. Because the basis of the fairness doctrine—the need to cover controversial and diverse issues of public importance and to include contrasting opinions—is contained in Section 315 of the Communications Act of 1934, legislation apparently is required for change or repeal, although this is an issue that currently is being debated. Major broadcasters who oppose the doctrine and foresee no fast Congressional action argue that Congress authorized but never mandated the doctrine, and that repeal is therefore within the jurisdiction of the FCC. There is apparent agreement, however, that rules adopted years ago by the FCC as auxiliary to the doctrine can be changed by the Commission itself. In 1983 the FCC proposed repeal of its rules on personal attack (that require a station to give reply time to groups or individuals who have been unjustly maligned during a discussion of controversial issues of public importance), and political editorializing (that require stations supporting or opposing a candidate to offer the candidate reply time). Before the FCC took action on this proposal, Senator Bob Packwood introduced a stronger measure in the form of a bill that would repeal the entire fairness doctrine. Support for this bill came from radio, television, and cable operators, news organizations, and advertisers. Opposition came from various organizations and public groups representing both political conservatives and liberals and including the UAW and the AFL-CIO. Lawrence Gold, AFL-CIO counsel, stated: "Over the years trade unions have found that the fairness doctrine, although feeble, is the best hope of assuring that commercial television and radio stations air labor's side on controversial issues of the day, most particularly collective bargaining disputes and other matters concerning workers' rights."[90]

In May, 1984, with the Packwood bill apparently bogged down in Congress, the FCC gave public notice of a new inquiry on the fairness doctrine, the purpose of which is to determine if the doctrine is continuing to provide the public with access to diverse ideas or whether it might now be causing fundamental conflict with the First Amendment goals upon which it is based. Carefully researched arguments presented at the end of the summer provided evidence that while those who represented nonbroadcasting interests saw continued public value in the doctrine, broadcasters viewed it as a violation of their First Amendment rights. The issue that now moves to the forefront of the controversy is who—Congress or the FCC—has the power to repeal the doctrine and what interpretations judicial decisions would give to disputes caused by the change.

In July, 1984, the Supreme Court handed down a decision granting public broadcasters who receive federal funds the right to editorialize (*Federal Communications Commission v. League of Women Voters of California*).[91] The decision was based on the premise that the law prohibiting such rights (the Public Broadcasting Act of 1967) was a violation of the First Amendment in that it restricted the expression of opinion. In justifying its decision, the Court relied on the existence of the fairness doctrine and on past cases, stating that Congress and the FCC are allowed to regulate the content of broadcast speech in support of First Amendment rights. Two footnotes in this case, however, seemed to indicate the willingness of the Court to look again at the scarcity argument, the fairness doctrine, and content regulations in the light of technological changes:

> The prevailing rationale for broadcast regulation based on spectrum scarcity has come under increasing criticism in recent years. Critics, including the incumbent Chairman of the FCC, charge that with the advent of cable and satellite television technology, communities now have access to such a wide variety of stations that the scarcity doctrine is obsolete. . . . We are not prepared, however, to reconsider our long-standing approach without some signal from Congress or the FCC that technological developments have advanced so far that some revision of the system of broadcast regulation may be required.[92]
>
> We note that the FCC, observing that "[i]f any substantial possibility exists that the [fairness doctrine] rules have impeded, rather than furthered, First Amendment objectives, repeal may be warranted on that ground alone," has tentatively concluded that the rules, by effectively chilling speech, do not serve the public interest, and has therefore proposed to repeal them. . . . Of course, the Commission may, in the exercise of its discretion, decide to modify or abandon these rules, and we express no view on the legality of either course. As we recognized in *Red Lion,* however, were it to be shown by the Commission that the fairness doctrine "has the effect of reducing rather than enhancing" speech, we would then be forced to reconsider the constitutional basis of our decision in that case.[93]

As of this writing, the controversy continues, with increasing conviction on the part of many people that the fairness doctrine and its related rules should be changed, but an inability to reach agreement on what, if anything, might substitute. Many of the arguments surrounding the degree to which the government has the responsibility to see that broadcasters inform the public stem from changes in the media industry itself.

MEDIA TECHNOLOGY

In spite of the concerns expressed by Justice Brennan over the absolute ban on editorial advertising allowed in *CBS,* labor unions have found that some stations are willing to give them air time, and they have been attempting to increase their use of this tool, especially on television. Obviously, if this is the route they choose to take, they will be constrained to some extent not only by policy, but also by the manner in which broadcasters perceive and execute their public trusteeship responsibilities, and the manner in which the Federal Communications Commission exercises whatever oversight responsibilities it continues to have.

At present, the only alternative to editorial advertising is reliance on what Benno Schmidt calls "contingent access rules,"[94] rules that exist only when triggered by something the broadcaster does (broadcasting a personal attack, airing only one side of a public issue). This is complicated by the fact that the rule is not automatically triggered: the party desiring access must first request airtime from the broadcaster and, if it is not supplied, must go to the FCC. That agency then must decide whether or not the broadcaster really did trigger any rule. The effort and delays and uncertainty involved are fundamental disadvantages of the legal and regulatory approaches.

An alternative to content regulation is represented by noncontingent structural approaches to media regulation that could be provided partially through media technology, especially cable television. Chief Justice Burger mentioned in his decision in *CBS* that the coming of cable would afford increased opportunities for the discussion of public issues and noted that the FCC, in its proposed rules for cable, had required the maintenance of a public access channel on cable systems in major television markets.

Burger also mentioned the difficulties of regulating the broadcast industry, which is "dynamic in terms of technological change; solutions adequate a decade ago are not necessarily so now, and those acceptable today may well be outmoded 10 years hence."[95] The communication industry has indeed been churning out technological innovations—not only by means of the steadily lengthening cable lines (central to the following discussion), but also in microwave transmission, low-power television stations, direct-to-home broadcast satellites, and other complex equipment that does have the capacity to fill both wires and airwaves with a diversity of voices, opinions, and ideas. What effect will all this potential actually have and how will it affect regulation of the over-the-air and print media with which we are now familiar?

Community Antenna Television (CATV) actually began as a rather minor offshoot of the present television system. The first cable system was installed to pull television signals into a valley community by means of a coaxial cable that connected a powerful antenna to customers' homes. The technique was successful and was repeated across rural America.

Subsequently, larger urban centers began to develop an interest; this was sometimes because channel capacity could be increased, but it was also because the quality of reception was vastly improved by the cable. The industry grew from 14,000 subscribers and 70 operating systems in 1952 to approximately 30 million total subscribers and approximately 5,000 operating systems at the end of 1983. Thirty-seven percent of U.S. homes were wired to cable television by 1984.[96]

In spite of the system's obvious popularity today, for many years cable was regarded as a development whose purpose was to improve and extend reception and to provide a transmitting function for existing programming. There has been only a gradual public awareness of the ways in which cable differs from the more familiar over-the-air system. As such awareness diffused, so did realization of the great potential offered by this medium. Cable television had broken free of the shackles imposed by a limited spectrum and could put an end to media arguments based on the premise of scarcity. Cable offered the promise of wide diversity in programming, broad choice by consumers, and greater ease of access by those who desired a mass media outlet. However, investors interested in profiting from the system realized its potential somewhat before the general public, and even before the FCC and Congress began to understand that media regulatory challenges were only increasing in complexity. The economic realities of cable, imposed by the industry's private ownership structure, make it questionable whether all of the imagined potential will be realized. The cable-related literature is a maze that deals with broad areas of conflict and confusion—local regulation, state regulation, federal regulation, deregulation, reregulation, technical problems, ownership, profit, public interest, copyright laws, pay cable, channel capacity, two-way capacity, leased channels, public access, liability construction, poles, franchises, market size—the list appears endless.

The FCC paid little attention to cable in its early years. This inattention, along with the reasons for cable growth, inhibited regulation. The FCC asserted jurisdiction over cable hesitantly and then primarily in order to protect broadcasters. As one commentator noted, between approximately 1958 and 1968, the FCC followed an objective of trying to discover the extent of jeopardy imposed by cable and of delegating cable control to the broadcast industry.

The FCC was responding to pressure brought by broadcasters who were concerned about the lack of payment by cable operators for material they were carrying and by local station operators concerned about the competition coming from the use of microwave relay facilities by cable operators that enabled them to bring in distant signals. The FCC first extended jurisdiction only to cable systems that were using microwave to import signals (in 1962); this jurisdiction gradually extended to all cable systems, a move that was upheld by the Supreme Court in 1968.[97] Definitive FCC rules regarding cable were not issued until 1972.

During the FCC rulemaking proceedings that led to the 1972 issuance of regulations, a number of groups presented proposals for effective means of access to cable systems; the FCC responded by requiring all cable systems located wholly or partially within the top 100 television markets to provide non-broadcast-designated access channels for public, educational, local governmental, and leased-access users and to furnish necessary equipment and facilities.

> The public access channel will offer a practical opportunity to participate in community dialogue through a mass medium. A system operator will be obliged to provide only use of the channel without charge, but production costs (aside from live studio presentations not exceeding five minutes in length) may be charged to users.[98]

The 1972 cable regulatory rules conceived by the FCC were impressively thorough, but were imposed before many of the potential problems facing cable had arisen. The rigorous nature of these regulations demonstrated the protectionist position the agency still maintained in general toward the broadcasting industry. During the remainder of the 1970s, however, these policies were gradually eroded both by court decisions and by the FCC itself. The public access rule was invalidated by the Supreme Court in 1979 when it affirmed a lower court decision won by a cable system, Midwest Video Corporation.[99] The Court's ruling was based upon the Communications Act (§ 3) that specifies broadcasters are not to be treated as common carriers. Justice White stated that access rules plainly impose common-carrier obligations on cable operators by requiring cable systems "to hold out designated channels on a first-come, nondiscriminatory basis."[100] It was the Court's position that such a regulation was an intrusion upon the journalistic integrity of broadcasters that would outweigh any benefits associated with resulting public access. The Court also found that Congress had not given the FCC the power to impose such requirements on the cable system. The decision did, however, leave the FCC free to seek such jurisdiction from Congress and free to suggest other, less intrusive, rules that might, in the Court's opinion, fall within the limits of the agency's authority. However, by the time this decision was passed down, public access channel provisions already had been written into the franchise agreements of a number of communities and the Court's decision did not rule out the possibility that state regulators might be able to enforce access requirements on their own upon cable operators.

In 1984, the fairness doctrine and equal time rules continued to apply to cable television, as they did to broadcasting, although the FCC requested public comment on this application. Generally, cable operators favor a lifting of such responsibilities, while public interest and other organizations—including the UAW—oppose the change. If legislation is passed abolishing the fairness doctrine entirely, the question no longer needs to be addressed. If, however, content regulation in some form continues, the FCC will need to examine the differences between cable television and broadcasters. One question, for example, is to what extent public access channels, where they exist, meet the objectives of the fairness doctrine.

The extent to which cable television can offer advantages to organized labor is questionable in light of three major issues: (1) control of the industry; (2) financial and technical barriers; and (3) audience dispersion.

The FCC generally has taken a relaxed position with respect to individuals and groups owning both cable systems and other media. The idea that radio and television were media of spectrum scarcity provides the theory upon which much policy has been built. In terms of media ownership, the rule of sevens was based on the concept that governmental oversight was necessary in order to avoid domination of the scarce airwaves by a few sources. With the ability of cable, satellite transmission, low-power television, and so on to provide viewers with a number of stations and channels, the threat of domination retreated. However, in 1970, the FCC made two rulings regarding cable ownership: (1) national television networks were not permitted to own cable systems anywhere in the country; and (2) in order to avoid the possibility of local cross-media monopoly, cable system ownership by telephone companies within their local exchange areas and by television stations within the same market were prohibited.

The television stations that already owned cable systems in the same market were ordered to divest. This order was greatly weakened, however—first by an extension of the divestiture limitation time and then by a 1975 Commission decision to require divestiture only in very concentrated markets. All of these rules were "designed to ensure vigorous competition among the mass media and to obtain for the public the greatest possible diversity of control over local mass communications media."[101]

In spite of these few regulations, a high degree of cross-ownership between cable and other media developed throughout the 1970s. A large number of broadcasters own cable systems, and there is increasing control of cable systems by newspapers and other publishers.

> Over the decade of the 1970s, broadcast stations held about a third of all cable systems, newspapers have generally increased their holdings (when combined with other publishers, print media holdings have better than doubled in relative terms while sharply increasing absolutely), program producers have owned about a fifth of all cable systems . . . , and TV/cable equipment manufacturers have held a declining number of cable systems.[102]

During the 1980s the feeling of the FCC has been that growth of the cable industry should be encouraged, unfettered by any regulatory restrictions. The growth of capital-intensive cable will require substantial investment. Accordingly, the Commission has proposed dropping the rule that television networks may not acquire cable systems. The proposal has attracted powerful support and many expect that it will be acted upon with little further delay. The questions surrounding cable ownership by telephone companies are somewhat more complex, however, and the FCC seems to be treading cautiously in this area. Both systems provide electronic information by wire, making possible cable system development by an established telephone company. Definitive answers to some questions of telephone-cable cross-ownership become even more difficult to provide since American Telephone and Telegraphs' divestiture. The economic pros and cons, the large number and variety of interests involved and the still-developing nature of the "new" telephone industry will make this cross-ownership area more resistant to change.

In assessing the impact of cable control, however, what is perhaps more important than the cross-ownership trends is the increasing power of the multiple system cable operators. Most communities have negotiated franchise agreements with one of a few large corporations that operate cable systems in a number of other cities. Sometimes local residents have partnership agreements of some sort with the franchise operator. Such a practice on the part of cable corporations usually gives some token appearance of local control and interest where in reality very little typically exists.

Growth of the top cable corporations has been achieved through system construction, but also through acquisitions and mergers. For example, American Television and Communications is owned by Time Inc., the corporation that also owns the country's largest pay-TV service, Home Box Office.

> Nicholas Johnson, the former head of the FCC, sees this type of vertical integration as one of the main threats to cable's potential as a medium of abundant diversity. "When a cable operator has an interest in one pay-cable service and can keep competing services off their system, that's a pretty brazen and outrageous violation of antitrust laws. It's as if the telephone company were controlling the conversation on all phone lines."[103]

Some cities have found alternatives. In St. Paul, Minnesota, for example, the cable system is municipally owned; and in 1981 the city of Davis, California franchised a cable cooperative, the first city to do so. Few minority groups own cable systems; in late 1981, only eight community cable systems were owned by minority groups[104] although the FCC, the Small Business Administration, and the National Association of Broadcasters have developed loan plans intended to encourage minority ownership.

In terms of programming, the hoped-for diversification is not happening. Diversification has come to mean more channels with more of the same programs and not a great variety of programs and speakers. Cable stations "appear to be carrying more national programming, via pay channels, the traditional broadcast network programs, or new syndicated programming [a taped program that is sold, or offered to television station licensees in more than one market for nonnetwork viewing] and 'superstations' that are local in the area of origination but are transmitted by satellite to cable systems all over the country, . . . "[105] It is doubtful that this type of programming, shown by cable systems with centralized control, will undergo much change in the near future.

Where public access channels do exist, they are often underused. Other than the fact that it is difficult to build, in a short period of time, a high degree of public use where the tradition has never existed, there are serious financial and technical problems. Labor unions and other groups who wish to use the channels must cope with both. Furthermore, the financial and technical problems may be even more complex for other communication innovations than they are for cable.

Public access channels themselves got off to a fairly good start in the early 1970s. Stations in New York City and in Reading, Pennsylvania, paved the way for other cities in a number of ways. In both cities equipment was provided by the cable systems. Volunteers operated on seed money from foundations and devoted time to a variety of activities aimed at acquainting the public with the potential of public access and encouraging program contributions from the area. Some people went out into communities with outfitted vans and microbuses to demonstrate equipment and to attempt to interest others in setting up media systems of their own. Tapes and informational newsletters were produced to share ideas and experiences and to broaden the popularity of public access.

The Fund for the City of New York conducted a study in 1973 which concluded that, based on the New York experience, critics were being overly harsh in saying that public access channels would neither be watched nor used. But the study stated that the medium had a long way to go.[106] One major problem was shortage of financing; researchers estimated that a half hour of programming could cost between nothing and $1,600. They recommended that these costs be shared by the city (through a grant of 1 percent of the franchise fee), federal and state governments, the cable operator, foundations, and the public. Undoubtedly, however, such shared control of the purse strings would ultimately lead to other areas of controversy. Obviously, no simple answer will suffice; more is needed than an ability to gain access; the financial and technical limitations are very restrictive to individuals and to groups and organizations who wish to use the medium.

Cable systems, therefore, are not fulfilling the objectives of diversifying content themselves and they are not solving the technical and financial barriers that interfere with diversification of content. What cable *is* doing, though, is fragmenting the audience. And it is really *access to audiences,* more than access to media, that is crucial to labor and other groups who are interested in communicating with someone other than themselves. As Jerome Barron stated, "What will happen to dissent when at last it is given a forum but no one listens?"[107] Dissent has not been "given a forum," but one suspects that should it be given, it would not be a mass-audience forum. Somewhat ironically, the big three television networks traditionally have been able to provide audiences to their advertisers, and still, in spite of a deteriorating combined audience share, they have an edge over competitors. Estimates are, however, that by 1990, even ABC, CBS, and NBC will have only a 59 percent prime-time audience share.[108] When ILGWU and AFSCME buy time on the networks, it is the audience that is important, just as it is for commercial advertisers. Labor has its own presses which provide an audience of members. But union leaders want and need to get their messages to people who are not waiting for them, who are not anticipating them, but who will be unexpectedly exposed. And it is to these large numbers of the random public that labor often wants to speak. But, "the access and diversity symbolized by public access cable may be no greater, as it turns out, than handing out mimeographed leaflets at a busy intersection or speaking to passersby from a soapbox."[109]

ORGANIZED LABOR AND MEDIA ACCESS

Discussion relating to print media, broadcast media, and new technology brings out a dizzying array of complex issues even when examined individually. But the coalescing of these issues also deserves mention. Policy differs for print media and broadcast media. The notion of limitations on available broadcast channels and a demand that exceeds supply has given rise to a perceived need for government regulation. The emergence of cable, however, has necessitated a rethinking of the issue because the notions of limitations are no longer so viable—the proliferation of coaxial cables and receivers makes the transmission of a much greater number of signals possible. Moreover, the print and broadcasting media are suddenly no longer the distinguishable entities they once were. Cable has taken on, not only the characteristics of television and radio, but also some of the characteristics of newspapers: newspapers can now be delivered by facsimile reproduction via cable. When they are so delivered, should the fairness doctrine apply as it does for broadcasting and for original programming done under the operator's control? Or should the fairness doctrine be declared invalid for cable as it has been for privately-owned, theoretically expandable newspapers? Or is there any need at all for the fairness doctrine and other media regulations? If regulation was initiated because of radio and television technology, it should be lifted when newer technology provides the diversity that regulation was originally intended to achieve. If there is no longer a need for regulation to assure democracy in the media, the answer is to deregulate.

On the other hand, the existence of 40 or more channels does not ensure diversity, especially when they are controlled by one corporation. Breaking up corporate control would necessitate regulation, but the mood of the country now does not seem to be moving toward regulation. And even if multiple owners existed, would they be diverse in terms of class? Could a common-carrier system overcome middle-of-the-road media homogeneity? Common carriers could provide anyone who wanted channel time the opportunity to purchase it and distribute whatever he or she wanted to distribute. But that cannot be the ultimate answer either, because lack of financial resources may be considered just as capricious a restraint as other policies used by media owners.

We are in a transition period; obviously some choices need to be made by the public, by the government, by media owners. The Communications Act is 50 years old and few would disagree that it is outdated. The question for labor is what changes would be most beneficial? What conclusions can be drawn about media access for organized labor?

No one has come up with new policy proposals that would provide real diversity of content (not even to mention assurance of quality). Any structural reform proposals dealing with ownership deconcentration measures plus diversity of industry control plus rights of access would not get far because of powerful opposition—not only from those who control the media, but also from legislators, administrators, and the courts. Nevertheless, deconcentration of the information industries would provide better opportunities for more equitable distribution of control over information. Admitting that minor changes won't come easily, and that significant major changes require a fundamental balance of power in society that does not exist at present, Bagdikian, nevertheless, makes a number of suggestions, both major and minor, for changes. Among these are the following: (1) be familiar with policies adopted in other democratic countries; (2) support legislative modernization of antitrust laws and tax policies; (3) encourage the granting of low-power television applications to individuals rather than corporations; (4) organize community support for cable franchises that include a public access channel; and (5) support regulation that would require public disclosure by each media corporation of its major outside financial interests.[110]

During its November, 1981 convention, the AFL-CIO adopted a policy resolution supporting the fairness doctrine. The primary reason for this support lay in the hope that it would provide a way to avoid media domination by broadcasters on issues of public importance. Since 1981, labor has upheld the resolution by commenting to the FCC and by giving testimony to Congressional committees. Such input attests to a defensive posture taken by those who want the fairness doctrine maintained because, as they perceive the situation, labor would be worse off without it.

It is not clear, however, on the basis of this research that labor would indeed be worse off without the fairness doctrine. The survey results presented in Chapter IV indicated that opinions regarding the doctrine were quite divided. Half of the unions questioned had never used it. And while the doctrine's "chilling effect" may be impossible to quantify, it does exist. Over half of the respondents agreed with the statement: "Though the fairness doctrine is intended to increase the diversity of opinions presented to the public, we have found that it has the opposite effect; broadcasters use it to exclude particular views." A number of unions have been denied media access either because the topic *is* controversial and may produce requests from the opposition for reply time, or because the topic is *not* controversial and earlier comments by others justify no reply time.

Survey respondents did indicate, however, strong feelings for the necessity of some form of media regulation. Most of the deregulation arguments are based on the premise that technological innovations have created structural change in the industry which has eliminated the scarce commodity argument upon which communication regulation is based. What too many deregulation advocates overlook, however, is that the limited spectrum rationale is not the *only* rationale for communications policy. Another primary basis of policy—and one which has received impressive judicial affirmation—is the right of the public to information—not just to information, but to diverse information. Justice White in *Red Lion* sums up the opinions of several court cases:

> It is the purpose of the First Amendment to preserve an uninhibited marketplace of ideas in which truth will ultimately prevail, rather than to countenance monopolization of that market, whether it be by the Government itself or a private licensee. . . . It is the right of the public to receive suitable access to social, political, esthetic, moral, and other ideas and experiences which is crucial here. That right may not constitutionally be abridged either by Congress or by the FCC.[111]

Justice Brennan, in suggesting a limited scheme of editorial advertising in his dissenting opinion in *CBS v. Democratic National Committee,* argues that full information requires public participation:

> Moreover, the Court's reliance on the Fairness Doctrine as the *sole* means of informing the public seriously misconceives and underestimates the public's interest in receiving ideas and information directly from the advocates of those ideas without the interposition of journalistic middlemen. Under the Fairness Doctrine, broadcasters decide what issues are "important," how "fully" to cover them, and what format, time and style of coverage are "appropriate."

The retention of such *absolute* control in the hands of a few Government licensees is inimical to the First Amendment, for vigorous, free debate can be attained only when members of the public have at least *some* opportunity to take the initiative and editorial control into their own hands.[112]

The scarce commodity argument and the public right to information argument are related only in that, with many channels, journalists can assume that any information they do not give the public can be acquired by switching channels. But there is no basis for this assumption.

Labor needs something more effective than the fairness doctrine. And the FCC itself laid out certain requirements for improvement in its report of the 1979 fairness doctrine inquiry. In order to serve the public interest, the new doctrine must assure "(1) that the quantity of response to available access time would be adequate; (2) that issues would be discussed; (3) that topics discussed would be important and timely public issues; (4) that a variety of viewpoints and issues would be discussed; (5) that presentations on issues would be balanced; and (6) that such presentations would be informative and comprehensible."[113]

Equal opportunity of access to all should be added. The preservation of licensee discretion is necessary to accomplish these additional requirements, but so would be government oversight to demonstrate the extent to which a licensee was fulfilling fairness responsibilities and so would be adequate means for the public to protest noncompliance.

At the present time, it appears that labor, in order most effectively to use the media, needs to reach a broad audience. And, although the networks' audience share is diminishing, the absolute number of people in the network audience is increasing. Therefore, for advertisers, network broadcasting still offers the most efficient means by which to communicate with a large, diverse audience. It seems that efforts might most effectively—at least in the near future—be directed at the networks and their affiliates. If the networks make the decision to allow use of the airwaves to air one advocacy advertisement, their expressed commitment to public interest standards might convince them of the need to develop fair requirements that apply to all who wish to advertise.

The AFL-CIO emphasis on improving internal communications and educating journalists about labor will continue to be highly important for all affiliates at all levels as well as for the Federation.

The fundamental problem, however, always seems to come back to media control and management and the way it affects minorities and other interests not represented in the owner-manager class. Complex interpretations of the First Amendment compound this problem. Lawyer John Taylor Williams wrote:

Strangely, it is the First Amendment that represents the greatest obstacle to minority access. On the one hand, without its protection, no minority could freely expound views which are abhorrent to those held by the majority. On the other hand, since the media of expression are primarily owned or dominated by nonminorities, governmentally decreed minority access rules for ownership, employment, or program content may not be so chilling as to affect the majority's exercise of its First Amendment rights.[114]

NOTES

[1] "Freedom of the press is guaranteed only to those who own one." A. J. Liebling, "The Wayward Press: Do You Belong in Journalism?" *New Yorker,* May 14, 1960, p. 109.

[2] *Chicago Joint Board, Amalgamated Clothing Workers of America, AFL-CIO v. Chicago Tribune Company,* 435 F. 2d 470 (7th Cir., 1970).

[3] Ibid., at 473n.

[4] Ibid., at 472.

[5] Ibid., at 478.

[6] *Retail Store Employees Union, Local 880, Retail Clerks International Association, AFL-CIO v. Federal Communications Commission,* 43b F. 2d 248 (D.C. Cir., 1970).

[7] Ibid., at 250.

[8] The text of one of these spots, evidently typical, is as follows: Announcer: Here is an important message from *Retail Store Employees Union Local 880*—regarding the picket line now at *Hill's Department Store* in Youngstown. The picket line is in support of the strike at *Hill's Department Store* in Ashtabula. This strike now in progress at *Hill's* comes after seven months of continuous negotiations, during which no agreement has been reached between the Retail Store Employees Union Local 880—and the management of HILL'S DEPARTMENT STORE. Important issues still unresolved include Union security, Arbitration and Grievance Procedures, Health and Welfare, Funeral Leave, and Visitation Rights to the store. These, and other issues are vital to the betterment of the store employees working conditions. *Some* Hill's employees are still working because if they all go out—the Company would try to replace them with non-union help who could be granted a vote in subsequent elections. The 2,000 members of Retail Store Employees Union Local 880 request that *all* union members, their families and friends observe and respect the picket line now at HILL'S DEPARTMENT STORE. Ibid., at 250n.

[9] Ibid., at 253.

[10] Ibid., at 258.

[11] David Wallace Anderson, "Access: An Analysis of the Development of an Affirmative Concept of the First Amendment in Broadcasting" (M.S. thesis, University of Illinois, 1974), p. 8. See generally Jerome A. Barron, "Access to the Press—A New First Amendment Right," *Harvard Law Review,* 80:8 (June, 1967), pp. 1641–1678.

[12] *Red Lion Broadcasting Company, Inc. v. Federal Communications Commission* 395 U.S. 367 (1969), at 386.

[13] Ibid., at 390.

[14] 47 U.S.C. § 307 (a), (d), (1976).

[15] 47 U.S.C. § 315 (a). See also *Report on Editorializing by Broadcast Licensees,* 13 FCC 1246 (1949) at 1258. [Hereinafter cited as 1949 *Report on Editorializing.*] See also *Handling of Public Issues under the Fairness Doctrine and the Public Interest Standard of the Communications Act,* 48 FCC 2d 1 (1974), at 10. [Hereinafter cited as 1974 *Fairness Report.*]

[16] *Rosenbloom v. Metromedia,* 403 U.S. 29 (1971), at 47n.

[17] Martin H. Redish, "The First Amendment in the Marketplace: Commercial Speech and the Values of Free Expression," *George Washington Law Review,* 39 (March, 1971), p. 443.

[18] Mark S. Massel, *Competition and Monopoly: Legal and Economic Issues* (Washington, D.C.: Brookings Institution, 1962), p. 154. To some extent deficiencies in the actual litigation may be ameliorated by analysis in law reviews; these publications are relied upon heavily among those in the legal profession. Such analyses may allow for greater independent inquiry, but the ultimate effect may only be to emphasize the "gamesmanship" aspect.

[19] *Valentine v. Chrestensen*, 316 U.S. 52 (1942).

[20] *New York Times v. Sullivan*, 376 U.S. 254 (1964).

[21] Ibid., at 266.

[22] *Pittsburgh Press Co. v. Pittsburgh Commission on Human Relations*, 413 U.S. 376 (1973).

[23] *Bigelow v. Virginia*, 421 U.S. 809 (1975).

[24] *Pittsburgh Press*, 413 U.S. at 385.

[25] *Konigsberg v. State Bar of California*, 366 U.S. 36 (1961), at 67. But see *Dennis v. United States*, 341 U.S. 494 (1941) at 520–25, 542–44 (Frankfurter, J., concurring). See generally Benno C. Schmidt, "*Nebraska Press Association*: An Expansion of Freedom and Contraction of Theory," *Stanford Law Review* (February, 1977), pp. 431–476.

[26] *Bigelow*, 421 U.S. at 822.

[27] *Virginia State Board of Pharmacy v. Virginia Citizens' Consumer Council*, 425 U.S. 748 (1976).

[28] Ibid., at 772n.

[29] Ibid., at 771.

[30] *Bates v. State Bar of Arizona*, 433 U.S. 350 (1977).

[31] *Ohralik v. Ohio State Bar Association*, 436 U.S. 447 (1978).

[32] A more recent Court pronouncement on commercial speech comes from *Metromedia Inc. v. San Diego*, 101 S.Ct. 2882 (1981) at 2892. The decision in this case was based on a four-part test that was used to distinguish protected commercial speech from unprotected commercial speech. The test originally came from *Central Hudson v. Public Service Communications*, 477 U.S. 557 (1980). The same test, which follows, was referred to again on March 3, 1982 in *Norton v. Arlington Heights*, 8 Med.L.Reptr. 2018 (1982) at 2020.
(1) the First Amendment protects commercial speech only if that speech concerns lawful activity and is not misleading. A restriction on otherwise protected commercial speech is valid only if it (2) seeks to implement a substantial government interest, (3) directly advances that interest, and (4) reaches no farther than necessary to accomplish the given objective.

[33] *First National Bank of Boston v. Bellotti*, 435 U.S. 765 (1978).

[34] Ibid., at 777.

[35] Ibid., at 802.

[36] Ibid., at 793.

[37] Ibid., at 813.

[38] *Abood v. Detroit Board of Education*, 431 U.S. 209 (1977).

[39] *Bellotti*, 435 U.S. at 814.

[40] *Associated Press v. United States*, 326 U.S. 1 (1945), at 20.

[41] Michael Pertschuk, "Opening Address," in *Proceedings of the Symposium on Media Concentration*, vol. I, U.S. Federal Trade Commission (FTC) (Washington, D.C.: U.S. Government Printing Office, 1979), p. 1.

[42] "Foreign Publishers Top U.S. Sales," *Editor and Publisher*, January 7, 1984, p. 40.

[43] Morris K. Udall, "Media Conglomerates—Will the Government Have to Step In?" in FTC *Symposium*, vol. I, p. 237; and Benjamin M. Compaine, "Newspapers" in *Who Owns the Media? Concentration of Ownership in the Mass Communications Industry*, 2nd ed., ed. Benjamin M. Compaine (White Plains, N.Y.: Knowledge Industry Publications, Inc.), p. 37.

[44] Ben H. Bagdikian, *The Media Monopoly* (Boston: Beacon Press, 1983), p. 4.

[45] *Standard and Poor's Industry Surveys*, April, 1984, p. Media 74.

[46] Bagdikian, *The Media Monopoly*, pp. 19–20.

[47] In 1976, Chief Justice Burger summed up prior restraint decisions: "The trend running through all these cases is that prior restraint on speech and publication are the most serious and the least tolerable infringement on First Amendment rights." *Nebraska Press Association v. Stuart*, 427 U.S. 539 (1976), at 559.

[48] See *Near v. State of Minnesota*, 283 U.S. 697 (1931). Public officials who feel they have been maligned by the press may seek sanctions under libel laws; there are few examples (this case is one) of attempts to impose prior restraints on publications in such a situation.

[49] See *Nebraska Press Association v. Stuart*, 427 U.S. 539 (1976).

[50] Courts are more likely to enjoin speech from being published in cases that involve invasion of privacy than in defamation cases. The issue in privacy cases centers on disclosure by the press of information about an individual that she/he would prefer to suppress. See, for example, *Commonwealth v. Wiseman*, 356 Mass. 251, 249 NE 2d 610 (1969), *cert. denied,* 398 U.S. 960 (1969).

[51] One of the best known of such cases is *New York Times Company v. United States*, 403 U.S. 713 (1971). This case involved the publication of the Pentagon Papers. After the *Times* had published three installments, the United States government sought an injunction to prevent further publication because such action would threaten national security. The Supreme Court, in a 6-3 decision affirmed the press's right to publish.

[52] *Miami Herald Publishing Company v. Tornillo*, 418 U.S. 241 (1974).

[53] Ibid., at 258.

[54] *Poughkeepsie Buying Service, Inc. v. Poughkeepsie Newspapers, Inc.*, 205 Misc. 982 (1954), at 985.

[55] *Chicago Joint Board*, 435 F. 2d 470 at 477.

[56] Jerome A. Barron, *Freedom of the Press for Whom? The Right of Access to Mass Media* (Bloomington: Indiana University Press, 1973), p. 17.

[57] *Lee v. Board of Regents*, 441 F. 2d 1257 (7th Cir., 1971).

[58] But see *Mississippi Gay Alliance v. Goudelack*, 536 F. 2d 1073 (5th Cir., 1976), *cert. denied*, 430 U.S. 982 (1977). This case demonstrates that rulings are not entirely consistent in this area and that conclusions often may be result-oriented.

[59] Barron, *Freedom of the Press*, p. 50.

[60] Everette E. Dennis, "The Rhetoric and Reality of Representation: A Legal Basis for Press Freedom and Minority Rights," in *Small Voices and Great Trumpets: Minorities and the Media*, ed. Bernard Rubin (New York, N.Y.: Praeger Publishers, 1980), p. 78.

[61] *In the Matter of the Mayflower Broadcasting Corporation and the Yankee Network, Inc. (WAAB)*, 8 FCC 333 (1941), at 340.

[62] Federal Communications Commission (FCC), 1949 *Report on Editorializing*, at 1253.

[63] *Red Lion*, 395 U.S. 367 (1969).

[64] *Red Lion*, 395 U.S. at 390.

[65] *Business Executives Move for Vietnam Peace v. Federal Communications Commission*, 450 F. 2d 642 (D.C. Circ., 1971).

[66] *Columbia Broadcasting System, Inc. v. Democratic National Committee*, 412 U.S. 94 (1973).

[67] Ibid., at 121.

[68] The protection of public health and safety has consistently had significant effects on patterns of legal remedies. Consider, for example, *Bigelow*, 421 U.S. 809 (1975); *Virginia State Board*, 425 U.S. 748 (1976); and *National Commission on Egg Nutrition*, 517 F. 2d 485 (7th Cir., 1975).

[69] *Applicability of the Fairness Doctrine to Cigarette Advertising*, 9 FCC 2d 921 (1967), at 925.

[70] *In Re Complaint by Friends of the Earth Concerning Fairness Doctrine Re Station WBNB-TV, New York, N.Y.*, 24 FCC 2d (1970).

71 The reasons for these confusing and apparent inconsistencies are explained further in *National Citizens Committee for Broadcasting v. FCC, 567* F. 2d 1095 (D.C. Cir., 1977).

72 *Green v. FCC*, 447 F. 2d 323 (D.C. Cir., 1974).

73 *Neckritz v. FCC*, 502 F. 2d 411 (D.C. Cir., 1974).

74 FCC, 1974 *Fairness Report*, at 26.

75 Ibid., at 23.

76 *Public Interest Research Group v. FCC*, 522 F. 2d 1060 (1st Cir., 1975). See also *In Re Complaint of Public Media Center*, 59 FCC 2d 494 (1976), *Georgia Power Project v. FCC*, 3 Med.L.Rptr. 1299 (1977), and *In Re Complaint of Energy Action Committee, Inc. against American Broadcasting Cos.*, 40 P & F Radio Reg 2d 511 (1977).

77 The most serious challenge to the FCC *Fairness Report* occurred in 1977 when several groups challenged parts of it in *National Citizens Committee for Broadcasting v. FCC*, 567 F. 2d 1095 (D.C. Cir., 1977). Friends of the Earth and Council of Economic Priorities challenged the FCC's decision to exempt *most ordinary* product commercials from the fairness doctrine as a violation of the Communications Act and as arbitrary, capricious, and an abuse of discretion. The Court of Appeals ruled that the Commission did not abuse its discretion by withdrawing most commercial advertisements from the purview of the fairness doctrine.

78 FCC, 1974 *Fairness Report*, at 22.

79 Ibid.

80 *In Re Complaint by Wilderness Society and Friends of the Earth Concerning Fairness Doctrine Re National Broadcasting Co.*, 30 FCC 2d 643 (1971).

81 Ibid., at 646.

82 FCC, 1974 *Fairness Report*, at 24.

83 *National Citizens Committee*, 567 F. 2d at 1110.

84 Ibid., at 1108.

85 *National Committee for Responsive Philanthropy v. FCC*, 7 Med.L.Rptr. 1530 (1981).

86 Ibid., at 1531.

87 *Columbia Broadcasting System*, 412 U.S. at 189.

88 *In the Matter of the Handling of Public Issues Under the Fairness Doctrine and the Public Interest Standards of the Communications Act*, 74 FCC 2d 163; 46 RR 2d 999 (1979). [Hereinafter cited as 1979 *Public Issues Report*.]

89 Monroe E. Price, "Taming Red Lion: The First Amendment and Structural Approaches to Media Regulation," in FTC *Symposium*, vol. I, p. 22.

90 "Broad Support for Repeal of 315," *Broadcasting*, February 13, 1984, p. 198.

91 *Federal Communications Commission v. League of Women Voters of California*, S.Ct. No. 82–912 (1984).

92 Ibid., at 11.

93 Ibid., at 13.

94 Benno C. Schmidt, *Freedom of the Press vs. Public Access* (New York: Praeger Publishers, 1976), pp. 212–13.

95 *Columbia Broadcasting System*, 412 U.S. at 102.

96 *Standard and Poor's Industry Surveys* (April, 1984), p. Media 76.

97 *United States v. Southwestern Cable*, 392 U.S. 159 (1968).

98 FCC, *Cable Television Report and Order* (Washington, D.C.: U.S. Government Printing Office, 1972), paragraph 122.

99 *Federal Communications Commission v. Midwest Video Corporation*, 440 U.S. 689 (1979).

100 Ibid., at 701.

101 FCC, *Regulatory Developments in Cable Television* (Washington, D.C.: U.S. Government Printing Office, April, 1976), p. 17.

102 Christopher H. Sterling, "Cable and Pay Television," in *Who Owns the Media?*, ed. Compaine (1982), p. 385.

103 "The Kings of Cable TV," *Mother Jones,* January, 1982, p. 6.

104 Sterling, "Cable and Pay Television," in *Who Owns the Media?,* ed. Compaine (1982), p. 401.

105 Sterling, "Cable," *Who Owns the Media?,* ed. Compaine (1979), p. 314.

106 "What New York has Learned About Public Access Channels in Two Years," *Broadcasting,* October 29, 1973, p. 30.

107 Barron, *Freedom of the Press,* p. 259.

108 "Bad Times for the Big Three," *Newsweek,* February 22, 1982, p. 77.

109 Compaine, "Introduction," in *Who Owns the Media?,* ed. Compaine (1979), p. 6.

110 Bagdikian, *The Media Monopoly,* pp. 229–237.

111 *Red Lion,* 395 U.S. at 390.

112 *Columbia Broadcasting System,* 412 U.S. at 188.

113 FCC, 1979 *Public Issues Report,* at 173.

114 John Taylor Williams, "Open and Closed Access: A Lawyer's Views," in *Small Voices and Great Trumpets,* ed. Rubin, p. 108.

CHAPTER VI

Three Media Campaigns: UFW's Grape Strike, Amalgamated's Farah Boycott, and the United Labor Committee's "Right-to-Work" Campaign

If the term "struggle" seems overused in discussions of labor history, a careful review of the circumstances of the labor force at any given moment during the expansion of a capitalist economy is likely to affirm its aptness. An obvious means of maximizing profits has been controlling the cost of labor. Employers accomplish this in various ways: industrialists often seek to isolate workers from their colleagues; farmers may utilize migrant labor; employers frequently hire illegal immigrants or ship work to low-wage countries. Although a comprehensive survey of the resulting difficulties that workers have confronted remains to be written, this chapter covers only the collective activity undertaken by members of two labor unions and one labor coalition, and methods they used to try to gain more equity in and control over their employment situations. And although collective bargaining and strikes are perhaps the most traditional forms of collective activity engaged in by organized labor, this chapter focuses on alternative methods, especially those where media played a vital role.

Utilization of media has, in the past, sometimes been well-thought-out in advance. More often, however, the potential ability of the media to influence opinion and thus to strengthen labor's case, although recognized by labor, has not been a well-defined part of collective action. Increased awareness, enhanced skill, and a gradually fortified legal foundation was demonstrated during the 1960s and 1970s when the United Farm Workers, the Amalgamated Clothing Workers of America, and the United Labor Committee, an ad hoc Missouri labor coalition, used the media successfully as part of collective actions. The methods used in these three cases are significant in that they contributed substantially to labor history and provided contours of the strategy that was later used by the Amalgamated Clothing and Textile Workers in their campaign against J. P. Stevens. The latter campaign has assumed major importance in this study because it touches on most of the issues that have been discussed. But it should not be viewed as an event isolated in time; it is instead interwoven with various long-term processes that are, in fact, still unfolding.

THE UNITED FARM WORKERS:
THE GRAPE STRIKE AND BOYCOTT

In December, 1964, Public Law 78 was terminated and an official end came to what was known as the *bracero* era in California. What had begun as a series of emergency labor agreements between the United States government and Mexico during World War II was not halted until 22 years later when strikes and politically active workers, especially Mexican-American workers, called attention to it.

During the World War II years, when the labor supply was scarce, farmers lost workers to higher-paying industrial jobs. In response to protests from the growers that their crops were rotting in the fields, the United States and Mexico worked out programs whereby Mexican farmhands (*braceros*) could enter the United States temporarily and go to contracting centers from where they could quickly and easily be sent out to farms as needed to harvest crops. The agreements stipulated that the Mexican workers were not to be used to displace American workers or to lower wage rates, and that there had to be minimum guarantees on wages and working conditions.[1] The plan seemed to work reasonably well: it supplied farmers with a cheap, able, dependable, and timely labor force and thereby saved valuable crops; and Mexico's unemployed found jobs at wage rates higher than they would have received in their own country. Understandably, employers objected to a 1946 plan to terminate the program. They managed to get it extended through bilateral agreements immediately after the war and as Public Law 78 in 1951.

At the war's end, however, U.S. labor was no longer scarce and U.S. workers who needed jobs began to agitate for an end to the supply of *braceros,* whose numbers were greatly swollen by illegal immigrants needing work. Their cause was supported by the increasing neglect of the *braceros'* working conditions by some of the growers who, in violation of the agreement, underpaid workers, supplied inadequate food and housing, and allowed mistreatment of workers in general.

Public Law 78 also made union organizing extremely difficult, a fact recognized by both employers and leaders among the workers. Besides the geographic dispersion of the farms and ranches, the large numbers of Mexican nationals and illegal immigrants and the temporary nature of their employment hindered organizing efforts. Steadily worsening working conditions, however, and the efforts of a number of activists, led to the formation of several organizations that were forerunners of the United Farm Workers of America. These were not stable organizations, but they did organize several large strikes during the 1950s and early 1960s which called attention to the burgeoning problems.

It was during the *bracero* years that Cesar Chavez, the Arizona-born member of a family of migrant workers and later the president of the United Farm Workers, displayed his talent for using the press to bring attention to the plight of workers. On one early occasion, for example, Chavez alerted a few reporters and television cameras and led a group of unemployed domestic workers into a field where *braceros* were working. The subsequently reported evidence that local domestics were being fired in order to hire *braceros* resulted in an investigation by the Department of Labor.[2] The situation itself was hardly unusual at that time, but Chavez's success in obtaining sympathetic news coverage was a noteworthy precursor of his later methods.

As American labor became increasingly undercut and displaced, the AFL-CIO Agricultural Workers Organizing Committee (AWOC) formed in 1959. The AFL-CIO, while recognizing the total inadequacy of the working and living conditions of farm workers, seemed rather stymied by the unique characteristics presented by problems of farm workers and offered little substantive support to the newly-formed group. In spite of this difficulty, which was augmented by low membership, lack of money, and the fact that its members found the scarce jobs were more readily given to those whose names were not associated with the organization, AWOC remained alive and active. It was a walk-out by rank and file members of the AWOC that started the Delano grape strike in 1965. The basic issue in the strike and subsequent boycott was the right of farm workers to bargain collectively for fair wages and working conditions. Cesar Chavez, who in 1962 had organized the National Farm Workers Association (NFWA) as a workers' cooperative rather than a trade union, decided to join the strikers' cause.

The early 1960s were a time of "movements" and Chavez turned the grapeworkers' cause into a movement-plus-union-organizing campaign. He was skillful at attracting support from other movement people—students, civil rights workers, and militant priests and ministers. "Respectable" trade union support came from the AFL-CIO itself; the Federation held a convention in San Francisco just two months after the strike had begun. Delegates adopted a resolution supporting the effort and promised moral and financial aid. Much of the credit for the passage of this resolution went to Walter Reuther, then president of the AFL-CIO Industrial Union Department, and Paul Schrade, UAW regional director and convention delegate, who had been involved in the strike from its inception. George Meany, AFL-CIO president, committed himself more reluctantly. The degree of support (especially financial) given to the farm workers was one of the conflicts between Reuther and Meany that eventually led to the dissociation of the UAW from the AFL-CIO.

The day after the convention, Reuther went to Delano to assure workers of support. Partly due to Chavez's maneuvering, Reuther was accompanied by a large contingent of newspeople, many of whom had been covering the San Francisco convention. Reuther's statement to workers plus a Reuther/Chavez-led march in Delano in defiance of city laws requiring parade permits made the trip of the labor reporters worthwhile and the cause of the farm workers was launched into national attention.

Chavez's efforts did not end with successful coalition-building and good media coverage. He was one of the first labor organizers to recognize the potential effectiveness of consumer boycotts, especially when given the right kind of publicity.

The relative scarcity of research on boycotts, organized efforts to withdraw and induce others to withdraw from social or business relations with another, cannot be attributed to the recent emergence of the technique. The technique is old and its forms are many and diverse.[3] There have been blacklists, trade boycotts, employer's boycotts, political boycotts, and international boycotts. One of the most familiar in the United States is the consumers' boycott. This type is usually organized by a national consumer group and has been used primarily as a protest against the poor quality or high cost of a product—meat or coffee, for example. Even though boycotts have been utilized in almost every field of endeavor, it is organized labor that has turned the strategy into what one author calls a "veritable science in recent years."[4] That comment was made after two major national labor boycotts had been organized—the grape and lettuce boycott by the United Farm Workers and the Farah pants boycott by the Amalgamated Clothing Workers of America. Both were undertaken on a larger scale and with more sophistication than had been attempted previously.

Early labor boycotts usually just involved labor in accord with the following perspective:

> Labor has a two-fold relationship with the employing class. It supplies that class with the labor power necessary to produce commodities. It also furnishes, to a considerable extent, a market for the commodities produced. In both relationships it can so conduct itself as vitally to affect the profits.[5]

Union members realized that through a boycott it was possible to apply economic pressure that could, in some instances, exceed the pressure developed through a strike. In a strike situation, union members use only their positions as producers; in a boycott situation labor union members' positions as consumers can also be used, and all of organized labor—rather than a single union—can be asked to support boycott efforts. The boycott can be used where strikes are not feasible, or in conjunction with strikes. The boycott is essentially nonviolent in character and possibly can be used relatively inexpensively. In addition to all this, labor union members can utilize not only their own consumer power, but also that of their families. And in the two major boycotts just mentioned, the use of third parties strengthened the strategy significantly; labor expanded its efforts and began to invite participation from all consumers.

A product boycott by organized labor is a form of secondary boycott—a boycott that involves a secondary neutral employer or some other third party not involved in the dispute. As compared with a primary boycott, one in which union members agree to refuse to purchase any product or service of a firm with which there is a labor disagreement, the secondary boycott often is unclear in both definition and legal status. Primary boycotts are generally legal unless their objectives are illegal, but they are also relatively ineffective. Union members therefore endeavor to engage others in their action. Boycotts of this type became increasingly important in the United States after 1880, although they have been subjected over the years to judicial scrutiny and many subsequent adverse decisions. The problem of course lies in the fact that, through secondary boycotts, labor conflicts can spread far beyond the spheres of influence of the primary parties and cause economic instability in businesses only indirectly related to the dispute.

The foundation for labor law in the United States is provided by the National Labor Relations Act (NLRA) of 1935. This act guarantees workers the right to form unions, requires employers to bargain in good faith, and prohibits unfair labor practices by management. There have been two major amendments to the act: the Taft-Hartley Act (1947) and the Landrum-Griffin Act (1959). Both of these were aimed at correcting alleged union misuses of the NLRA, one of which was seen as secondary boycotts. Both the Taft-Hartley and Landrum-Griffin amendments were intended to restrict severely secondary boycott activity and to clarify situations in which such activity was illegal. A large number of secondary boycotts have occurred since Landrum-Griffin, however, especially in the construction industry. The resulting court cases have produced fairly complex legal interpretations and precedents and many areas are still disputed.

Before the mid-1960s labor had used boycotts primarily as a last-resort tactic, usually when it looked as though strikes were not going to be successful. Accordingly, they were almost always doomed as a really effective means of achieving desired results and, therefore, not often used. Chavez therefore did not launch directly into a successful nationwide consumer boycott overnight. He started on a small scale by announcing a boycott against the Schenley Company, a major liquor manufacturer that produced only two brands of wines that used California grapes.

It was primarily this small-scale boycott that troubled George Meany and made him somewhat less than eager to advocate the resolution of support for the grape strike. He had several reservations. One was that Schenley was a union company—completely organized by several AFL-CIO affiliated international unions, among them the Distillery Workers Union. The second was that what the UFWA was doing was clearly a secondary boycott; most unions would never have proposed such an action, recognizing the shaky legal grounds upon which they would have been standing. The reason that NFWA could dare to be different was that farm workers are excluded, along with several other categories of employed people, in the definition the National Labor Relations Act applies to employees. Because farm workers were not covered by federal labor laws, they had to struggle separately for the right to bargain collectively, a right that other individual workers obtained through the NLRA. But at the same time, because farm workers were excluded, they were not affected by the NLRA sections that made secondary boycotts illegal. The NFWA action caused Meany to think once more about the unique nature of this group of workers and how they fit into Federation structure. The AFL-CIO resolution of support in 1965 was for the strike alone—not the boycott.[6]

Nevertheless, Chavez achieved nationwide support, mostly from union members, for the boycott. Because Schenley had a reputation as a prolabor company, the boycott of its products by farm workers and union members proved damaging. The boycott was short-lived; in spring, 1966, Schenley signed a contract with NFWA.

The Schenley boycott laid the foundation for the large nationwide consumer boycotts of table grapes and lettuce by the United Farm Workers. Moreover, it established another precedent:

> It was also in the Schenley drive that the NFWA began to develop a tactic which seemed to reverse the traditional trade-union approach. It went after the large companies first, not the smaller ones. In the conglomerate age an effective boycott had suddenly taken on a new significance. Schenley's, a large company with only a small part of its investment in grapes, was the first to throw in the towel—the cost of the boycott was too high for its other products.[7]

The AWOC and NFWA merged in 1966 under the name United Farm Workers Organizing Committee (UFWOC). The strike continued for four more years and the national consumer boycott against table grapes was launched. Good press coverage for UFWOC resulted from gaining support from the politically powerful Kennedy family, from a 25-day fast by Chavez in 1968 to protest the increasing violence in the strike, and an International Grape Boycott Day that sparked demonstrations in more than 100 cities. The boycott became international in scope as union members in Canada joined in and then even dockworkers in London refused to unload California grapes. Leaders of farm workers who often had argued that farm workers should be included in federal labor laws began to realize advantages of not being included. AFL-CIO leaders, however, continued to fight to get federal labor law protection extended to farm workers.

The grape agreement between all of the major fresh grape producers and UFWOC was accompanied by much ceremony, many celebrations, and excellent newspaper, radio, and television coverage. Growers admitted that the wide publicity and the boycott had hurt them; unionized grape ranches began to stamp each box of grapes with the "union label," a black eagle.

UFWOC immediately extended its tactics to vegetable crops—primarily lettuce. In spite of the jurisdictional and political problems many AFL-CIO leaders had with UFWOC's activism, its coalitions with militants, and its independent attitude and secondary boycotts, massive attacks on the UF-WOC by the independent Teamsters led to an official UFWOC-AFL-CIO affiliation in 1972. In 1973 a first convention was held and the union's name officially became the United Farm Workers of America, AFL-CIO.

That same year, as many of the UFW contracts were lost to the Teamsters, Chavez initiated a new boycott of all California grapes and lettuce not harvested by UFW members. For the first time AFL-CIO approval—and even active assistance—was gained, but in order to gain that approval this boycott had to be clearly a boycott of nonunion lettuce and grapes and not a boycott of the stores that carried the produce.

THE AMALGAMATED CLOTHING WORKERS OF AMERICA: FARAH PANTS BOYCOTT

The second major product boycott that contributed to the process of turning such collective activity into a "veritable science" also enjoyed extensive public support and reasonable success. In many ways the 1972–1974 boycott of the Farah Manufacturing Company in El Paso, Texas, by the Amalgamated Clothing Workers of America was more similar to the J. P. Stevens boycott discussed in Chapter VII than the UFW boycott. At any rate, it serves to bridge the two and demonstrates the development of some previously-used tactics plus the acquisition of new ones.

The Amalgamated, one of the two unions that merged to form the Amalgamated Clothing and Textile Workers Union in 1976, was a much older union than the UFW and its public relations and media skills went back a long way. It certainly never depended so much on the ideas and drive of one person as had the UFW. The Amalgamated was formed by a group who were originally members of the United Garment Workers, a men's apparel union that was formed in 1891 and affiliated with the AFL. Unhappy with that organization, these individuals struggled against what they perceived to be ineffective and dishonest leadership and were finally disenfranchised and denied convention seats at the United Garment Workers meeting in 1914.

The splinter group formed a new union, the Amalgamated Clothing Workers of America, that same year.

The same sweatshop conditions that existed in the women's apparel industry and that had led to the formation of the ILGWU prevailed in the men's industry as well. And just as the Triangle Shirtwaist Company fire marked a well-known turning point in the organization of the women's apparel industry, so did the 1910 Hart Schaffner and Marx strike in the men's apparel industry. In that incident, intolerable working conditions, apparently ignored or mishandled by United Garment Workers leaders, caused a group of women to walk out of a Hart Schaffner and Marx plant. Because worker discontent and restlessness were prevalent throughout the industry, this action gained rapid support and soon the majority of Chicago's 35,000 garment workers had joined the protest. The strike was lost after several months of chaos, bitterness, and violence. What is significant about this effort, however, is the fact that a limited agreement was negotiated with Hart Schaffner and Marx, and this agreement laid the foundation for an effective arbitration system, one of the first in U.S. industries; the system is based on the simple premise of a neutral arbitrator.

The strike also brought out the leadership abilities of a number of the workers, among them Sidney Hillman, who was elected president of the Amalgamated after its formation in 1914. Dedicated leaders were all the more important because the new organization lacked finances and AFL support (which lay with the United Garment Workers) and faced an industry that had united in a firm anti-union position. In spite of this, the Amalgamated proceeded to organize the men's clothing industry on an industry-wide basis, and in the process achieved a notably peaceful labor-management relationship.

Hillman is credited with outstanding leadership from 1914 until 1946. His efforts extended to a number of welfare projects to benefit workers, including cooperative housing, camps, a comprehensive insurance and retirement system, and labor banks. Moreover, recognizing that gains made at the bargaining table could be lost quickly because of an unsympathetic government, Hillman encouraged a course of political activism for the Amalgamated and founded the Political Action Committee of the CIO.

Jacob Potofsky succeeded Hillman as Amalgamated's president in 1946. Potofsky served until 1972 and is considered to have been a capable and effective leader who saw the union through a period when the structure of the garment industry was undergoing considerable change. Small tailor shops gave way to large publicly owned corporations, some of which became parts of giant conglomerates. This trend did not make the industry easier to organize, because it was accompanied by decentralization in terms of production processes and plant location. The industry remains basically labor-intensive, requiring a variety of skill levels and job classifications and, as noted below, this provides management with additional incentive to seek an inexpensive—and relatively compliant—labor force. One of the ways union leaders responded to these circumstances was to emphasize outreach to industry workers and to the general public.

The Amalgamated established a separate public relations department in 1945. The purpose of this department was external rather than internal relations. It put out news releases, newspaper advertisements, pamphlets, and planned radio and television shows—all intended to gain public attention for Amalgamated's gains for members and role in politics and community affairs. Closely related to these two departments was Amalgamated's union label department, established in 1948. At that time, the union label was redesigned and an advertising agency was retained to promote it. The campaign began with advertisements placed in national magazines, leading newspapers, and in the labor and trade press (Figure 17).

The Amalgamated's history of concern for workers, political activism, and capable handling of communications came together in its experiences with the Farah Manufacturing Company of El Paso, Texas. The boycott was preceded by an unsuccessful strike against the company, a fact that encouraged many union members and sympathizers to devote their energies to a massive campaign urging the public not to buy Farah products.

Del Mileski, former director of ACTWU's union label department, has stated that he believes the Amalgamated Clothing Workers of America is the only union in the country that has had a full-time boycott staff since 1949. The boycott staff actually was part of the union label department created less than a year earlier. The close relationship between boycott leadership and the union label department is not only organizational but also logical in that a boycott requires identification of union-made goods. And the activities of the union label department in the 1950s and 1960s gave its members valuable experience that was utilized in the Farah campaign. Howard D. Samuel, now president of the Industrial Union Department of the AFL-CIO, served as director of Amalgamated's union label department during this period. Del Mileski, who worked with Samuel for almost 30 years, served as regional representative and field director before becoming director himself.

Organizing at Farah began in 1969, but with a lack of significant progress until a combination of factors coalesced—some by sheer accident, some by poor Farah management decisions, some due to good union planning—resulting in victory for Amalgamated. In May, 1972, six workers were fired in one Farah plant, allegedly because they were active in the union. When the news spread, a large number of employees walked out, most of them Mexican-American women. Amalgamated called a boycott to

FIGURE 17.   Advertisement in *Collier's*, January 21, 1950, p. 9; ad sponsored by ACWA.

supplement the strike action and obtained the active aid of the AFL-CIO. As with the grape and lettuce boycott, the Federation approached this boycott cautiously.

The legal ground for the Farah boycott, however, was firmer than that of the UFW, even though the garment workers come under the full jurisdiction of federal labor laws. One section of the Landrum-Griffin Act, known as the "publicity proviso," directly affects the kind of boycott activity undertaken by the Amalgamated and later by ACTWU.[8] The difficulties with secondary boycotts recede when emphasis is placed upon consumers and moved further away from directly involving secondary neutral employers (e.g., retail stores). Union members not only have a right to refuse to purchase products from a firm with which there is a labor disagreement, but they also have the right to inform the public of the labor dispute. Consumers in turn have the right to join the boycott and refuse to buy certain products if they are sympathetic with labor. The reason such product boycotts are a form of secondary boycott is, of course, that other neutral firms usually *are* involved, even if only indirectly.

Although both were product boycotts, to the AFL-CIO there was a big difference between the UFWA's Schenley boycott and the UFWA's consumer boycott. The Schenley boycott was a boycott that asked union members to stop buying all Schenley products. Schenley products were, however, union-made, even though *some* ingredients in *some* Schenley products were not union-produced (i.e., grapes). The consumer boycott of table grapes informed consumers of the union grievance and asked consumers to stop purchasing nonunion products. Consumers were not asked to boycott grocery stores where the grapes were sold, many of which were union stores. To do so would have affected other (neutral) companies and possibly the jobs of other union members. The Schenley boycott was a direct form of illegal secondary boycott while the grape boycott targeted nonunion farmer-employers. No other company was directly involved.

In reality, the distinction between the two types of product boycotts is rather fine because, of course, consumers may refrain from entering a store in conjunction with the decision not to buy a particular product. Moreover, withdrawal of business from stores carrying the targeted product may be encouraged by local boycott sympathizers. Nevertheless, the central legal question remains what the union has asked consumers to do. A separate issue that is examined by the AFL-CIO is whether the purposes of the boycott are likely to be acceptable to the public. For example, secondary boycotts used to demand that unneeded workers be hired or prefabricated materials used, probably would elicit far less sympathy than boycotts intended to eliminate undesirable working conditions. Union leaders also recognize that boycotts can affect an involved union just as negatively as the targeted company. This, however, is true of most union weapons, simply because the fate of union members is inextricably entangled with that of the company—the difference being that when the company suffers, workers usually suffer, but when the company prospers, they often do not. The Farah case clearly demonstrated that when sales are down workers are laid off. In addition, labor officials are concerned that boycotts can have unfortunate long-term effects—some people won't buy products from a boycotted company even after the boycott is over.[9] Such an effect is rare with a strike action. AFL-CIO officials regard the best boycott as a simple boycott threat that in itself is sufficient to bring both sides to the bargaining table.

For all of these reasons, a "Federation-approved boycott strategy," though highly desirable, is not easy for unions to obtain. Legally, however, AFL-CIO approval is irrelevant. In the Amalgamated's case Federation approval was secondary to federal law. The necessary legal leg that the Amalgamated stood upon was the publicity proviso contained in the Landrum-Griffin Act. This proviso states that a union may truthfully advise the public that a primary employer with whom the union has a dispute is producing a certain product or products. The union may also inform the public regarding distributors of the products and request that the public show support by boycotting the product. The appeals may not, however, result in the stoppage of deliveries or pickups at the secondary site.[10] Although the original proviso stated that picketing was the one method that could *not* be used to inform consumers, certain picketing received judicial approval in a 1964 National Labor Relations Board case.[11] The court decided at that time that if the picketing is peaceable and advises only that a specific company's products should not be purchased, it is permissible.

Although objections to the publicity proviso have been widespread, the AFL-CIO eventually did grant its approval to the Farah boycott. It even took an active part by organizing, through state labor federations, "informational leafleting and picketing" across the country at stores where Farah products were sold. The message picketers carried was phrased, of course, to urge shoppers to boycott the product, not the stores.

Active and effective support also came from the International Confederation of Free Trade Unions; Farah's foreign affiliates and distribution subsidiaries located abroad made the firm vulnerable to international trade action.

In separate action, the Amalgamated filed several complaints against the Farah Company and its anti-union policies with the National Labor Relations Board. Some of these resulted in NLRB decisions against the company; others favored the company, however, and several more were reversed on appeal. The decision on the six workers fired in May, 1972 (the action that had initiated the strike), was issued later that same year by administrative law judge Walter H. Maloney, Jr., who severely criticized Farah for violating not only labor laws, but also the Ten Commandments. The media attention generated by the decision was distinctly valuable to Amalgamated and devastating to Farah. In October, 1974, *after* the boycott had ended, the NLRB reversed Judge Maloney's decision, finding that the six workers had not been discharged but had been asked to leave the plant when they refused to work. According to Farah's annual report for 1974: "The NLRB also decided to 'disavow and repudiate' the comments throughout the Maloney decision which intemperately characterized the Company; it found what he had said to be unwarranted and injudicious."[12]

Amalgamated broadened the scope of the campaign by introducing such social justice issues as racial discrimination, women's rights, and workers' dignity. A coalition seemed to come together as easily as it had for the UFW in the 1960s; endorsements were received from religious groups, liberal politicians, and city officials. Union leaders admit that the social justice issues that proved helpful during the Farah boycott were the result of fortunate circumstances rather than careful planning. The strike and boycott occurred so suddenly that Amalgamated had little time for strategic planning. Recalling the situation, Del Mileski stated:

> The Farah boycott really was our training ground for the Stevens campaign, although we had had numerous boycotts in the past. But the Farah campaign was really a learning experience. It was the first time, for example, that we actually hired clergy people on our own staff to organize different institutes. We had a women's coordinator, a student coordinator, a Jewish coordinator, a Catholic coordinator, a Protestant coordinator, a Black coordinator, and we really had a machine.[13]

The labor press of course helped spread the word, but this effort was vastly augmented by the mass media. As one author reports; "The media were drawn to the situation by scenes of Mexican-Americans fighting for human dignity in the desert towns of Texas and reports of bishops and political leaders joining in demonstrations and walking picket lines."[14]

The Farah struggle thus became more than an effort to get Farah to hire union members and to allow employees to join a union. The public, largely through the media, began to see it as a struggle for human rights and dignity as well as economic well-being. The 21-month campaign caused the Farah Company severe difficulties and ended in union recognition.

> In 1971, prior to the strike and boycott, Farah (one of the largest manufacturers of men's trousers) operated 10 plants in Texas and New Mexico with about 9,500 employees—mostly Mexican-Americans. By the time the battle ended in February 1974, five Farah plants had closed and more than 2,000 workers had lost their jobs.
>
> Company officials acknowledge that the effect of the boycott had been devastating. An impressive profit of $6 million in 1971 had turned into a [sic] $8.4 million loss in 1972; Farah stocks fell from $30 a share to $3 a share at one point.[15]

For Amalgamated, the Farah experience was valuable, but it also came at an extremely high price. The union spent at least $4 million on the campaign. Farah reopened only two of the four plants that had been closed during the boycott. Employment levels continue to remain far below pre-boycott numbers—meaning that many workers had to seek permanent employment elsewhere and there was a greatly diminished number of prospective members for the union.

THE UNITED LABOR COMMITTEE:
THE MISSOURI "RIGHT-TO-WORK" AMENDMENT

Partly because no such costs in jobs and union membership were incurred, people who worked on defeating a right-to-work referendum that appeared on Missouri ballots in November, 1978, enjoy talking about it. They remember that it was an uphill struggle, that the time element alone almost defeated them, that a number of talented people became involved, and that several successful strategies were employed. Many still express some amazement at the victory their efforts produced.

Whoever coined the phrase "right-to-work" and made it stick deserves great appreciation from all who are antilabor. Even union members use the term now in order to avoid confusion, but they do so unhappily and usually preface the term with "so-called" or surround it with quotation marks in order to indicate that the term has nothing to do with full employment or to any person's right to a job. Under U.S. laws, a union that is selected as a bargaining agent for a majority of workers must represent all workers in the bargaining unit. Benefits that accrue to workers as a result of union efforts are received by all workers. Members argue that those who do not join the union reap the benefits while contributing nothing and assuming no responsibilities. Nonmembers counter that no one should be forced to join a union. A "union shop" contract provides union security by requiring that any individual who is hired by an employer for a job must become a union member. Such a contract operates only when a majority of the workers have selected a particular union as a bargaining agent and the employer has agreed to a union security contract. Section 14-b of the Taft-Hartley Act allows states to opt for bans on the union shop and about 20 states, mostly in the South, have passed such legislation.

Missouri labor knew that right-to-work legislation was developing as a state issue and there had been low-key educational efforts aimed at union members in order to counteract when it became necessary. Many were caught by surprise, however, when the Missouri Freedom to Work Committee, following the rejection of a right-to-work law by the state legislature, circulated an initiative petition in mid-1978 in order to get the issue placed on the November ballot. Unions did rally in time to get educational leaflets printed. These were distributed to members along with instruction sheets explaining how most effectively to deal with petitioners. Such efforts were not enough to keep the referendum off the ballot, however, and at that point the crisis appeared so severe that many felt there was little use in doing anything.

For one thing, there was no organized effort to respond to the already well-organized opposition: besides the Missouri Freedom to Work Committee, there was another state group, the Missourians for Right to Work; both had the backing of the National Right-to-Work Committee, based in Washington. Another problem was that there were about 550,000 union members in the state of Missouri, representing only about 10 percent of the total state population. To make it worse, less than half of the union members were registered to vote. A registration drive was begun, but with the realization that labor's numbers were not enough to defeat the proposed amendment. A third problem lay in the widespread confusion that existed over the issue. One person who actively worked on the referendum said that it was determined that fewer than 17 percent of the people in the state could actually explain what a right-to-work law was. The results of a poll conducted by a state labor newspaper illustrated some of the confusion. One question asked: "Do you feel that Missouri should have a right-to-work law?" Of those who responded, 66 percent said yes, 13 percent said no, and 21 percent had no opinion. Another question (same poll) rephrased the question: "Should a worker be required to join the union in order to receive the benefits which the union gains from the company for its members?" Answers to this were 59 percent yes, and 41 percent no.[16]

At the outset of the campaign, there was very little money. Moreover, all these problems were intensified by lack of time. Labor did begin to mobilize efforts during the summer—first by responding to the petition drive, and then by organizing to get members registered. Labor also began to do some polling of Missouri residents in August; as explained below, the results of this poll proved to be extremely useful later in the campaign. However, in late September, with only about six weeks until election day, labor interests still had financial problems, plans but no coordinated campaign, and only a scattered form of statewide organization—and the polls showed that an overwhelming number of Missourians planned to vote for right-to-work.

But there were a few things that were going labor's way. The state labor organizations and locals had done well in their registration drives. Union members were not only registered, but the political interest of many had been stirred. The intensive August and September voter registration drive had yielded 100,000 new registrations[17]—not only in Kansas City and St. Louis, but in small towns and rural areas as well. And labor had many energetic volunteers. Requests for donations to support the effort were also extremely successful; they came not only from individuals and organizations within the state, but from unions nationwide. They were so successful, in fact, that a newspaper article published just before the election said that opponents of the amendment outspent the advocates three to one. Based on public records required by a new (August, 1978) campaign disclosure law, labor spent $400,000 on media advertising.[18] A somewhat lower figure was given by Ron Waggener, head of a public relations firm formed to help fight the amendment; Waggener stated that the total television cost was less than $125,000; radio, $70,000; and newspaper, $47,000.[19]

To pull the statewide efforts together, the state labor federation created an ad hoc umbrella committee called the United Labor Committee (ULC). At first it was composed primarily of AFL-CIO staff, staff members of various labor bodies, and union members; strong support came from the UAW, the United Mine Workers, and the Teamsters, and few labor organizations in the state remained uninvolved. The AFL-CIO sent staff people to Missouri to lend their support and talents. Gradually, the labor coalition developed a much broader support base, similar in many ways to that of the Amalgamated in Texas and the UFW in California. According to Waggener, Catholic bishops signed a statement against the amendment and held public seminars to explain that statement; black organizations worked hard to defeat the amendment, as did women's groups, consumer groups, civic organizations, and farmers belonging to the American Agricultural Movement. It was, in the words of an AFL-CIO report, "a classic example of organized labor and its natural allies working together for the defeat of anti-worker legislation."[20] The goals of the United Labor Committee were to inform and educate voters and to get them to turn out on election day.

Strategies went in several directions. Probably most noteworthy was the skillful way in which political marketing was used. Besides Ron Waggener, the ULC hired independent political consultants. A core group of union leaders, AFL-CIO staff members, and these professional consultants, headquartered in Jefferson City, Missouri, decided to target efforts in order to avoid the strongly pro-right-to-work people insofar as possible. Besides being cost- and time-effective, it was hoped that such targeting would also help avoid making the right-to-work proposition a big issue in areas where voters already supported its passage. In other words, ULC sought not only to get the right voters convinced and to the polls, but to suppress voter turnout in other areas.

The targeting system used had been developed for direct mail marketing; in essence it combined polling data with computerized demographic data that defined cluster groups—units of about 280 households that shared socioeconomic characteristics and reacted in similar ways to commercial marketing techniques. Demographic clusters were correlated with opinion and attitude data in order to identify profiles of "persuadable" voters. With "persuadables" thus identified and located, messages could be targeted to them. Areas that had few voters of this type were avoided as much as possible. Telephone, mail, face-to-face messages, and media were used to communicate with these voters.

One AFL-CIO staff member who arrived in Missouri late in September and stayed through election day reported that when he arrived virtually nothing had been accomplished. A slogan had been selected by ULC, but even that slogan, "'Right-to-work' is a rip-off," was soon replaced by one telling voters what to do: "Vote No on Amendment 23." Another union media specialist who devoted full-time effort to the campaign noted that on October 1 not one radio or television spot or newspaper advertisement had been produced. Not only did ULC proceed to produce its own spots, but they targeted them to the "persuadables" in terms of spokesperson, message content, medium, and audience.

There was, for example, a "Harry Truman" television spot (containing Truman quotes, delivered in a Truman-like style and widely popular); a "Grandpa" radio spot (the Missouri "voice of reason" who spoke like the Missourian he was and became a campaign symbol); a radio spot done by Slim Wilson (a country and western television personality in Missouri); and radio spots by Coretta King, Bayard Rustin, and Ben Hooks (to get out the black vote). Printed press releases were supplemented by ULC-produced voice actualities in which people's speeches, opinions, and news events could be taped and sent to radio stations in the hope that they would be accepted and used on news programs. An effort was made to come out regularly with timely newsworthy events; the biggest of these was an October 17 rally in Columbia at which Senator Edward Kennedy spoke against the amendment.

Newspaper advertisements were widely used and also varied to appeal to different target groups. Small towns used both the ULC ads and locally-created ads. One ad in Aurora, Missouri, for example, stated at the bottom: "This ad is paid for by the area wage earners."[21] The newspaper ads were used to make key points about the campaign and to educate and inform more thoroughly than could be done on radio and television spots.

Wisely, the ULC leaders did not concentrate efforts on St. Louis and Kansas City while neglecting other areas in the state, although to do so would have simplified their task in many ways. Besides targeted messages in newspapers, and on television and radio, a great deal of time was spent designing and writing leaflets explaining why those other than union members—the general public, farmers, students, and so on—would be disadvantaged should the amendment be passed.

On the Sunday before election day, the *Kansas City Star* published results of its latest poll on page one. It showed that a sizeable 58 percent of the voters were opposed to the amendment while only 30 percent favored it.[22] In the final vote the state rejected the constitutional amendment that would have made Missouri a "right-to-work" state by a margin of over 300,000 votes, or 60 percent of the total.

SUMMARY

All three efforts discussed above were chalked up as successes by organized labor. And in each case the successful outcome could not have been achieved in the absence of significant mass media involvement. The role of media was determined partly by unionists' strategic efforts. Chavez in particular was a master at creating situations of interest to news people: confrontation of workers in a field, a "spontaneous" march without a parade permit, a fast against strike violence. He provided visual interest, action, and color. But he also backed up actions and allegations with substantive evidence to prove his points and give reporters something to write about as well as an increased understanding of the situation from labor's point of view. In addition, Chavez gained the support of key public figures, including especially the Kennedy family. With this support came the media attention that such individuals typically attract and the media skills that they often have acquired.

In order to implement the consumer boycott of table grapes, more direct media support was sought by the United Farm Workers. Their success in this effort was mixed. Advocacy for the grape strike was provided mostly by the labor press, union members, and coalition activists. Their picketing, leafleting, and demonstrations attracted media attention, but frequently not media support.

On the other hand, labor and coalition support for the Farah boycott was extremely effective in terms of the media. The major difference between the two campaigns was that Amalgamated was able to broaden the scope of its messages. Rather than a labor-management struggle, the conflict in El Paso was cast in terms of more general human rights issues. The Amalgamated assembled a team representing and capable of generating support from a number of labor unions and other social groups. Working with the boycott staff, this team used the mass media as well as trade publications, professional journals, and ecumenical newspapers with unprecedented success. The union also received media support by filing claims with the NLRB against Farah. Judgments did not always receive publicity, nor was attention always favorable. However, when the NLRB ruled in favor of Amalgamated, the media coverage received fit in nicely with the broad scope of the campaign.

Faced with a different kind of challenge in Missouri, the United Labor Committee charted a somewhat different course with its media campaign. Here the carefully planned and targeted newspaper advertising, radio and television spots, and voice actualities had a dramatic effect upon the outcome of the referendum. The Committee's efforts demonstrated to labor that they could gain media access—at least during a political campaign— and that they could use what are typically considered the tools of the corporate world to their own advantage.

Clearly, not all activity that affected the outcome of these cases was planned by labor. Media support was often gained indirectly—because the union did something else right and the media recognized it. Sometimes the outcome was influenced because labor leaders took the time to educate and explain the situation to newspeople. Helpful coverage occasionally was the result of sheer happenstance or good fortune. But, however, it came about, its importance was noted, sometimes after the fact, by labor leaders. These three campaigns thus contributed significantly to recognition of the value of expanded utilization of mass media.

NOTES

[1] Matt S. Meier and Feliciano Rivera, *The Chicanos: A History of Mexican Americans* (New York: Hills and Wang, 1972), p. 205.

[2] Sam Kushner, *Long Road to Delano* (New York: International Publishers, 1975), p. 117.

[3] Harry W. Laidler, *Boycotts and the Labor Struggle: Economic and Legal Aspects* (New York: Russell and Russell, 1913, reprint ed., 1968), p. 27.

[4] Daniel D. Cook, "Boycott! Labor's Last Resort," *Industry Week*, June 28, 1976, p. 24.

[5] Laidler, *Boycotts and the Labor Struggle,* p. 56.

[6] American Federation of Labor—Congress of Industrial Organizations (AFL-CIO), *Proceedings of the Sixth Constitutional Convention,* 2 vols. (Washington, D.C.: AFL-CIO, 1965), 1:622–627.

[7] Kushner, *Long Road to Delano,* p. 156.

[8] *Labor-Management Reporting and Disclosure Act of 1959* (Landrum-Griffin Act), *Statutes at Large,* vol. 73, sec. 704 (a) (1959).

[9] Albert Zack, former AFL-CIO publicity director, quoted in Cook, "Boycott!," pp. 26–27.

[10] *Labor-Management Reporting and Disclosure Act of 1959.*

[11] *NLRB v. Fruit and Vegetable Packers and Warehousemen, Local 760,* 377 U.S. 58 (1964).

[12] *Farah Manufacturing Co., Inc. Annual Report,* 1974, p. 5.

[13] Del Mileski, Director, ACTWU Union Label Department, interview, New York City, June 3, 1982.

[14] Cook, "Boycott!," p. 26.

[15] George Sanderson, "The Product Boycott: Labour's Latest Tool," *The Labour Gazette,* July, 1974, p. 477.

[16] Mary Elkuss, Education Director, S.W. Regional Joint Board, Amalgamated Clothing and Textile Workers Union, "The Missouri Campaign to Defeat Right-to-Work," unpublished paper, 1978.

[17] AFL-CIO, *Proceedings of the Thirteenth Constitutional Convention,* 2 vols. (Washington, D.C.: AFL-CIO, 1979), 2:281.

[18] "Right-to-Work Foes Have Big Spending Lead," *St. Louis Post-Dispatch,* November 11, 1978, p. 4A.

[19] Ron Waggener, "Right-to-Work—The Missouri Decision," *AFL-CIO American Federationist,* January, 1979, p. 21.

[20] AFL-CIO, *Proceedings* (1979), 2:281.

[21] Elkuss, "The Missouri Campaign."

[22] "Poll Gives Big Edge to Right-To-Work Foes," *Kansas City Star,* November 5, 1978, p. 1.

CHAPTER VII

The ACTWU Campaign
Against J. P. Stevens Company

INTRODUCTION

In June of 1976 the Amalgamated Clothing and Textile Workers Union (ACTWU) was formed by the merger of the Amalgamated Clothing Workers of America (Amalgamated) and the Textile Workers Union of America (TWUA). The merger produced a union affiliated with the AFL-CIO with a membership of 500,000. Its members make all varieties of items of men's and boys' apparel, plus a variety of textile products (yard goods, carpets, knit goods, hosiery) made from all types of natural and synthetic textile fibers. In addition, some ACTWU members work in dyeing, laundry, and dry cleaning plants, and in retail stores.

The stated goals of the new union were to fight high unemployment, seek favorable legislation (especially in the areas of imports, minimum wages, and occupational safety and health), step up organizational efforts, and reduce anti-union sentiment in the south and southwestern United States. As an immediate move toward implementing these latter two objectives, ACT-WU declared a large-scale campaign against the J. P. Stevens Company, Inc., the second largest textile manufacturer in the United States and, at the time of the merger, a company with 45,800 nonunion workers on the payroll.[1] The 1976 declaration actually marked the beginning of a second phase of the Stevens campaign. The Textile Workers Union of America, supported by the AFL-CIO Industrial Union Department, had been struggling since 1963 to organize workers in Stevens' plants, located primarily in North Carolina and South Carolina. After the TWUA-Amalgamated merger the campaign was reorganized and revitalized with additional resources and commitment. ACTWU put new strategies into motion to supplement what up to that point had been rather standard organizing tactics. These consisted of an extensive legal campaign, a national consumer boycott, and what is now known as a corporate campaign, an attack on Stevens' business relationships.

The purpose of this chapter is to present an in-depth analysis of the entire campaign. Although the ACTWU-Stevens case is not perfectly representative of organized labor's use of the media to achieve political and economic objectives—indeed, the case has been referred to by some as "classic"—to the extent that there has been a trend toward greater sophistication and commitment to media utilization, the J. P. Stevens campaign by ACTWU probably was a watershed.

The background to this case bears directly on legal and practical matters pertaining to mass media access. In addition, the case provides an account of a labor organization that changed its traditional bargaining strategies and tactics in response to changes that had taken place within an American company. J. P. Stevens has grown into a giant, multinational corporation relatively unaffected by certification votes, strikes, and even the decisions of administrative law judges. These trends in institutional relationships have their counterparts in other segments of the social and political system; the interaction of capitalist expansion and media power is a major source of many emerging policy issues.

Data were collected primarily by means of personal interviews with a wide range of individuals from media, public relations firms, the AFL-CIO, and ACTWU. The objective of the relatively unstructured interviews was to elicit from each interviewee discussion of topics that he/she felt were relevant and important to the campaign and media-related goals during the campaign. These interviews were supplemented by examination of union documents, journalistic accounts of the campaign, related court and congressional hearings, and other relevant materials such as films and advertising.

THE AMALGAMATED TEXTILES AND CLOTHING WORKERS UNION

[W]e have much to learn from industry when it comes to uniting and consolidating their forces against the labor movement. The last two decades have been marked by the birth and growth of conglomerates which develop when giant corporations merge and acquire companies in a variety of industries. We have seen this in textiles. . . .

The net effect is that the unions in the chemical, oil, rubber, clothing and textile industries are beginning to have jurisdictions that overlap. This is a problem common to almost every union. Fortunately, the leaders of other unions that are similarly affected by conglomerate corporations recognize the problem and they, too, are willing to do something about it.

A plan must be devised by which the efforts, the resources and the energies of all such international unions are either coordinated, combined or consolidated to meet this challenge.[2]

With these considerations in mind, TWUA president Sol Stetin reported to delegates at the 1974 convention that the executive council had asked union officers to explore merger possibilities. Although some preliminary overtures were made to unions in other related industries, more serious discussions were initiated with the Amalgamated. The alliance between the two unions was longstanding and their relationship of interest had been close even before the industry mergers that were increasingly threatening to both.

The Amalgamated was the older of the two unions and the larger, adding 350,000 members to TWUA's 160,000. Both unions had solid experience in public relations and publications. The longstanding activities of Amalgamated's Union Label Department, especially those related to boycotts, were noted in Chapter VI. Although today the ILGWU is far better known for its union label campaign that ACTWU, it was Amalgamated's steadfast and successful promotion of its label that provided the initial inspiration to ILGWU to have a nationwide label designed.[3] When the ILGWU launched its label program in 1959, it was Amalgamated's example that was followed and with Amalgamated's assistance. Advertising had for years played a major role in Amalgamated's success, and not only in achieving public recognition of the label. During the 1950s, the label campaign was also viewed as a counterbalance to the antagonistic press that had, in some areas, influenced the public against unionism. Amalgamated's ads were frequently targeted to retailers; such efforts resulted in an award in 1964 from American Business Press, Inc., for the "Most Effective Use of Advertising in Merchandising Business Publications."[4]

The TWUA, however, was far less successful in promoting its own label, which had been used on piece goods since 1939. This is partially explained by the differences in the industries initially represented by the two unions. The textile industry is more diverse than the apparel industry. It includes fiber production, yarn production, and fabric production and finishing. Even when all fibers were natural—mostly cotton, wool, silk, and linen— the industry included diverse sectors. Since each of these fibers was produced and processed in different ways, corresponding segments of the industry developed relatively autonomously. In this century the explosion of chemically synthesized fibers that were used alone as well as blended with other fibers or yarns at some stage of production complicated the industry even further. The TWUA union label department, established in 1957, encountered major obstacles just in working out methods of attaching the label to the variety of items manufactured in the textile industry and in getting manufacturers to sign agreements. Furthermore, approximately 80 percent of the industry did not produce a finished product that reached consumer hands. Partly for these reasons, TWUA in the early 1970s pushed for the creation and adoption of *one* union label for all of organized labor.[5]

Unionization in the textile industry came more slowly than in the clothing industry for reasons that must be explained largely in terms of the evolving structure of the industry. U.S. textile mills, once small and simple installations, became more complex and specialized as the number of industrial jobs expanded. Fibers had to be spun into yarns of varying sizes, some of which were distributed as yarns to retail markets while others went to weavers and knitters to be processed into unfinished fabrics. The latter were usually sold to converters who were responsible for keeping up with demand and having the fabrics finished in ways that met the needs of other industries primarily, ultimate consumers secondarily. It was not at all uncommon for textiles to be sent back and forth across the country to mills that provided some additional processing and then sent off again.

People of many different nationalities were employed in mills that were scattered in almost every state. Natural fiber mills originally were located close to supply sources, whereas synthetic fiber mills were located close to adequate supplies of raw chemicals, power, and labor. Because, like the garment industry, textile production has traditionally been labor intensive, this last factor was especially important. While many U.S. mills had originally located in the northeastern part of the United States, movement to the south began to occur after World War II because of the availability of labor at low wages.

It was not until the CIO was formed that textile workers were able to get the support they needed to form a strong union. In 1937 the Textile Workers Organizing Committee (TWOC) was formed within the CIO; Sidney Hillman, Amalgamated's president, chaired the committee. The Amalgamated had long recognized the need for a strong textile union, not only because of the benefits it would bring to the people in the textile industry and to labor in general, but also because of the related nature of the textile and apparel industries. A fund of $1,000,000, half contributed by the Amalgamated, was raised to launch an organizing campaign. Organization was carried on simultaneously in all branches of the industry in all major production areas. In May, 1939, leaders felt that an effective foundation for a permanent organization had been established, and the locals joined to form the Textile Workers' Union of America, affiliated with the CIO.

The Union grew rapidly in spite of vigorous anti-union opposition. Defense production during World War II helped; mills operated 24 hours a day. Membership increased, and collective bargaining methods were established and refined. At the same time, new problems were emerging. In addition to organizational maintenance, advocacy of bread and butter concerns, and membership recruitment, union leaders had to give increasing attention to such problems as recurring depression (to which this industry is especially vulnerable), automation, import competition, occupational safety and health issues, and antilabor sentiments in the southeastern states. Burlington Industries, expanding through vertical and horizontal integration and conglomeration, established a pattern that other textile companies emulated. There are now fewer but much larger firms, many of which process fiber to finished fabric.

In addition, the industry has experienced considerable product diversification. Burlington, which remains the largest U.S. textile manufacturer, now has divisions that produce all kinds of natural and synthetic fibers, spun and textured yarns, woven and knitted fabrics, and finished and unfinished fabrics. Most of what is produced in this industry continues to be distributed to apparel manufacturers, producers of home furnishings, government, and other industrial sectors rather than directly to consumers.

A publicity department was included in TWUA's initial organization. This department published a newspaper, *Textile Labor,* made early use (1941) of the radio for organizing, and began advertising (1943) in conjunction with its collective bargaining efforts. Even so, it did not bring to the merger any media experience comparable to the Amalgamated's experience in the successful Farah campaign and boycott, which had ended just two years before the merger. As Sol Stetin admitted at TWUA's nineteenth—and last—convention, "a consumer boycott by a united, single union of textile and clothing workers will evidently have far greater impact and effectiveness than one conducted by our union alone."[6]

In June, 1976, the merger was accomplished. Amalgamated's president, Murray H. Finley, was named president and the TWUA president Sol Stetin was named senior executive vice president of the new union. The first ACTWU convention was held in California in 1978.

THE J. P. STEVENS CAMPAIGN

With the merger, Amalgamated agreed to throw the weight of its resources and boycott expertise into the battle to organize textile giant J. P. Stevens, a battle that TWUA had been waging for 13 years. Stevens is a broadly diversified international conglomerate engaged in textile production in Canada, Mexico, Great Britain, France, and New Zealand, as well as the United States. Headquartered in New York, the firm produces woven, nonwoven, and knitted fabrics; yarns; hosiery; and other end products for apparel, home, and industry.

Apparel fabrics, which represented approximately 50 percent of the company's business in 1976, are sold primarily to converters, garment manufacturers, and retailers. Home furnishings fabrics, including sheets, towels, tablecloths, draperies, bedspreads, upholstery fabrics, and carpeting, represented about 33 percent of sales; these are sold primarily to government, industry and retailers. Industrial products manufactured by Stevens include insect screening, automobile accessories, and filtration products. In addition, Stevens operates in the areas of commercial printing, chemicals and plastics, and aircraft sales and maintenance. In 1976, when the boycott against the company was announced, Stevens realized net sales at a record level of $1,421,386,000, an increase of 27 percent over 1975.[7]

In 1976 Stevens employed approximately 45,800 persons[8] in 85 manufacturing plants in the United States; 36 plants were in South Carolina, 27 in North Carolina, 8 in Georgia, 6 in Virginia, and the remaining 8 were located in Alabama, California, Connecticut, Florida, Massachusetts, and Tennessee.[9]

Stevens had actively and openly fought TWUA's organizing efforts. When the newly formed ACTWU announced its consumer boycott, the company summarized its position in its annual report for 1976:

> The objectives of the boycott are to inhibit our sales, to disrupt our business operations, and to interfere with our customer relations to obtain our acceptance of a collective bargaining agreement dictated by the Union. The Company regards the boycott as improper and unjustified, and we will use every lawful means available to us to protect our rights and those of our employees. With the support which we believe we can expect from our employees, our customers, and our shareowners, we have no doubt about the ultimate outcome.[10]

The textile union's struggle with J. P. Stevens is popularly considered to have begun in 1976, with the merger and the announcement of the boycott, and to have ended when a settlement was reached in October, 1980. In actuality, however, the ACTWU campaign against Stevens had not one, but four major interrelated components and two of these began long before the merger. The four components were organizing, litigation, the consumer product boycott, and the corporate campaign. Concentrated organizing efforts began, as stated above, in 1963. Litigation against Stevens had begun even before that; Stevens' alleged unfair labor practices were one reason the company had been targeted for its organizing efforts.

Organizing and litigation gained impetus in 1974 when TWUA won an important certification election in Roanoke Rapids, North Carolina, but it was not until after the 1976 merger that the multifaceted nature of the Stevens campaign really emerged and gathered momentum. Although the campaign often is referred to simply as the "J. P. Stevens boycott," the boycott was only one segment of the overall plan.

Each of the four major components of ACTWU's campaign against J. P. Stevens is described in the sections that follow. Special attention is given to the way media utilization entered into each component, for it was a crucial determinant of the outcome.

Organizing the Textile Mills

The struggle of the Textile Workers to organize the approximately 800,000 unorganized textile workers in the United States and Canada gained some support when, in December, 1962, the AFL-CIO Industrial Union Department authorized a "'comprehensive, cooperative, coordinated organizing drive' aimed at gaining social and economic justice for the millions of Americans still denied the benefits and protection of trade unionism."[11] To the TWUA, this meant additional funds and organizers, both sorely needed, as well as the incentives provided simply by the verbal support of the united labor. TWUA leaders decided to target Stevens, and particularly Stevens' plants located in North and South Carolina, as these states had been designated by the Industrial Union Department as being a specific target area.

In 1963 the total number of persons employed by Stevens was approximately 35,000[12] and the company was rapidly expanding. In that year Stevens acquired a menswear converting firm, A. and M. Karagheusian (a leading carpet manufacturer with three plants in North Carolina and Georgia), and a yarn manufacturing plant in North Carolina. The company also was building a new workclothing fabric plant in South Carolina. The J. P. Stevens annual report for 1963 asserted, in addition, the following indications of corporate health and vitality: the company had been commended by several state legislatures, among them North Carolina and South Carolina, for contributions the company had made to progress of their states; the company maintained excellent employee relationships and a good safety record; employee wage increases had been announced during the year that were "in line with the pattern generally established in the industry."[13]

The pattern generally established in the industry is, however, a pattern that has resulted in textile workers being among the lowest paid industrial workers in the United States. Average weekly earnings in the U.S. textile mill products category consistently have been lower than the average weekly wages paid to U.S. production or nonsupervisory workers. In 1963 production workers in all industries had an average weekly income of $88.46; textile mill production workers earned a weekly average of $69.43.[14]

The TWUA was not only concerned about the low wages that existed in the southern textile industry, however. Fringe benefits also were poor— pensions were small and vacations were one week a year regardless of the length of employment. Many employees worked a six-day week. Levels of cotton dust in factories were associated with increasing frequency of byssinosis or "brown lung," and accidents were frequent. Stevens itself had been repeatedly accused and several time convicted of racial discrimination in employment practices. No J. P. Stevens plants were union plants.

In fact, throughout the textile industry in the southeastern United States, less than 10 percent of the industry was organized. In 1956 management at a Deering-Millikin textile mill located in Darlington, South Carolina, declared the plant would be closed if workers won a union representation election. After the TWUA-affiliated workers achieved an election victory, the plant was closed as threatened.[15] This tactic was repeated by Stevens in its Statesboro, Georgia plant. Capital investment in the textile industry was so small that it usually was possible to move equipment and work associated with specific plants, and the industry as a whole was able to relocate fairly easily—from the northeastern United States to the south where taxes and the cost of land and labor were low. When a mill closes in a small, isolated southern town, as did the Millikin plant at Darlington, workers have particular difficulty finding other jobs. Under these circumstances threats of closure—and a record of enforcing such threats—effectively discourage organizing.

In 1963, Stevens owned fewer mills, a total of 65, approximately 40 of which were located in the Carolinas. Prior to this time, TWUA's typical organizing procedure had been to concentrate efforts on one factory. Strategy changed for the Stevens campaign, however, when TWUA decided to try to organize 25 mills concurrently.

Stevens made no secret of its strong anti-union position. Shortly after the campaign was begun, a notice appeared on company bulletin boards and was mailed to all employees stating the company's "positive intention to oppose this union and by proper means to prevent it from coming in here."[16]

Between 1963 and 1976, the union experienced one election defeat after another in Stevens plants. Out of 12 separate elections held during that time, all NLRB-supervised and in Stevens facilities, only one victory was achieved. This occurred during August, 1974 in the seven J. P. Stevens plants in Roanoke Rapids, North Carolina. Because the vote was close—1,685 to 1,448—and the workers covered by the election represented only about 10 percent of total Stevens workers, the union's victory was limited.

The election at Roanoke Rapids did produce some good publicity for the union. Achievement of even a slim victory after so many years of hard work was viewed as an accomplishment. Reporters from major U.S. newspapers and television crews appeared in Roanoke Rapids. Gloria Steinem arrived to do a televised program on a woman who worked in one of the mills. Such publicity represented a change from the stories that often appeared in the dailies of southern mill towns that berated the "outside agitators" who had descended on the locality. But it did not alter the fact that the TWUA had to rely heavily on essentially defensive arguments about the company's fear-inducing intimidation tactics. A negotiated contract agreement seemed out of the question as relations between the principals deteriorated; and, to add to the general discouragement, the union suffered another election loss in Wallace, North Carolina in February, 1975.[17]

Although results of bargaining elections indicate that the union was overwhelmingly defeated in its 13-year-old war, the union was chalking up some victories in legal battles that ultimately proved to be vitally important. The outcome of the legal encounters was a series of judgments showing that J. P. Stevens regularly engaged in unfair labor practices. Because the cases were slowly litigated and often appealed, the significance of these victories was not immediately apparent. In fact, to many involved in the union campaign, specific decisions against the company appeared inconsequential and thus demonstrated the ineffectiveness of labor laws. What had begun in 1963 as an organizing campaign, conventional except for the number of plants targeted, expanded quickly to include the unrelenting and crucial court battles during the 1970s. By 1976, the legal strategy had gained visibility both because of the merger and because of a cumulative record that dramatically supported union charges made against J. P. Stevens.

The Legal Strategy

The National Labor Relations Act of 1935 was criticized in the 1940s and 1950s by those who perceived that it tipped the balance of labor-management relations too heavily in the direction of labor. The Taft-Hartley Act (1947) and the Landrum-Griffin Act (1959) were passed as an attempt to correct this alleged imbalance. Labor law reform bills were introduced into Congress in 1977 and subsequently were defeated; there have, therefore, been no reforms in labor-management legislation since 1959, and no reforms aimed at curbing management abuses since the National Labor Relations Act was passed. Although the NLRA does give the NLRB regulatory power,[18] NLRB practice has been to make decisions on a case-by-case basis. This practice results in long procedural delays in establishing policy. One object of the 1977 labor reform legislation was to equalize the results of such procedural delays, which in administrative law typically benefit the defendant.

In order to initiate NLRB action, charges of an unfair labor practice must be filed with a regional NLRB office. The NLRB sends a board agent, either a field agent or an attorney, out to investigate the charges. Based on this investigation, which includes versions of facts from both sides and sworn statements from witnesses, the NLRB regional director or general counsel determines whether or not a *prima facie* case exists. If evidence suggests that a violation of the act has occurred, a complaint is issued against the company involved. This is followed by a hearing before an administrative law judge, followed by submission of briefs, after which a decision is made by the judge. This decision may be appealed to the NLRB, which can affirm, override, or modify the judge's decision. These procedures consume a good deal of time, but even then the process is incomplete because NLRB decisions are not self-enforcing. Enforcement comes by order of the court of appeals. Subsequent to an NLRB decision

> someone, either the respondent will file a petition for review, or the National Labor Relations Board will file a petition for enforcement in the circuit court of appeals, and then the case is briefed to the court of appeals, and argued to the court of appeals, and then there is approximately another year of delay. This process takes approximately 2—if it is fast—2 years to 30 months. It can take 3 years.[19]

Recent testimony given to a House subcommittee indicated in fact that currently three years is the *average* length of time spent just from the filing of an unfair practice charge to the court enforcement of a remedy.[20] Decisions by the circuit court of appeals may, of course, be appealed to the Supreme Court. Moreover, additional delays may be caused by referrals back to bodies that have previously considered the case for reconsideration.

The legal tactics initially employed by TWUA were those common in any organizing campaign. It is the responsibility of union organizers to be in constant contact with workers. An organizer hearing of an incident that is a potential unfair labor practice follows up with an investigation. Sometimes the organizer files charges with the regional NLRB office, sometimes the organizer aids workers in filing charges.

Due to the extensive efforts the union was investing in the Stevens campaign, and in anticipation of possibly intense legal action, the TWUA (and later the ACTWU) legal department closely monitored the filing of charges against Stevens. Their clearing-house role in this regard kept the union lawyers informed of patterns of alleged violations, and, consequently, of some aspects of company strategy. Such patterns, when perceived, were reported to the NLRB so that each regional office was aware of violations of similar kinds.

The 1976 ACWA-TWUA merger resulted in a strengthened legal department under the direction of general counsel Arthur M. Goldberg, assisted by deputy general counsel Joel R. Ax, both of whom had been with Amalgamated. Probably the best summary of the legal cases against J. P. Stevens up to 1977 is provided by the ACTWU statement on the labor reform act before the Senate Subcommittee on Human Resources. To support testimony urging passage of the bill, the union submitted seven and a half pounds of material that comprised the record of Stevens' NLRB cases between 1959 and September, 1976.[21] Union officers also submitted a chart that summarized the litigation in tabular form. This chart lists Stevens cases as Stevens I (1965) through Stevens XX (1977), with each "case" representing multiple violations. One case might, for example, include 20 complaints, involving perhaps 50 violations of the labor act.[22]

Fifteen of the 20 Stevens cases were decided by the NLRB at the time of the hearings, all with findings of guilty. Eleven of the 15 were brought by the NLRB before the court of appeals in an effort to enforce its orders. The court of appeals upheld the NLRB's conviction of Stevens in 9 of these 11. Stevens appealed three of the cases to the Supreme Court and was denied on each occasion. [23] This was the record that earned for Stevens the reputation of being the nation's number one labor law violator.

The most frequent cause of complaints to the NLRB in these cases was that workers had been discriminated against, intimidated, and terminated from their jobs because they were union supporters. When the NLRB decides that a company has engaged in illegal terminations, it is allowed to impose only two penalties: the company can be ordered to rehire the employees and to reimburse them for the wages they would have earned had they not been fired. If a worker has found employment elsewhere (and this is virtually a necessity given the duration of the procedures), the earnings made on the other job during this period are deducted from the amount the company must pay. The effect of the penalties is further mitigated by the fact that such wage reimbursements are tax deductible as a legitimate business expense.

Worker intimidation and firing, although the most common charges, were not the only charges of which Stevens was found guilty in Stevens I through XX. Others included threatening plant closings, economic reprisals, firing workers who testified before the NLRB, refusing to bargain in good faith, and electronic spying on organizers.[24]

To add to this record, the NLRB filed a number of contempt citations against Stevens for violating court decrees. In 1971, eight years after the Stevens campaign had been launched by TWUA, the consistent pattern of violations by Stevens caused one judge to note that "neither the passage of time nor the admonishments of judicial tribunals have caused the Company to alter its now all too familiar perseverance of full-scale war against unionization.[25] And, in August, 1977, in finding J. P. Stevens guilty of contempt, the court described the company as the "most notorious recidivist" in the field of labor law;[26] this phrase, as well as "the nation's number one labor law violator," were strongly emphasized in labor publicity.

Continuing violations by Stevens, even when the company was facing contempt charges, resulted in some extraordinary remedies. Monetary fines against the company were not that severe. Stevens' fines totalled $1.3 million by 1977. It is probably true that this amount, even when legal costs are added, still represents a far lower financial outlay by the company than the costs of higher wages and fringe benefits that organized workers would demand. NLRB remedies got increasingly tough, however, often because of the diligent and persistent efforts of the ACTWU legal department. Administrative law judge Joel A. Harmatz gave the following opinion of ACTWU's legal efforts:

> The ability of the administrative-judicial system to withstand the Stevens assault upon its integrity is owing, in large measure, to the Union's vigilance, and unrelenting will to commit its legal resources to the fray. Were it to succumb, the exploits of J. P. Stevens would serve as an historic touchstone for those who would defy the law by subjecting employee organization to the type of endurance struggle experienced here.[27]

After the court of appeals found Stevens guilty of contempt in the fall of 1977, the court said that any future violations would result in compliance fines of $100,000 for each occurrence and $5,000 per day for each day the violations continued. The court order also required that the company allow union organizers access to all the parking lots, canteens, and nonwork areas of each plant in the Carolinas.[28] Union organizers were allowed this plant access for the first time in May, 1978, giving them an advantage that leaders feel greatly helped their organizing efforts.

In December, 1977, the ACTWU legal department persuaded the NLRB general counsel to combine a number of unfair labor practice charges and complaints from different regional areas into one major complaint and seek a nationwide injunction in federal court against Stevens. This injunction would bar Stevens from using illegal tactics in any of its plants. The ACTWU legal staff felt that this injunction would have been a major legal achievement. Even injunctions at specific plants are seldom utilized by the NLRB, and this request for a nationwide injunction against a company appears to have been unprecedented.[29] The request, however, was later withdrawn by the NLRB under terms of a settlement worked out between the Board and Stevens.

In January, 1978, the Fifth Circuit Court of Appeals threatened Stevens not only with heavy fines stipulated earlier by the Second Circuit Court, but also stated that company representatives would be jailed unless they complied with court orders. In the same month administrative law judge Bernard Ries found Stevens guilty of bargaining in bad faith in Roanoke Rapids. According to ACTWU counsel Joel Ax, the union attached a great deal of importance to this trial, the first major Stevens trial after the union merger. Ax thought, at the trial's onset, that the bad faith bargaining charge could be proven but was concerned about the issuance of a meaningful remedy. He was not disappointed, however; the remedy again was precedent-setting. Judge Ries, after stating that "The record as a whole indicates that [Stevens] approached these negotiations with all the tractability and open-mindedness of Sherman at the outskirts of Atlanta,"[30] directed the company to pay all costs incurred by the union in its negotiation efforts and in NLRB hearings. He also ordered the company to pay costs incurred by the NLRB on the case.

In August, 1979, the NLRB ordered Stevens to reimburse ACTWU for costs of organizing in Wallace, North Carolina, and to bargain with the union even though the union had *lost* the election in Wallace. In January, 1980, the Board ordered Stevens to pay court costs of the NLRB and of ACTWU in an unfair labor practices case involving the company's West Boyleston, Alabama plant. And for the second time in history Stevens was ordered to pay the union's organizing costs. That same month, the Fourth Circuit Court upheld an NLRB order that Stevens cease and desist from engaging in unfair labor practices on a nationwide basis; also affirmed was the court order that the company must mail a copy of the cease and desist order to all its 45,000 workers. This decision, as well as the court order for union access, was appealed to the Supreme Court. The Court refused, however, to stay the ruling.

Other than appealing these decisions and issuing brief statements to the press after decisions had been handed down, Stevens did little to support its case during these legal battles. The firm turned down an invitation to testify before the Labor-Management Relations Subcommittee of the House of Representatives when the committee held one day of hearings in Roanoke Rapids. It did, however, gain access to motel rooms of the visiting legislators and press in order to leave a company packet. And the firm did issue a press release and place several advertisements in southeastern newspapers explaining its side of a union surveillance case that later was settled out of court.[31]

The large number of court cases resulted in the establishment by the NLRB of an entire Stevens task force that did nothing but work on the pending Stevens cases. On the other side, in order to decrease the number of allegations against them, and on the advice of a newly retained law firm, Stevens assigned an attorney to each group of plants. When a worker asked a supervisor a question about the union, supervisors were instructed to write the question down and take it to the personnel office. The personnel supervisor had to call the lawyer, get the answer to the question, and take it back to the supervisor who read it to the worker.

By 1980, the NLRB had found Stevens guilty in 22 out of 23 separate cases. The steady legal campaign had the effects of entangling Stevens in a web restricting its activities, producing certain extraordinary remedies, and, finally, generating news stories that the media found useable and the union found welcome. As with the entire legal strategy, the overall effect of publicity in combination with the broadening scope of the cases benefited the union substantially. This positive cumulative effect was not just a consequence of the number of cases won by ACTWU, but also the length of time involved. Much attention was placed on the company's repeated and protracted violations of the labor act—first by ACTWU's legal department and then by the press.

Even when a single case is won in court, that decision alone may influence the type of media coverage received. ACTWU lawyers noted, for example, that it is not unusual to find evidence of an anti-union press bias at the outset of an NLRB proceeding; this is especially true in the largely rural, nonindustrial, polically conservative areas where textile mills are located. Typically, in this situation, there were headlines about the trial opening accompanied by a story that included numerous quotes from company spokespersons claiming innocence of the charges. Readers might have found, buried in the text, a short quote from a union spokesperson. A year or so later, however, when a legal decision had been handed down that favored the union, the news story, occupying approximately the same space on the same page of the same newspaper, often written by the same reporter, would have a different focus. This time the headlines would proclaim the union victory, the story would have numerous quotes from union officials and one might see, at the bottom, a short quote from a company spokesperson.

Victory in the courtrooms confers credibility. And when one party's victories occur repeatedly the credibility of that side grows. (Stevens, of course, was subject to the converse of this proposition.) The ACTWU was also aided by the similarity of the cases. Newspeople and the public alike became reasonably well acquainted with the issues simply because of their repetitiveness. And because the overall issue was ongoing for so long, media people rarely chose to give a final decision inconspicuous converage on the basis that the public "had forgotten" or was "no longer interested."

In terms of the union's relationship with the media, the duration of the battle was also a positive element. Although it is doubtful that any union would purposely choose to negotiate for six years simply in order to give lawyers more than an adequate opportunity to educate the press about the issues, ACTWU did have this time. It was used continually to better press relations, especially with the southern dailies. Reporters who work for small southern newspapers are not labor reporters. They often lack labor expertise. In the words of Joel Ax: "Labor is a speciality just as cooking is a specialty and just as cooking has a language of its own, so labor relations and labor law have a language of their own. If I found someone who knows absolutely nothing about cooking and asked that person to write about making a souffle, I could not really expect him or her to do an accurate first-rate job. That person doesn't know the language and could not write well about the subject unless real effort was put forth."[32]

Ax found, though, a number of people willing to put forth that effort. One such person in Roanoke Rapids was "just a reporter, but he was willing to spend time and willing to talk with us and willing to learn. He started to learn the language and reported things accurately. If you read his reports, they express a certain understanding of what these cases are about and what the impact of these cases really is to the people and to the campaign."[33]

Other media people, initially openly hostile to the union and its organizers, began to realize, as the years passed, that a number of people in their communities were union members or supporters and that their point of view should be represented. In Roanoke Rapids, virtually the whole town reacted to the upheaval that occurred in the community and few people did not take a side. Editors of daily newspapers in mill towns often found themselves in difficult positions. They found that one way to reduce their vulnerability was to run wire service stories rather than to write their own news stories.

The lengthy negotiations allowed people nationwide to develop the kind of understanding of the issues for which ACTWU hoped. The public was interested not only because of ACTWU's courtroom maneuverings and the fact that the case did not disappear quickly, but also because the story became so broad in scope. More was at stake than wages and benefits. Questions that long had been taken for granted by most of the American public were surfacing—questions regarding a worker's right to join a union and a union's right to exist. Stevens anti-union stance attracted audiences on both sides of the labor-management fence. Ed McConville, in a 1976 article in *The Nation* expressed his opinions:

> It is commonly supposed that the American labor movement has every-where become just another stodgy sector of the Establishment. Wilfred Sheed gave expression to this conventional wisdom in 1973 when he wrote in the *Atlantic Monthly* that "in 1935, after much bloody skirmishing with the management, the Wagner Act was passed, defining the right to organize, strike, and close a shop, all the prerogatives that now seem prehistoric."
>
> In sober fact, unions hold none of these historic prerogatives in the South. Strikes there are virtually futile since judges routinely hand down anti-picket-ing injunctions and local and state police escort strikebreakers safely into and out of struck plants. Under "right to work" laws authorized by the Taft-Hartley Act in 1947, the closed shop is illegal in all but one Southern state. As for the Wagner Act's forty-year-old guarantee of workers' "right-to-orga-nize"—"It ain't worth the paper it's printed on south of the Mason-Dixon," snapped an old union organizer recently. He was perhaps trying a little too hard to be vivid, but he is essentially right.[34]

A very different view came from a cover story in *Clothes* magazine, a trade publication:

> [T]he government already ha[s] taken much of the wind out of organized labor's sails—thanks to demands by organized labor for child labor laws and minimum wage laws and social security and unemployment compensation and health insurance for the needy and the aged and occupational safety regulations.
>
> In other words, the ACTWU—like the rest of organized labor—has very little to offer. . . . [The methods used by J. P. Stevens] must be seen in the light of the continual onslaught experienced by the company since 1963 and the fact that the union has seized upon every possible infraction—probably to the point of inciting some of them.[35]

Union officials believe breadth of the issues caused them the most trouble in their legal campaign/media relationship. As one example of a situation in which misinterpretations were made by media personnel, Joel Ax cited news stories that appeared at the time the NLRB began proceedings for the issu-ance of the national injunction against Stevens. Trouble started when the NLRB and Stevens worked out a settlement under which the NLRB would drop its injunction motion and Stevens would rehire a number of workers who allegedly had been discharged illegally. The NLRB's position was that "any injunction order granted by the court would have provided virtually the same affirmative relief as was obtained through the settlement agreement but only after substantial delay attributable to prolonged litigation.[36] The only active parties to the injunction were the Board and Stevens, even though ACTWU had issued the original complaint, so the decision was up to the Board. They decided to settle.

On April 29, 1978, the *New York Times,* in a story headlined "J. P. Stevens Settles with Labor Board in Antiunion Acts," stated that "Both Stevens and the union involved, the Amalgamated Clothing and Textile Workers, regard the settlement as a victory."[37] A similar story appeared in the *Wall Street Journal* on May 1, this one with the headline "NLRB Cancels Bid for Injunction Against Stevens; Textile Firm Agrees to Take Action Required; Right to Join Unions Involved." This article included the following statement: "A union official said Friday that union leaders consider the settlement a 'win,' but are disappointed that the agreement doesn't have the force of a court decree."[38]

ACTWU's reactions both to the settlement itself and to media coverage of the situation were negative. Later that same month the union officially— by means of press statements and a letter to NLRB chairman John Fanning—found the settlement "unacceptable." To some extent this position was a tactical response to the fact that, since news of the settlement had been released, the union had received numerous congratulatory messages from persons who interpreted the news stories to mean the entire Stevens-ACTWU campaign had been settled. In reality, the company had simply been put under a court restraint to cease labor violations or face a reopening of the case. However, when media stories came out reporting union displeasure with the settlement (the headline that appeared in the trade publication *Women's Wear Daily* was "NLRB, Stevens in Pact; Union Objects"),[39] a good portion of the attentive public probably was even more confused.

Although this situation was cited by ACTWU officials as an example of misinterpretations made by media personnel, it was an exceptionally complicated and confusing story. The main point is that the ACTWU, presumably like a wide range of institutions and interests, was limited in the extent to which it could shape media coverage. And the public relations department's efforts along these lines were frustrated partly by the tactics developed by the union's own legal department.

Labor lawyer Joel Ax also expressed some disappointment that the media throughout the campaign placed minimal emphasis on the ways in which the legal victories achieved by ACTWU affected people.

There didn't seem to be a real effort made to analyze the impact of these decisions on the people who were involved. There are a lot of good stories about the mill workers and the media did a good job on those. But some major legal decision would come down which would in reality have tremendous impact on the people working in that shop. If it didn't mean someone was being reinstated with backpay, they didn't register any of these cases as having an impact on people.[40]

Ax did credit legal periodicals and law journals that published a variety of articles discussing the legal implications of the precedent-setting remedies and relief for workers that had been achieved. Because many of these were legal "firsts," they have a continuing potential impact that goes far beyond the Stevens situation.

ACTWU officials outside the legal department felt that the legal strategy was the segment of the Stevens campaign that was least appreciated by the public. This public relations problem may derive from the fact that the legal strategy did not appear to be part of the "campaign." Yet this somewhat isolated and obscure role of the legal strategy also helps explain a fundamental benefit that it yielded. ACTWU lawyers understandably may feel somewhat frustrated that the press gave credit for much of their effort not to them, but to the NLRB. But, there can be little doubt that NLRB involvement added legitimacy to the union's campaign. The pro-union decisions made by the courts and the NLRB added the authority of these "neutral" government institutions to the union's endeavors.

The Boycott Strategy

The Stevens boycott was undertaken because the intransigent stance of the company had been unaffected by more ordinary collective action. ACTWU also felt that Stevens' policies had moved the controversy away from a pure labor-management dispute and into the broader arena of social justice. The boycott thus was aimed at Stevens' generally antisocial activities as well as activities—for example, intimidation and refusal to bargain—that were more clearly in the domain of labor relations.

A number of parallels can be drawn between the Farah case and the Stevens case. But there are also some fundamental differences. In the words of one ACTWU staff member, comparing Farah to Stevens is like comparing a firecracker to a stick of dynamite.

Stevens is a much larger and wealthier company than Farah. ACTWU officials estimated at the outset that costs would total at least two to three times the costs for Farah. They also expected AFL-CIO support in this financial expenditure. The long history of the organizing campaign gave the union a thorough knowledge of its opponent, and the record of NLRA violations upheld on appeals gave the union solid legal and judicial encouragement. The fact that Stevens sells approximately two-thirds of its products not to ultimate consumers but to industry as raw material for finished goods could be interpreted two ways. On the negative side, a consumer boycott, even if extremely successful, could not possibly have much economic impact on the company. On the positive side, however, continued sales of Stevens products to industry meant continued need for mill workers. The union was hopeful that the large numbers of employee discharges that occurred at Farah would not occur at Stevens.[41]

An additional source of difficulty for ACTWU related to the Stevens product. A boycotted product needs to be identifiable, but not indispensable. Of the 34 percent of Stevens products that reached consumers, few carried a J. P. Stevens label; identification was possible, but difficult. Stevens' sheets and pillowcases carry the brand names Utica, Tastemaker, Yves St. Laurent, Beauticale, and Peanuts. Other consumer products are Contender, Gulistan, and Tastemaker carpets, Spirit and Finesse hosiery, and a variety of textiles designed and/or licensed by well-known designers and television personalities. It would be much more difficult to get consumers to boycott all these than simply to boycott Farah pants. These products were also more broadly distributed in Europe and Asia than Farah products had been.

The boycott plan for Stevens was laid out even before the June, 1976, merger and boycott announcement. Rather than a boycott in reaction to a specific development or situation, ACTWU had time to develop a plan and even a schedule of activities. Regional staff members around the country immediately began surveys of retail stores in order to provide information about sales patterns of Stevens products and retailers' promotional practices. Plans were made for a certain number of additional staff people to be hired and trained by certain dates. Special coordinators were employed as in the Farah boycott, but this time they were hired before the boycott. As before, there was a women's coordinator, a students' coordinator, and coordinators of national religious constituencies. In addition to these national coordinators, city coordinators were located in approximately 27 major urban areas throughout the country. The number of national boycott staff members varied, starting small and peaking in 1978 at about 35 people. In localities where ACTWU had no field staff, the AFL-CIO's community services and union label departments used their resources to extend ACTWU's efforts. ACTWU had the AFL-CIO's sanction and union staff members credit the Federation for excellent support and cooperation given throughout the Stevens campaign.

Del Mileski, former director of ACTWU's union label department, emphasized the importance of the communication network that was established through the specialists. It was the specialists who knew how to communicate with people in their areas and who knew how to increase their numbers, or their active support, etc. Mileski stated:

> I really couldn't tell Father Sullivan, who was our Catholic liaison, how to get the Bishops' Council to support the boycott or how to get the Maryknoll Sisters into our boycott. I don't know these things. I couldn't tell the Protestant coordinator how to get the National Council of Churches on board or how to get the Presbyterian Church Council. But the specialists would come in and tell me what they thought should be done and I relied on their judgment. My role was like that of a traffic policeman—directing and coordinating. And it was amazing the way this worked.[42]

The national boycott staff activities were directed from ACTWU's union label department and the staff met periodically in New York.

The communications network was also maintained by means of a monthly newsletter, *Social Justice,* that was published, sometimes irregularly, until the boycott ended. This newsletter, primarily a join effort by the union label department and the ACTWU public relations department under the directorship of Burt Beck, was devoted exclusively to the Stevens campaign and provided readers with news, information, and photographs. It included the growing lists of prominent Americans who supported the boycott, boycott groups that had been formed, news of speeches, rallies, marches, news about J. P. Stevens, and news of related campaign segments. *Social Justice* was mailed to boycott supporters; by 1980, when the last newsletter was mailed, it was reaching nearly 50,000 readers.

The boycott was officially launched in November, 1976, with rallies in the downtown shopping areas of Philadelphia, Detroit, and St. Louis. By that time the ACTWU had received active endorsement of the campaign by a number of government officials, church, civil rights, and labor leaders. Community leaders in the three kick-off cities participated in the distribution of informational leaflets and cards that listed brand names under which Stevens products were sold. The leaflets emphasized Stevens' long record of labor law violations and disregard for workers.

Unlike the Farah campaign, the Stevens boycott involved very little picketing. Signs appeared at rallies and marches, but picket lines in front of retail stores that carried Stevens products were not used. This decision was based on advice from ACTWU's lawyers, who were extremely anxious that all union supporters abide by the letter of the law. They tried, in Joel Ax's words

> to advise our people in a way that they can impact in the way they want to impact with the least amount of risk. That sometimes is very difficult to do. It makes us enemies of field people if they want to do more than we can recommend. We don't ultimately make the decisions as to what they are going to do,

but we get credited for making the decisions of what they are not going to do. In reality, we just advise the risks that we see in the various courses of conduct from leafleting to picketing to demonstrating. The risks increase in that order. Your least risk is leafleting. It increases with picketing and increases considerably with large demonstrations."[43]

The picket line was avoided because the union leaders felt there was too much association in people's minds about "crossing picket lines." Because the union legally was allowed to boycott the product only, and not even to imply that a shopper should not enter stores that carried the products, the decision was made to use leafleting instead of picketing. This activity was supplemented by mail and phone campaigns to retailers, and by delegations of local consumers who talked with store management.

In March, 1977, more than 3,000 ACTWU supporters marched in front of J. P. Stevens Tower, company headquarters in New York City, during the annual stockholders' meeting. Inside, Coretta Scott King, Bayard Rustin, and others spoke in support of two resolutions presented to management by five major religious groups that held well over 44,000 shares of Stevens stock.

Such stockholders' actions—the presentation of resolutions and stockholders' lawsuits (based essentially on the idea that a company is showing disregard for the welfare of its stockholders by spending large sums of money fruitlessly in union-busting efforts)—were undertaken on several occasions during the campaign. Concerted efforts were made to ensure the presence of representatives from sympathetic groups at these stockholders' meetings. ACTWU often was involved, sometimes actively, sometimes more passively, in the organization of such drives. Planning for such actions necessarily involved experts from different parts of the campaign—legal, corporate, boycott, public relations, and so on.

The resolutions presented in the March, 1977, actions sought disclosure of information on company policy and practice regarding labor and minority hiring. Management held the overwhelming majority of proxy votes and the resolutions received only a small percentage of the total vote. The action outside the meeting, however, gave evidence of a rapid build-up of support for the boycott and the breadth of that support.

The issues that generated such support were issues of social justice and human dignity. ACTWU named its newsletter *Social Justice* in order to resonate with such statements as that prepared by 14 southern ministers. Interpreting and relating the issues to their beliefs and principles as religiously committed people, they answered their own question "Is an economic boycott justified?" in this manner:

We believe that we must ask this question primarily in our role as concerned Christian persons who use textile products. We recognize some justice in the arguments that "the union's threat of a boycott is no less coercion than the company's threat of plant-closings." The use of economic power, in the service of a benefit for some group of people over against another group, often involves the danger that some innocent party will get hurt. We find it hard to be enthusiastic about a national boycott against the products of the J. P. Stevens Company, but we confess that we are even less enthusiastic about the buying of any products manufactured at the cost of avoidable human suffering. If, as may happen, the widespread unionization of the textile industry should result in rising costs for textile production, the industry will surely feel free to pass those costs on to the buyer; and, as textile users who are also Christians, we feel some obligation to count those higher prices as the cost we may have to pay for the increase of justice in the textile industry. Further, we remember that defenders of the American competitive economic system have frequently urged citizens to "vote with dollars" for products that they like. Should the quality of a company's labor relations enter into a citizen's judgment on the quality of its products? It is the *right* of the American citizen to answer this question with the vote of dollars as well. . . . In our judgment, the boycott is necessary and just. It is the last tool available to the workers in this struggle. It must be supported if the rights of workers are to be secured and advanced.[44]

The National Council of Churches, after months of its own independent research, written up in a 21-page report, reached similar conclusions, as did other religious groups.

Bayard Rustin, president of the A. Philip Randolph Institute and newspaper columnist, linked the boycott with civil rights:

Like many companies in the South, Stevens continues to discriminate. In December 1975, a federal judge ruled that Stevens was guilty of hiring on the basis of race, reserving clerical jobs for white employees, discrimination against blacks in job assignments, discrimination in layoffs and recalls and other discriminatory employment practices. The judge discovered that blacks with ten years seniority were making less than whites with only two years seniority, while blacks with a twelfth grade education were paid less than whites with a third grade education. . . .

Only by mobilizing the concern of all people all over the country in support of the boycott of J. P. Stevens can a start be made to bringing economic and social justice to the working people of the South, both black and white.[45]

In October, 1977, the AFL-CIO organized a meeting of labor leaders from Mexico, Australia, France, New Zealand, Japan, and Belgium, and began the coordination of worldwide labor support for the boycott. This international group drafted and issued a statement promising to "bring Stevens' disgraceful oppression of its employees"[46] to the attention of unionists in their countries and to aid in the American struggle for justice.

A dramatic instance of such support came in January, 1978, from Japan. Members of Zensen Domei, the 470,000-member Japanese Federation of

Textile, Chemical, Distributive and Allied Industry Workers demonstrated and picketed clad in black robes and skull masks. Stevens products were cleared out of retail stores in Japan with remarkable haste because, as one union official explained:

> In Japan there is one single wholesale distributor of Stevens' products. The Japanese labor people went after that distributor and got an agreement that the firm would stop importing Stevens' products until the labor problem ended.[47]

The same individual added that such results were not obtained in Europe because the products were so widely distributed.

The campaign did not reach the smaller towns and cities in the United States until much later than the major cities. But ACTWU officials envisioned eventual mobilization of local sponsors who would, with the assistance of regional boycott representatives, lead boycott efforts in communities throughout the nation. In Champaign-Urbana, Illinois, a mid-sized city typical except for the influential presence of a large university, these sponsors were primarily the Twin City Federation of Labor and the Champaign-Urbana Democratic Socialist Organizing Committee. These two bodies garnered additional support from the Champaign-Urbana Student Association, the Champaign-Urbana National Organization for Women, and various church groups. In January, 1979, the Urbana city council voted to support the boycott. "The city council resolution 'urges all citizens to join in the J. P. Stevens boycott to achieve economic justice and human and safe working conditions.' "[48]

Why should a southern textile dispute concern a city council in central Illinois?

> This issue affects people's lives. . . . Beyond that, the issue affects jobs—here and elsewhere—because if a large company like J. P. Stevens can thumb its nose at the law in the south, it may encourage other like-minded companies to move there. From here.[49]

By the end of 1978 students from at least 75 universities and colleges across the country had organized boycott support committees.

> Student leaders of the boycott say their campaign centers on "the moral and social issues" raised by Stevens' policies, rather than on the specific issue of unionization.
>
> "The company is evil, its approach medieval," says Joshua I. Miller, a graduate student in political theory at Princeton University. "A nationwide boycott is the only way to bring relief to hundreds of workers who have no right to strike."[50]

The boycott issues had immediate appeal for women's groups. Representatives of 30 national women's organizations formed the National Women's

Committee to Support J. P. Stevens Workers in 1978. Eleanor Smeal, president of the National Organization for Women, explained the alliance as follows:

"[The consumer boycott] so ties in with everything that the women's movement is doing that it is part and parcel of it." She noted that about half of Stevens' employees are women and that women consumers, as the major purchasers of bedding and towels, have the power to assure the success of the boycott.[51]

Politicians who publicly supported the boycott included not only the liberal politicians who had supported the Farah boycott, but also a number of more conservative politicians. Active support on the part of legislators resulted in moves that barred Stevens from entering into contracts or subcontracts with several cities and states. Some of the bills passed by local and state governments did not mention Stevens specifically, but rather barred contracts with any persons or firms that repeatedly violated NLRA laws or repeatedly had been found in contempt of court.

The participation of these various sympathetic groups and individuals was perhaps the best measure of ACTWU's planning and strategy. Issues were presented to individuals and organizations in a way that made the campaign important to them and emphasized values that they held to be important. The numbers of these individuals and organizations became so large that they were able to gain further support even from some very unexpected sources. The American Civil Liberties Union, for example, broke tradition and supported the boycott. A coalition of stockholders was prepared to challenge the longstanding neutrality in such matters of the giant retailer R. H. Macy, but the issue was averted by the eventual settlement between ACTWU and Stevens.

Eventually, this pressure made retailer after retailer decide to remove J. P. Stevens products from their shelves or to cut back on purchases of Stevens products. Union officials are quick to say that cooperation from retailers is both difficult to obtain and critical to the success of a boycott. Occasionally, the social justice themes suffice to convince store owners to take action against one of their vendors; Del Mileski was aware of only one case where this occurred in the J. P. Stevens boycott. Retailers usually respond to their customers, however, especially if consumers do more than simply boycott the product in their purchases. Personal boycotts by individual shoppers have little impact. As Howard Samuel, president of the AFL-CIO Industrial Union Department and experienced boycott specialist, put it:

You've got to have direct action before it's going to work. If you are depending on ordinary consumers not to buy, the store people won't even know it. Their sales are not going to go down.[52]

There are other viewpoints, however. Another union leader explained how, in his opionion, the consumer level can have some impact:

> In terms of national impact, the fact that there were consumers—unknown numbers of consumers, unnamed consumers in quantities all over the country—that were potentially dangerous to the company created a psychological effect that was every bit as important as the community leaders.[53]

In reality, however, the basic problem with a consumer boycott is that such an impact is difficult to achieve because the necessary level of consumer participation is so high. Without massive numbers of boycotters, the retailer won't be aware of what is happening, the huge corporation won't be aware of it—how could it be effective? Even if on some levels the strategy might be judged to be appropriate and potentially effective, it is very difficult to get consumers to change their buying habits. It is much simpler to gain their expressions of support. Howard Samuel is forthright in his evaluation of consumer boycotts:

> Most boycotts are time-wasters. Amalgamated may be the only union that understands that. Unless the issue is overwhelmingly important and no strike or labor situation is ever going to reach that level of importance. No matter how often you drum it into people's minds, there are other things on their minds that are going to take precedence when they make a purchase—whatever the purchase is. Obviously quality and suitability of the product and the price of the product are going to take priority. By the time they get by these things, there's not going to be any time left to decide whether this is a union- or non-union-made product, and then purchase the union one.[54]

In the Stevens boycott, as in the Farah boycott, retailers were usually convinced to stop buying Stevens products by delegations of people who personally went in and made the request and explained why they believed such action important. These delegations were composed of community leaders—city council members, rabbis, priests, and ministers, state legislators, civil rights leaders, and so on. Samuel commented; "Even if some consumers observe a boycott religiously, and a store stops purchasing that product, it is not because consumers don't buy, but because consumers go in and make a fuss."[55] And if the consumers happen to be politically significant people, so much the better.

The boycott strategy was so carefully conceived and implemented that few surprises occurred. One of these surprises—a good one for ACTWU—was the staying power of retail commitments.

> In previous boycotts, including Farah and over the years, a retailer would make a commitment not to sell a product, but you would find that if the boycott continued for any length of time—two months, three months—you would find the product back in the store. So it was a constant hassle of rechecking, talking again with management and this type of thing. In the

Stevens campaign we checked retailers on a regular basis. We computerized all of the retail activities so this task was simplified. To my knowledge, no major retailers ever reneged on a commitment to drop the line.[56]

One reason this might have occurred was because of the responsibility the retailers felt to the types of people with whom they had made the initial agreement. The ACTWU staff supported these local activities by coordinating efforts directed at national retail chains located throughout the country.

The economic effect of the boycott was negligible, as expected. A *Business Week* survey in several major cities found that Stevens products were not being displayed and advertised as frequently as they had been before the boycott.[57] Nevertheless, Stevens' annual reports show that company sales increased every subsequent year of the boycott. Stevens' net income experienced ups and downs, but this figure was influenced by a variety of factors. In 1978, James D. Finley, chairman of the board at Stevens, attributed the decline to escalating costs and increasing imports, factors that were indeed causing industry-wide declines. Some decisions made by Stevens' management during this time may have been related to the effects of the boycott, but it would be difficult to demonstrate that this was so. At any rate, no one explains Stevens' decision to come to an agreement with ACTWU as being caused by the economic impact of the consumer boycott. In order to appreciate more fully the pressure generated by the boycott, its political impact, as mediated largely through the opinions of various portions of the public and the mass media, must be examined.

In the early, carefully constructed plans for the boycott, media planning occupied a central position.

> We had a media strategy when we started. And the strategy was never to portray the Stevens campaign as a battle between big labor and a giant corporation. Our plan was to make it more of a social justice crusade—bringing in all the elements we could: the exploited workers of the south and the impact on the economy of a region of the country, as well as the impact on the individual lives of the people. That we were able to maintain throughout the entire campaign, starting in June of 1976.[58]

Between June, 1976, when the boycott was publicly announced, and November, 1976, when the boycott was publicly launched, a good deal of the attention that had been gained initially was maintained by ACTWU's public relations department. It was that department's responsibility to make sure that the issue was not forgotten during this relatively inactive period. Subsequently, according to Burt Beck, ACTWU public relations director, publicizing the boycott was more a matter of interdepartmental and interorganizational teamwork.[59]

Media relations were maintained by ACTWU through press releases, press conferences, and by "carefully cultivating the media." The union tried to ensure that press releases had a legitimate purpose—that is, that they communicated some hard news, some story of unusual public interest, or that they were accompanied by action of some type that would attract local media attention. By following up press releases with additional contacts—telephone reminders on the day of the action event, or telephone calls to see if there were questions—the type of media relationship that ACTWU wanted to develop was gradually created. ACTWU staff members worked to provide their supporters with answers to as many anticipated questions as possible—or to tell them where they or media personnel could get the answers.

An early example of media strategy was provided at the March, 1977, annual J. P. Stevens stockholders' meeting. An advertisement "to the shareholders of J. P. Stevens . . . to the leaders of the retail business community . . . to every fair-minded American" appeared the day of the meeting in major newspapers (Figure 18). The presentation of resolutions inside the meeting and the march outside the meeting were accompanied by a press conference. The chairperson and the speakers at this press conference were not ACTWU leaders, but were well-known public figures and representatives from various anti-Stevens groups. The meeting was chaired by the director of the Interfaith Center on Corporate Responsibility, which underscored the fact that the reolutions were presented by a religious coalition. One of those who spoke in favor of the resolutions was the president of the New York City Council.

All over the country, at all levels of the campaign, the same technique was utilized: union leaders organized the media-related plans, and then the large network of support groups activated the plans. For example, telephone calls that were made to follow up press releases were not made by ACTWU field people, but by local people who were active in ACTWU-support groups; so the call to the local newspaper might come from a senior citizen, a local political leader, or a religious leader. These same people often arranged for local press conferences. ACTWU officials believed that this method would stimulate good media interest and have a greater impact than would have been possible had labor leaders been doing all the work.

Human interest was added to this strategy by bringing into a city, when possible, a Stevens mill worker. Local leaders arranged for the worker to speak before interested groups, arranged advance news releases and publicity, and, when possible, arranged for local media people to be present during the talk and to interview the worker personally. This proved to be especially worthwhile in areas with large and widely viewed television stations and when used in conjunction with some other local activity, such as presentation of an anti-Stevens resolution to a city council.

The public launching of the boycott also was given a great boost by the airing of two television programs on the subject, both of which were consid-

To the shareholders of J.P. Stevens…
to the leaders of the retail business community…
to every fair-minded American:

TODAY, THE J.P. STEVENS COMPANY WILL PRESENT ITS ANNUAL REPORT.

WE FEEL THERE ARE TWO OTHER REPORTS YOU OUGHT TO HAVE.

1. A report to all shareholders pertaining to equal employment opportunity at the J. P. Stevens Company.

2. A report to all shareholders pertaining to the labor policies and practices of the J. P. Stevens Company.

What are J.P. Stevens labor policies?

What is J.P. Stevens attitude toward equal employment opportunity?

J.P. Stevens shareholders have a right to know.

The public has a right to know.

The retail business community has a right to know.

Church groups are asking for facts and for the truth. For non-competitive information. For complete and accurate reports that will help explain why more and more critical national attention has been focused on the Stevens Company, which the Amalgamated Clothing and Textile Workers Union has declared to be the number one labor law violator in the country!

Why has the national consumer boycott of Stevens products which has been initiated by the Amalgamated Clothing and Textile Workers Union, been receiving the growing support of important political, civic and religious groups and individuals around the nation?

Why has the National Labor Relations Board found Stevens guilty in fifteen separate cases?

Why has more than 1.3 million dollars in back pay been ordered by the courts to be paid to Stevens workers?

Why did former chairman Boyd Leedom of the NLRB, as early as ten years ago, in January 1967, state that Stevens practices are "so out of tune with a humane, civilized approach to industrial relations that it would shock even those least sensitive to honor, justice and decent treatment."

Why?

Only J.P. Stevens can tell us.

We want to know. We want not just the company's profit figures. We are entitled to know the human facts behind them.

ACTWU
AMALGAMATED CLOTHING AND TEXTILE WORKERS UNION
AFL-CIO, CLC
15 Union Square, New York, N.Y. 10003

FREEDOM AND JUSTICE FOR J.P. STEVENS WORKERS

In support of Protestant and Catholic shareholders working through the
INTERFAITH CENTER ON CORPORATE RESPONSIBILITY
475 Riverside Drive, New York, N.Y. 10027

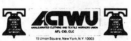

FIGURE 18. Advertisement in *Social Justice*, March 1977, pp. 2–3 (also in major newspapers, March 1, 1977); ad sponsored by ACTWU.

ered "fine wrap-ups from [ACTWU's] point of view."[60] The first of these was the "MacNeil/Lehrer Report," produced by public television and shown on 200 stations around the country. On December 22, 1976, this program carried a half-hour examination of issues involved in the Stevens campaign. On Sunday, March 13, 1977, CBS devoted a segment of "Sixty Minutes" to the ACTWU-Stevens situation.

Both of these television programs summarized events leading up to the boycott announcement and included interviews with Stevens workers who were both pro- and anti-union. James Finley, chairman of Stevens' board of directors, and other Stevens executives were given an opportunity to appear, but refused. Films and transcripts of these programs were circulated to field workers by ACTWU's public relations department.

On his program, Robert MacNeil mentioned the social justice appeal that the union was so eager to stress ("The Union knows it can't mobilize wide public support for just a labor dispute; it must attack industrial paternalism in the name of civil rights and social justice"),[61] but Mike Wallace of CBS defined the problem more narrowly ("This is the story of big labor versus J. P. Stevens").[62] Both reports, however, cited the legal cases against Stevens and emphasized the poor working conditions, low wages, and poor benefits provided by the company. This segment of Mike Wallace's interview with an anti-union worker provides a feel for the tone of the "Sixty Minutes" treatment:

> WORKER: If a man wants to get out there and work for a living, he can make a living here.
> WALLACE: How much do you make?
> WORKER: I make $4.53 an hour. I've been here 37 years.
> WALLACE: Thirty-seven years!
> WORKER: Thirty-seven years.
> WALLACE: So you must be in your middle fifties?
> WORKER: Fifty-five.
> WALLACE: Okay. Now, then, if you were to leave tomorrow, how much of a pension would you get from J. P. Stevens?
> WORKER: Tomorrow? Oh, now—that's something else. It'd probably be ten dollars a month. (LAUGHS)
> WALLACE: What?
> WORKER: Ten dollars a month, probably, if I leave tomorrow.
> WALLACE: After 37 years?
> WORKER: Yes.
> WALLACE: Well, that's not much of a pension, is it?
> WORKER: If I stay until I'm 65, I can get $60.00 a month.
> WALLACE: You've got to stay another ten years, and then you'll get $15.00 a week.
> WORKER: Sixty dollars a month, right.
> WALLACE: Well, that's not very much either.

WORKER: No, it's not very much.
WALLACE: Plus the factor—that would be after 47 years in.
WORKER: Right.
WALLACE: And if the union could get you a better pension—?
WORKER: If they could get the better pension without the other things to go with it.
WALLACE: What other things?
WORKER: Well, they go raising our wages, we don't get it, those in the higher tax bracket. We have to pay union dues, and the union has—I mean the company has been good to us. With no more education than people got around here, we're not the college type person.[63]

The same month that this "Sixty Minutes" program was aired, ACT-WU's public relations department released a color film that was sponsored by the National Citizens Committee for Justice for J. P. Stevens Workers and entitled *Testimony—Justice vs. J. P. Stevens*. As described by the *Social Justice* newsletter

> the 28-minute documentary is a shockingly intense portrayal of the struggle by textile workers in the south to win social and economic justice. It focuses on workers at Stevens' seven plants in Roanoke Rapids, N.C., many of whom vividly describe the inhumane conditions under which they toil.[64]

Audiences at the premiere showings of the film in New York and Los Angeles were greeted by the mayors of New York and Los Angeles, other government, religious, civil rights, and labor leaders, show business personalities, and some of the workers who had appeared in the film. The film was then made available to civic, church, labor, and other groups who requested it. According to Burt Beck, at one time at least 225 prints of *Testimony* were moving around the country. In his opinion, the project was an "eminently worthwhile" undertaking that had resulted in an excellent film. For those unable to see it, the public relations department printed a booklet that summarized *Testimony* and sent hundreds of copies out nationwide to be distributed by the union's informal communications network.

ACTWU's media efforts were simplified to some extent by the general silence maintained by J. P. Stevens executives. Media people came to ACT-WU to ask questions rather than to Stevens because they found ACTWU staff members willing to provide answers. Some people feel that William "Willie" Farah, head of Farah Manufacturing, made the same tactical error when his company was being boycotted.

> Mr. Farah aided the opposition with his refusal to answer the union's charges. His silence seemed, at least to some extent, to be an admission of guilt. "We should have fought back from the first," one company official now says. "But that isn't the way Willie [Farah] does things. The union's charges were completely false, but Willie just wouldn't dignify them with a rebuttal. He felt his people (employees) would stay loyal and do his talking for him."[65]

Early in the campaign, Stevens officials were seldom willing to comment publicly about the union or its boycott, as Robert MacNeil stated during his television program. Burt Beck believes that the company position was that there would be less turmoil if they just kept quiet. Their position also was consistent with policy established in previous years when their only response to questions about their legal problems was a denial that any illegal activities had occurred. To many media people this response, in the light of campaign-related events, simply did not make sense. So they publicized the denials less frequently, and many of them finally stopped asking for a response from Stevens altogether.

Stevens' position apparently underwent some changes, however, as the years passed and the campaign continued. The company printed a pamphlet entitled *Straightening Things Out* that was distributed on a limited basis, but updated regularly. Stevens also produced a 27-minute film—an answer to *Testimony*—entitled *The Issue: Freedom of Choice*. Later in the campaign, Stevens hired persons whose responsibility it was to travel around the country speaking on behalf of Stevens and refuting ACTWU's arguments. In some parts of the country, debates were arranged between these Stevens representatives and ACTWU staff members. In November, 1978, a long article was published in *Women's Wear Daily* on the Stevens company and Stevens' top executives, Robert Stevens, James Finley, and Whitney Stevens.[66]

Generally, however, Stevens' silence meant that ACTWU enjoyed the offensive in dealing with media. Rarely did they have to defend themselves or their anti-Stevens arguments. There were two significant exceptions to this generalization. The first involved claims by the J. P. Stevens Employees' Educational Committee that the majority of Stevens workers actually rejected the union. The second was a widely publicized report by the Heritage Foundation that concluded that it was workers who resisted organization efforts rather than industry.

On both occasions, ACTWU vigorously joined the issue, mainly by questioning the source of funding of the organization involved. In the first instance the union's principal target was a self-styled "employees' committee," the Employees' Educational Committee, organized in 1976 in order to end the boycott and defeat the union. The committee emphatically denied that it was company-supported, though members refused to account for their funds.[67]

At ACTWU's request the Labor Department subpoenaed the group to disclose both membership and contributor information under the Labor Management Reporting and Disclosure Act. The employees' committee appealed, and in November, 1981, after a refusal by the Fourth Circuit Court to block the subpoenas, asked the Supreme Court to hear the case. In a telephone interview for the *New York Times* in October, 1981, a spokesperson for the group stated that the ACTWU would be disappointed with the information if and when it should become available because committee funds had come mainly from the sale of pro-Stevens T-shirts.[68]

The August, 1977, report of the Heritage Foundation, a tax-exempt research group in Washington, D.C., was entitled "Unionization of the Textile Industry: A Case Study of J. P. Stevens." This Foundation, which has a conservative reputation and whose officials admit to an anti-union position, keeps names of contributors confidential, although officials stated, when the report came out, that neither J. P. Stevens nor any other textile firm funded their research.

ACTWU put out a nine-page response to the report, arguing each of its major sections, and the ACTWU research department issued a critique of the economic analysis in the report. These materials were distributed throughout the country. The union publicized its charges during a press luncheon sponsored by Fairchild Publications (publishers of numerous trade publications, including *Daily News Record*) in New York. The union charge that received the most publicity was that author David Williams had copied sections of Stevens' pamphlet *Straightening Things Out* and other company materials without crediting the source and that little independent research had been done.

In September, 1979, James Finley announced that he would step down as chairman of Stevens on January 1, 1980. He was succeeded by Whitney Stevens, who represents the family's fifth generation in the textile industry. There was speculation at that time that this change had implications for a new approach to Stevens' labor problems. When questioned about this, Finley's reply was, "This move represents an evolutionary change in the management of this company and does not represent any change in its policy."[69]

Perceptions of company willingness to bargain more seriously, however, gradually gained strength from the time Stevens succeeded Finley until the agreement was reached in October, 1980. Company policy may have been unchanged, but Finley and Stevens definitely approached business matters in different ways: "If Finley could be considered Stevens' iron fist, Whitney might well be its velvet glove."[70]

Some of the publicity originating with the union grew out of the advertising campaign initiated by ACTWU in June, 1977. The campaign involved a series of advertisements that centered on individual experiences of former Stevens workers who explained, in their own words, their grievances against the company. Although referred to by ACTWU as "informational advertisements," each ad specifically advocated boycott action by stating "Boycott These J. P. Stevens Products" and "We ask all concerned citizens to join the fight for freedom and justice for J. P. Stevens workers" (Figures 19 and 20). The ads appeared in trade publications and metropolitan daily newspapers.

Although an advertising agency was retained by ACTWU, the public relations staff did most of the work on the ads themselves. They had a great deal of material close at hand—information on people involved in the boycott, quotations and stories from workers, and photographs. While the early ads placed emphasis upon the workers themselves, later ads emphasized the

200 YEARS AGO AMERICANS FOUGHT HARD FOR FREEDOM AND JUSTICE...TODAY J.P. STEVENS WORKERS ARE STILL FIGHTING!

J.P. Stevens is the second largest textile manufacturing corporation in America. It is also America's number one labor law violator, keeping workers down and wages low, suppressing freedom and justice. Help J. P. Stevens workers achieve social justice and full economic opportunity!

Boycott

J.P. STEVENS TEXTILE PRODUCTS

FIGURE 19.   Advertisement in *Social Justice,* June–July 1977, p. 4 (also in trade publications and metropolitan daily newspapers, 1977–1980); ad sponsored by ACTWU.

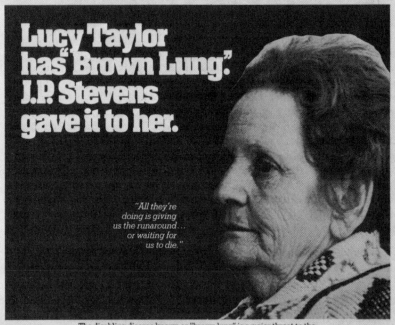

There are J. P. Stevens employees who work in cotton dust levels three times higher than allowed by the Government. The result: dread "brown lung" disease (byssinosis) threatens thousands of Stevens workers.

Lucy Taylor has "Brown Lung." J.P. Stevens gave it to her.

"All they're doing is giving us the runaround... or waiting for us to die."

The disabling disease known as "brown lung" is a major threat to the health of workers in J.P. Stevens mills throughout the South. The cause is cotton dust levels far in excess of the Occupational Safety and Health Act standard. Noise is also a serious problem—with levels much higher than permitted by law. These and other unsafe, inhumane practices persist—and J.P. Stevens workers continue to suffer at the hands of America's No. 1 Labor-Law-Breaker!

BOYCOTT J. P. STEVENS PRODUCTS SOLD AT RETAIL STORES.

We ask all concerned citizens to join the fight for freedom and justice for J. P. Stevens workers.

FIGURE 20. Advertisement in *Social Justice*, June–July 1977, p. 4 (also in trade publications and metropolitan newspapers, 1977–1980); ad sponsored by ACTWU.

social justice theme by quoting public leaders who had spoken out "for justice" (Figure 21).

Although the services of the advertising agency were helpful in placing the ads in the media, ad placement in general remained a problem for ACTWU.

> We had some problems with getting advertising across. The issue of paid advertising caused us problems in many areas. We could not get ads placed in many newspapers; they refused to take them. Radio stations would not accept our spot announcements. I can't think of any place where we managed to advertise on the radio except for Philadelphia where some sixty- or ninety-second pre-recorded pitches for the boycott were aired. All kinds of reasons were given to us. One of the toughest regions was Cincinnati, Ohio, where we had a very active campaign. It was an important area because Federated Department Stores is headquartered there and their stores were part of our national campaign throughout the country. We had a big media blitz planned one year during the time Federated's stockholders were meeting in Cincinnati. Part of that included advertising on city buses. Our ads just asked for boycott support—don't buy Stevens products—that type of thing. But they would not sell to us under any conditions. I think it was because of the strength Federated has in that city—advertising power.[71]

Newspapers in smaller towns were especially reluctant to carry advertisements, and this was a sore point with many local boycott committees. In Champaign-Urbana, University of Illinois students who supported the boycott and who had formed a group called the J. P. Stevens Boycott Committee undertook the task of placing an ad in the local newspaper. The ad itself was drafted by a student and funds (about $320 for a 9-inch by 12-inch ad) were obtained from the Student Organization Resource Fee (SORF) board.

People at the local newspaper, the *News-Gazette,* initially agreed to run the ad, but later rejected it on the basis of a policy allowing no controversial ads to be printed. The student group recruited support from the Twin City Federation of Labor, and they finally got the newspaper staff to agree to print the advertisement. First, however, the newspaper required the committee to obtain a letter of indemnification from ACTWU that indemnified the *News-Gazette* from all claims against it that might arise out of the ad's publication.

Such requirements became familiar to the ACTWU legal department, which responded with its own legalistic procedures, including signed consent from individuals and organizations listed in ads as boycott supporters. In the view of union officials the motives of reluctant dailies were probably mixed. Some of their concerns about legal liabilities were legitimate, and could be assuaged by careful and patient responses. Usually this approach was successful because, "They were embarrassed not to take it. You see, the press likes to think of itself as very fair and impartial and unbiased."[72] On the

ANOTHER OUTSTANDING AMERICAN ADDS SUPPORT TO THE GROWING CONSUMER BOYCOTT AGAINST J. P. STEVENS PRODUCTS.

MAYOR TOM BRADLEY OF LOS ANGELES JOINS THE FIGHT FOR JUSTICE FOR J.P. STEVENS WORKERS.

All over the country, civic, religious, student and community groups, as well as leading citizens representing every aspect of American life are joining in the struggle for justice for J. P. Stevens workers... victims of social and economic injustice, of repression of human rights, of scornful disregard for the laws of the land.

In newspapers, on TV, on radio, everywhere across the nation we're calling on America to listen to the call for freedom and justice: "Don't buy J.P.Stevens products."

ALMALGAMATED CLOTHING AND TEXTILE WORKERS UNION
AFL-CIO, CLC

15 Union Square, New York, N.Y. 10003

FIGURE 21. Advertisement in *Women's Wear Daily,* January 9, 1979; ad sponsored by ACTWU.

other hand, the requirements imposed by newspapers could be regarded as bad faith chicanery, an opinion more predominant outside the legal department.

> Here you are in a boycott situation and are willing to pay to express your point of view and the newspapers—especially the newspapers—keep insisting on modification, modification, modification. If labor would only set up media committees in their local cities—number one, to try to develop and maintain a decent relationship with the press, and, if that fails, to develop some means of dealing with the lack of response from the press.[73]

Because of the consent requirements and the time that was passing, the student committee in Champaign-Urbana decided to use only local names in the ad rather than including national supporters as originally planned. The ad finally was printed on July 30, 1980, not in the first section of the paper as had been agreed, but in the third section. After protests and further discussion, the paper reprinted the ad in the first section on August 27, 1980, at no extra charge (Figure 22).

In general, and in retrospect, ACTWU people were not overly impressed with the advertising they did. It served a purpose in some towns where little media attention was given to the boycott or where a local committee found that the only way to get its point of view across was by means of advertising. Union leaders also believed that advertising in trade publications had some positive effects in that it increased retailers' knowledge of the issues and of the individuals and organizations who supported the boycott. Trade press advertising was considered especially helpful in smaller towns where there was less news coverage of the situation.

But advertising was often difficult; it was time-consuming, and it was expensive. Burt Beck said that relative to other campaign expenditures the amount spent on advertising was small, but what had been spent was, in his opinion, not well-spent. It could have been better used elsewhere—for example, to put more people in the field. Moreover, no real efforts were made to evaluate the effectiveness of the advertising at any time during the boycott. Evaluation had been discussed from time to time and was being fairly seriously considered by the union and its ad agency when the settlement was reached. In the absence of systematic evaluations, union leaders continued to believe that paid advertising was not as effective as a good news story. Mileski said:

> The media look for news stories. I can understand a certain degree of reluctance on the part of the press to get involved in fighting "capital" because that's where money comes from, from advertising. But they can safely print a news story and if you give them a good news story, they will print it.[74]

Although the campaign itself showed that this generalization is not always accurate, both Mileski and Ray Rogers, who worked primarily on the corporate campaign, felt that the J. P. Stevens situation provided numerous

DON'T SPOIL THE 1980s FOR SOUTHERN TEXTILE WORKERS

The J.P. Stevens Co., Inc., is the nation's second largest textile company, with 83 plants and more than 44,000 employees. If you've seen the movie NORMA RAE, you have some idea about the working conditions that J P. Stevens employees face every day. NORMA RAE was based on the experiences of J.P. Stevens workers.

In its factories, the Stevens Company has had cotton dust levels which were three to twelve times the level permissible by law. Cotton dust causes the deadly brown lung disease which disables hundreds of workers every year. Furthermore, the average J.P. Stevens employee makes only ⅔ of what an average American factory worker earns.

Employees of Stevens who have attempted to change these and other conditions by trying to join the Amalgamated Clothing and Textile Workers Union have failed because, over the past two decades, "the Stevens Co.," one judge from the National Labor Relations Board recently stated, "has engaged in a massive, multi-state campaign to deny its employees their legal rights . . . to seek collective bargaining representative of their own choosing." (15-CA6297, May 1977)

Indeed, Stevens has been found guilty of more violations of federal labor law than any other company in American history. Because of these violations, Stevens has been ordered to pay over 1.3 million dollars in back pay to nearly 300 employees who were discriminated against or illegally discharged by the company.

But J.P. Stevens has gotten off cheap! It is much more profitable for the Stevens corporation to disobey the law and pay relatively small fines than to comply with the National Labor Relations Act and occupational, health, and safety standards. By denying its employees their legal right to decent wages and safe working conditions, the Stevens company has reaped millions of dollars in extra profits. That's why the employees of the J.P. Stevens Co. are asking for your help. If the courts can't make the J.P. Stevens Co. obey the law of the land it is our duty as law-abiding Americans to help.

J.P. Stevens' workers are asking you not to buy any products made by that company. Your power as a consumer can help create public and economic pressure on the Stevens corporations to obey the law. The Stevens Co. tries to hide its products under other brand names. But by bringing the list below with you when you shop for textile products you can identify Stevens Co. products easily.

So please don't spoil the 1980s for J.P. Stevens textile workers and their families. Bring them closer to decent wages and safe working conditions. PLEASE SUPPORT THE CONSUMER BOYCOTT OF J.P. STEVENS CO. PRODUCTS.

LOCAL ENDORSEMENTS OF THE J.P. STEVENS BOYCOTT

URBANA CITY COUNCIL
MAYOR JOAN SEVERNS, CHAMPAIGN
TWIN CITY FEDERATION OF LABOR (AFL-CIO)
CHAMPAIGN-URBANA DEMOCRATIC SOCIALIST ORGANIZING COMMITTEE
CHAMPAIGN-URBANA NEW AMERICAN MOVEMENT
GREATER CHAMPAIGN NATIONAL ORGANIZATION FOR WOMEN
CHAMPAIGN-URBANA GRAY PANTHERS
McKINLEY PRESBYTERIAN CHURCH

WHEN YOU SHOP FOR SHEETS, TOWELS, CARPETS, AND OTHER TEXTILE PRODUCTS, BOYCOTT J.P. STEVENS CO. PRODUCTS UNDER ALL STEVENS CO. LABELS:

SHEETS, TOWELS, LINENS, & BLANKETS

J.P. Stevens	Utica	Meadowbrook
Tastemaker	Simtex	Beauti-Blend
Forstmann	Fine Arts	

DESIGNER LABELS

| Hardy Amies | Dinah Shore | Yves. St. Laurent |
| Angelo Donghia | Suzanne Pleshette | Snoopy or Peanuts |

DRAPERIES & CARPETS

| J.P. Stevens | Merryweather | Tastemaker |
| Gulistan | Contender | Pinehurst |

I SUPPORT THE STRUGGLE FOR JUSTICE FOR J.P. STEVENS CO. WORKERS AND THE CONSUMER BOYCOTT OF J.P. STEVENS CO. PRODUCTS. I WILL:

☐ Boycott J.P. Stevens Co. products under all Stevens Co. labels listed above.

☐ Volunteer to distribute J.P. Stevens boycott information to my church or civic organization.

☐ Request that a member of the J.P. Stevens Co. Boycott Support Committee speak before my group.

Please send this coupon to the **J.P. STEVENS CO. BOYCOTT SUPPORT COMMITTEE, P.O. BOX 2182 STATION A, CHAMPAIGN, IL 61820**

ADVERTISEMENT PAID FOR BY THE CHAMPAIGN-URBANA J.P. STEVENS BOYCOTT SUPPORT COMMITTEE.

FIGURE 22.   Advertisement in the *Champaign-Urbana News-Gazette,* July 30, 1980, p. C7, and August 27, 1980, p. A6; ad sponsored by Champaign-Urbana J. P. Stevens Boycott Support Committee.

examples of ways good news stories could be generated and good press relationships developed.

Reams of leaflets, pamphlets, brochures, bumper stickers, fact sheets, and so on, that were continually sent out to field staff and active supporters were the work of ACTWU's union label department and the public relations department. News releases, photographs, and specially written background articles on Stevens workers and boycott leaders were provided to staff, active supporters, and media—that is, newspapers, trade journals, the labor press, and radio and television networks. While there was nothing particularly novel in such endeavors, several factors are noteworthy. First, the material was supplied in *large* quantities; wide distribution of the materials was achieved by utilizing the broad support network. Second, ACTWU regularly produced *new* material, an especially important factor because of the length of the campaign—new issues were brought out, old issues were kept alive. Third, "people stories" were emphasized. There were, for example, personal stories from underpaid black workers, workers afflicted with byssinosis, workers who had been injured on the job, and stories from workers who received few benefits from Stevens and no support during times of personal crises in spite of many years of employment. Accounts of the ways Stevens' policies and practices affected the personal lives of workers were effective for ACTWU because individual stories of personal difficulty can produce an amazing show of public support and sympathy which in this case articulated well with the emphasis on social and economic justice.

The stories of essentially the same group of people were first issued as news releases. ACTWU staffers wished to respond to Stevens' regular claims in its annual reports that the company enjoyed "an excellent relationship" with its employees. The people stories were subsequently used in the *Testimony* film, for boycott leaflets, and as the basis for an advertising campaign. In addition, some of these people told their stories before the Congressional committee hearings on labor law reform. The number of workers actively involved was very small; the media impact was large and varied.

Of course the union's access to and ability to make use of the media were far from perfect. Boycott supporters put strenuous and time-consuming work into activities aimed at the ultimate goal of convincing retailers to stop buying J. P. Stevens products or to reduce such purchases. When they were successful and a retailer agreed to alter purchasing patterns because of public pressure, the agreement typically specified that this action not be made public. Retailers were concerned that such publicity would attract lawsuits charging conspiracy to restrain trade.

Media reached through ACTWU's efforts included the magazines, journals, and newsletters published by national and regional organizations that supported the boycott. Articles in these publications typically included statements on why boycott resolutions had been adopted by the organization and how the boycott issues affected the members of the organization. The *National NOW Times,* for example, included articles that stressed the similarity in objectives between the women's organization and labor. The newspaper kept readers updated on boycott events and, in November,

1978, published a recently adopted convention resolution to "continue to support the Boycott against J. P. Stevens products and urge active participation in planned actions around the country. . . "[75]

Similarly, supportive articles and columns appeared in publications subscribed to by a certain narrow segment of the population. For example, the *Chronicle of Higher Education,* a journal with some visibility among college and university administrators and faculty, published an article describing boycott activities of students and faculty at various colleges and universities.[76] The *Georgia Bulletin,* published by the Catholic Archdiocese of Atlanta, printed articles on the bishops who were actively supporting the campaign.[77] The *Baltimore Afro-American* printed a pro-union statement by a state representative.[78]

Editorials in metropolitan daily newspapers that supported the boycott became increasingly visible. The culmination of the editorial trend occurred when ACTWU and J. P. Stevens finally were able to come to an agreement. At that time, numerous editorials hailing the union's achievements appeared in newspapers across the country. A *New York Times* editorial stated:

> It took 45 years, but at last law and history have caught up with the J. P. Stevens Company. Stevens, one of the country's largest textile makers, has belatedly acknowledged the authority of the National Labor Relations Act of 1935.[79]

The *Detroit Free Press* said:

> One Stevens is enough. If the nation is really serious about protecting the rights of workers to have a voice in their destinies, it is time to dust off the Labor Reform Act of 1977 and start over. Its principal purpose is simply to prevent the kind of unfair labor practices Stevens engaged in for so long, and to permit employees to decide whether or not they want a union.[80]

The *Chicago Sun-Times* observed:

> The relief is almost palpable—a stunning labor victory after 17 years of bitterness and obstruction.[81]

The following came from an editorial in the Raleigh, North Carolina *News and Observer:*

> The ACTWU proved tough and inventive in its own strategy against Stevens, but even more credit for the contract goes to the Roanoke Rapids workers. They persisted in the face of adversity to assert their right to a union agreement. . . . [T]he Roanoke Rapids workers struck a large blow for labor justice. And they may help usher the nation's second largest textile company back to the ranks of law-abiding corporations.[82]

Between the boycott years of 1976 and 1980 there was one media coup that played a most significant part in ACTWU's campaign—and one that was, in this carefully planned and systematic course of activities, a total surprise to ACTWU. This was the release in 1979, by Twentieth Century Fox, of the film *Norma Rae*, a film based on the true story of Crystal Lee Sutton, a former Stevens worker, and her struggles to unionize the company where she worked. Perhaps it should not have been the surprise it was because ACTWU had provided some technical assistance to the filmmakers. According to labor leaders, however, technical assistance to Hollywood in previous years certainly had not ensured a product that labor would consider to be friendly or of high quality.

The technical assistance rendered by ACTWU involved little more than helping to arrange the film location and efforts aimed at making the plant where the film was made look like a J. P. Stevens plant.[83] In addition, the extras and the textile workers in the film were union members. ACTWU leaders knew that the basic story line of the film was going to be based on a book about Crystal Lee Sutton, but very little beyond that. One staff member reported that when the film came out he certainly was not expecting much from it and was not even particularly interested in seeing it.

> After seeing the film, though, I was stunned at the number of issues that we were trying to project through the campaign that were touched upon in the film—brown lung, racial discrimination, the control over the whole life of the community that the mill in the mill town has. All those issues were there. Of course, they were not fully developed. But all in all, we couldn't have asked for a better portrayal of what it was like to work in the Stevens plant.[84]

The ACTWU General Executive Board report described the film as "a fictionalized, but vivid and largely accurate, portrayal of a crucial period in the Stevens workers' organizing struggle in the early '70s."[85] Good reviews of the film and an Oscar award to Sally Field as best actress for her starring role increased audience sizes all over the country.

The union lost little time in taking advantage of this serendipitous windfall. Staff members from the union label department and the public relations department again pooled their efforts. A New York freelance publicist was hired whom a union leader described as being

> very good, very aggressive, very sharp and very hard working. And we didn't miss a beat in that public relations campaign. I think we got total coverage in every possible piece of media. We were able to ride on the back of the film and we saturated media outlets in every major city."[86]

The union arranged for the film to be shown all over the country to audiences composed of labor boycott support groups. These groups used their membership lists, telephones, and newsletters to assemble large audiences. The showings frequently were highlighted by the appearance of the "real Norma Rae," Crystal Lee Sutton.

Here again, the union leaders feel they were lucky. Sutton, in their opinion, stepped naturally into her public relations role. She made numerous appearances on national and local telecasts, radio shows, and gave numerous interviews that appeared in magazine and newspaper articles. She toured the United States and Canada. Photographs were widely circulated of her first meeting with Sally Field at a reception sponsored by the Screen Actors Guild, the AFL-CIO, and ACTWU in March, 1980. Sutton displayed naturalness and ease in responding even to unexpected and difficult questions.

The timing of the film's release could hardly have been better had it been part of ACTWU's overall strategy. Because of ACTWU's already well-organized network, it was able to take immediate advantage of the film. And Crystal Lee Sutton's personal story attracted public sympathy for what she was trying to achieve in the same way that the other "people stories" had: the campaign issues were presented in an understandable, personal way. In addition, however, Sutton's story became inextricably interwoven with the more romantic, fictionalized film version of her life; and both stories were communicated to an extraordinarily large public, many of whom knew little about the J. P. Stevens boycott, well-publicized though it was.

When a settlement was reached between J. P. Stevens and ACTWU in October, 1980, Stevens requested that a specific promise to terminate the boycott be part of the agreement. Moreover, the company requested that the media be used to publicize this section of the agreement:

> To effectuate the termination of the boycott, the Union shall state publicly that the boycott has ended, cease all efforts to affect adversely the sales of Stevens' products, and take the necessary steps to insure that all boycott activities by the Union are terminated promptly. The Union will also advise all organizations which have supported the boycott that it is the desire of the Union that they cease all boycott activities. To that end, the Union will prepare and make available, to all news and media sources to which boycott news has been normally made available a press release stating that the boycott has been terminated; . . . and, if requested, place mutually agreed upon advertisements in not more than five publications selected by Stevens announcing the termination of the boycott, the cost of such advertisements to be borne by Stevens.[87]

This provision emphatically expresses the depth of the company's concern about the boycott as it related—regardless of its narrow economic impact—to the company's public relations.

The Corporate Campaign

The "corporate campaign" aimed at J. P. Stevens by ACTWU was a unique labor tactic and one that engendered controversy and some opposition both inside and outside of ACTWU headquarters. The tactic's success is not disputed, however. It was successful enough that, along with the consumer boycott, it was mentioned specifically in the ACTWU-Stevens settlement.

Paragraph 3 of the settlement includes what is sometimes called the "Ray Rogers" clause, a provision requiring the union to agree to refrain from engaging "in any 'corporate campaign' against the company" and from any

> attempt to effectuate the resignation of members of the Board of Directors of Stevens or to effectuate the resignation or removal of Stevens executives from the boards of directors of other companies, or to restrict the availability of financial or credit accommodations to Stevens, or by deliberate conduct to affect materially and adversely the relationship between Stevens and any other business organization.[88]

The strategy was primarily the brainchild of Ray Rogers, who was, until December, 1980, an ACTWU organizer and a veteran of Farah and other Amalgamated campaigns. Rogers' philosophy might best be summed up in one of his favorite phrases: "You have to confront power with power." This he did by analyzing Stevens' power base, a base made up of other corporate and financial institutions. The goal of the corporate campaign was to alienate and isolate the targeted institution (i.e., J. P. Stevens) from this power base, thereby removing its crucial foundation and causing it to topple—not totally, but in the direction of the bargaining table.

Rogers believed that while the social justice theme was essential to the total campaign, it needed to be translated into corporate language, the language of profit and loss, dollars and cents, in order to have an ultimate effect. Individuals who had leading roles in the Stevens situation—the chief executive officer of Stevens, the workers who told their stories and others— were important, but power existed at the institutional level. And, Rogers explained, Stevens at the institutional level was not a multinational corporation with 83 plants, thousands of employees, and a complex web of financial lines that could not be untangled, but was, instead, the 13 persons who composed the Stevens board of directors.

> It is these people who make the policy and hand down the decisions that will bring the company to a settlement with ACTWU and force them to recognize the dignity and rights of workers. Stevens had begun to maneuver around our legal strategy. And they could sit out bad public relations from now until doomsday. They were not being hurt economically.[89]

Rogers' concept called for the separation of the targeted institution from those organizations that composed its power base. Such an action must be concentrated and carefully coordinated.

> I had a group of people that were working on putting pressure on the banks to pull money out of South Africa. So they came and said, "Here's our plan of attack: we've lined up a half a dozen banks here in New York and we're going to hold a demonstration at one bank and then right after that one we're going to hold a demonstration against another bank." I said to them, "Look, after you run your second demonstration you have just negated what you did at the

first. When you run your third, you've just negated what you've done at the last two." You don't create any alternatives; you spread the pressure over everybody so it's not really affecting any one particular institution. The best thing to do would be to pick out the biggest, most powerful institution, draw your battle lines there, and literally go out to annihilate that institution."[90]

Rogers essentially did this in the Stevens campaign; his divisional method exploited the corporate tradition of interlocking directorates (and, to a lesser extent because of secondary boycott laws, of interlocking investments and loans), a practice that is typically regarded as one that provides corporations with strength and power. He started with Manufacturers Hanover Trust Company.

The selection of Manufacturers Hanover and the implementation of a strategy aimed at them should be viewed as part of a larger and somewhat uneven process. The basics for the corporate campaign were developed by Rogers even before the merger of TWUA and Amalgamated, at the same time the boycott strategy was being developed. Disagreements between Rogers and the merging unions caused him to leave the organization for a period of about six months. When he returned, he began to work on what he considers the first real action of the corporate campaign, the Stevens stockholders' meeting that was held in New York in March, 1977. This was the same meeting that had provided the boycott with national media attention.

Stockholders' actions are not new to labor, but past efforts had not provided examples of power confronting power, in Rogers' opinion.[91] So plans were made to have thousands of people present and to have over 600 people lined up with stock proxies. Rogers gives three reasons for the large-scale confrontation:

> One was that I wanted to appeal to a large number of people, to intimidate management in the same way that they had intimidated workers for so many years. The stockholders' meeting was the only place that I could be guaranteed to be at the front—eyeball-to-eyeball, face-to-face with the company's highest officials. Secondly, I wanted to raise the issues to the consciousness of the national press. Most importantly, I wanted a media display. I wanted the business community to read in their newspapers, to see on television the large coalition of support we had and to realize that anyone closely tied to Stevens' interests would be held accountable for the company's policies and actions by the coalition.[92]

Stevens moved its next three annual stockholders' meetings to Greenville, South Carolina. This was the first time since the 1940s that the meetings were not held in New York City.

Rogers was pleased with the success of this first action, but was frustrated subsequently because although he wanted to take immediate steps to operationalize his corporate strategy, others had misgivings. ACTWU's legal staff was concerned about secondary boycotts and lawsuits. This, of course, was equally true for the boycott strategy; the boycott, however, was not a new strategy. Rogers was sailing into uncharted waters and union staff and officers found it difficult to advise on the likely consequences of his proposed directions.

While waiting for the legal staff to investigate ramifications of a corporate campaign, Rogers targeted Manufacturers Hanover. This was a large, powerful institution and James Finley, Stevens' chief executive officer, was on its board. In addition, David Mitchell, chairman and top executive officer of Avon Products, Inc., was on the Stevens board and the Manufacturers Hanover board. Manufacturers Hanover was headquartered in New York and Rogers knew that many unions and union members had deposits there and that union funds were invested in Manufacturers Hanover stock. As Rogers said; "It's incredible that Manufacturers Hanover—a bank with lots of union deposits and pension-fund accounts—is lending so much money to an anti-union company like Stevens. How is that in any union's interest?"[93]

Although he was advised against organizing another big action at the Manufacturers Hanover stockholders' meeting, Rogers did attend the meeting, accompanied by 100 supporters—the ACTWU legal staff felt that more than that number would be unwise—and he was able to raise the issues regarding Stevens at the meeting. This action was followed by letters that were sent to international unions, explaining the Stevens-Manufacturers Hanover connections and asking for information about union deposits and investments with the bank.

In November, 1977, Rogers received a thick memo from ACTWU's legal department explaining the legal problems and advising that the corporate campaign not be undertaken. Rogers nevertheless proceeded by organizing a postcard, letter-writing, and telephone campaign, drawing on ACTWU's own power base, the coalition of labor and other organizations that supported ACTWU in the Stevens campaign. These organizations were supplied with information about Manufacturers Hanover and with preprinted postcards demanding that the targeted interlocking director be removed from Manufacturers Hanover board. Rogers says he was faithful to his no-boycott agreement with the union—he never asked anyone to threaten withdrawal of financial support from the bank or any other institution. He didn't have to, because the suggestion was implicit in the campaign and crucial to it. Individuals threatened Manufacturers Hanover themselves, and the numbers of letters, postcards, and telephone calls made it clear to officials at Manufacturers Hanover that they were deeply embroiled in the controversy and that hundreds of thousands of dollars were involved.

On March 7, 1978, it was announced that James Finley and David Mitchell had resigned from the board of Manufacturers Hanover. Two weeks later David Mitchell also resigned from the Stevens board.

The next target was New York Life Insurance Company. In September, 1978, Ralph Manning Brown, Jr., New York Life's chairman and chief executive officer, resigned from the board of Stevens and James Finley resigned from the board of New York Life.

In addition to the procedures used against Manufacturers Hanover, Rogers proposed contesting Finley's and Brown's seats on the New York Life board; mutual insurance policy holders are considered the owners of the insurance company and have the right to nominate people to the board. This is something that policy holders rarely do as a matter of course. But for New York Life, a contested election would have meant an extremely large financial outlay for legal costs and mailing costs to all its policy holders. Sister Ann Patrick, a national ecumenical leader, and Clarence B. Jones, an attorney and businessman, were nominated to run for the two seats on the board; they withdrew their candidacies when Finley and Brown resigned.

In 1979 activity slowed. Corporate campaign activities were directed at E. Virgil Conway, chairman and president of the Seamen's Bank for Savings. The strategy linked Conway's generally conservative politics to his opposition to a bill that had been proposed in the New York state legislature. This bill, opposed by mutual savings banks, provided for elections of savings bank trustees by their depositors. This campaign also involved an allegation that Seamen's Bank was investing most of its money out of the state of New York rather than meeting the credit needs of the community for mortgage loans, in order to receive a better rate of return. Conway, however, proved to be a resistant target. He did not give up his Stevens directorship, but evidently did use his influence to get some talks going between Stevens and ACTWU. These talks were slow-moving and desultory, and Rogers was eager to keep his campaign moving.

The New York Life campaign had made Rogers realize how strategically crucial Metropolitan Life and Equitable also were. Both of these companies were deeply involved financially with Stevens and with the management of union pension funds and union members' insurance policies. However, Rogers could not figure out a way to get to them. There were no interlocking directorates and any attempts to cut off financial relationships could possibly involve ACTWU in the uncertain realm of secondary boycott legalities.

Rogers finally got at Metropolitan Life while actively targeting Sperry Corporation, the giant computer manufacturer on whose board James Finley sat. Richard Shinn, head of Metropolitan Life, was on Sperry's board and had been a member of the nominating committee that had renominated Finley to the Sperry board. At that time, Shinn had received letters critical of the nomination and his part in it. In September, 1980, attorneys representing ACTWU filed a petition with the New York State Department of Insurance for access to the Metroplitan Life policy holder list, thereby indicating they were going to run a contested election for Metropolitan's board—just as they had done with New York Life. The action was so unprecedented (the union had not gotten to this stage in the New York Life case) that the Department of Insurance decided to hold a hearing before releasing the list.

According to Rogers, Shinn moved quickly, not waiting for the outcome of the hearing. He met with ACTWU's president, Murray Finley, on September 30, and then with Stevens' executives. Rogers was told later that day that negotiations would continue nonstop until a settlement was reached. The agreement was reached within the next two weeks and was ratified by Stevens workers on October 19.

In reporting the settlement, the *Wall Street Journal* observed: "The union recently had apparently put considerable fear in the hearts of Stevens executives when it paraded this corporate weapon in front of a major Stevens leader." The article explains Richard Shinn's situation and concern over the threat of a contested election. This threat, it says, led Shinn to meet with Whitney Stevens.

> Mr. Shinn says he applied "absolutely no pressure" on Mr. Stevens. "I merely wanted to find out how the negotiations with the union were going," he says. "It was an exchange of information."
>
> But overt pressure undoubtedly wasn't necessary. Metropolitan last year held $97 million of the textile company's $226 million in long term debt, public records indicate.
>
> "Without my ever having to say anything," Mr. Shinn says, J. P. Stevens "realized that if in the course of good business dealings they could settle with the union, it would minimize our election problems" with the textile workers [i.e., ACTWU].[94]

Shinn's influence on the timing of the settlement agreement was undoubtedly important. On the other hand, it should not be overemphasized. The complex agreement could not have been reached quickly. As far back as June, 1980, press stories had reported that ACTWU and Stevens were hammering out a pact and that the end was in sight.

There were at least three parts to the relationship between media and the ACTWU in connection with the corporate campaign: Rogers worked with media people to establish good lines of communication; the corporate campaign generated news stories and editorials; and Rogers was able to use the media to help him achieve certain of his short-term goals. Although Rogers says he views publicity as "icing on the cake," it is clear that his strategy would have been less successful without it. He was able to apply the economic pressure he wanted, but the public attention that the media focused on corporate interlocks served as the catalyst that produced results—often surprisingly quickly.

The media target market for the corporate campaign was not so much the general public that the boycott had targeted, but the business and financial community. Rogers says that he identified key newspapers and magazines—*New York Times, Wall Street Journal, Business Week, Time, Newsweek, Fortune, Forbes,* and so on—and key writers for each of these. He met with as many as he could and explained his strategy early in the campaign. He told them he would always be glad to answer questions and would keep them informed, but would only come to them when he really had something newsworthy to report.

The news that was generated by the corporate campaign actually began, not with the demonstration at Stevens Tower in March, 1977, but a year later. In 1977, the corporate campaign had no separate identity and was primarily in the discussion stage at ACTWU headquarters. It was not until March, 1978, when Finley and Mitchell resigned, that news writers and commentators became interested in this particular segment of the overall campaign against Stevens. Interest centered on the strategy and Rogers himself—his background and his philosophy.

A *Business Week* article on Stevens' March, 1978 stockholders' meeting in Greenville reported:

> [T]he most important news of the day was not mentioned in the meeting. In response to reporters' questions, Stevens' chairman said he would drop from the Manufacturers Hanover board. For the past year the ACTW has been mobilizing the support of the bank's union customers in threatening to withdraw from the bank a reported $1 billion in union deposits, individual members' deposits, and pension funds. Finley said he recently discussed the situation with the bank's senior management and other directors, and decided "not to go where you're not wanted." The bank would say only that "while we regret the need for [Finley's] decision, we understand the considerations that led him to make it." In addition, David W. Mitchell, chairman of Avon Products, Inc. and a Stevens director who had also been a target of the ACTW campaign, said he would bow out as a Manufacturers Hanover director. He wants to spent more time on other activities, he said.[95]

The *Journal of Commerce* explained the strategy: "The union, joined by a coalition of religious, civil rights and labor leaders, is urging corporations directly tied with Stevens—with interlocking directorships and large shareholdings—to sever these ties."[96]

Women's Wear Daily speculated about what would come next:

> Rogers said he was not about to reveal his specific strategy or targets other than Brown and Conway. He suggested a look at Stevens' proxy statement to provide a clue.
> "Just check the list of directors and look at the interlocks," he says.
> If the past is any guide, this can bring in a wide range of companies that could be impacted.[97]

This article proceeds to do what Rogers suggested; it discusses the directors and the interlocks.

Rogers enjoyed the kind of suspense that the corporate campaign generated. Rather than having to call the news people, they called him: "I would have ten major publications calling me wanting to know what the next step was going to be. That's the kind of interest generated."

Rogers was concerned about the way the strategy was explained to the public in light of his promise to the union not to ask people to boycott banks. The above excerpt from *Business Week* illustrates the basis of his concern. The statement about withdrawal of funds appears to say that the union was threatening to withdraw its deposits and was mobilizing support of customers who were being asked to threaten to withdraw their own deposits as well.

Women's Wear Daily clarifies this by quoting Rogers:

> Rogers says that despite all the talk about pension funds, "We have never suggested to anyone to withdraw pension funds. I read somewhere that our union had threatened to withdraw its money from Manufacturers Hanover. We never had a cent in Manufacturers Hanover.
>
> "Never did anyone suggest threatening a boycott against the bank or Avon. We simply exposed the links between them and Stevens."[98]

Not all media coverage on the corporate campaign was good, however. Rogers expected this; the strategy was new and it was a pressure strategy intended to cause concern in corporate circles. It had also caused concern within the ACTWU. Such doubts were bound to be echoed in the press. A paragraph in the *American Banker* stated:

> These events are causing concern in the banking and corporate communities, some observers calling them "dangerous precedents." Many have raised the question as to what might happen if these tactics were applied to other issues.[99]

The following is from *Women's Wear Daily:*

> The latest pressure tactics of the Amalgamated Clothing and Textile Workers Union, in its long battle with J. P. Stevens has drawn angry charges of illegality from textile manufacturers. They term such actions "blackmail," and insist they must be stopped. . . .
>
> Said Donald F. McCullough, chairman of Collins and Aikman: "These actions by the union and its associate organizations have many negative ramifications. In fact, they smack of being a secondary boycott. Let's face it, if successful, it won't stop there. Later, it could involve all American industry. Or a charitable group, or another union. No one could tell who would be the next victim. If they don't like what you're doing, they just threaten to withdraw support. . . .
>
> Robert E. Coleman, chairman, Riegel Textile Corp., said he doubted very much that the union was within its legal rights in seeking to use pension funds to further its ends.

"It's a blatant misuse of their delegated powers," he charged.

If the industry does not wake up to this "blackmail," he declared, then it deserves whatever happens in the months ahead.[100]

The *Greenville News* (South Carolina) said:

> The success of organized labor in forcing the resignations of members of corporate boards is alarming—a word that even if it is overused best describes the deplorable situation. The harassment of J. P. Stevens directors represents a low point in the history of the American labor movement.[101]

The same kind of criticism was expressed in the *Wall Street Journal:*

> It is not often that we stick our nose into a strictly private conflict between management and labor. . . .
>
> But the beef between the Amalgamated Clothing and Textile Workers Union and J. P. Stevens and Co. . . . has gotten out of hand. The union has essentially lost its long fight to organize Stevens. . . .
>
> The union has lost a fortune in its long drive, and its frustration and bitterness are not hard to understand. But we can't sympathize with the union's last-ditch tactics. Because Stevens can't be beaten in a fair and square stand-up fight, Amalgamated has now resorted to terrorizing businessmen who do business with Stevens. The object is to starve Stevens into submission by isolating it from the rest of the business and financial community. . . .
>
> Labor's problems are serious. But it will solve them sooner by looking inward, not trying to threaten individual corporate directors with the novel weapon of the secondary blacklist.[102]

Rogers defended his methods, stating that putting together power coalitions was something that corporations had done for years. Labor unions had just been slower to realize how these methods could be turned around and utilized against the business world. Of course, the Stevens directors who resigned board directorates were frustrated and angry, but Rogers points out that they were probably no more frustrated and angry than Stevens workers were when their efforts to secure fair employment benefits were ignored. Rogers is quoted in *Time* as saying: "Unions must confront giant corporate power with interlocking workers' power."[103]

Rogers reports that heated discussions with the ACTWU legal department continued throughout the campaign, but he began to get some firm support from within from some ACTWU officers and staff members. For example, after Finley resigned from the New York Life board, ACTWU secretary-treasurer Jacob Sheinkman said: "It is our feeling that this action on the part of New York Life is concrete evidence that the insurance company is certain its policies in supporting J. P. Stevens wouldn't stand the scrutiny of its policy holders or the general public."[104]

In an interview with *Working Papers,* Rogers provided a detailed example of how he used the press to help his campaign move in the desired direction. Early in the campaign, while doing research on Manufacturers Hanover, he sent out one mailing to unions, support groups, and so on, describing links between Manufacturers Hanover and Stevens. As a result of this mailing, he received extensive information concerning union deposits in Manufacturers Hanover, and copies of letters that organizations and individuals had written to Manufacturers Hanover threatening to withdraw their funds. Rogers wanted to take these letters to the press, feeling the response and the amount of money involved would make an excellent story. Union lawyers advised against such a move, saying Rogers could easily be accused of instigating secondary boycott activity if he did so.

> I reminded the lawyers that earlier I had written a letter that said that periodically I would publish a list thanking everybody who writes a letter to Manufacturers Hanover for what they had done. When I reminded them of this, the lawyers said, "OK, you can go ahead." But I also sent the list over to certain key people in the press. I told them that I had all these letters from all these organizations, and I told them frankly, off the record, Manufacturers Hanover is being threatened with a situation that could make their profitable relationship with J. P. Stevens no longer profitable.
>
> Well, one thing led to another, I told them off the record what was contained in the letters and, of course, they wanted copies. I told them that there were particular unions that they would probably be most interested in contacting, and if they called enough unions, they would find that the money added up to hundreds of millions of dollars.[105]

After the settlement, in December, 1980, Ray Rogers left ACTWU and formed his own company, Corporate Campaign, Inc. During the Stevens campaign Rogers had advised some other unions (most notably, the United Food and Commercial Workers' Union), and his successes made him eager to continue and use the experience he had gained. His relationship with ACTWU remained good, though there clearly was some tension between Rogers and some other ACTWU staff members. Specifically, Rogers was critical of the other segments of the campaign because he felt they were going nowhere. He was unhappy with union spokespersons when the settlement agreement was signed; he felt that very little credit, if any, was given to the part the corporate campaign had played in bringing about the settlement. Whether or not this was true, the press gave the corporate campaign a great deal of credit.[106] The scarcity of editorial criticism of the tactics ACTWU utilized to obtain a settlement suggests that much of the negative publicity that Rogers had caused in 1978 had apparently vanished.[107]

Other ACTWU staff members express the opinion that Rogers did not give them credit for providing him with the support that he needed to make his campaign successful. As one said: "The corporate campaign got a lot of press as it was supposed to, and it was extremely important in the late stages of the campaign, but I feel it wouldn't have had the success it had unless it built on a lot of the other less newsworthy aspects of the campaign earlier on."[108]

Rogers agrees that the public feeling engendered against Stevens by both the legal and boycott strategies was extremely important and played a big part in providing him with an organized network and with quick support in his requests for information and in his letter-writing campaigns. His expanded definition of what a corporate campaign is expressed a keen appreciation of the necessity of a multifaceted campaign:

> A corporate campaign attacks an adversary from every conceivable angle. . . . Corporate campaign activities focus on a company's highest officials, its corporate headquarters, its consumer products and on persons and institutions heavily supportive of and tied into its interests through interlocking directorates, large stockholdings and multimillion dollar loans. . . . A total corporate campaign strategy encompasses all legitimate means of pressure and might include a strike, a consumer boycott, or other traditional tactics. However, each tactic would be timed and coordinated as part of an overall conceptualized strategy to maximize the campaign's effectiveness.[109]

The precise role and impact of media coverage of the corporate campaign is impossible to measure. Even a skeptic like Rogers himself, however, who, as noted above, purports to regard publicity as "icing on the cake," says:

> The bank was facing a huge pull-out of union funds. That wasn't the key thing, though, because the huge pull-out of funds threat was really the result of a much greater threat: this was this broad campaign that was creating so much friction. And it was exploding, mushrooming. So that every time the bank officials would go somewhere someone would raise the issue: what are you going to do about the Stevens situation? They saw their image, their reputation of credibility that many years and millions of dollars had built, being destroyed overnight.[110]

Moreover, the significance of media coverage emerged very clearly from such accounts of the corporate outlook as *Textile World's* quote from Whitney Stevens:

> Whitney Stevens is clearly exasperated: "The press has handled this entire story in a most peculiar way, especially in the *[Wall Street] Journal*. I don't understand why they would write a story that is so very inaccurate even with the facts at hand. One of their reporters got me aside yesterday and kept asking about the situation with Dick Shinn. Finally I said, 'Look, you're trying to get me to say that Dick Shinn and the Met had a great deal to do with what happened, when in fact it had nothing to do with it.' "[111]

Of course the postcards and letters connecting Stevens and the other institutions contributed to the corporate perception that the company's image had been damaged. In some corporate campaigns, these and some kind of solid, hard-working coalition may conceivably be all that is necessary. The media may not be essential. In the Stevens campaign, however, the media broadened the public support for the endeavor, which in turn resulted in more economic pressure being placed upon corporations connected to Stevens. The media also educated the business and financial audience on the corporate campaign methods, an outcome that may not have been especially relevant to Rogers in this case, but may have some positive or negative effect in the future.

The Settlement

Settlement discussions were conducted between union officials, Stevens officials, and attorneys from both sides over a period of about two years. They became more substantial starting in January, 1980, and particularly intense during the summer of that year. On October 19, the settlement, in the form of two separate documents, was concluded.

One of these documents was a fairly typical labor union contract that was negotiated with a workers' committee, ratified at a union meeting, and signed by company and union officials in Roanoke Rapids. On the same day, October 19, in New York City, three union officers and two corporate officials (Stevens' chairman of the board and the president), signed a shorter document. The former document usually is referred to as the "contract," while the latter is the "settlement agreement."

The settlement agreement is somewhat novel in that the issues covered in it are not typical collective bargaining issues (e.g., wages, benefits, and adjustment of grievances), but issues that essentially derived from the unusual and lengthy battle between the two sides and the diverse strategies each had utilized in its war. Both documents had a life span of two and a half years, and both sides made significant concessions in order to settle.

Perhaps the biggest concession made by J. P. Stevens leaders consisted in their willingness to sign an agreement and thus recognize the union after vowing for years that the company never would do this. Among other things, the company also agreed to do the following:

1. Execute union contracts at plants where the union had gained bargaining rights through NLRB certification or through court order.
2. Pay Roanoke Rapids workers and former workers approximately $3 million in pay increases that had been withheld in 1979 and 1980 (union workers were denied general wage increases of 8.5 percent in 1979 and 10 percent in 1980).
3. Institute a "check-off system," whereby union dues would be deducted directly from employees' paychecks.
4. Allow workers to grieve issues with management and to accept an outside arbitrator to settle disputes; the rulings of the arbitrator would be "final and non-appealable."

5. Rehire and give backpay to workers in the West Boyleston plant who had been terminated for union activity; to destroy adverse personnel files of those who had been terminated or disciplined for union activity.
6. Hold an election within 90 days at any plant where the workers petitioned.
7. Consult with the union when making decisions regarding improvements or the institution of any corporate-wide benefits and to make announcements of such jointly with the union; such benefits would be installed simultaneously in union plants as well as non-union plants.

The union agreed to discontinue many of the segments of its multifaceted campaign against Stevens. As has been mentioned, it agreed to end its boycott, end its corporate campaign, and, further, agreed that it would not single out Stevens as its primary organizing target in the textile industry. Other concessions made by ACTWU included the following:

1. To suspend for 18 months the extraordinary access remedies that had been ordered by the Second Circuit Court in 1978.
2. To drop its lawsuit in the Milledgeville case of widespread industrial espionage conducted by the Milledgeville police department.
3. To enter into formal settlements of certain other pending NLRB cases against Stevens.
4. To terminate the publication of *Social Justice*.

The agreement covered workers at the seven Roanoke Rapids plants, plus the plants in High Point, North Carolina; Allendale, South Carolina; and West Boyleston, Alabama, a total of only 10 of Stevens plants and covering only about 10 percent of all Stevens workers. These figures confirm that the agreement, while celebrated by ACTWU, could hardly be regarded as the end of one of the longest labor-management disputes in history, but, rather, as a significant move in the right direction.

The ACTWU public relations department organized media coverage and press conferences in Roanoke Rapids and in New York City on October 19 to announce the settlement shortly after the documents were ratified by workers. At the New York press conference, ACTWU president Murray Finley said, "This union has borne the brunt of the struggle. . . . We have committed our resources, energies and prestige more than any other union to bring organization to southern workers. Every ACTWU member can take pride in the struggle we have waged and the victory we are announcing today."[112] According to ACTWU's newspaper, *Labor Unity*, Finley praised the "groundbreaking" legal work that had been done by Arthur Goldberg and the union's legal staff and the "unprecedented" world-wide consumer boycott organized by Del Mileski and his union label department. ACTWU secretary-treasurer Jacob Sheinkman added that everyone was intensely proud of the accomplishments, but at the same time realized that the struggle with Stevens necessarily would continue. And AFL-CIO president Lane Kirkland praised ACTWU, saying that the victory was one for all working people.

Whitney Stevens, chairman of J. P. Stevens, said little to the media after the contract was signed. He did state, however, that he believed that large numbers of Stevens employees did not want the union; but, where the union had won elections, the company would live with the union successfully.[113]

> While it was clearly a union victory, Whitney Stevens . . . predicted that within five years the union would be eliminated from Stevens plants. He said the agreement cost the company nothing more in wages and fringe benefits than had already been given to the company's non-union workers.
>
> Stevens said the company "continues to be openly and strongly opposed to unions" at its more than 70 other non-union plants.[114]

Generally, the settlement brought wide media editorial support for ACTWU. Publications targeted to specific audiences took fairly predictable positions based either upon the side that had been taken publicly earlier in the campaign, or the general orientation of the publication and its readers. The following, for example, was printed in the trade publication *Retail-week:*

> [L]et no one envy the situation of the organizer peddling unionism in the South's textile belt today—especially not after the contract that the Amalgamated Clothing and Textile Workers Union (ACTWU) signed with J. P. Stevens last month.
>
> Picture the scenario: arrives the out-of-towner, probably sporting a foreign northern accent, and settles himself into a modest motel on the outskirts of town. Bright and early the next day, he wanders out in search of prey, mentally reviewing his new pitch: "Hey, did you hear about our victory at Roanoke Rapids? Did you hear how we brought the mighty J. P. Stevens to its knees?"
>
> "Yeh," says a disgruntled mill operative, "tell me how much y'all socked it to 'em. How big a raise; more vacation and sick days; better health and pension benefits?"
>
> "Oh, much more than that," explains the organizer. We won a moral victory; we won a symbolic victory; we won check-off of union dues; we won binding arbitration."
>
> "You mean," asks the most vocal among the small crowd gathering around, "that you got 'em nothing the other Stevens' workers don't have? And, for this, they're paying dues?"
>
> "You don't understand," comes the patient reply, "Arbitration is very important when it comes to seniority and compensation disputes."
>
> *Try feeding your kids or paying your mortgage or buying gas on that.*"[115]

As a part of the settlement agreement, ACTWU agreed to state publicly that the boycott had ended—to prepare a press release and make it available to news and media sources and to notify its network and support institutions, including state and local governments. This work was undertaken primarily by union staff members in the union label and public relations departments.

The last issue of the *Social Justice* newsletter came out in December, 1980, with a brief note by editor Joe Pilati;

> Since November, 1976, *Social Justice* has brought news of the J. P. Stevens workers' struggle and the consumer boycott, now ended, to hundreds of thousands of people. You, the readers, translated that news into activism and action that culminated in the victory scenes published here, in our final issue. Future campaigns will bring us together again, no doubt, but for now we pause to celebrate and consider how far we have come. . . and how far we have to go. . . proudly, sustained by the Stevens workers' example.[116]

The relationships between the media and ACTWU that were developed during the Stevens campaign reflect characteristics of all of the segments of the campaign and the leadership in those segments: the skill and persistence of the legal department; the unprecedented commitment of the label and public relations departments and the cohesion of the coalition they formed; and the innovativeness and flamboyance of the corporate campaign.

Update

A great deal has happened in the years since the 1980 contract was signed. In regard to the relationship shared by ACTWU and Stevens, top ACTWU officials summed up the years as having produced "a maturing of the collective bargaining process in which both parties demonstrated a willingness to live with each other and cooperate."[117] J. P. Stevens attorney Robert T. Thompson, Sr. stated: "We have an understanding that we will deal with each other within the law and, in the future, that is what we expect to do. . . . I hope that we are entering a new age because I think the age that we (hopefully) just left is one that we can't always be proud of. . . . I think J. P. Stevens has entered a new age for sure."[118]

In April, 1983, the original two-and-a-half year contract between Stevens and ACTWU was renegotiated in a short time and with few difficulties. The 25 month contract covers approximately 3,500 workers in nine plants in North and South Carolina. Two plants in Wallace, North Carolina were organized as a result of a court bargaining order which had been handed down before the original 1980 agreement because of Stevens' prior labor law violations. In January, 1983, Stevens and ACTWU signed a 30-month contract that covers about 550 workers in Wallace. Both the Wallace contract and the renegotiated contract covering the original plants expired and were replaced by a new three-year contract in May 1985. Both Stevens and ACTWU are struggling with problems engendered by a changing textile industry. Increasing automation and an unprecedented flood of textile and apparel imports have caused job losses, a dwindling existing and potential membership for ACTWU, and rising costs and decreasing profits for Stevens.

Stevens experienced a net loss in 1981, a year in which the company announced plans to "redeploy assets" in order to improve its long-term profits. Since then, as part of that plan, Stevens has closed plants, phased out some product lines, introduced others, and expended millions in relocations, machinery, and other modernization investments. Total employment figures dropped from 49,000 in 1969 to 35,300 in 1983.[119] (Not all of these workers are textile workers, however, as Stevens also has interests in printing and aviation.) Earnings fell in both 1982 and 1983, but increased moderately in 1984. Company leaders believe the major costs are behind them; they feel good about the changes that have been made, and are optimistic about the level of market activity and the future of the company. One of the changes made by Stevens was the closing of the plant in West Boyleston, Alabama, one of the plants covered in the original agreement. At the same time, however, the company has invested in major remodeling and modernization at the Roanoke Rapids, High Point, and Wallace plants.

Stevens has, as promised in 1980, continued to resist vigorously (and legally) union attempts to organize other plants. But also as promised in 1980, ACTWU has placed top priority on organizing. Its efforts continue, but more quietly. No longer is Stevens singled out; ACTWU devotes attention to it as deemed necessary. The union has also had to watch its budget; it was estimated that the union spent between $13 and $14 million on the Stevens campaign between 1963 and 1980, most of this amount being spent between 1976 and 1980.

The final chapter in the original campaign was written in October, 1983, when Stevens and ACTWU reached a comprehensive settlement that ended all the outstanding unfair labor practice cases against Stevens. Under its terms, Stevens agreed to pay the union $1 million to settle claims arising out of the cases and an additional $200,000 in backpay to employees. In return, ACTWU agreed to drop all 13 of the unresolved NLRB cases against the textile company, each of which was in some phase of the judicial process.

Media attention directed toward ACTWU during its Stevens campaign has diminshed to a point where the union now has a low profile typical of organized labor. To the extent that communications are emphasized, this is done primarily in support of ACTWU's organizing efforts. A principal goal of such communications is to keep current members well-informed. In December, 1981, ACTWU reorganized its publications and public relations departments. There is now a department of communications, whose responsibility it is to disseminate information and news to members and to the news media. The new arrangement is regarded as simpler and more workable and represents an attempt to address some of the organizational problems that accompanied the merger and were ignored or received little attention because of the intensity of the Stevens campaign.

The department of communications, which remained under the directorship of Burt Beck until his retirement in 1983, publishes the union newspaper, *Labor Unity,* pamphlets, newsletters, and so on. It is also responsible for press releases, the preparation of background material—information, statistics, photographs, and so on—media reports, and the maintenance of personal contact with members of the working press. The department actively assists ACTWU locals in their communications efforts. Several publications have been distributed to officers, joint boards, and locals outlining the union's rights to access to radio and television and providing tips on effective use of the media.

At the ACTWU convention in June, 1981, retiring senior executive vice president Sol Stetin emphasized the need for effective media usage. In addition to more and better media use, Stetin discussed the importance of interpersonal communications—both among workers and through the use of the powerful networks that had been so important in the Stevens campaign.

Some ACTWU locals have become skilled in their media relationships. One outstanding example was provided by Local 1855 in Columbus, Georgia. The local's interest in publicity started when members established a local newsletter because they were having difficulty with management concerning the use of company bulletin boards. Subsequently, they held several press conferences, each attended by representatives from the local press, radio, and television. Subjects at the press conferences included byssinosis, union gains, and Reagan administration policies. Members reported good local coverage of issues of interest to them and of their point of view.

ACTWU recently has been able to give more time to goals other than organizing that were stated at the time of the merger: to seek favorable legislation and to reduce anti-union sentiment, especially in the south. Following the Stevens campaign, the union was successful in generating news about byssinosis, cotton dust, the decline in OSHA's performance during the Reagan administration, and OSHA's reopening of the cotton dust standard. The union also has generated news through its activism in protest of the Labor Department's order to eliminate homework restrictions in the knitted outerwear industry and through its position on unregulated imports and fair trade.

Some advertising has been undertaken. Because ACTWU's union label department was so involved in the Stevens campaign, ordinary union label efforts received little attention. After the merger, a new label was designed; the need to promote it was met through an advertising campaign developed by the public relations department after the termination of the Stevens campaign. The advertisement appeared in national magazines and, following the Machinists example, on the flashing sign in New York's Time

Square during the November, 1981 AFL-CIO convention (Figure 23). At its third convention in June, 1984, the union stressed better promotion of the union label as well as political activity, a variety of crucial legislative issues, programs for the unemployed, workplace chemical and other health hazards, and economic parity for women.

CONCLUSIONS

The J. P. Stevens campaign as conducted by ACTWU was unprecedented in a number of ways. One of these was the media relationship that was established. Had this relationship not been developed, it is doubtful that ACTWU could have achieved its goal of reaching an agreement with J. P. Stevens. In achieving this relationship several factors were important.

First, there was the multifaceted nature of the campaign—the organizing, the legal segment, the consumer product boycott, and the corporate cam-

FIGURE 23. Advertising on flashing sign in Times Square, New York City, November 1981, sponsored by ACTWU; from *Labor Unity,* January 1982, p. 16.

paign. Each of these segments involved a separate strategy, but all were oriented toward achieving a single well-defined objective and all received strong guidance from ACTWU's New York headquarters. This guidance had to be and was skillfully administrated. In retrospect, some of the leadership in New York have regarded this fact with a certain amount of wonder.

It is clear that there were internal conflicts. Given the complexity and crisis quality of the situation, this might have been true in any case, but it was compounded by the fact that the two unions had just merged. The merger did not result in an automatic coalescing of two unions into one. The Stevens campaign required unity, however, and ACTWU leaders apparently put aside narrower self-interest and postponed less important problems. The determination of ACTWU leaders to achieve their primary goal resulted in strong internal cohesion.

The union's internal communication system was vital to the smooth administrative process that was achieved. Bulletins, memos, meetings, and discussion kept those in the New York office and in the field very aware of the latest developments, plans, and so on.

Second, ACTWU leaders developed the issues of the campaign. Union leaders wanted to raise those campaign issues that had salience to a public that exceeded labor. They wanted to avoid portraying the campaign as another labor-management battle. They sought to do more than provide information about a corporation that was, in their opinion, unfair to employees. The social justice issues were ideological issues that were salient to a large number of people and thus broadened the appeal of the campaign considerably.

Next, the union developed an effective coalition that formed an active nationwide network and took the issues outside of ACTWU. The key to the coalition was the specialists who were recruited to be staff members of ACTWU. These specialists communicated with others with whom common interests were shared and many of these people, including people at the local level and people who thought the social justice arguments were important for a whole variety of reasons, communicated with the media.

The ACTWU staff members provided good examples for this coalition in working with the media. Those involved in the various segments of the campaign worked to develop personal contacts and close cooperation with the media. A mutuality of interest did exist: ACTWU wanted to obtain media coverage and the media wanted new information. The multifaceted nature of the campaign also enabled ACTWU to reach numerous specialized publications.

Serendipity boosted the campaign: there was limited media opposition from the opponent and there was the success of *Norma Rae*. ACTWU was on the offensive and this gave a positive thrust to the campaign.

Finally, the fact that the campaign leaders within ACTWU agreed that the media coverage they were able to generate was more effective than the advocacy advertising that was done deserves emphasis. Burt Beck stated flatly that he felt that the money spent by ACTWU for advertising was not well spent. David Dyson remembered little about the advertising though he said he thought several ads had been placed in newspapers and on radio previous to planned marches and rallies in order to raise consciousness and gain support. Dyson said that advertising certainly was not used extensively—it was a relatively minor part of the campaign, and, even so, the ACTWU staff had had some disagreements about its use and questioned its potential effectiveness when weighed against the costs involved. These latter included not only money, but the difficulties encountered and time spent trying to convince media that a given ad should be carried.

Ray Rogers stated:

> I am just pretty much opposed to buying advertising. Advertising may gain the attention of the public, but it won't make much of an impression. This is because you write it yourself—or pay someone to write it for you—and it's self-serving and the public knows this. But, especially in any kind of campaign, it is better to generate newsworthy stories.[120]

While agreeing with this assessment in general, however, union leaders pointed out that some of the advertisements served a valid purpose. Advertising placed in trade publications was regarded rather favorably.

> We placed ads in *Daily News Record, Women's Wear Daily,* and perhaps one other publication—I'm not sure. At any rate, trade publications generally have lower advertising rates than the daily press. And these ads were well-targeted—they were aimed at retailers and I think they were effective. These trade publications go out all over the country and they probably were most helpful when they were seen by retailers in some of the smaller towns and cities where few news stories got into the daily press. They served as sort of an introduction to our people who were talking with retailers.[121]

The trade publication ads typically carried an endorsement of the boycott by some well-known person. They were, therefore, probably not only well-targeted, but carefully conceived to give the campaign increased legitimacy. The campaign had succeeded in gaining the support not only of people who were willing to be actively involved in the network, but also of high-status people who had no inclination or time to be active but who were willing to have their endorsement used by ACTWU.

As for advertising in more general circulation media, especially newspapers, the purposes and results were somewhat different but also considered useful. Of these ads, which were intended to increase attention, provide additional information, or express a different point of view, a union staff person said: "There was a reason for this kind of advertising and it took persistence, but the ads usually were accepted by the media and were beneficial to the overall campaign."[122]

ACTWU leaders learned a great deal about the use of mass media during the Stevens campaign. This case, however, was unique in many respects. The next challenge for this union—and other internationals—is to take the knowledge gained during the campaign years and reapply it to immediate objectives. While the media may not be necessary—or even useful—in achieving some objectives, organizing is certainly not in that category. More difficult, of course, is the question regarding *how* the media should be used. And on this issue the debate continues. However, ACTWU Executive Vice President Scott Hoyman, a seasoned organizer who put a great deal of effort into the Stevens campaign, believes that the emphasis, at least for organizing, must be on issues. " 'Selling the union like you would sell a refrigerator' is a tactic he opposes."[123]

Debate also continues regarding the effectiveness and potential usefulness of corporate campaigns. Many believe they can rarely be effective because they are time-consuming, costly, and generally cumbersome. However, Ray Rogers and Vic Kamber, founder of the Washington public relations and political consulting firm called the Kamber Group, believe that this tactic is worthwhile enough to dispute over the use of the phrase "corporate campaign." Both are using the strategy for labor clients. Rogers is working on campaigns against RCA, a soup company, a book publisher, and a Wisconsin newspaper chain. Kamber has hired a director for corporate campaigns who has been devoting efforts to a campaign in Illinois for the United Steelworkers. Those who support the strategy believe that it is a necessary response by labor to the growth of multinational corporations. They also believe that while it is based on power politics, the part the media plays is vital to its success.

NOTES

[1] *J. P. Stevens Annual Report,* 1976, p. 1.

[2] Textile Workers Union of America (TWUA), *Proceedings, Eighteenth Biennial Convention* (New York: TWUA, 1974), p. 14.

[3] International Ladies' Garment Workers' Union (ILGWU), *Report and Record, Twentyninth Convention* (New York: ILGWU, 1956), p. 365. This source argues that the union label can be an effective force for labor, an adjunct to organizing, and claims that Amalgamated got 12 holdouts in the men's clothing industry to sign agreements as a result of the label campaign.

[4] Amalgamated Clothing Workers of America (ACWA), *General Executive Board Report, Twenty-fifth Biennial Convention* (New York: ACWA, 1966), p. 50.

[5] This idea goes back as far as 1909, according to AFL-CIO reports. (See the AFL-CIO *Executive Council Report, Ninth Constitutional Convention,* 1971, p. 401.) In the 1970s there was renewed interest in the concept of a universal label because of the growth of multinational

companies and the impact of imports on the U.S. economy. TWUA's support for it is understandable, but the idea has never been favored by all unions and it appears to lack practical application—probably in just the same way the TWUA's own label did.

6 TWUA, *Executive Council Report, Nineteenth Biennial Convention* (1976), p. 12.

7 *J. P. Stevens Annual Report, 1976,* pp. 23, 3.

8 Ibid., p. 1.

9 *Moody's Industrial Manual,* vol. II (New York: Moody's Investors' Service, 1976), p. 3289.

10 *J. P. Stevens Annual Report, 1976,* p. 10.

11 American Federation of Labor-Congress of Industrial Organizations (AFL-CIO), *Proceedings, Fifth Constitutional Convention,* vol. II (Washington, D.C.: AFL-CIO, 1963), p. 304.

12 TWUA, *Proceedings* (1964), p. 240.

13 *J. P. Stevens Annual Report,* 1963, p. 7.

14 United States Department of Labor, Bureau of Labor Statistics, *Employment and Earnings, United States, 1909–78,* Bulletin 1312–11 (Washington, D.C.: United States Government Printing Office, 1979), p. 505.

15 The Darlington case, after years of litigation, finally reached the Supreme Court in 1981. The Supreme Court upheld the NLRB decision that Deering-Milliken had broken the law when it closed its Darlington plant in 1956. The Court ordered backpay to be sent to the 525 former workers or to their heirs. The amount of the settlement totaled nearly $5 million. (See "First Backpay Checks Sent to Darlington Mills Victims," *AFL-CIO News,* August 1, 1981, p. 8.)

16 Representative Frank Thompson, Jr., remarks delivered to the U.S. House of Representatives, May 24, 1966. Reprinted in "A Case History of Union Busting . . . J. P. Stevens in the South," *AFL-CIO American Federationist,* July, 1966, p. 3.

17 Bargaining efforts with Stevens were not discontinued in Roanoke Rapids, however, despite all the setbacks. Scott Hoyman, formerly TWUA southern regional director and currently ACTWU executive vice president, who led the negotiations throughout, reported that bargaining continued in an "unusual process—the process of bargaining on an initial contract with a continuing series of meetings once every two or three weeks, for two or three days at a time, from 1974 until October 1980." (From a speech, "J. P. Stevens and Organizing," made by Hoyman at the Institute of Labor and Industrial Relations Colloquium, University of Illinois, December 5, 1980).

18 National Labor Relations Act, 49 Stat. 452, ch. 372 § 6a, 29 U. S. C. § 156 (July 5, 1935).

19 *Hearings before the U.S. Senate Subcommittee on Labor of the Committee on Human Resources on the Labor Reform Act of 1977* (testimony of Arthur M. Goldberg, ACTWU General Counsel), 95th Cong., 1st Sess., pt. 1 at 208 (1977).

20 "Unions Denounce Perversion of U.S. Labor Law's Objectives," *AFL-CIO News,* June 30, 1984, pp. 1, 3.

21 The Labor Reform Act of 1977 (H. R. 8410, S. 1883) was cosponsored by Representative Frank Thompson, Jr. (N. J.), Senator Harrison Williams (N. J.), and Senator Jacob Javits (N. Y.). Thompson said that the actions of the J. P. Stevens Co. were one of the "inspirations" for his bill. During the House and Senate hearings a number of Stevens workers testified, as well as union officials, clergy, state legislators, and civic leaders. Company representatives declined an invitation to testify. Among other things, the bill called for expansion of the NLRB from five to seven members, a faster representation election process, the NLRB to seek an injunction against an employer for one unfair labor practice, exclusion of labor law violators from federal contracts (Defense Department contracts awarded to Stevens between 1965 and 1977 totaled about $118.5 million, according to ACTWU's statement during the Senate hearings), and increased settlements for workers discharged for union activities.

[22] See, for example, the complaints received by the Senate subcommittee in 1977, in the *Hearings* (1977), pp. 909–19.

[23] Senate *Hearings* (1977), pp. 221–28.

[24] The latter case resulted in a criminal trial against two Stevens employees, the only one of its kind. The two were charged with federal violations resulting from wiretap activities of a union organizer's telephone during the organizing campaign in Wallace, North Carolina. Both were found guilty in December, 1973, though this decision was later overturned on a technicality. A civil suit also was filed in this case. It was settled out of court. Stevens denied its guilt, but settled the lawsuit with a payment of $50,000.

[25] *J. P. Stevens and Co. v. NLRB,* 441 F. 2d 514 (5th Cir., 1971), at 521.

[26] *NLRB v. J. P. Stevens and Co., Inc.,* 563 F. 2d 8 (2nd Cir., 1977), at 13.

[27] *NLRB v. J. P. Stevens and Co., Inc.,* 244 NLRB (1979), at 459.

[28] This decision was appealed to the Supreme Court by Stevens, but the Court refused to hear the case.

[29] A national injunction was issued in 1948 in a labor case against a union, the International Typographical Union, according to *Time,* December 12, 1977, p. 76, but evidently never before against a company.

[30] *NLRB v. J. P. Stevens and Co., Inc.,* 239 NLRB (1978), at 738.

[31] This union surveillance case started in 1978 at the Stevens plant in Milledgeville, Georgia. ACTWU agreed to drop the case when the settlement was reached in 1980.

[32] Joel Ax, ACTWU Associate General Counsel, interview, New York City, June 3, 1982.

[33] Ibid.

[34] Edward M. McConville, "The Southern Textile War," *The Nation,* October 2, 1976, p. 294.

[35] "On the Road Again: the Textile/Apparel Union," *Clothes,* September 15, 1976, pp. 67, 65.

[36] Letter of NLRB Chairman John Fanning and General Counsel John Irving to Amalgamated Clothing and Textile Workers' Union on J. P. Stevens Settlement. Reprinted in the *Daily Labor Report* (Washington, D.C.: Bureau of National Affairs, Inc., May 25, 1978).

[37] "J. P. Stevens Settles With Labor Board on Antiunion Acts," *New York Times,* April 29, 1978, p. 29.

[38] "NLRB Cancels Bid for Injunction Against Stevens; Textile Firm Agrees to Take Action Required; Right to Join Unions Involved," *Wall Street Journal,* May 1, 1978, p. 14.

[39] "NLRB, Stevens in Pact; Union Objects," *Women's Wear Daily,* March 13, 1978, P. 13.

[40] Ax interview.

[41] There are few certainties in the textile industry, however, as *Clothes* magazine points out: "Although Stevens is a strong company, it has certainly experienced dips as a member in full standing of the volatile textile industry and even showed a loss in 1971. Should one of those dips occur during the boycott, the combination might boomerang—discrediting the boycott as an organizing tool. After all, workers are not likely to take kindly to the idea that they might lose their jobs but at least some of their former fellow workers are organized." (See "On the Road Again," September 15, 1976, p. 64).

[42] Del Mileski, Director, ACTWU Union Label Department, interview, New York City, June 3, 1982.

[43] Ax interview.

[44] "What Is At Stake In the Stevens Union Struggle," Statement by Fourteen Southern Ministers, pamphlet (1976).

[45] Bayard Rustin, "Labor's Struggle At J. P. Stevens Promises Justice for All in South," *Social Justice,* May, 1977, p. 4.

[46] "Unions of Six Nations Back Boycott," *Social Justice,* October, 1977, p. 1.

[47] Mileski interview.

48 Peter Selkowe, "Council Makes Its Bed with Union-Made Sheets," *The Morning Courier* (Champaign-Urbana, Illinois), January 14, 1979, p. 30.

49 Ibid.

50 Noreen McGrath, "Boycott of Textile Companies Supported at 75 Colleges," *Chronicle of Higher Education,* November 6, 1978, p. 10.

51 "Women Renew Drive Against J. P. Stevens," *Social Justice,* May, 1978, p. 4.

52 Howard D. Samuel, President, AFL-CIO Industrial Union Department, interview, Washington, D.C., May 24, 1982.

53 David Dyson, Field Director ACTWU Union Label Department, interview, New York City, June 2, 1982.

54 Samuel interview.

55 Ibid.

56 Mileski interview.

57 "A Gathering Momentum Against J. P. Stevens," *Business Week,* March 20, 1978, p. 147.

58 Mileski interview.

59 Burt Beck, Director, ACTWU Department of Communications, interview, New York City, June 3, 1982.

60 Memo from Burt Beck, January 11, 1977. The memo accompanied a transcript of the "MacNeil/Lehrer Report" that was sent to a number of ACTWU field workers.

61 Transcript of "MacNeil/Lehrer Report—J. P. Stevens," Educational Broadcasting Corporation and GWETA, 1976, p. 2.

62 Transcript of "Sixty Minutes—Target: J. P. Stevens," CBS Television, March 13, 1977, p. 1.

63 Ibid., pp. 5–6.

64 "Film Exposes 'Real' J. P. Stevens," *Social Justice,* April, 1977, p. 1.

65 Daniel D. Cook, "Boycott! Labor's Last Resort," *Industry Week,* June 28, 1976, p. 26.

66 Marvin Klapper, "Through the Mill with J. P. Stevens," *Women's Wear Daily,* November 20, 1978, pp. 4–5.

67 There was also a "sister" organization to the Employees' Education Committee in Roanoke Rapids that was also involved in the quest for contributor information. This group, located in Greenville, South Carolina, was called "Stevens People and Friends for Freedom."

68 Sandra Salmans, "J. P. Stevens: One Year After the Truce," *New York Times,* October 18, 1981, p. F9.

69 "Finley to Leave Stevens' Top Post," *Women's Wear Daily,* September 21, 1979, pp. 1, 14.

70 "J. P. Stevens: Change Ripples the Fishbowl," *Women's Wear Daily,* October 8, 1980, p. 44.

71 Mileski interview.

72 Ax interview.

73 Mileski interview.

74 Ibid.

75 "First Bi-annual Issues Conference," *National NOW Times,* November, 1978, p. 13.

76 McGrath, "Boycott Supported at 75 Colleges," p. 10.

77 "Bishops Support Boycott of J. P. Stevens," *The Georgia Bulletin,* March 13, 1980, p. 1.

78 Parren Mitchell, "J. P. Stevens Co., Blacks and Unions," *Social Justice,* February, 1977, p. 4. Reprinted from the *Baltimore Afro-American.*

79 "Pulling J. P. Stevens, and Labor, Into 1980," *New York Times,* October 21, 1980, p. A18.

[80] "J. P. Stevens: Labor Wins a Hardball Contest in the South," *Detroit Free Press*, October 24, 1980, p. 10A.

[81] "Son of 'Norma Rae,'" *Chicago Sun-Times*, October 22, 1980, p. 75.

[82] "Victory for Workers," *News and Observer* (Raleigh, North Carolina), October 21, 1980, p. 4.

[83] The film *Norma Rae* was made in a plant in Opelika, Alabama that is a division of Opelika Mfg. Corp., and an active union plant.

[84] Dyson interview.

[85] Amalgamated Clothing & Textile Workers Union (ACTWU), *Report of the General Executive Board, Second Constitutional Convention* (New York: ACTWU, 1981), p. 69.

[86] Mileski interview.

[87] Settlement Agreement, J. P. Stevens Co., Inc. and the Amalgamated Clothing and Textile Workers Union, October 20, 1980, pp. 2–3.

[88] Ibid., p. 3.

[89] Ray Rogers, Director, Corporate Campaign, Inc., interview, New York City, June 1, 1982.

[90] "An Interview with Ray Rogers," *Working Papers Magazine*, January-February, 1982, p. 50.

[91] TWUA had organized a small stockholders' action a year before the merger. According to Rogers, there were only about 30 people outside Stevens headquarters and only about 11 on the inside with stock proxies. In his opinion, this action only made the union look weak and its cause unimportant.

[92] Rogers interview.

[93] Judith Coburn, "J. P. Stevens Plays by Its Own Rules," *Village Voice*, May 2, 1977, p. 35.

[94] Gail Bronson and Jeffrey H. Birnbaum, "How the Textile Union Finally Wins Contract at J. P. Stevens Plants," *Wall Street Journal*, October 20, 1980, p. 1.

[95] "A Gathering Momentum Against J. P. Stevens," *Business Week*, March 20, 1978, pp. 147–48.

[96] Susan Fass, "A Look at Labor's Chief Strategist," *Journal of Commerce*, March 24, 1978, p. 15.

[97] "Putting the Squeeze on J. P. Stevens," *Women's Wear Daily*, March 27, 1978, p. 6.

[98] Ibid., pp. 6–7.

[99] Teresa Carson, "Stevens Attack Based on Aligning Power," *American Banker*, March 29, 1978, p. 2.

[100] "Putting the Squeeze on J. P. Stevens," pp. 6–7.

[101] "Low Point," editorial, *Greenville News* (Greenville, South Carolina), September 14, 1978. Reprinted in Ray Rogers, "How to Confront Corporations," *Business and Society Review*, Summer, 1981, p. 61.

[102] "Labor's Blacklist," editorial, *Wall Street Journal*, March 24, 1978, p. 8.

[103] "New Weapon for Bashing Bosses," *Time*, July 23, 1979, p. 71.

[104] "Stevens Chairman Resigns from Insurance Board," *Women's Wear Daily*, September 13, 1978, p. 12.

[105] "An Interview with Ray Rogers," pp. 53–54.

[106] See, for example, the following accounts: Gail Bronson and Jeffrey H. Birnbaum, "Rogers' Tough, Unorthodox Tactics Prevail in Stevens Organizing Fight," *Wall Street Journal*, October 21, 1980, pp. 37, 42; James Warren, "How the Union Conquered Stevens," *Chicago Sun-Times*, October 26, 1980, pp. 7, 42; Lance Gay, "Labor Activist Engineers Union's Corporate Battle," *Washington Star*, November 28, 1980, pp. D13, D14.

[107] See, for example, the *Wall Street Journal*. In its 1978 editorial the corporate strategy

was criticized for terrorizing businessmen. (March 24, 1978, p. 8) In its 1980 editorial entitled, "Patching Up," no mention was made of Rogers' tactics in helping to bring about the settlement. The editorial focused on discussion of unions winning the right to represent workers in fair elections. (October 22, 1980, p. 32)

[108] Dyson interview.

[109] Ray Rogers, "Corporate Campaign Highlights," unpublished summary of the campaign, October, 1980.

[110] Rogers interview.

[111] "'Corporate Campaign No Factor,' says Stevens," *Textile World,* November, 1980, p. 23.

[112] "Victory!" *Labor Unity,* November, 1980, p. 1.

[113] "Stevens, Union Finally Settle on Contract," *Women's Wear Daily,* October 20, 1980, p. 11.

[114] "Stevens Chief—Battle Not Over," *Chicago Sun-Times,* October 21, 1980, p. 17.

[115] "Whose Victory?," *Retailweek,* November 1, 1980, p. 16.

[116] Joe Pilati, *Social Justice,* December, 1980, p. 4.

[117] "Union Ratifies New Contract at Nine J. P. Stevens Plants," *Labor Unity,* May, 1983, p. 11.

[118] Robert T. Thompson, Sr., Attorney for J. P. Stevens Company, "CBS Morning News," CBS Television, November 1, 1983.

[119] *J. P. Stevens Annual Report,* 1969, 1983.

[120] Rogers interview.

[121] Mileski interview.

[122] Ax interview.

[123] William Serrin, "The Unsung Heroes of America's Labor Movement," *New York Times,* August 14, 1983, p. 6F.

CHAPTER VIII

In Conclusion: Contemporary Counterstrategy

Since the 1930s a variety of changing circumstances has forced unions to yield bargaining initiatives to management. Management has developed what Jack Barbash identifies as four strategy models to deal with this situation. These are (1) positive bargaining (more collaborative than adversarial methods are used to restructure working conditions); (2) hard bargaining (concessions are demanded and threats such as plant closing are used); (3) normal bargaining (a more prosperous company such as American Telephone and Telegraph negotiates a 1970s-type contract in the 1980s); and public sector bargaining (normal contracts are negotiated, but at the cost of job contraction).[1] In order to deal with these, unions have developed counterstrategies:

> The essence of the general union counterstrategy is orderly retreat, reflecting the first principle of unionism: a union is, in the first instance, only as effective as its product markets allow it to be. . . .
>
> To compensate for weaknesses in collective bargaining power, unions are moving to fall-back positions in politics, public relations, pension power, and organizing. The payoffs for these strategies are still to be realized. Their main significance at this moment is that they are in place and are being actively pursued.[2]

The preceding chapters have described and analyzed labor's public relations position by considering historical trends, the full range of factors that shape the labor-media relationship, and specific cases in which that relationship was maintained during periods of labor-management conflict. Public relations and media strategies are not new to labor, but what labor leaders have accomplished in the 1980s in this regard has formed a contemporary counterstrategy that implies a good understanding of their circumstances. As Barbash says, the results are not yet in, but the strategy is being actively pursued. The purpose of this final chapter is to place the counterstrategy in a framework that may be useful in generalizing labor's media usage to a variety of bargaining situations and to provide a summation of considerations suggested by the research that may be helpful as labor's counterstrategy evolves.

MEDIA COUNTERSTRATEGY IN COLLECTIVE BARGAINING

At certain points the preceding analysis was influenced by the work of Michael Lipsky, whose account of the dynamics of rent strikes in New York City suggested some useful ways of conceptualizing aspects of this study. The framework clearly demonstrates not only the type of relationship that existed between labor and management in a particular bargaining situation, but also the importance of the maintenance of that relationship. The following section assesses Lipsky's framework in light of the material presented mainly in Chapter VII.

Models—simplified, often diagrammatic representations of reality—are intended to aid in the understanding of relationships, to allow the conceptualization of relationships, and to allow formulation of generalizations about relationships. The Lipsky model presented in Chapter I—both as originally designed and as adapted to the ACTWU-J. P. Stevens case—has some interesting implications for organized labor. Lipsky was interested in the limitations inherent in situations where protest leaders are relatively powerless. He explains that these limitations occur because protest leaders must appeal to four audiences at the same time:

> [P]rotest leaders must nurture and sustain *an organization* comprised of people with whom they may or may not share common values. They must *articulate goals and choose strategies* so as to maximize their *public exposure* through communications media. They must *maximize the impact of third parties* in the political conflict. Finally, they must try to maximize chances of success among those capable of granting goals.[3]

During its conflict with J. P. Stevens, ACTWU did find it necessary to work with these four components and Lipsky's discussion therefore proved helpful not only in identifying them, but also in suggesting the relationships that might exist between them. However, as was suggested in Chapter I and became increasingly clear as the investigation of the case proceeded, the data and the model did not always coincide. Figure 24 presents a revision of Lipsky's framework that better represents the protest activity pursued by ACTWU. Much of the following discussion emphasizes limitations that ACTWU encountered and are perhaps generalizable to other labor situations, but that do not pertain to protests against government policy, as Lipsky's case did. Particular attention is directed toward the role played by the communications media.

Protest Leadership and the Protest Target

In the ACTWU/J. P. Stevens case the relationship between the union and the corporation is, of course, one of fundamental conflict. If ACTWU had been able to put direct pressure on J. P. Stevens and achieve its organizational goals, the case would have been relatively simple. However, Lipsky's as-

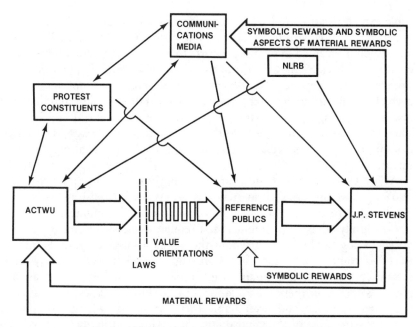

A Revised Model of the ACTWU/J.P. Stevens Interaction
FIGURE 24.   A Revised Model of the ACTWU/J. P. Stevens Interaction

sumption that protest is a highly indirect process obtains in the ACTWU case. The communications media and the reference publics of J. P. Stevens did play critical roles. Moreover, because of the legal barriers existing between the reference publics and ACTWU, the process was even more indirect than in the cases Lipsky observed.

In Lipsky's framework, the protest leader must activate reference publics—groups whose value and/or goal orientations differ significantly, in direction or intensity, from those of the protest leaders. The goal orientations of the reference publics are more aligned with those of the protest target, and the reference publics are in a position to apply pressure on the target in ways that could help the protest leaders. In the ACTWU case, the best examples of reference publics were the retailers who carried J. P. Stevens products and institutions such as Manufacturers Hanover that had financial and corporate ties to J. P. Stevens. In the legal phase of the conflict, the National Labor Relations Board acted as a reference public in some respects, but there are sufficient differences between the NLRB and other reference publics that it is treated separately below.

Certainly the value orientations of ACTWU and Manufacturers Hanover, for example, are different, and this alone would have constrained ACTWU from enlisting Manufacturers Hanover's aid against J. P. Stevens to some extent, if not completely. More significantly, secondary boycott laws impeded ACTWU both in the boycott and corporate campaigns. The union was legally restrained in its direct efforts to involve Macy's or Manufacturers Hanover because these institutions were only secondarily involved in the primary dispute between ACTWU and J. P. Stevens. The union might have been able to justify such direct action on the basis that retailers and financial institutions doing business with J. P. Stevens are not "neutral" to the case. The law, however, is not clear in this area, and ACTWU lawyers advised caution. In the case of retailers, restraint of trade laws was also a potential threat.

ACTWU's way around this barrier is suggested by the "publicity proviso" in the Landrum-Griffin Act; that is, ACTWU could appeal not to retailers, but to consumers. The union could use the communications media to "truthfully advise" the public that a retailer was distributing goods produced by an employer with whom there was a labor dispute. Similarly, ACTWU could inform the public, through the media, of the ways that certain corporations and financial institutions were involved with an employer with whom there was a labor dispute. In both cases, the public is becoming informed and presumably then can decide whether or not to continue patronage of the neutral company. The legal implications of this approach were particularly unclear in the corporate campaign. Ray Rogers, former ACTWU staff member who was primarily responsible for putting the corporate campaign together, assured ACTWU lawyers that he would not ask anyone to threaten withdrawal of financial support from any institution. He found it necessary only to "truthfully advise" the public about certain relationships and let things proceed from there.

In Figure 24 the broken arrow that follows the legal and orientations barriers indicates that ACTWU had some effect upon the reference publics that was not channeled through consumers or other parties. For example, ACTWU did directly approach some retailers and was successful in convincing them to stop buying from J. P. Stevens or to reduce their J. P. Stevens inventory. So the barriers are not impenetrable. Consideration of counterstrategies provoked by the legal barrier reveals the greatly increased importance not only of protest constituents—those consumers, labor groups, women's groups, civil rights groups, and so on, who shared certain value orientations with ACTWU—but of the communications media who were critical in disseminating the information. These provided the crucial routes around the barriers.

The Protest Leader and Its Constituents
ACTWU activated its protest constituents as one means of approaching its reference publics. Protest constituents differ from reference publics primarily in that "the value orientations of [protest constituents] are suffi-

ciently similar to those of the protesting group that concerted or coordinated action is possible."[4] Coalitions or alliances can be formed that not only may prove useful to the protest leader in one situation, but sometimes can lead to longer-term relationships. The protest constituents of ACTWU in the J. P. Stevens case represented a wide variety of interests. There were religious groups, women's groups, campus groups, civil rights groups, and so on. In terms of general value orientations, the only thread linking such groups to ACTWU is that they all were relatively liberal in orientation. In fact, the protest constituent alliance in the J. P. Stevens case did not exist before the boycott.

As ACTWU began to recruit allies on an ad hoc basis, it was discovered that only a few associations had such strong pro-union outlooks that they sympathized with ACTWU's position immediately. Instead, most organizations were motivated to support ACTWU because ACTWU chose to develop issues that had a social justice/human dignity emphasis, rather than emphasize the "bread-and-butter" issues of labor relations. ACTWU's success with the campaign thus was due largely to its ability to frame the campaign issues in a way that portrayed J. P. Stevens as a giant, powerful corporation that violated labor laws, cared little about worker safety and health, discriminated against blacks and women, and provided few company benefits. Moreover, ACTWU gave a great deal of attention to presenting these issues to different societal groups and organizations in ways that emphasized values that the groups held important; this strategy made the campaign especially salient to the individual protest constituent groups. To accomplish this, ACTWU hired special national field staff coordinators to work with different potential support groups. Recruiting was highly successful because the issues were explained in terms of compelling social values. For example, sympathy from the National Organization of Women was gained by informing NOW members that textile workers are predominantly women, most of whom are underpaid and otherwise disadvantaged. Such explanations served as effective inducements.

In this case, the coalition between ACTWU and its protest constituents proved to be a short-term rather than a long-term relationship. When the settlement agreement was signed, the coalition's purpose ended and its organizational structure ceased to function. In the period immediately following the signing of the agreement, some labor activists expressed the opinion that an effort should be made to maintain cohesion among such a well-organized and effective coalition. Others, however, recognized the value inherent in ad hoc alliance formation. One of these was Scott Hoyman, ACTWU's executive vice-president, who stated:

> It is the association itself and the willingness to trust each other that develops gradually in the give and take of deciding on a program that gives such a coalition strength and cohesion—things like how it will be financed, how

described to others, how launched, etc. This way it gradually develops into something useful. Nothing seems to be lost—and perhaps gains are made—by not having a large, formal, permanent organization.[5]

In the J. P. Stevens case, the protest constituents could legally and directly take the issues of the case to the reference publics. In both the boycott and corporate campaign, the protest constituents were activated because (1) they were aware of the campaign issues and sympathized with ACTWU and (2) they had financial connections with groups that were reference publics of J. P. Stevens. In the boycott, the protest constituents formed groups that went directly to retailers and explained the situation, why they supported ACTWU, and what they hoped to see retailers do about the problem. These protest constituents were also, of course, consumers, and therefore their requests and their voice in the community had a more direct effect on retailers than ACTWU ever would have. A retailer who might have paid little attention to representatives from a local labor body was more inclined to listen and respond when he or she was visited by a delegation of local citizens, one of whom might have been a minister, another a city council member, another a leader of a local retired persons association, and so on.

Ultimately retail cooperation is crucial to a boycott. The basic problem with a consumer boycott is that impact is difficult to achieve because of the extremely high level of participation necessary. Without massive numbers of boycotters, no economic effect will occur or be noticed by large retailers—not to mention huge multinational corporations. Consumer activism and support is needed even more than consumer agreement not to buy a product. In ACTWU's corporate campaign, the numbers of letters, postcards, and telephone calls that Manufacturers Hanover and New York Life got made it clear to officials of those companies that they were involved in a serious and potentially damaging conflict.

Such alliances as ACTWU managed to form cannot be put together by organizations that have no power whatsoever. The high ideals and volunteer efforts of many individuals in the constituent groups notwithstanding, certain resources are necessary. ACTWU spent a great deal of money on the campaign. The union needed extensive professional advice, much of which fortunately was supplied from within—from regular staff members. Because it has a regular, full-time legal staff, for example, ACTWU did not have to retain outside legal assistance. It also has departments staffed with people experienced in labor organizational strategy, research, photography, film-making, journalism, and so on. Nevertheless, these resources are extremely limited relative to the resources of the union's adversaries. And Lipsky's description of the political handicaps of what he calls protest groups still applies to most labor unions and specifically to ACTWU:

That some relatively powerless groups do succeed in obtaining the services of volunteer professionals, or succeed in receiving federal funds and private philanthropy does not detract from the generalization that these resources are not usually commanded by political groups which lack status, expertise, or the experience which frequently begets the opportunity to gain still further experience.[6]

The Protest Leader and the Communications Media

ACTWU used internal resources to increase public understanding and visibility of the protest. The union produced a film, for example, and printed newspapers, fact sheets, bumper stickers, pamphlets, and so on. Yet the role played by the mass media was certainly critical to the case and indeed may have been absolutely necessary to the outcome.

Figure 24 shows that ACTWU reached the media in two ways—one is direct, the other is through the protest constituents. Lipsky's model shows the same relationship between protest leader and media, but it differs in that it shows the media having an effect on the protest constituents, but not vice versa. Lipsky also has placed the media in the center of his model and depicts them as being influenced from all directions by actors in the protest situation. Such a representation suggests that the media have no significant degree of autonomy. In reality, however, what the media choose to publicize and the way that issues are presented in a given situation primarily are determined not by the participants in that situation, but rather by the structure and values of the media industries themselves. Media structure is an overriding, separate issue, and it is discussed further below. In an attempt to clarify the model to some degree, media are not placed in the center of the model in Figure 24, but apart from the main line of protest activity, and not surrounded on all sides by direct influences from the protest activity. This implies a degree of autonomy that applies also to the protest constituents and the NLRB.

The direct relationship between ACTWU and the media was a two-way relationship in the J. P. Stevens situation. ACTWU leaders saw the necessity of establishing an active, direct line to the media, and they worked hard to accomplish this. This active contact occurred in all four phases of the campaign. Leaders of each phase went to media people and explained, presented their side, issued press releases, held press conferences. In the early years of the campaign, the media were not particularly interested, especially outside the southern localities where J. P. Stevens plants were located. And in those places, protest publicity sometimes was granted by the media, but it was not the kind ACTWU needed nor was it the type that would activate many others to take labor's side. Even the legal campaign was routine news and was given little attention until ACTWU courtroom successes began to accumulate and attract more news attention. Through these successful legal cases involving individual workers ACTWU began to emphasize the social justice issues. Subsequently, the social justice/human dignity emphasis was maintained and expanded in the boycott. ACTWU recognized that such a focus provided a good opportunity not only to broaden the campaign, but to frame the campaign issues in such a way as to attract sympathetic media coverage. While the views and opinions of the powerless and relatively powerless social groups appear to be systematically excluded from the media,[7] it is also true that

> [i]n theory, the professional skill of news editors and subeditors is the skill of knowing what the readers will be interested in, what is important, how to present it interestingly. And that, frequently, is precisely what they do.[8]

ACTWU gradually began to improve its media relationship because of several factors. First, there was the growing number of courtroom successes that gave legitimacy to ACTWU's claim that workers were being unfairly treated. Next, news coverage of individuals who have faced or are facing great difficulties in their lives generally attracts a good deal of sympathetic public attention, especially if the individuals display courage or ingenuity in facing the difficulties. Also, as Lipsky points out: "Communications media and potential allies will consider more soberly the complaints of people who are understood to be placing themselves in jeopardy."[9] The J. P. Stevens workers who told their stories publicly were facing difficulties, and appeared to be displaying courage in that their jobs could be lost or their work situation could become more unpleasant as a result of what they were doing. The news media were able to "humanize" such problems and to dramatize them quickly and effectively.

The advertising that ACTWU did in the media, while not extensive, was another example of the way the union utilized the media. Union leaders in general, however, viewed this strategy as the least effective means of communicating campaign issues to the public. It was not always easy to gain access and when they did, costs were high and effectiveness largely unknown. On one side people praised the advocate's stand that was taken by the union. On the other side, ACTWU was criticized because the advertisements appeared self-serving and defensive. ACTWU, however, did demonstrate an increasing sophistication in the types of appeals used in the advertisements, and, partially on the basis of this, other unions have increased the amount of advertising they are doing; and leaders see it as something that they would like to do more often in the future.

The active steps that ACTWU took to establish good lines of communication with media personnel had a fairly unusual payoff: the media started going to ACTWU to get *not* just the "union's side" of the story, but also information and a reading on "what was going to happen next."

The Protest Constituents and the Communications Media

The relationship between the protest constituents and the media also deserves mention. The work of ACTWU's national coordinators—those specialists who recruited particular groups of constituents, such as religious groups, women's groups, and so on—was greatly facilitated by the early media attention given to ACTWU-J. P. Stevens court cases. That is, at the outset of the boycott, many people already were aware of J. P. Stevens' growing reputation as the "nation's number one labor law violator" and were quite willing to lend active support against Stevens, especially when the issues were explained to them in terms of significant social values.

Activated protest constituents then proceeded to establish direct relationships with the media much in the same ways that ACTWU did—with news releases, press conferences, and so on. But the impact was greater and the message had more emphasis and legitimacy because it was coming from another source, a source having no apparent vested interests. Where the media were concerned, the coalition of protest constituents did not act as one single group; representatives of the various associations contacted the media separately. This activity may have been especially important in obtaining media attention in geographical areas far removed from the site of the ACTWU-J. P. Stevens conflict.

One thing not immediately apparent when relating ACTWU with its protest constituents and the media is the substantial costs borne by the union in order to achieve an effective level of "protest noise." The development of the coalition of protest constituents may have enabled the union to share the financial burden, but it created new demands on the energy and time of union leaders. This dimension of the costs involved includes not only organizational expertise, but also the ability to, as Lipsky says, "juggle the conflicting demands of groups in the protest process."[10] ACTWU needed not only media attention and not even only sympathetic media attention, but media attention that did not alienate other constituents. And although every "third party" that the union added to its alliance could be potentially helpful, each added constraints and different "role requirements" on ACTWU. Lipsky provides an example that is perhaps especially appropriate given remarks made in Chapter I regarding labor and its retreat from militancy.

> [T]he demands of the media may conflict with the needs of protest group maintenance. Consider the leader whose constituents are attracted solely by pragmatic statements not exceeding what they consider political "good taste." He is constrained from making militant demands which would isolate him from constituents. This constraint may cost him appeal in the press. However, the leader whose organizing appeal requires militant rhetoric may obtain eager press coverage only to find that his inflammatory statements lead to alienation of potential allies. . .[11]

ACTWU and the NLRB

In Figure 2 (see Chapter I), the NLRB is diagrammatically represented as a reference public. This is because the NLRB appears to be in a position where it can exercise a considerable amount of influence on J. P. Stevens, the protest target. Yet clearly the NLRB does not fit neatly into this category and its role in this case deserves further attention.

The National Labor Relations Board is a federal agency that has been granted authority to regulate labor-management bargaining and oversee unfair labor practices. The primary difference between the NLRB and the other reference publics lies in this authority. NLRB interaction with other institutions tends to involve the use, or threat of use, of administrative sanctions. The difficulties involved in activating this authority were discussed in Chapter V and do not need to be repeated. What is important in the ACTWU-J. P. Stevens case is that the agency indeed was activated; it did repeatedly use its authority in ACTWU's favor; and its decisions usually won court support. However, the kind of pressure applied to J. P. Stevens through the NLRB appeared to have little direct effect. The corporation did reinstate employees and pay its fines, but seemed relatively unaffected by such penalties—even when their severity was increased.

According to Lipsky, protest strategies vary "depending upon the relative congruence of the goals of protest groups and the goals of reference publics of target groups."[12] Up to this point in the discussion, the reference publics in this case (as in Lipsky's treatment) have exhibited goal orientations quite dissimilar from those of the protest leader. But the NLRB does not. One distinguishing feature is in the ostensible neutrality that it, as a government agency, holds. Many people view the government in this country as providing both a stable and predictable arena where opposing groups can engage in battle, and agencies such as the NLRB serve as neutral referees to decide outcomes. In opposition to this view is the notion that the agencies are in reality instruments of the state that serve to benefit only the existing economic system. Both arguments focus on administrative agencies as serving instrumental functions. Instrumentally, in the ACTWU case, the NLRB did provide a mechanism through which ACTWU was able to obtain some favorable outcomes. It should be remembered, though, that as they related to the union and the industry in general, these outcomes involved mainly the rights to organize and bargain, rights that are preliminary to the attainment of tangible benefits. The difficulties of achieving this much have been discussed, as have the limited economic effects on Stevens. And it is instructive to note that had the NLRB and court decisions been made in favor of J. P. Stevens, the economic effects on ACTWU undoubtedly would have been devastating.

The alleged neutrality of government—and of the NLRB—is largely a myth, however, and therein lies its real significance. Being widely believed by the American public, it serves a function that is other than instrumental. Murray Edelman calls this the expressive function; the myth of governmental neutrality creates and sustains "an impression that induces acquiescence of the public in the face of private tactics that might otherwise be expected to produce resentment, protest, and resistance."[13] The significance of the NLRB from this point of view has less to do with its (instrumental) specific decisions and policies than with its more expressive function of representing the procedural fairness and neutrality of the state.

> To let the adversary groups oppose each other through the workings of an administrative agency continuously resolving the conflicts in "decisions" and policies replaces tension and uncertainty with a measure of clarity, meaning, confidence, and security. This is precisely the function performed in more primitive societies by the rain dance, the victory dance, and the peace pipe ceremony, each of which amounts to an acting out of contending forces that occasion widespread anxiety and a resolution that is acceptable and accepted.[14]

The real importance of the NLRB in this case was in the symbolic reassurance it provided to the public, but especially to ACTWU, the protest constituents, and even to the reference publics as these groups began to pressure J. P. Stevens. This symbolic role of the NLRB more than any other factor helps to explain the discrepancy between the sense of victory—or at least satisfaction—experienced by ACTWU and its supporters on the one hand and the very limited tangible benefits won by the union on the other.

Pressure on J. P. Stevens

Figure 24 shows that pressure was being applied on Stevens from three different sources. J. P. Stevens, however, was not a vulnerable target. For years the company remained aloof from the intense political activity directed against it; executives could draw a good deal of reassurance from the knowledge that such activity cannot be sustained indefinitely by a protest leader. In spite of this, however, they eventually became convinced that bargaining with ACTWU was in the best interests of the company.

The reference publics were undoubtedly the most directly persuasive elements in bringing this about. J. P. Stevens, being the large corporation that it is, has continuing business relationships with numerous other institutions, each of which shares some goal orientations with the textile manufacturer. During the boycott, many retail firms cut back on their orders of J. P. Stevens products, usually in response to pressure put on them by consumers. While such cutbacks had little economic effect on Stevens, the deteriorating relationships with these firms must have been disturbing to company leaders. A similar situation existed with some of the financial institutions with whom Stevens was connected, and in these cases there was the added possibility that very effective economic pressure could be placed on J. P. Stevens.

The effect of the roles played by the NLRB and the courts was undoubt-

edly felt in different ways by company officials. The "instrumental" pressures—the decisions against Stevens, the fines, and so on—may have been
little more painful financially than judicial slaps on the corporate wrist. But
here again the actions of these groups probably were more effective in an
expressive or symbolic sense. The symbolic reassurance given by the NLRB
and the courts to ACTWU and its constituents had exactly the opposite
meaning for J. P. Stevens. The continuing signals of displeasure that Stevens
received from these authoritative institutions was symbolic punishment that
laid corporate integrity open to question and probably was more difficult to
explain to stockholders than the heavy fines. Regarding the latter, J. P.
Stevens' *Annual Report, 1978* provided a standard phrase to the effect that
resolution of legal matters "will not, in the opinion of management, have a
material adverse effect on the financial position of the company,"[15] along
with a statement that "Stevens' determination to comply with the orders of
both Courts of Appeal and with the requirements of the National Labor
Relations Act is unqualified. We have constructed a compliance program
intended to prevent the occurrence of future unfair labor practices. . . "[16]

While labor has long been aware that its public relations efforts prove
least effective during strikes and other collective actions, business has not
had to pay much attention to its public relations during such periods. The
media as well as the inconvenienced public typically side with business.[17] In
the Stevens situation, ACTWU was able to turn things around. The communications media were amplifying the protest in a way that helped ACTWU
and put increasing pressure on J. P. Stevens. Stevens had a difficult time
responding to this situation. At first, almost no response came from the
corporation. By the time management realized its silence was only making
things worse, media personnel were not very interested in Stevens' story. A
direct line from J. P. Stevens to the communications media was never really
established—even when some media personnel sprang to the company's
defense during the corporate campaign. Had Stevens made itself available to
the press at the outset, had it utilized opportunities and resources available
to it as a huge corporation, it might have avoided the deprivations it experienced—even if these were largely symbolic.

Rewards

Such questions of timing are inadequately represented by the model. The
ACTWU campaign against J. P. Stevens took place over a number of years,
and during this time relationships among the actors underwent constant, if
sometimes subtle, changes. Although Stevens did not establish a direct two-
way relationship with the media, for example, the corporation did not
consistently ignore the media throughout the duration of the campaign. J. P.
Stevens' silence early in the campaign had its own meaning. It meant to

convey the message that the problem was trivial—not worthy of attention, and certainly not warranting any defense.

Later, however, Stevens leaders changed their tactics as they felt increasing need to respond in some manner to the protest. Stevens' responses parallel Lipsky's description of tactics available to protest targets who are unwilling to give in to the material demands of the protest leader, but need to satisfy their reference publics. First, Stevens needed to reassure these reference publics. It needed to let them know that in spite of all they might be hearing, there were no problems of a serious nature at J. P. Stevens, that J. P. Stevens was a progressive, profitable, forward-moving corporation. This could be—and was—done directly by J. P. Stevens through normal available business channels and business communications. The annual reports, quarterly reports, and so on, are typical means of conveying symbolic reassurances to reference publics. But Stevens gradually realized that it needed to go beyond giving symbolic reassurance to the reference publics. The media attention received by the campaign had caused a deterioration in the J. P. Stevens image that could not be mended through business channels alone. Stevens also needed to "reassure unorganized political group interests," and to "reduc[e] the anxiety level of organized interests and wider publics which [were] only tangentially involved in the issues."[18] These ends could only be accomplished through the media.

While J. P. Stevens executives continued to refrain from talking to the media about the ACTWU feud, they began to issue press releases on the general health of the corporation and the various positive steps the corporation was taking in terms of its position with other segments of society. The public thus was informed by the media that J. P. Stevens expected record annual sales or had just experienced a 6 percent increase in quarterly earnings, or that Stevens had made certain contributions to a community program or an educational institution. Stevens also could provide what Lipsky calls "symbolic aspects of material rewards" through the media. That is, it could exemplify its good employee relations through publicized expressions of concern about issues related to the campaign such as occupational health and safety. The resulting publicity provided symbolic reassurances not only to the reference publics but to the general public as well. To the extent that such activity satisfies reference publics and maintains a reasonably good corporate image, the dispensation of material rewards to the protest leader—that is, the union—can be delayed. Unfortunately for the company, the symbolic media reassurances were too few and came too late. Stevens' reassurances appeared to many to be an attempt either to avoid the situation because it was uncomfortable, or to trivialize the conflict by ignoring it. The reassurances lacked substance because they did not deal directly with the already well-publicized issues.

The Revised Framework

This study supports earlier findings conducted by Michael Lipsky and James Q. Wilson[19] that protest is a strategy adopted by relatively powerless groups for the purpose of increasing their bargaining ability. Lipsky's analysis emphasizes that the success of the protest is dependent upon the activation of reference publics of protest targets in ways that support protest goals. In the ACTWU case the roles of the protest constituents and the communications media had greater weight because of the legal barriers that existed between the labor union and the reference publics. Both protest constituents and communications media also must be activated to enter the conflict in ways that support protest goals. It is a complex and difficult process. The resources needed and the tensions that may arise as the protest leader balances demands of participants must be recognized at the outset of protest activity and weighed against estimated chances of a successful outcome.

Of course the particular circumstances within which such groups operate vary greatly, and in the case of ACTWU its ability to participate in a struggle for rights and benefits and to utilize the media in this struggle was profoundly shaped by the historical relationship between labor and the media. This historical relationship affects all unions, but certainly not all unions in exactly the same way. Each union that uses the media as an essential part of collective bargaining will need to determine the type of media relationship that would seem to be most beneficial and proceed from there. The model and cases provide no simple answers.

COMMUNICATIONS COUNTERSTRATEGY: STRUCTURAL, POLITICAL, AND INTELLECTUAL INITIATIVES

In the 1940s the typically sporadic public relations activities that were undertaken by unions sought primarily to portray unionism simply as an integral part of the American way of life. More recently, approaches intended to build the union "image" in the public mind are being abandoned and replaced by a more realistic activist media approach. In the words of AFL-CIO Department of Information director Murray Seeger:

> Recently . . . I was asked by a TV reporter . . . was I trying to change the image of labor?
>
> No, I replied; I am trying to change the media's perception of organized labor. My point was that I see organized labor, the labor movement and the AFL-CIO as a reality. And I see my main mission to make the media, and through them, the general public, more conscious of what we are and what we do. I don't like the concept of image-making because it connotes something fraudulent.[20]

The four large international unions whose past and present public relations programs were examined in Chapter III all provide illustrations of the trend toward an activist stance. During the period these four were studied, each was maintaining its public relations program in the absence of any highly unusual or stressful situation. Their activism was expressed through political advertising (such as AFSCME's advertisements that criticized the Reagan administration's budget and tax cuts and the UAW's trade reform advertisements) and by IAM's media monitoring projects.

On the other hand, ACTWU's public relations program was examined during a period in which that union was engaged in an unusual campaign against a large manufacturer. This case proved to be an especially interesting selection because of its four parts (the initial and underlying organizational efforts, the legal campaign, the boycott, and the corporate campaign), each of which provided examples of an unusually active approach to the media. ACTWU's activism was manifested in the improvement of communications with individual journalists, the organization of press events and the use of regular press releases, and advocacy advertising in which the union point of view was expressed and a product boycott was endorsed.

In exploring the extent to which such counterstrategies as public relations will lead to permanent change in industrial relations, Barbash notes:

> [T]his much can be said: many of the changes at work in the strongholds of collective bargaining are structural, not temporary. . . . We are witnessing basic alterations in political alignments, in market and wage structures, in technologies, and in the geographic distribution of the industry. These changes cannot help but alter, in consequence, the dimensions of industrial relations[21]

The most obvious structural changes related to public relations have been in the AFL-CIO Department of Information. The changes made by LIPA (Labor Institute of Public Affairs) especially, in the short time it has existed, undoubtedly will have long-term impact. Certainly the AFL-CIO intends this to be true. LIPA has provided a bridge between all of labor and electronic media. Its activist stance is apparent, but its emphasis has not been on political activity. Its notable series "America Works" was produced as a public affairs series; recognition of the program as one that presents broad issues of concern to working people (rather than a more narrow "labor program") was gained when the series was adopted for fall, 1984, by over 150 public broadcasting stations.

To the extent that LIPA can become involved in public opinion research and marketing techniques such as those used in Missouri, it will be able to provide further ongoing services to labor. LIPA and the Department of Information can establish central computer banks of information on the mass media and on legislative issues that pertain to labor use of the media.

Time and money are required, but these are projects that can be undertaken and accomplished gradually.

LIPA and the Department of Information have the potential to solve many of labor's most troublesome public relations problems. But, while the Federation and a number of international unions can be seen to be moving in the direction of greater media activism in ways explained above, the same cannot be said for all—or even most—international unions. As Chapter IV indicated, the internationals vary greatly in terms of public relations, objectives, experience and expertise, philosophy, internal organization, financial resources, and so on.[22] The most prevalent problems appear to be financial resources, internal organization and public relations expertise, and inexperience with media technology. Regarding the latter, it appears that some labor leaders unconsciously equate "media" with "newspapers," thereby forgetting radio, television, and magazines;[23] the improvement of journalistic skills that has accompanied development of a professional labor press also has resulted in ability to deal more comfortably with the general press. But it continues to be true that comparatively little use is made of radio and television; public service time has been underused in the past, and apparent unfamiliarity with technology has led to some avoidance. Continued efforts directed toward marketing LIPA to labor organizations are necessary in order first, to stimulate the interest and support of unions that have been relatively inactive in public relations in the past, and, second, to get affiliates to use electronic media comfortably, effectively, and regularly.

LIPA is not the only unit that is making an effort to broaden the use of media by labor. The George Meany Center for Labor Studies regularly offers courses on media studies. State labor press associations, joint boards, and federations sponsor workshops and training conferences. For example, sessions in which union leaders are videotaped in simulated press conferences or actual panel discussions, after which their performance is criticized by themselves and others more experienced in media skills, have been quite successful.

Probably the most basic structural change relates to media ownership by labor. The data presented in this study do not suggest that labor must own media in order to be heard effectively. Certainly labor is achieving a degree of success without involving itself in the complexities that media ownership would entail. That is not to say, however, that ownership might not be a useful alternative. Although past efforts have not proven fruitful, new technologies will make a difference. The experiences the UAW is undergoing in its LPTV efforts will be instructive. Other competitors of cable such as direct broadcast satellite (DBS) and subscription television (STV) also are undergoing rapid change and development, and it is difficult to say how they might or might not help special interest groups. Such alternatives do offer the advantages of little governmental red tape and relatively low start-up costs.

Cable possibilities for labor programming cannot be discounted. The great potential that cable offered the viewing public was new programming aimed at small but selective audiences. Currently perhaps, only Music Television (MTV) really does this, but if LIPA continues to produce programs, cable is a possible outlet. What makes this avenue difficult is the fact that programming is not enough. Cable operators—owners of the hardware—still control the medium. Cable will become increasingly expensive as more networks get organized. Cable networks are supported either by subscribers or advertisers; both present problems for labor. Access at the local level undoubtedly will continue to be more easily obtained.

As for political intervention, the inability of many special interest groups and legislators to shape revisions of the Communications Act was discussed. It is important to be aware, however, that policy changes have taken place with *no* legislative action whatsoever. An example is the fact that broadcasters no longer need to make public service time available.

Bagdikian's suggestions for improving diversity of media content were presented in Chapter V. Suggestions of another sort come from the Glasgow University Media Group, whose television study is concluded with suggestions for restructuring the broadcasting system in Great Britain:

> *Aims of Broadcasting:* Broadcasters should be required to represent fairly and accurately the divisions within our social world resulting from class, race or sex, and programmes should be made from the perspectives which result from these divisions.
>
> *Control:* To put the new aims into practice, the present Board of Control should be made more representative of the class, racial and sexual composition of our society. Ultimately, Boards should be elected at local and regional levels.
>
> *Access:* A major part of the output should be given to forms of access programming, with proper budgets allocated to these. Material from non-professional sources should also be featured, and broadcasting authorities should encourage the development of resources in the community to produce this.
>
> The background and affiliations of the professionals who at present make programmes, should be broadly representative of the outside society. There must be positive discrimination in the recruitment of women and ethnic minorities to rectify existing imbalances.[24]

These are ambitious proposals, and the prospects for their realization hinge on any number of questions warranting further investigation.

Change also occurs by way of judicial decision. There is strong evidence that the best judicial-constitutional leg for labor to stand on in the access argument is the right of the public to full and diverse information. But court decisions, like other forms of policy, are likely to be influenced by the general political climate. The Reagan administration has not provided an encouraging climate for labor. The myth of government neutrality mentioned earlier seems to be losing ground even as a myth. Fundamental differences exist between administration personnel and policies and organized labor. The Department of Labor has not provided a pipeline from labor to the president. And, as noted by one AFL-CIO official: "The promise of timely NLRB remedies and sanctions against employers who trample on workers' rights has become a cruel hoax."[25] Yet it is helpful to remember what past experience has shown: the myth of government neutrality can be used from time to time to labor's advantage, particularly if labor can mount an effective intellectual initiative.

The two preeminent intellectual challenges are (1) educating media personnel and (2) taking a public stand on issues. Regarding the importance of the education of media personnel, Murray Seeger stated:

> I find ignorance to be a bigger problem in trying to explain what we are and what we do. Just the other day, a senior reporter from one of the major news organizations asked: "What is it, 15 member unions?" At our February meetings, a local television reporter watching the 33 AFL-CIO vice-presidents assemble asked: "Where are the Teamsters?"
>
> Clearly, one of the first things we have to do is simply tell our story better. And we have to push and shove a little to get more attention in the heavy competition for space and time in the media. . . . So far, we have started a process of reaching beyond the small group of reporters who are assigned to cover labor as a beat. This beat has fallen on lean days, for many reasons. But *we* have been mesmerized by the old concept that you had to expect a labor reporter to cover everything we did because we are a labor organization. We are now reaching a wider group of reporters.[26]

And regarding AFL-CIO activism in terms of speaking out on issues, Seeger added:

> We have something to say on nearly every public issue facing this country. Nuclear disarmament? We have a position. Caribbean basin development? We have a statement. Food stamps, welfare programs, Social Security? We're prepared to speak on those. Poland, South Africa, El Salvador? Trade with the Soviet Union? ERA? Taxes? We are there in spades.[27]

The directions organized labor has taken in its advertising campaigns have been of interest throughout this study. Advertising separates itself from other media coverage in that labor controls the contents of the purchased time and/or space and, in so doing, provides an obvious indication of desired directions and objectives. In Chapter I, the question was raised whether labor could use advertising to provide members with a sense of vigor, aggressiveness, and advocation of change while at the same time providing general public appeal by creating an understanding of labor as a responsible institution, fully integrated into the American system. Although the advertising that has been undertaken by the AFL-CIO and by various international unions differs widely in purpose, theme, and style, making generalizations dangerous, the answer to the question appears to be yes. Accordingly, labor is not using advertising simply to create awareness or a favorable image. LIPA does produce what it calls "image spots." But even these are described as "powerful messages that feature union contributions to all America." Look-for-the-union label also goes beyond creating awareness because it endorses action. When ILGWU's campaign was first conceived, the intention was merely to create awareness of the label. Recently, however, disputes have arisen over international textile and apparel trade policy, the ILGWU has endorsed the "Buy American" and the newer "Crafted with Pride in the U.S.A." campaigns, and even the old look-for-the-union label slogan has taken on a newer, more controversial meaning.[28] So it now appears that even the "mildest" union advertising educates, informs, and encourages action.

Respect for advocacy advertising was shared even by questionnaire respondents who represented unions having relatively inactive public relations programs. About the only drawback expressed was the expense: not all international labor unions are able to afford advertising and therefore staff members are not able to consider it seriously—though they see it as a trend of the future. Yet not everyone shares such a high opinion of advertising as a tool for organized labor. As Chapter VII revealed, several ACTWU leaders did not believe that advertising had contributed much to the Stevens campaign. And Murray Seeger's opinion is reserved:

> I'm very dubious about it. People often ask us why we don't do more advertising. They don't understand our financial limitations. Shortly after I took this position we did two ads in the *New York Times* and the *Washington Post;* the fee was over $30,000. That is so high that I was not tempted to try to raise the money to do it again.
>
> I do feel that in certain specific ways advertising works. I can see a use for television advertising. I think some very successful efforts have been made— by AFSCME, UAW, the Carpenters, the Postal Workers. These were dedicated to a particular issue for which there was a great deal of reinforcement. The timing was well-chosen, the ads well done. Under certain circumstances, I think advertising also can be used effectively for organizing. I question the function of image ads; they may do nothing more than achieve better name recognition for a union. I like the generic ads that are informative, that explain what a union is, what it does. To make an impact, however, a lot of money needs to be spent. But I think, if I had a lot of money, that would not be my top priority.[29]

Organized labor's commitment to an increasingly active labor-media relationship has provided media with greater amounts of labor information, much of which is more realistic, substantial, and consistent than in past years. But insofar as labor's public relations problem derives from external rather than internal structural characteristics, it cannot be eliminated simply through improved organization—or any other act of volition. John Henning introduced the 1979 convention resolution referred to in Chapter II with a stark reference to this problem: "Whereas, Television, radio and the printed medium are owned by private corporations which shape and dominate the coverage of news events and the discussion of vital public issues. . ."[30] Henning's resolution proposed to establish a special media education fund intended to provide financial assistance to international unions to purchase media space and time. The resolution was foresighted and, in a sense, has been acted upon. But it does not resolve the fundamental problem: in order to purchase space and time, unions still must deal with the media industries. Access is not guaranteed, as some unions and the AFL-CIO have discovered when they tried to advertise. And it is equally true that the nature of the media structure provides a framework that can render education of journalists by labor fairly useless.

The communication industries in the United States have become highly concentrated, owned by private businesses and operated to acquire maximum profits. The media are managed within a narrow conceptual framework. When media executives defend the First Amendment, they are referring to *their* understanding of the First Amendment. When they defend the free flow of information, it is the free flow of *their interpretation* of information. Controversial views do appear in the media in the United States and certainly their worth and significance cannot be underestimated. But realistically there is more to consider. As Ralph Miliband explains:

> [T]he notion of pluralist diversity and competitive equilibrium is, here as in every other field, rather superficial and misleading. For the agencies of communication and notably the mass media are, in reality, and the expression of dissident views notwithstanding, a crucial element in the legitimation of capitalist society. Freedom of expression is not thereby rendered meaningless. But the freedom has to be set in the real economic and political context of these societies; and in that context the free expression of ideas and opinions *mainly* means the free expression of ideas and opinions which are helpful to the prevailing system of power and privilege.[31]

The Glasgow University Media Group, in a six-year study that is reported in three volumes, examined the historical and social factors that have shaped British television news, especially in terms of the nation's industry and economy. The study provided evidence that television news in Great Britain not only tended to trivialize and sensationalize much labor news, but also tended to be "organized into highly selective patterns that implied a definite way of seeing and understanding industrial life." The report went on to explain: "We refer to these patterns as the interpretive framework, within which the flow of information and reporting is organized and the dominant views of particular stories created."[32]

Evidence in the United States is similar. The IAM study discussed in Chapter III found that corporate America's views on selected issues consistently prevailed on network news by means of selection of interviewees, visuals used, and reporter comments. The study showed also that the union issue that receives most attention is a strike, though reasons for strikes are not given and background information is not included.

Gallup opinion polls show that approval of labor unions by professional and business people has been declining. A 1978 poll showed that although 53 percent of people in this category approved of labor, it also is true that "[u]nions find their strongest opposition in the upscale groups—those people in the higher education and income brackets as well as those in the professions and business."[33] And by 1981, approval by this group had edged downward slightly to 50 percent.[34] More specifically, polls of media executives apparently are even more discouraging. A recent poll of attitudes of narrow leadership groups in the United States showed that, among executives of news organizations, the anti-union bias is high.[35] Nor are such feelings confined to high executive levels; research shows how top leaders in formal organizations not only make policy, but secure and maintain conformity to that policy at lower organizational levels.[36] So the "interpretive framework" filters down and dominates an organization like a television station or newspaper.

For the most part, ACTWU was able to gain favorable publicity by working within this interpretive framework. It did this by turning attention to issues that were broader than labor-management issues. It makes a good deal of practical sense to link labor's public relations programs to broader issues whenever possible—both in ongoing programs and in those programs that are developed to meet special circumstances. It must be realized, however, that when this is done, basic labor-management issues often become submerged. The problems are humanized and dramatized by the media and short-term solutions satisfy a concerned public. But the overall bias in labor coverage by the media is not significantly changed.

Labor's activist media stance has been accompanied by a more consistently aggressive disposition, however. The media are more regularly challenged when access is denied and when blatant instances of the existence of media's narrow interpretive framework come to light. An example of one such challenge occurred in 1982 and 1983 in an exchange between Murray Seeger and producers of CBS's "Sixty Minutes." In September, 1982, a segment of "Sixty Minutes" was devoted to a report of the labor boycott against the Adolph Coors Company. The presentation was characterized as "shoddy journalism" by Seeger who based his complaints on the facts that (1) AFL-CIO headquarters was not given the opportunity to explain labor's position, in spite of requests that it be allowed to do so; (2) the program gave no background on the origins or basis of the boycott; (3) the comments of an AFL-CIO field representative were edited unfairly and he was given no chance to rebut management accusations; and (4) none of the union employees at Coors (where the 1977 strike vote had been unanimous) were included in the interviews.[37] After extensive efforts by Seeger to persuade CBS that the show had been unfair, a small portion of one of his letters finally was mentioned on the air.

Another example was provided in 1982 when *Forbes* magazine printed an article about the relationship between former Labor Secretary Ray Donovan and organized labor.[38] According to Seeger, the article printed an incorrect AFL-CIO annual membership dues increase figure.[39] Even more troublesome, however, was the implication that the Federation misused dues and federal grant monies. Requests to the magazine that corrections or a letter to the editor be printed were ignored. The Department of Information then filed a complaint against the publication with the National News Council, a group composed of professional journalists and citizens. The National News Council not only upheld the complaint, but conducted its own investigation regarding the alleged source of *Forbes'* information and could find no one who admitted providing the information.

Often it is difficult to distinguish between bias and ignorance in the media. The latter is the easier problem with which to deal and offers more hope for improvement. Seeger is hopeful that AFL-CIO responses to media problems such as the two described will at least educate news people about reasons why the AFL-CIO feels that labor's side was not presented fairly and alert them to the fact that he intends to continue to approach such matters with all the serious attention they deserve. Still, no systematic method has been established by labor to monitor the media in order to maintain its more aggressive behavior and regularly to challenge perceived inaccuracies and distortions.[40]

The importance of the media can hardly be overstated and is apparent in the general effects it has upon popular opinions, attitudes, beliefs, and actions.

> One of the great truisms of our era is that we live in an age of communications. Battles for political turf, for social and economic advancement, for power and position, are fought these days in the realm of the public media. Key decisions affecting our lives are still made in smoke-filled rooms, legislative halls and in the streets where the older battles were fought, but it is rare that these conflicts can long be shielded from the omnipresent gaze of the printed or electronic media.[41]

Further research on labor and communications policy, technology, and so on, may be broad in scope, but it surely will need to take careful account of this study's finding that, although the class structure of the media industries apparently has changed little since the days when labor decided to ignore it and publish its own newspapers, labor's methods of dealing with the media have changed and are changing. Indeed, counterstrategies are in place and are being pursued. And in becoming more active and aggressive, labor improves its probability of achieving at least some media successes, some strengthening in collective bargaining, and of continuing to sensitize people to the fact that there are other ways of interpreting issues than the way they conventionally have been interpreted by the media.

NOTES

[1] Jack Barbash, "Trade Unionism from Roosevelt to Reagan," *Annals of the American Academy of Political and Social Science* 473 (May, 1984), pp. 11–22.

[2] Ibid., pp. 18–19.

[3] Michael Lipsky, *Protest in City Politics: Rent Strikes, Housing and the Power of the Poor* (Chicago: Rand McNally & Company, 1970), p. 163.

[4] Ibid., p. 3.

[5] Scott Hoyman, ACTWU Executive Vice-President, in a speech entitled "J. P. Stevens and Organizing," Institute of Labor and Industrial Relations Colloquium, University of Illinois, December 5, 1980.

[6] Lipsky, *Protest in City Politics*, p. 168.

[7] Graham Murdock and Peter Golding, "Beyond Monopoly: Mass Communications in an Age of Conglomerates," in *Trade Unions and the Media*, eds. Peter Beharrell and Greg Philo (London: The Macmillan Press Ltd., 1977), pp. 93–117. See also Ralph Miliband, *The State in Capitalist Society* (New York: Basic Books, Inc., 1969), pp. 219–238.

[8] Francis Beckett, "Press and Prejudice," in *Trade Unions and the Media*, eds. Beharrell and Philo, p. 44.

[9] Lipsky, *Protest in City Politics*, p. 166.

[10] Ibid., p. 171.

[11] Ibid.

[12] Ibid., p. 3.

[13] Murray Edelman, *The Symbolic Uses of Politics* (Urbana: University of Illinois Press, 1967), p. 56.

[14] Ibid., p. 61.

[15] *J. P. Stevens Annual Report*, 1978, p. 22.

[16] Ibid., p. 10.

[17] In the words of Ralph Miliband: "Similarly, and consistently, the press for the most part has always been a deeply committed anti-trade union force. Not, it should be said, that newspapers in general oppose trade unions as such. Not at all. They only oppose trade unions, in the all too familiar jargon, which, in disregard of the country's welfare and of their members' own interests, greedily and irresponsibly seek to achieve short-term gains which are blindly self-defeating. In other words, newspapers love trade unions so long as they do badly the job for which they exist. Like governments and employers, newspapers profoundly deplore strikes, and the larger the strike the greater the hostility: woe to trade union leaders who encourage or fail to prevent such manifestly unsocial, irresponsible and *obsolete* forms of behavior. The

rights and wrongs of any dispute are of minor consequence; what counts is the community, the consumer, the public, which *must* be protected, whatever the cost, against the actions of men who blindly obey the summons of misguided and, most likely, evil-intentioned leaders." Miliband, *The State in Capitalist Society*, p. 222. See also Paul Walton and Howard Davis, "Bad News for Trade Unionists," in *Trade Unions and the Media*, eds. Beharrell and Philo, pp. 118–134; and Glasgow University Media Group, *Bad News* (London: Routledge and Kegan Paul, 1976), chaps. 5 and 6.

[18] Lipsky, *Protest in City Politics*, p. 176.

[19] James Q. Wilson, "The Strategy of Protest: Problems of Negro Civic Action," *Journal of Conflict Resolution*, V (September, 1961), pp. 291–303. Lipsky cites this work by Wilson as being helpful to his (Lipsky's) examination of protest. Lipsky specifically mentions Wilson's recognition of the utility of the bargaining framework for examining protest movements.

[20] Murray Seeger, Director, AFL-CIO Department of Information, "Address to the Public Relations Society of America," Washington, D.C., April 20, 1982.

[21] Barbash, "Trade Unionism," p. 22.

[22] Research done in Great Britain by the Glasgow University Media Group showed there were considerable differences among unions in terms of the relative effort each put into contacting and utilizing media. The differences appeared especially great when blue collar unions and white collar unions were compared. No similar comparative work has been done on unions in the United States, though results of the present study would lead to the conclusion that such differences would not be found between blue-collar and white-collar unions. In fact, the distinction itself is inappropriate; many labor unions in this country could not be categorized as either blue collar or white collar because of the diversity of their membership. AFSCME is a good example. The Glasgow University Media Group recognized this problem in Great Britain as well and suggested that a better distinction might be made between what they called elite or vertical unions (those whose membership was composed of both top management and low-paid workers) and non-elite or horizontal unions. See Glasgow University Media Group, *Bad News*, chap. 6.

[23] Ibid. The Glasgow University Media Group also found this to be true of some people they interviewed.

[24] Glasgow University Media Group, *Really Bad News* (London: Writers and Readers, 1982), p. 159.

[25] Alan Kistler, "Union Organizing: New Challenges and Prospects," *Annals of the American Academy of Political and Social Science* 473 (May, 1984), p. 103.

[26] Seeger, "Address to the Public Relations Society," April 20, 1982.

[27] Ibid.

[28] The most recent legislative/industry turmoil concerns country-of-origin labels. Congress agreed in October, 1984, on a country-of-origin labeling bill for all domestic and imported textiles and apparel; it requires explicit and conspicuous labeling of an article's country of origin. This legislation is significant for two major reasons: (1) redefining "country of origin" may cause imports to decrease due to quota limitations; and (2) for the first time in history, textiles and textile products made in the U.S. must be so labeled.

[29] Murray Seeger, interview, Washington, D.C., May 25, 1982, and November 9, 1983.

[30] American Federation of Labor-Congress of Industrial Organizations (AFL-CIO), *Proceedings and Executive Council Reports of the AFL-CIO, Thirteenth Constitutional Convention*, 2 vols. (Washington, D.C.: AFL-CIO, 1979), 1:153.

[31] Miliband, *The State in Capitalist Society*, p. 220.

[32] Glasgow University Media Group, *Bad News*, p. 229.

[33] George H. Gallup, *The Gallup Poll: Public Opinion, 1978* (Wilmington, Delaware: Scholarly Resources Inc., 1979), p. 53.

[34] "Approval of Labor Unions Remains At Low," *The Gallup Report*, No. 191 (August, 1981), p. 7.

[35] Seeger, "Address to the Public Relations Society," April 20, 1982.

[36] See, for example, Warren Breed, "Social Control in the Newsroom: A Functional Analysis," in *Conformity, Resistance, and Self-Determination: The Individual and Authority*, ed. Richard Flack (Boston: Little, Brown and Company, 1973), pp. 153–160.

[37] "CBS Report on Coors Boycott Branded 'Shoddy Journalism,'" *AFL-CIO News*, November 13, 1982, p. 4.

[38] Allan Dodds Frank, "Argumentum ad hominem," *Forbes*, August 2, 1982, pp. 37–38.

[39] Seeger, "Remarks to the Texas AFL-CIO Convention," July 27, 1983.

[40] Suggestions were made by Philo, Beharrell, and Gewitt for establishing a monitoring/research unit for use by labor in Great Britain. The authors felt that it was important for trade unions wishing to monitor media output to be involved themselves in the financing and organization of such a unit. They provide details for the unit that could perhaps be adapted and utilized in this country as well. Anyone involved in such a task would need to be committed, as Seeger is, to the idea that such an endeavor is worth serious attention. Greg Philo, Peter Beharrell, and John Gewitt, "Strategies and Policies," in *Trade Unions*, eds. Beharrell and Philo, pp. 138–142.

[41] Seeger, "Remarks to the Texas AFL-CIO Convention," July 27, 1983.

Bibliography

This bibliography is divided into five major sections arranged in the following order: books; documents; periodicals; pamphlets, reports, speeches, and unpublished materials; and personal sources.

BOOKS

General
Bagdikian, Ben H. *The Media Monopoly*. Boston: Beacon Press, 1983.

Bakke, E. Wight, Kerr, Clark, and Anrod, Charles, W., eds. *Unions, Management and the Public*. 1st, 2nd, 3rd eds. New York: Harcourt, Brace and World, Inc., 1948, 1960, 1967.

Barbash, Jack. *American Unions: Structure, Government and Politics*. New York: Random House, 1967.

———. *Labor Unions in Action: A Study of the Mainsprings of Unionism*. New York: Harper and Brothers, 1948.

———. *The Practice of Unionism*. New York: Harper and Brothers, 1956.

Barron, Jerome A. *Freedom of the Press for Whom? The Right of Access to Mass Media*. Bloomington, IN: Indiana University Press, 1973.

———. *Public Rights and the Private Press*. Toronto: Butterworths, 1981.

Beharrell, Peter and Philo, Greg, eds. *Trade Unions and the Media*. London: The Macmillan Press Ltd., 1977.

Billings, Richard N. and Greenya, John. *Power to the Public Worker*. Washington-New York: Robert B. Luce, Inc., 1974.

Bookbinder, Hyman H. and associates. *To Promote the General Welfare*. New York: The Amalgamated Clothing Workers of America, 1950.

Bureau of National Affairs, Inc. *The McClellan Committee Hearings—1957*. Washington, D.C.: Bureau of National Affairs, Inc., 1958.

Compaine, Benjamin M., ed. *Who Owns the Media? Concentration of Ownership in the Mass Communications Industry*, 1st, 2nd eds. White Plains, NY: Knowledge Industry Publications, Inc., 1979, 1982.

Day, Mark. *Forty Acres: Cesar Chavez and the Farm Workers*. New York, N.Y.: Praeger Publishers, 1971.

Dolbeare, Kenneth M. and Edelman, Murray J. *American Politics: Policies, Power, and Change*. Lexington, MA: D. C. Heath and Company, 1971.

Dubinsky, David and Raskin, A. H. *David Dubinsky: A Life with Labor*. New York: Simon and Schuster, 1977.

Dunn, S. Watson and Barban, Arnold M. *Advertising: Its Role in Modern Marketing*, 4th ed. Hinsdale, IL: The Dryden Press, 1978.

Edelman, Murray. *The Licensing of Radio Services in the United States, 1927 to 1947: A Study in Administrative Formulation of Policy.* Illinois Studies in the Social Sciences, Vol. XXXI, No. 4. Urbana, IL: University of Illinois Press, 1950.

———. *The Symbolic Uses of Politics.* Urbana, IL: University of Illinois Press, 1964.

Flack, Richard, ed. *Conformity, Resistance, and Self-Determination: The Individual and Authority.* Boston: Little, Brown and Co., 1973.

Franklin, Marc A. *Cases and Materials on Mass Media Law.* Mineola, NY: The Foundation Press, Inc., 1977.

Fusfeld, Daniel R. *The Rise and Repression of Radical Labor USA—1877–1918.* Chicago: Charles H. Kerr Publishing Company, 1980.

Glasgow University Media Group. *Bad News.* Vol. I. London: Routledge and Kegan Paul, 1976.

———. *More Bad News.* Vol. II. London: Routledge and Kegan Paul, 1980.

———. *Really Bad News.* London: Writers and Readers, 1982.

Goldstein, Robert Justin. *Political Repression in Modern America: 1870 to the Present.* Cambridge/New York: Schenkman Publishing Co., Inc.; Two Continents Publishing Group Ltd., 1978.

Gorman, Robert A. *Basic Text on Labor Law: Unionization and Collective Bargaining.* St. Paul, Minn.: West Publishing Co., 1976.

Hardman, J. B. S., and Neufeld, Maurice F., eds. *The House of Labor: Internal Operations of American Unions.* New York: Prentice-Hall, Inc., 1951.

Harris, Herbert. *American Labor.* New Haven: Yale University Press, 1938.

Hemmer, Joseph J., Jr. *Communication Under Law.* Vol. II: *Journalistic Freedom.* Metuchen, N.J.: and London: The Scarecrow Press, Inc., 1980.

International Advertising Association. *Controversy Advertising: How Advertisers Present Points of View in Public Affairs.* New York: Hastings House, 1977.

Kennedy, Robert. *The Enemy Within.* New York: Harper and Brothers, 1960.

Konecky, Eugene. *Monopoly Steals FM from the People.* New York: Provisional Committee for Democracy in Radio, 1946.

Kotler, Philip. *Marketing for Nonprofit Organizations.* Englewood Cliffs, N.J.: Prentice-Hall, Inc., 1975.

Kramer, Leo. *Labor's Paradox—The American Federation of State, County, and Municipal Employees, AFL-CIO.* New York: John Wiley and Sons, Inc., 1962.

Krasnow, Erwin G., Longley, Lawrence D., and Terry, Herbert A. *The Politics of Broadcast Regulation.* 2nd, 3rd eds. New York: St. Martin's Press, 1978, 1982.

Kushner, Sam. *Long Road to Delano.* New York: International Publishers, 1975.

Laidler, Harry W. *Boycotts and the Labor Struggle: Economic and Legal Aspects.* New York: Russell and Russell, 1913; reissue, 1968.

Lens, Sidney. *Radicalism in America.* New York: Thomas Y. Crowell Company, 1960.

Lester, Richard A. *As Unions Mature: An Analysis of the Evolution of American Unionism.* Princeton, NJ: Princeton University Press, 1958.

Levin, Harvey J. *Fact and Fancy in Television Regulation: An Economic Study of Policy Alternatives.* New York: Russell Sage Foundation, 1980.

Levy, Jacques E. *Cesar Chavez.* New York: W. W. Norton and Company, Inc., 1975.

Lipset, Seymour Martin. *The First New Nation: The United States in Historical and Comparative Perspective.* Garden City, NY: Doubleday and Co., Inc., 1967.

Lipsky, Michael. *Protest in City Politics: Rent Strikes, Housing and the Power of the Poor.* American Politics Research Series. Chicago: Rand McNally and Co., 1970.

Lofton, John. *The Press as Guardian of the First Amendment.* Columbia, SC: University of South Carolina Press, 1980.

McClellan, John L. *Crime Without Punishment.* New York: Duell, Sloan and Pearce, 1962.

Massel, Mark S. *Competition and Monopoly: Legal and Economic Issues.* Washington, D.C.: Brookings Institution, 1962.

Meier, Matt S., and Rivera, Feliciano. *The Chicano: A History of Mexican Americans.* New York: Hill and Wang, 1972.

Miliband, Ralph. *The State in Capitalist Society.* New York: Basic Books, Inc., 1969.

Parenti, Michael. Democracy for the Few. 3rd ed. New York: St. Martin's Press, 1980.

Rohrer, Daniel M. *Mass Media, Freedom of Speech, and Advertising: A Study in Communication Law.* Dubuque, Iowa: Kendall/Hunt Publishing Co., 1979.

Rubin, Bernard, ed. *Small Voices and Great Trumpets: Minorities and the Media.* New York: Praeger Publishers, 1980.

Schmidt, Benno C., Jr. *Freedom of the Press vs. Public Access.* New York: Praeger Publishers, 1976.

Sethi, S. Prakash. *Advocacy Advertising and Large Corporations.* Lexington, MA: Lexington Books, D. C. Heath and Co., 1977.

Simmons, Steven J. *The Fairness Doctrine and the Media.* Berkeley: University of California Press, 1978.

Stieber, Jack. *Governing the UAW.* Science Editions. New York: John Wiley and Sons, Inc., 1967.

Stolberg, Benjamin. *Tailor's Progress: The Story of a Famous Union and the Men Who Made It.* Garden City, NY: Doubleday, Doran and Co., Inc., 1944.

Strong, Earl D. *Amalgamated Clothing Workers of America.* Grinnell, Iowa: Herald-Register Publishing Co., 1940.

Tyler, Gus. *The Political Imperative: The Corporate Character of Unions.* New York: The Macmillan Company, 1968.

Wolfe, Alan. *The Limits of Legitimacy: Political Contradictions of Contemporary Capitalism.* New York: The Free Press, 1977.

Articles in Collections

Beckett, Francis. "Press and Prejudice." *Trade Unions and the Media.* Edited by Peter Beharrell and Greg Philo. London: The Macmillan Press Ltd., 1977.

Breed, Warren. "Social Control in the Newsroom: A Fundamental Analysis." *Conformity, Resistance, and Self-Determination: The Individual and Authority.* Edited by Richard Flack. Boston: Little, Brown and Company, 1973.

Cole, Gordon. "The Union's Public Relations." *The House of Labor: Internal Operations of American Unions.* Edited by J. B. S. Hardman and Maurice F. Neufeld. New York: Prentice-Hall, Inc., 1951.

Compaine, Benjamin M. "Introduction." *Who Owns the Media? Concentration of Ownership in the Mass Communications Industry.* Edited by Benjamin M. Compaine. White Plains, N.Y.: Knowledge Industry Publications, Inc., 1979.

———. "Newspapers." *Who Owns the Media? Concentration of Ownership in the Mass Communications Industry.* Edited by Benjamin M. Compaine. White Plains, NY: Knowledge Industry Publications, Inc., 1982.

———. "Who Owns the Media Companies?" *Who Owns the Media? Concentration of Ownership in the Mass Communications Industry.* Edited by Benjamin M. Compaine. White Plains, NY: Knowledge Industry Publications, Inc., 1982.

Dennis, Everette E. "The Rhetoric and Reality of Representation: A Legal Basis for Press Freedom and Minority Rights." *Small Voices and Great Trumpets: Minorities and the Media.* Edited by Bernard Rubin. New York: Praeger Publishers, 1980.

Murdock, Graham, and Golding, Peter. "Beyond Monopoly: Mass Communications in an Age of Conglomerates." *Trade Unions and the Media.* Edited by Peter Beharrell and Greg Philo. London: The Macmillan Press Ltd., 1977.

Owen, Bruce M. "Structural Approaches to the Problem of TV Network Dominance." *Proceedings of the Symposium on Media Concentration*. Vol. I. Federal Trade Commission. Washington, DC: Government Printing Office, 1979.

Pertschuk, Michael. "Opening Address." *Proceedings of the Symposium on Media Concentration*. Vol. I. Federal Trade Commission. Washington, DC: Government Printing Office, 1979.

Philo, Greg; Beharrell, Peter; and Gewitt, John. "Strategies and Policies." *Trade Unions and the Media*. Edited by Peter Beharrell and Greg Philo. London: The Macmillan Press Ltd., 1977.

Price, Monroe E. "Taming Red Lion: The First Amendment and Structural Approaches to Media Regulation." *Proceedings of the Symposium on Media Concentration*. Vol. I. Federal Trade Commission. Washington, DC: Government Printing Office, 1979.

Sterling, Christopher H. "Cable and Pay Television." *Who Owns the Media? Concentration of Ownership in the Mass Communications Industry*. Edited by Benjamin M. Compaine. White Plains, NY: Knowledge Industry Publications, Inc., 1982.

———. "Television and Radio Broadcasting." *Who Owns the Media? Concentration of Ownership in the Mass Communications Industry*. Knowledge Industry Publications, Inc., 1982.

Udall, Morris K. "Media Conglomerates—Will the Government Have to Step In?" *Proceedings of the Symposium on Media Concentration*. Vol. I. Federal Trade Commission. Washington, DC: Government Printing Office, 1979.

Walton, Paul and Davis, Howard. "Bad News for Trade Unionists." *Trade Unions and the Media*. Edited by Peter Beharrell and Greg Philo. London: The Macmillan Press Ltd., 1977.

Williams, John Taylor. "Open and Closed Access: A Lawyer's View." *Small Voices and Great Trumpets: Minorities and the Media*. Edited by Bernard Rubin. New York: Praeger Publishers, 1980.

Proceedings, Annuals, and Yearbooks

Amalgamated Clothing Workers of America. *General Executive Board Report*. New York: Amalgamated Clothing Workers of America, 1954–1972.

Amalgamated Clothing and Textile Workers Union. *Report of the General Executive Board*. New York: Amalgamated Clothing and Textile Workers Union, 1978–1983.

American Federation of Labor. *American Federation of Labor History, Encyclopedia and Reference Book*. Vol. III, Parts 1 and 2. Washington, DC: American Federation of Labor and Congress of Industrial Organizations, 1960.

American Federation of Labor. *Report of the Executive Council of the American Federation of Labor to the Annual Convention*. Washington, DC: American Federation of Labor, 1942–1955.

American Federation of Labor-Congress of Industrial Organizations. *Proceedings of the AFL-CIO Constitutional Convention*. Vols. I and II. Washington, DC: American Federation of Labor-Congress of Industrial Organizations, 1955–1984.

American Federation of State, County and Municipal Employees. *Proceedings of the International Convention*. Washington, DC: American Federation of State, County and Municipal Employees, 1954–1980.

Cable and Station Coverage Atlas. Washington, DC: Television Digest, Inc., 1982, 1983.

Congress of Industrial Organizations. *Proceedings, Fourteenth Constitutional Convention*. Washington, DC: Congress of Industrial Organizations, 1952.

Farah Manufacturing Co. *Annual Report*. Various years.

Gallup, George H. *The Gallup Poll: Public Opinions, 1978*. Wilmington, Delaware: Scholarly Resources Inc., 1979.

Gifford, Courtney D., ed. *Directory of U.S. Labor Organizations: 1982–83 Edition.* Washington, DC: The Bureau of National Affairs, Inc., 1982.

International Association of Machinists and Aerospace Workers. *Officers' Report to the Grand Lodge Convention.* Washington, DC: International Association of Machinists and Aerospace Workers, 1952–1980.

International Association of Machinists and Aerospace Workers. *Proceedings, Grand Lodge Convention.* Washington, DC: International Association of Machinists and Aerospace Workers, 1956–1980.

International Ladies' Garment Workers' Union. *Report and Record.* New York: International Ladies' Garment Workers' Union, 1953–1980.

J. P. Stevens Co., Inc. *Annual Report.* Various years.

Moody's Industrial Manual. New York: Moody's Investor's Service, 1976, 1981.

Standard and Poor's Industry Surveys. New York: Standard and Poor's Corporation, April, 1984.

Textile Workers Union of America. *Executive Council Report.* New York: Textile Workers Union of America, 1941–1976.

United Automobile, Aerospace and Agricultural Implement Workers of America. *Report of the President to the Constitutional Convention.* Detroit: United Automobile, Aerospace and Agricultural Implement Workers of America, 1953–1980.

DOCUMENTS

Statutory and Congressional Materials

Labor-Management Reporting and Disclosure Act of 1959 (Landrum-Griffin Act). *Statutes at Large,* Vol. 73 (1959).

National Labor Relations Act. U.S. Code, Vol. XXIX (1935).

Telecommunications. Code on Federal Regulations, Title 47, Part 73: "Radio Broadcast Services," 1981.

Telegraphs, Telephones, and Radio Telegraphs. U.S. Code, Title 47, Vol. 11 (1976).

U.S. Congress. Senate. Committee on Human Resources. *Labor Reform Act of 1977. Hearings* before the Labor Subcommittee of the Committee on Human Resources, Senate, 95th Cong., 1st sess., 1977.

U.S. Congress. Senate. Select Committee on Improper Activities in the Labor or Management Field. *Improper Activities in the Labor or Management Field. Final Report* of the Select Committee on Improper Activities in the Labor or Management Field, pts. 1–4, Senate 86th Cong., 2nd sess., 1960.

U.S. Congress. Senate. Select Committee on Improper Activities in the Labor or Management Field. *Improper Activities in the Labor or Management Field. Hearings* before the Select Committee on Improper Activities in the Labor or Management Field, pts. 1 and 2, Senate, 85th Cong., 1st and 2nd sess., 86th Cong., 1st sess., 1960.

Executive Agency Documents

U.S. Department of Labor. Bureau of Labor Statistics. *Directory of National Unions and Employee Associations, 1979.* Bulletin 2079. Washington, DC: Government Printing Office, 1980.

U.S. Department of Labor. Bureau of Labor Statistics. *Employment and Earnings, United States, 1909–78.* Bulletin 1312-11. Washington, DC: Government Printing Office, 1979.

U.S. Federal Communications Commission. *Annual Report*. Washington, DC: Government Printing Office, various years.

U.S. Federal Communications Commission. *Cable Television Report and Order and Reconsideration*. Washington, DC: Government Printing Office, 1972.

U.S. Federal Communications Commission. *Regulatory Developments in Cable Television*. Washington, DC: Government Printing Office, 1976.

U.S. Federal Trade Commission. *Proceedings of the Symposium on Media Concentration*. Vols. I and II. Washington, DC: Government Printing Office, 1979.

Cases, Decisions, and Orders

Abood v. Detroit Board of Education, 431 U.S. 209 (1977).

Applicability of the Fairness Doctrine to Cigarette Advertising, 9 FCC 2d 921 (1967).

Associated Press v. United States, 326 U.S. 1 (1945).

Bates v. State Bar of Arizona, 433 U.S. 350 (1977).

Bigelow v. Virginia, 421 U.S. 809 (1975).

Business Executives Move for Vietnam Peace v. FCC, 450 F. 2d (D.C. Cir., 1971).

Central Hudson v. Public Service Communications, 477 U.S. 557 (1980).

Chicago Joint Board, Amalgamated Clothing Workers of America v. Chicago Tribune Co., 435 F. 2d 470 (7th Cir., 1970), *cert. denied*, 402 U.S. 973 (1971).

Columbia Broadcasting System, Inc. v. Democratic National Committee, 412 U.S. 94 (1973).

Commonwealth v. Wiseman, 356 Mass. 251, 249 NE 2d 610 (1969), *cert. denied*, 398 U.S. 960 (1969).

Dennis v. United States, 341 U.S. 494 (1941).

Federal Communications Commission v. League of Women Voters of California, S.Ct. No. 82–912 (1984).

Federal Communications Commission v. Midwest Video Corporation, 440 U.S. 689 (1979).

First National Bank of Boston v. Bellotti, 435 U.S. 765 (1978).

Georgia Power Project v. FCC, 3 Med.L.Rptr. 1299 (1977).

Green v. FCC, 477 F. 2d 323 (D.C. Cir., 1971).

Handling of Public Issues Under the Fairness Doctrine and the Public Interest Standard of the Communications Act, 48 FCC 2d 1 (1974).

In Re Complaint by Friends of the Earth Concerning Fairness Doctrine Re Station WBNB-TV, New York, N.Y., 24 FCC 2d 743 (1970).

In Re Complaint by Wilderness Society and Friends of the Earth Concerning Fairness Doctrine Re National Broadcasting Co., 30 FCC 2d 643 (1971).

In Re Complaint of Energy Action Committee, Inc., against American Broadcasting Cos., 40 P & F Radio Reg 2d 511 (1977).

In Re Complaint of Public Media Center, 59 FCC 2d 494 (1976).

In the Matter of the Mayflower Broadcasting Corporation and the Yankee Network, Inc. (WAAB), 8 FCC 333 (1941).

In the Matter of the Handling of Public Issues Under the Fairness Doctrine and the Public Interest Standards of the Communications Act, 74 FCC 2d 163 (1979).

J. P. Stevens and Co. v. NLRB, 441 F. 2d 514 (5th Cir., 1971).

Konigsberg v. State Bar of California, 366 U.S. 36 (1961).

Lee v. Board of Regents, 441 F. 2d 1257 (7th Cir., 1971).

Metromedia Inc. v. San Diego, 101 S.Ct. 2882 (1981).

Miami Herald Publishing Co. v. Tornillo, 418 U.S. 241 (1974).

Mississippi Gay Alliance v. Goudelack, 536 F. 2d 1073 (5th Cir., 1976), *cert. denied*, 430 U.S. 982 (1977).

National Citizens Committee for Broadcasting v. FCC, 567 F. 2d 1095 (D.C. Cir., 1977).

National Commission on Egg Nutrition, 517 F. 2d 485 (7th Cir., 1975).

National Committee for Responsive Philanthropy v. FCC, 7 Med.L.Rptr. 1530 (1981).

National Labor Relations Board v. Fruit and Vegetable Packers and Warehousemen, Local 760, 377 U.S. 58 (1964).

National Labor Relations Board v. J. P. Stevens and Co., Inc., 563 F. 2d 8 (2nd Cir., 1977).

National Labor Relations Board v. J. P. Stevens and Co., Inc., 239 NLRB 738 (1978).

National Labor Relations Board v. J. P. Stevens and Co., Inc., 244 NLRB 407 (1979).

Near v. State of Minnesota, 283 U.S. 697 (1931).

Nebraska Press Association v. Stuart, 427 U.S. 539 (1976).

Neckritz v. FCC, 502 F. 2d 411 (D.C. Cir., 1974).

New York Times v. Sullivan, 376 U.S. 254 (1964).

New York Times Co. v. United States, 403 U.S. 713 (1971).

Norton v. Arlington Heights, 8 Med.L.Rptr. 2018 (1982).

Ohralik v. Ohio State Bar Association, 436 U.S. 447 (1978).

Pittsburgh Press Co. v. Pittsburgh Commission on Human Relations, 431 U.S. 376 (1973).

Poughkeepsie Buying Service, Inc., v. Poughkeepsie Newspapers, Inc., 205 Misc 982 (1954).

Public Interest Research Group v. FCC, 522 F. 2d 1060 (1st Cir., 1975).

Red Lion Broadcasting Company, Inc. v. Federal Communications Commission, 395 U.S. 367 (1969).

Report on Editorializing by Broadcast Licensees, 13 FCC 1246 (1949).

Retail Stores Employees Union, Local 880, Retail Clerks International Association, AFL-CIO v. Federal Communications Commission, 436 F. 2d 248 (D.C. Cir., 1970).

Rosenbloom v. Metromedia, 403 U.S. 29 (1971).

United States v. Southwestern Cable, 392 U.S. 159 (1968).

Valentine v. Chrestensen, 316 U.S. 52 (1942).

Virginia State Board of Pharmacy v. Virginia Citizens Consumer Council, 425 U.S. 748 (1976).

PERIODICALS

Scholarly and Professional

Barbash, Jack. "Trade Unionism from Roosevelt to Reagan." *Annals of the American Academy of Political and Social Science* (May, 1984), pp. 11–22.

Barron, Jerome A. "Access to the Press—A New First Amendment Right." *Harvard Law Review* 80:8 (June, 1967), pp. 1641–78.

Brinker, Paul A. and Taylor, Benjamin J. "The Secondary Boycott Maze." *Labor Law Journal* (July, 1974), pp. 418–27.

Carson, Teresa. "Stevens Attack Based on Aligning Power." *American Banker* (March 29, 1978), p. 2.

Christiansen, L. A. "Diagnoses of Stevens Agreement: No Epidemic." *Textile World.* Editorial (November, 1980), p. 15.

Fass, Susan. "A Look at Labor's Chief Strategist." *Journal of Commerce* (March 24, 1978), p. 15.

Geller, Henry. "FCC Media Ownership Rules: The Case for Regulation." *Journal of Communication* (Autumn, 1982), pp. 148–56.

Green, Paula. "Huge Growth Expected in Issues-Causes Advertising." *Advertising Age* (November 13, 1980), pp. 66–68.

Hall, Burton. "Gingold's Law; or Why Does the ILGWU Continue to Decay?" *New Politics* 11:3 (Winter, 1976), pp. 69–79.

Kistler, Alan. "Union Organizing: New Challenges and Prospects." *Annals of the American Academy of Political and Social Science* (May, 1984), pp. 96–107.

Klapper, Marvin. "Through the Mill with J. P. Stevens." *Women's Wear Daily* (November 20, 1978), pp. 4–5+.

Le Duc, Don R. "Deregulation and the Dream of Diversity." *Journal of Communication* (Autumn, 1982), pp. 164–78.

Margolies, Ken. "Silver Screen Tarnishes Unions." *Screen Actor* (Summer, 1981), pp. 42–52.

McGrath, Noreen. "Boycott of Textile Companies Supported at 75 Colleges." *Chronicle of Higher Education* (November 6, 1978), p. 10.

Mushkat, M., Jr. "Implementing Public Plans: The Case for Social Marketing." *Long Range Planning* (August, 1980), pp. 24–29.

Pomper, Gerald. "The Public Relations of Organized Labor." *Public Opinion Quarterly* 23 (Winter, 1959–60), pp. 483–94.

Redish, Martin H. "The First Amendment in the Marketplace: Commercial Speech and the Values of Free Expression." *George Washington Law Review* 39 (March, 1971), pp. 429–73.

Sanderson, George. "The Product Boycott: Labour's Latest Tool." *The Labour Gazette* (July, 1974), pp. 477–80.

Schmidt, Benno C. "*Nebraska Press Association:* An Expansion of Freedom and Contraction of Theory." *Stanford Law Review* (February, 1977), pp. 431–76.

Sethi, S. Prakash. "Institutional/Image Advertising and Idea/Issue Advertising as Marketing Tools: Some Public Policy Issues." *Journal of Marketing* 43 (January, 1979), pp. 68–78.

Shorto, Russell. "Machinists Tool Up for TV." *Washington Journalism Review* (September, 1980), p. 9.

Straub, J. Kurt. "Problems in the Application of the Fairness Doctrine to Commercial Advertisements." *Villanova Law Review* 23:2 (January, 1978), pp. 340–65.

Westen, Tracy. "The First Amendment: Barrier or Impetus to FTC Advertising Remedies?" *Brooklyn Law Review* 46:3 (Spring, 1980), pp. 487–512.

Wilson, James Q. "The Strategy of Protest: Problems of Negro Civic Action." *Journal of Conflict Resolution* V (September, 1961), pp. 291–303.

General Magazines and Newspapers

"A Gathering Momentum Against J. P. Stevens." *Business Week*, March 20, 1978, p. 147.

"An Interview with Ray Rogers." *Working Papers Magazine*, January-February, 1982, pp. 48–57.

"Approval of Labor Unions Remains at Low." *The Gallup Report*, August, 1981, p. 7.

Arnold, Jay. "Study: TV Has Bad View of Businessmen." *Champaign-Urbana News-Gazette*, April 24, 1981, p. B8.

"Bad Times for the Big Three." *Newsweek*, February 22, 1982, p. 77.

Banker, Steven. "Look for the Union Label . . . and Much, Much More." *TV Guide*, March 31, 1984, pp. 30–33.

"Bishops Support Boycott of J. P. Stevens." *Georgia Bulletin*, March 13, 1980, p. 1.

Bronson, Gail, and Birnbaum, Jeffrey H. "How the Textile Union Finally Wins Contracts at J. P. Stevens Plants." *Wall Street Journal*, October 20, 1980, p. 1.

———. "Rogers' Tough, Unorthodox Tactics Prevail in Stevens' Organizing Fight." *Wall Street Journal*, October 21, 1980, pp. 37, 42.

"The Business Campaign Against 'Trial by TV.'" *Business Week*, June 2, 1980, pp. 77, 79.

Coburn, Judith. "J. P. Stevens Plays by Its Own Rules." *Village Voice*, May 2, 1977, p. 35.

"Confidence in Organized Labor." *Gallup Report*, October, 1983, p. 13.

Cook, Daniel D. "Boycott; Labor's Last Resort." *Industry Week*, June 28, 1976, pp. 23–32.

"First Bi-annual Issues Conference." *National NOW Times,* November, 1978, p. 13.

Frank, Allan Dodds. "Argumentum ad hominem." *Forbes,* August 2, 1982, pp. 37–38.

Gay, Lance. "Labor Activist Engineers Union's Corporate Battle." *Washington Star,* November 28, 1980, pp. D13–D14.

"How Unions Try to Clean Up Their Image." *U.S. News and World Report,* October 22, 1979, pp. 69–70.

"J. P. Stevens: Labor Wins a Hardball Contest in the South." *Detroit Free Press.* Editorial, October 24, 1980, p. 10A.

"The Kings of Cable TV." *Mother Jones,* January, 1982, pp. 6, 8.

"Labor Violence and Corruption." *Business Week,* August 31, 1957, pp. 77–90.

Liebling, A. J. "The Wayward Press: Do You Belong in Journalism?" *New Yorker,* May 14, 1960, pp. 105–12.

McConville, Ed. "The Southern Textile War." *The Nation,* October 2, 1976, pp. 294–99.

Myerson, Michael. "ILGWU: Fighting for Lower Wages." *Ramparts* (October, 1969), pp. 51–55.

"New Weapon for Bashing Bosses." *Time,* July 23, 1979, p. 71.

"The Pinch on Public Employees." *Business Week,* June 23, 1980, pp. 71–77.

"Poll Gives Big Edge to Right-to-Work Foes." *Kansas City Star,* November 5, 1978, p. 1.

"Public Workers' Powerhouse." *Time,* May 21, 1973, p. 90.

"Right-to-Work Foes Have Big Spending Lead." *St. Louis Post-Dispatch,* November 11, 1978, p. 4A.

Rogers, Ray. "How to Confront Corporations." *Business and Society Review,* Summer, 1981, pp. 60–64.

Salmans, Sandra. "J. P. Stevens: One Year After the Truce." *New York Times,* October 18, 1981, pp. F8, F9.

Selkowe, Peter. "Council Makes Its Bed with Union-Made Sheets." *Morning Courier* (Champaign-Urbana, Ill.), January 14, 1979, p. 30.

Serrin, William. "Ailing ILGWU Is Facing More Problems." *New York Times,* November 29, 1981, p. 29.

———. "The Unsung Heroes of America's Labor Movement." *New York Times,* August 14, 1983, pp. 4F, 6F.

Shapiro, Fred C. "How Jerry Wurf Walks on Water." *New York Times Magazine,* April 11, 1976, pp. 59–84.

"Son of 'Norma Rae.'" *Chicago Sun-Times,* October 22, 1980, p. 75.

"Stevens Chief—Battle Not Over." *Chicago Sun-Times,* October 21, 1980, p. 17.

"Union Network." *Business Week,* December 17, 1949, pp. 92–93.

"U.S. Injunction Against Stevens?" *Time,* December 12, 1977, p. 76.

"Victory for Workers." *News and Observer* (Raleigh, NC). Editorial, October 21, 1980, p. 4.

Warren, James. "How the Union Conquered Stevens." *Chicago Sun-Times,* October 26, 1980, pp. 7, 42.

"Why Advertisers are Rushing to Cable TV." *Business Week,* November 2, 1981, p. 96.

Other Periodicals

The following periodicals have been useful for either news items on a regular basis or general background information. Citations for specific articles from these will be found in the notes for each chapter.

AFL-CIO American Federationist.

AFL-CIO News.

Chicago Sun-Times.

Daily Labor Report.

Justice.
Labor Unity.
Machinist.
New York Times.
Public Employee.
Social Justice.
Solidarity.
Wall Street Journal.

Pamphlets, Reports, Speeches, and Unpublished Material

American Federation of Labor and Congress of Industrial Organizations. *Policy Resolutions.* Pamphlet. Washington, DC: American Federation of Labor and Congress of Industrial Organizations, various years.

American Federation of State, County and Municipal Employees. *A Model of Vitality and Democracy.* Pamphlet. Washington, DC: American Federation of State, County and Municipal Employees, n.d.

————. *Who Speaks for Public Employees: Jerry Wurf Debates William Buckley.* Pamphlet. Washington, DC: American Federation of State, County and Municipal Workers, 1975.

Anderson, David Wallace. "Access: An Analysis of the Development of an Affirmative Concept of the First Amendment in Broadcasting." M.S. thesis, University of Illinois, 1974.

Barnes, Gregory Allen. "The Impact of the McClellan Investigations on the Bakery and Confectionery Workers International Union of America." M.S. thesis, University of Illinois, 1959.

Beck, Burt. *A Brief History of the Amalgamated.* Pamphlet. New York: Amalgamated Clothing Workers of America, n.d.

————. Memorandum. Attached to transcript of "MacNeil/Lehrer Report" and sent to ACTWU field workers, January 11, 1977.

Elkuss, Mary. "The Missouri Campaign to Defeat Right-to-Work." Paper, 1978. Mimeographed.

Hoyman, Scott. "J. P. Stevens and Organizing." Speech presented at colloquium, Institute of Labor and Industrial Relations, University of Illinois, December 5, 1980.

IAM Media Project TV Trainers' Manual. Prepared by William M. Young and Associates, Chicago, n.d.

International Association of Machinists and Aerospace Workers. *IAM Television Entertainment Report, Part II: Conclusions and National Summary of Occupational Frequency in Network Primetime Entertainment for February, 1980.* Washington, DC: International Association of Machinists and Aerospace Workers, June 12, 1980.

————. *Network News and Documentary Report: A Member Survey and Analysis.* Washington, DC: International Association of Machinists and Aerospace Workers, July 30, 1980.

"MacNeil/Lehrer Report." Educational Broadcasting Corporation and GWETA telecast: "J. P. Stevens," 1976. Transcript.

National Association for Better Broadcasting. *Broadcasting Law and the Consumer.* Series of ten papers, June, 1979–March 1982.

Rogers, Ray. "Corporate Campaign." Paper prepared in New York, n.d. Mimeographed.

————. "Corporate Campaign Highlights." Paper prepared in New York, October, 1980. Mimeographed.

————. "Remarks Presented by Ray Rogers to the Executive Board of the United Food and Commercial Workers Union in Miami, Florida on March 14, 1980." Mimeographed.

Seeger, Murray. "Address to the Public Relations Society of America." Washington, DC, April 20, 1982. Mimeographed.

———. "Remarks to the Texas AFL-CIO Convention." July 27, 1983. Mimeographed.

———. "Report to the Executive Council: Institute of Public Affairs." Washington, DC, April, 1982. Mimeographed.

———. "Report to the Public Relations Committee." Washington, DC, May 27, 1982. Mimeographed.

"Settlement Agreement, J. P. Stevens Co., Inc. and the Amalgamated Clothing and Textile Workers Union." New York, October 20, 1980.

"Sixty Minutes." CBS telecast: "Target: J. P. Stevens," March 13, 1977. Transcript.

Thompson, Robert T. "CBS Morning News." CBS Television, November 1, 1983. Cassette tape.

The TWUA Story: *They Said It Couldn't Be Done.* Pamphlet. New York: Textile Workers Union of America, 1964.

What Is At Stake In the Stevens-Union Struggle: A Statement by Fourteen Southern Ministers. Pamphlet. 1976.

PERSONAL SOURCES

Ax, Joel. Associate General Counsel, Amalgamated Clothing and Textile Workers Union. Interview, New York, June 3, 1982.

Beck, Burt. Director, Department of Communications, Amalgamated Clothing and Textile Workers Union. Interview, New York, June 3, 1982.

Cole, Gordon. Instructor, George Meany Center for Labor Studies. Editor, *Machinist,* retired. Interview, Silver Spring, Md., May 26, 1982.

Conn, Dick. Press Relations Wire, Inc. Interview, Washington, DC, May 27, 1982.

Conn, Harry. Press Relations Wire, Inc. Interview, Washington, DC, May 27, 1982.

Dyson, Dave. Field Director, Union Label Department, Amalgamated Clothing and Textile Workers Union. Interview, New York, June 2, 1982.

Fleisher, Henry C. Maurer, Fleisher, Anderson and Conway, Inc. Interview, Washington, DC, May 24, 1982.

Hoyman, Scott. Executive Vice President, Amalgamated Clothing and Textile Workers Union. Interview, New York, June 2, 1982.

Kamber, Victor. The Kamber Group. Interview, Washington, DC, May 25, 1982.

Kirkman, Larry. Director, Labor Institute of Public Affairs. Interview, Washington, DC, November 9, 1983.

Mileski, Del. Director, Union Label Department, Amalgamated Clothing and Textile Workers Union. Interview, New York, June 3, 1982.

Miller, Saul. Director, Department of Publications, AFL-CIO, retired. Telephone interview, Washington, DC, May 26, 1982.

Parker, David. Communications Director, Industrial Union Department, AFL-CIO. Interview, Washington, DC, May 24, 1982.

Rogers, Ray. Director, Corporate Campaign, Inc. Interview, New York, June 1, 1982.

Samuel, Howard. President, Industrial Union Department, AFL-CIO. Interview, Washington, DC, May 24, 1982.

Seeger, Murray. Director, Department of Information, AFL-CIO. Interview, Washington, DC, May 25, 1982, November 9, 1983.

Stetin, Sol. Senior Executive Vice President, Amalgamated Clothing and Textile Workers Union, retired. Interview, St. Louis, September 23, 1982.

Zack, Allen. The Kamber Group. Interview, Washington, DC, May 26, 1982.

Author Index

Subject Index